DATE DUE

OC 4'99			
DE 20'00			
JE 11'01			
OC 12'01			
NO 2'01			
AP 16'02			
AP 21'03			
OC 07'03			
JE 9'04			

DEMCO 38-296

Asians in America

*The Peoples of East, Southeast, and South Asia
in American Life and Culture*

Series Editor

Franklin Ng
California State University – Fresno

A GARLAND SERIES

Contents of the Series

R

Asian American Family Life and Community

Edited with introductions by

Franklin Ng
California State University – Fresno

GARLAND PUBLISHING, INC.
A MEMBER OF THE TAYLOR & FRANCIS GROUP

New York & London
1998

Library of Congress Cataloging-in-Publication Data

Asian American family life and community / edited with introductions
by Franklin Ng.
p. cm. — (Asians in America ; 2)
Includes bibliographical references.
ISBN 0-8153-2691-2 (v. 2 : alk. paper). — ISBN 0-8153-2689-0
(6 vol. set : alk. paper)
1. Asian American families. 2. Asian Americans—Social
conditions. 3. Asian Americans—Economic conditions.
I. Ng, Franklin, 1947– . II. Series.
E184.O6A8275 1998
305.895073—dc21   98-10881
                                                      CIP

Printed on acid-free, 250-year-life paper
Manufactured in the United States of America

Contents

Series Introduction

As the fastest growing segment of the U.S. population since the mid-1960s, Asian Americans encompass Chinese, Japanese, Koreans, Filipinos, Asian Indians, Pakistanis, Sri Lankans, Bangladeshis, Vietnamese, Lao, Hmong, Cambodians, Iu-Mien, and others. Their remarkably diverse ethnic, social, historical, and religious backgrounds and experiences enrich the cultural fabric of the United States. The study of Asian Americans offers many insights on such issues as immigration, refugee policy, transnationalism, return migration, cultural citizenship, ethnic communities, community building, identity and group formation, panethnicity, race relations, gender and class, entrepreneurship, employment, representation, politics, adaptation, and acculturation.

This collection of articles presents contemporary research that examines such issues as the growing political power of Asian Americans, the empowerment of emigrant women, the rise of youth gangs, relations between ethnic groups, the migration of highly educated Asians, and other important subjects. The writings are drawn from a wide variety of disciplines to provide a broad but informative array of insights on this fascinating and diverse population. The volumes give in-depth exposure to important issues linked to the different communities and impart a greater understanding of Asian Americans in the United States.

This series consists of six volumes, and its coverage cuts across many disciplines. The first volume focuses on the history and immigration of Asian Americans. The second volume treats various themes relating to Asian American family life and community. The third volume is complementary and considers vital issues pertaining to Asian American women and gender. A fourth volume explores the processes of adaptation and acculturation, as well as the continuing significance of transnational ties for Asian Americans. The fifth volume addresses the complex subject of interethnic relations and Asian American politics. Finally, the last volume examines issues associated with labor, employment, entrepeneurship, enclave economies, and socioeconomic status.

In preparing this anthology, I have had help from many individuals. I would especially like to acknowledge assistance from Leo Balk, Paul Finkelman, and Carole Puccino. Their patience, encouragement, and guidance helped to ensure the success of this project.

Volume Introduction

Families constitute the building blocks of communities and are an important aspect of the Asian American experience. In the migration to the United States, Asian families had to wrestle with traditional ideas of socialization as opposed to the changes that came with the adjustment to the new environment. Families became the sites for the negotiation of issues pertaining to cultural values, enculturation, and economic activity. Immigration policies set forth by the United States and the cultural practices of the immigrant homeland also affected the nature of the families that were transplanted.

Given the diversity of Asian groups that came to the United States, there were to be a variety of Asian families over time. Restrictive immigration laws before World War II, for example, helped to ensure a predominance of men versus women in the Chinese, Filipino, and Asian Indian communities. This resulted in the appearance of bachelor communities for the Chinese and Filipinos. In locales where there were no antimiscegenation laws, intermarriage was an option. Many Asian Indians married Mexican women in California, Filipinos married European immigrant women in Illinois, and Chinese married native women in Hawaii. The immigration barriers also helped to promote split household families among some Chinese and Asian Indians. In this case, the male spouse labored in the United States while the female counterpart resided in the immigrant homeland. Remittances were sent across the Pacific to support the wives and family members. Japanese male immigrants, in contrast, formed families by sending for picture brides as did some Koreans.

Major changes among Asian American families and communities occurred after 1965 and after the Vietnam War. This volume takes note of these changes and examines issues such as the role of the family, generational changes, and the significance of kinship, networks, newspapers, and credit associations in various Asian American groups.

Families are often seen as a key element behind the success of Asian immigrant achievement. Going beyond the cultural factors versus opportunity structures debate, Victor Nee and Herbert Wong try to account for socioeconomic mobility of the Chinese and the Japanese in America. Public policy does have an impact upon families in the United States, especially for the refugees from the Vietnam War. However, David W. Haines notes that federal policy is not aware of the importance of kinship for Southeast Asians and how it can impact their economic adjustment and bases of social support.

Nazli Kibria indicates how household structure and family ideology play a critical role in how the Vietnamese adapt economically. By emphasizing family collectivism, the Vietnamese devise strategies by which they can share economic and social resources. Kenneth A. Skinner follows by pointing out that Vietnamese youth, women, and others may have diversity in their adaptation to America. Finally, in the Asian American population, Japanese Americans are the only group that is primarily American-born in composition. Colleen Johnson explains how social mechanisms help to reinforce the solidarity of extended family structures among Japanese Americans. In another article, she discusses how the concept of generation is linked with ethnicity for Japanese Americans.

The nature of Asian American communities varies according to ethnic group and locale. They may have different degrees of institutional completeness with institutions such as churches, schools, voluntary associations, mutual aid societies, and newspapers. Jonathan Y. Okamura examines the proliferation of Filipino hometown or locality associations in Hawaii since 1965. He investigates their membership and the roles that they play in the Filipino community. Eleanor Yu complements his treatment by exploring the relationship between migration and community organization among Filipinos in the United States. Ivan Light, Im Jung Kwuon, and Deng Zhong focus on the *kye* or rotating credit associations in the Korean American community. They suggest that rotating credit associations, which can also be found among other Asian American groups, can help in the development of ethnic entrepreneurship and business. Pyong Gap Min describes how immigrant churches and concentration in a limited range of small businesses are important bases for Korean Americans. In her study of the Chinese American Citizens Alliance, Sue Fawn Chung draws attention to an organization that has sought to improve the status of Chinese Americans in the United States.

Although the term community often conjures up the idea of a neighborhood or enclave, Anne K. Fleuret observes that the Sikhs in Los Angeles do not live as a clustered group. They are territorially dispersed, but maintain ties through social networks. This fits in well with scholarship that indicates communities need not be residential or geographical. Instead, they can also be based on shared practices or ideas and be "imagined communities" or "communities of memory." Leadership is also a key factor in the dynamics of a community. Bernard Wong, for example, emphasizes how competing elites among the Chinese in New York can hold different views about interethnic relations and define the ethnic boundaries of a community. George M. Scott Jr. cites an intriguing situation in San Diego, in which the Hmong leadership is trying to direct their community. They are espousing assimilation to learn marketable skills even as they are also encouraging the maintenance of their ethnic identity. He alludes to this as an "assimilation-contra-assimilation paradox." Lastly, context can influence the character of a community. Jonathan Y. Okamura investigates why many people in Hawaii do not refer to themselves as Asian Americans, preferring instead to use the term "local." They opt for a local identity—a form of panethnic identity—as a way of reacting to external forces and change.

FURTHER READING

Books:

Almirol, Edwin B. *Ethnic Identity and Social Negotiation: A Study of a Filipino Community in California*. New York: AMS Press, 1985.

Anderson, Robert N. *Filipinos in Rural Hawaii*. Honolulu: University of Hawaii Press, 1984.

Bacon, Jean. *Life Lines: Community, Family, and Assimilation among Asian Indian Immigrants*. New York: Oxford University Press, 1996.

Fugita, Stephen S., and David J. O'Brien. *Japanese American Ethnicity: The Persistence of Community*. Seattle: University of Washington Press, 1991.

Kibria, Nazli. *Family Tightrope: The Changing Lives of Vietnamese Americans*. Princeton: Princeton University Press, 1993.

Kim, Illsoo. *New Urban Immigrants: The Korean Immigrants in New York*. Princeton: Princeton University Press, 1981.

Kwong, Peter. *The New Chinatown*. New York: Hill & Wang, 1987.

Matsumoto, Valerie J. *Farming the Home Place: A Japanese American Community in California, 1919–1982*. Ithaca: Cornell University Press, 1993.

Nee, Victor G., and Brett de Bary Nee. *Longtime Californ': A Documentary Study of an American Chinatown*. New York: Pantheon, 1972.

Yanagisako, Sylvia Junko. *Transforming the Past: Tradition and Kinship among Japanese Americans*. Stanford: Stanford University Press, 1985.

Articles:

Bach, Robert, and Rita Carroll-Sequin. "Labor Force Participation, Household Composition and Sponsorship among Southeast Asian Refugees." *International Migration Review* 20 (1986).

Shin, Steve S. "Community Orientations and Newspaper Use among Korean Newcomers." *Journalism Quarterly* 67 (1990).

Smith, Christopher J. "Asian New York: The Geography and Politics of Diversity." *International Migration Review* 29 (1995).

Starr, Paul D., and Alden E. Roberts. "Community Structure and Vietnamese Refugee Adaptation: The Significance of Context." *International Migration Review* 60 (1982).

Yanagisako, Sylvia Junko. "Two Processes of Change in Japanese-American Kinship." *Journal of Anthropological Research* 31 (1975).

Yuan, D. Y. "Voluntary Segregation: A Study of New York Chinatown." *Phylon* 24 (1963).

ASIAN AMERICAN
SOCIOECONOMIC ACHIEVEMENT
The Strength of the Family Bond

VICTOR NEE
HERBERT Y. WONG
University of California, Santa Barbara

The analysis emphasizes the need to examine structural and cultural factors in the sending and receiving countries over a historical process to understand how immigrants are incorporated in American society. The article argues that Chinese were slower to make the transition from sojourner to immigrant due to structural characteristics of Chinese village society; whereas Japanese immigrants were not tied by strong family bonds to Japan and made a more rapid transition. The differential timing of family formation and family-run businesses in America account for the more rapid assimilation of Japanese Americans. Changing labor markets after World War II provided new opportunity structures favorable to the socioeconomic mobility of native-born Chinese and Japanese Americans.

Asian American socioeconomic achievement has stimulated increased attention for its implication in understanding the dynamics of ethnic inequality in America. New interest in Asian Americans stems from the perception that Asians as a nonwhite minority group have achieved parity with whites, despite a history of discrimination (Sowell, 1981). If minority status has been typically associated with socioeconomic dis-

---

AUTHORS' NOTE: *We gratefully acknowledge the careful criticism by Leonard Broom and Beverly Duncan and take responsibility for the continuing problems in the article. The article grew out of a seminar taught by Harvey Molotch and Victor Nee on "Economy and Ethnicity in American Society."*

SOCIOLOGICAL PERSPECTIVES, Vol. 28 No. 3, July 1985 281-306
© 1985 Pacific Sociological Assn.

advantage due to racial discrimination, why have Asians been the exception? Whereas social scientists have reached considerable agreement in explaining differential attainments of white ethnics and blacks (Lieberson, 1980), there has been considerably less consensus in explanations of Asian American socioeconomic achievement.

There is widespread agreement that in the post World War II period Asian Americans have made significant socioeconomic gains (Nee and Sanders, 1985; Petersen, 1971; Sung, 1967). The occupational profile of Japanese Americans roughly approximated that of whites by 1970, while Chinese Americans were disproportionately represented in professional occupations (Wong, 1982). Hirschman and Wong (1984) argue that in general, Asian Americans approach socioeconomic parity with whites due to overachievement in educational attainment. Indeed, the fact that Japanese households have the second highest income next to Jews has made Japanese Americans part of the American folklore of successful ethnic groups (Sowell, 1981). The picture for Chinese Americans has been complicated by large-scale immigration beginning in the 1960s, which resulted in more than 60% foreign-born among Chinese Americans. The large influx of new immigrants has had the effect of lowering the overall socioeconomic profile of Chinese, compared to Japanese, a predominately native-born population. The fact that native-born Chinese and Japanese share similar socioeconomic profiles, however, suggests that status attainment processes for the native-born of these two ethnic groups were closely parallel.

Various theoretical formulations have been suggested to explain Asian American socioeconomic attainment that can be roughly conceptualized as cultural versus structural. The cultural argument emphasizes attributes of Asian Americans, whereas structural arguments examine the occupational structure of the host society. Here we will argue that such ahistorical formulations fail to capture the dynamic nature of immigrant groups as they respond to historical situations and changing economic structures.

2

CULTURAL EXPLANATIONS

The most popular and recurrent explanations for Asian American socioeconomic attainment have been cultural. Japanese American success, for example, has been attributed to Japanese values that are compatible, if not similar, to those of middle-class Americans. As Kitano (1969: 3) wrote: "Japanese-American values, skills, attitudes, and behavior apparently do not differ markedly from those of the average American. 'Scratch a Japanese American and find a white Anglo-Saxon Protestant' is a generally accurate statement." The problem with such cultural explanations, as Lieberson (1980: 8) pointed out, is that they rely on a subtle form of circular reasoning: "The argument then frequently involves using the behavioral attribute one is trying to explain as the indicator of the normative or value difference one is trying to use as the explanation."

The cultural argument, in order to break away from the circular reasoning, must start at the point of departure, viewing immigrants as a special group of people who decided to leave their homeland to improve their living standard. The immigrants' willingness to endure hardship for economic gains, together with the socioeconomic background at the time of immigration, set the stage for possible upward mobility not only for themselves, but also for the second and third generations (Chiswick, 1977).

Thus a more rigorous cultural argument must begin by examining historical context of immigration as a "background variable" with two components. The first component reflects the cultural characteristics that enable the immigrant group to cope with host hostility and compete more effectively once its members arrive in America. These cultural characteristics reflect not the essence of white Protestant ethic, as suggested by Petersen (1971) and Kitano (1969), but the influence of neo-Confucianism, which was dominant in the East Asian cultural sphere from which the Chinese, Japanese, Korean, and Indo-Chinese immigrants came. Neo-Confucianism stressed the legitimacy of status attainment through education and membership and obligation to an interdependent family and kinship unit.

The second component concerns the socioeconomic background of the immigrant group in the creation of opportunities for upward mobility. Later, we will demonstrate that attributes of Chinese and Japanese immigrants differ cross-sectionally between places of origin and across historical periods. The socioeconomic and cultural characteristics of the different immigrant groups affected their timing of family formations and the availability of resources, which had important consequences for status attainment and experience of discrimination. In short, an adequate cultural argument must account not only for the ideological component of the immigrant group but also for the availability of resources in combating discrimination in the host society.

It may be useful at this point to introduce a metaphor from economics, placing the cultural attributes of immigrant/minority groups in a broader context—supply side of the labor market. A cultural explanation is a supply side argument because of its emphasis on what the immigrant groups brought with them for competition in the American labor market. It is linked to a human capital perspective in which status attainment is seen as a result of the actors' ability to generate resources. For the Asian Americans, the process of differential family formation between Chinese and Japanese immigrants played a critical role in the timing of socioeconomic attainment of these groups in American society. From the supply side argument, the family unit not only provides socialization and support, but also serves to generate "physical" capital through household production.

STRUCTURAL FACTORS

From the structural perspective, the role of immigrant labor has historically served to fill the need for low-wage labor at the bottom rung of the occupational structure and to disrupt labor union activities of domestic workers by maintaining a reserve supply of low wage labor (Bonacich, 1972; Castles and Kosack, 1973; Rosenblum, 1973; Buraway, 1976). Prior to World War II, the structure of demand in California was for cheap labor to fill positions required to build the transportation, agricultural, and industrial infrastructure of the Western states (Cheng and Bonacich, 1984). These jobs could not be sufficiently filled by white labor. The use of low-wage labor rendered the cheaper labor force structurally vulnerable to a "split-labor" market ethnic antagonism (Bonacich, 1972). The split-labor market hypothesis suggests that ethnic antagonism first developed in a labor market split along ethnic lines. Because split labor markets exist when there are at least two groups of workers whose price of labor for the same work differs, the introduction of cheap labor along ethnic lines threatened local workers' security and income. In many instances, the threat to security is sufficient to generate hostility, and local workers organize politically to limit the opportunities for immigrant groups (Li, 1977).

However, the structure of demand changes in different historical periods, resulting in changes in the composition of immigrant groups and therefore the relationship between the immigrant group and local workers. For example, after World War II, the difference in purpose served by the "brain drain" immigration in augmenting the skilled labor force is reflected in the differential experience of immigrants who were incorporated into the primary labor market, including jobs with relatively high wages, good working conditions, chances of advancement, and above all employment stability. Available studies of professional and technical immigrant workers have not produced evidence of systematic discrimination in salaries and work conditions. Immigrants in these conditions frequently do as well or better than domestic workers (Portes, 1981), in which case, for the latter immigrant group, there is no split labor market and, therefore, less ethnic antagonism. Skilled workers recruited into the primary labor force to fill professional and technical positions, whether immigrants or minorities, generally settle outside of segregated enclaves and are more assimilated than immigrants or minorities locked in the secondary labor market.

5

Whereas the supply side focuses on the attributes of immigrant groups, the structural argument examines the market condition of the host society. The structural argument examines the discriminatory practices of the host society and its impact on immigrant groups' status attainment process. Like the supply side argument, the structural argument is often ahistorical, failing to deal with the changing economic condition of the expanding market economy in North America. We will introduce another economic metaphor—the demand side of the labor market—and will argue that labor market demand needs to be examined from a historical perspective. Rather than conceptually separating cultural explanations from structural explanations, we will argue that the status attainment of Asian Americans is a result of the historical interplay between the supply and demand of labor.

There is a third category of theoretical formulation pointing to the interplay between the supply and demand side of the labor market and its impact on status attainment for immigrant groups. The Wilson and Portes (1980) study of the Cuban enclave in Miami has identified a third "enclave" sector that shares characteristics of both the primary and secondary labor market. Like work in the secondary labor market, the jobs in the enclave economy are low-paying and low in prestige; yet like the primary sector, enclave jobs provide a more favorable return on human capital investment and internal mechanisms for socioeconomic mobility. However, from the supply side, both human and physical capital are needed for an enclave economy to survive. As both Light (1972) and Wilson and Portes (1980) pointed out, the key to the development of ethnic enclaves depends on the ethnic minorities' ability to generate capital, utilize cheap labor supply, utilize cultural specific institutions such as rotating credit association, and develop ethnically sympathetic sources of supply and consumer outlet.

The existence of a thriving enclave economy creates an ethnically controlled demand structure that encourages the immigration of entrepreneurial talent in addition to unskilled and skilled labor necessary to fill the more complex division of labor developed in an enclave economy. The concentration of family-run small businesses in the enclave economy also provides an economic basis for stable family life, and resources to support the high educational attainment associated with children of Asian American immigrant/minority groups. On the other hand, the enclave economy perpetuates a segregated residential pattern, which studies have shown is associated with cultural isolation and lower income (Duncan and Lieberson, 1959; Nee and Sanders, 1985). The close proximity of work and residence and the social interdependence fostered by enclave economies provide the structural basis that perpetuates ethnicity (Yancey et al., 1976).

In order to understand the socioeconomic mobility of Chinese and Japanese Americans, it is necessary to view the changing mix of supply-side and demand-side factors over a historical process. Unlike the ahistorical explanations for socioeconomic achievement (Rosen, 1959; Caudill and DeVos, 1965; Petersen, 1966), we maintain that there is continuous change and transformation of both cultural attributes and labor market conditions that has bearing on the socioeconomic attainment of immigrant and ethnic groups. An analysis that views cultural attributes as unchanging, or that does not account for the changing labor market demands, cannot explain the differential socioeconomic achievement of Chinese and Japanese Americans prior to and after World War II nor account for the differences between Asian Americans and other ethnic and minority groups.

Historically, from the supply side, we will show that formation of family in the host society was critical for the formation of household production units, which in turn opened the way for social and economic mobility. Unlike working under a labor contract where most of the profit went to the labor contractor, profit generated from the household production unit funneled back to the families as accumulation of capital for the development of small businesses. Cheap labor generated by household units allowed these ethnic businesses to be competitive in the dominant society; formation of family businesses coincided with the development of an enclave economy, which opened ethnically controlled avenues for socioeconomic mobility, and provided a stable environment for family life and the socialization and education of an upwardly mobile second generation. With the changes in the structure of opportunity following World War II, native-born Asian Americans entered the primary labor market in increasing numbers.

VILLAGE SOCIAL STRUCTURE AND
EARLY CHINESE IMMIGRATION

The characteristic features of the first wave of Chinese immigration from 1850 to 1882 to California were molded by the social structure of the peasant society of South China. The early Chinese immigrants came from impoverished rural counties in the Pearl River Delta. In rural Kwangtung province, villages were exogamous single or multilineage communities (Freedman, 1966). Ancestor worship, widely practiced by peasants, reflected the strength and importance of lineage solidarity (Hsu, 1948). So central was family and lineage to the social organization of peasant life that scholars have characterized Chinese peasants of this period as "familist," lacking a developed sense of national identity (Fei, 1939; Freedman, 1964; Johnson, 1962).

This strength of family and lineage bonds of village society resulted in a pattern of domestic and international migration in which males left for economic opportunities in Canton, Hong Kong, or distant lands—Southeast Asia and America—leaving wife and children behind in the village. According to the Chinese system of patrilineal descent, the household property and land were divided equally among adult sons, usually upon the marriage of the youngest son. Responsibility for support of parents in old age was thus shared by all sons; whereas daughters married out of the village, did not inherit property, and were not responsible for the support of elderly parents. Ownership of land and property provided a strong tie to the village of emigration. However, peasants who emigrated abroad typically came from poorer families in which landholding was modest. Indeed many peasants from impoverished families were landless when they emigrated to America. To ensure a continuing bond to family and village for both the land-owning and landless, emigrating men were expected to leave their wives and children behind (Nee and Nee, 1973). Thus cultural sanctions against women accompanying their husbands to distant lands had an economic basis in the interest of parents to guarantee that emigrating sons would continue to send back remittances to support them in old age (Glick, 1980). The few women who emigrated to California from 1850 to 1882 came either as prostitutes or wives of the small group of urban merchants who came from Canton to establish businesses in California (Lyman, 1977: 69). Though the sex ratio of Chinese emigrant society in America was dramatically masculine, most male migrants were married, but lived their lives in America as "bachelors." Chinese women were legally able to enter the United States before the passage of the Chinese Exclusion Act in 1882, but the sex ratio in 1880, three decades after the start of immigration, was still 2,106 males to 100 females (Lyman, 1977). The Chinese "bachelor" immigrant thus lived a lonely life in America, working to save money to remit back to villages in Kwangtung and to accumulate sufficient capital to enable him to return to his village to retire as a returned overseas Chinese. Without the establishment of families in America, there was little incentive for early Chinese immigrants to invest in acquiring the cultural and social skills necessary to get on in white society (Siu, 1952). Instead the Chinese lived among fellow sojourners in Chinatowns and the smaller "China camps" that were scattered throughout the Western states.

Confucianism was the product and inspiration of a rich literary tradition, yet illiteracy was very high among Chinese peasants. In village society, only the landed gentry could afford the long years of study necessary to acquire knowledge of classical Chinese for the Chinese examination system (Fei, 1953). The gentry was also affected by rural social disorder in Kwangtung, but they did not participate in the migration abroad (Barth, 1964). Compared to the high educational attainment of Japanese immigrants and of Chinese Americans after World War II, the literacy of the early Chinese male migrants was among the lowest of the immigrant groups in California. As long as Chinese remained sojourners, failing to establish families and produce a sizable second generation in America, low educational attainment and high illiteracy continued to characterize this group. Their children in China, supported by remittances sent back by their fathers abroad, generally did not pursue scholarly ambitions, and instead remained within the peasant class, though in many cases they were economically better off than peasants without money from abroad (Chen, 1940).

The supply side of early Chinese immigrant labor, as determined by the socioeconomic factors at the point of departure, thus sets the stage for the problem of social mobility in America. Low education level coupled with lack of family formation in America for the early Chinese immigrants resulted in demoralization as well as holding down the accumulation of capital and resources for social mobility in America.

On the demand side, the emergence of a capitalist economy in California and the Western states in the mid-nineteenth century stimulated new migrations of people (Cheng and Bonacich, 1984). The search for a ready source of cheap and efficient labor to develop the rich resources of the new state was a central issue for California's early capitalists. Sources of cheap labor were in fact quite limited because indigenous Indian labor proved unsatisfactory, slavery was foreclosed, and the Americans who came to California as settlers provided unreliable and expensive labor for the large-scale infrastructure projects. The attraction of Chinese labor for California's early capitalists was not only that Chinese were cheap relative to white labor, but that they were also hard working and, above all, thought to be temporary. The cheapness of Chinese labor was rooted in the low cost of reproduction of labor because the sojourner supported his family at much lower costs than would have been possible had his family joined him in California (Bonacich, 1973).

The opportunity structure for Chinese in nineteenth-century California was primarily defined by this demand for cheap labor. Controlled by labor contractors, and facing a growing anti-Chinese movement, only a few were successful in leaving laboring jobs to establish viable small businesses in ethnic enclaves. These small Chinese businesses survived because they filled niches in noncompetitive areas, such as laundries and Chinese restaurants. However, the majority of the sojourners drifted from mining to heavy construction, to farm labor, and finally into manufacturing (Saxton, 1971).

The qualities that made Chinese labor so attractive to capitalists, however, contributed to the eruption of a split-labor market conflict with the California working-class movement two decades after the start of large-scale Chinese immigration, culminating in the passage of the Chinese Exclusion Act in 1882 (Saxton, 1971). The ethnic antagonism and violence of the nineteenth-century anti-Chinese movement far exceeded subsequent anti-Oriental movements directed against the Japanese and was only approached by the anti-Filipino movement in the 1930s (Melendy, 1980). The outcome of the anti-Chinese white working-class movement was the erection and consolidation of a caste-like system, which spatially and legally separated Chinese from white society in the enclaves of Chinatowns. Chinese labor was excluded from most labor markets by white labor unions and legislation that they sponsored.

In the early Chinese immigration, from the supply side, peasant culture and the social structure of immigration locked Chinese laborers in a split labor market conflict that resulted in violent exclusion. For those who remained in America after exclusion, their continued status as poorly educated "bachelor" sojourners foreclosed any appreciable socioeconomic gain in America. It was over eighty years after the start of large-scale immigration and the formation of immigrant families in America before substantial socioeconomic gains occurred.

VILLAGE SOCIAL STRUCTURE AND THE JAPANESE IMMIGRATION

The early history of Japanese immigration to California paralleled that of the Chinese in many respects. Like the

Chinese laborers, Japanese immigrants were young peasant men from several prefectures in southern Japan and Okinawa; they came as sojourners, with the intention, as temporary residents, to earn the higher wages available in America and return to Japan upon completion of their work contracts; and they lived in bachelor societies, often next to Chinatown, where prostitution and gambling were also prevalent.

Despite these similarities, differences in Japanese rural social structure resulted in a weaker tie to family and village for Japanese immigrants. The peasant household *(ie)*, the basic unit of the rural society, was both a kin group and an economic corporation, a "continuing entity transcending individuals" (Fukutake, 1967). With the emphasis on the continuity of the household unit, centered on the house, fields, and agricultural implements, the Japanese inheritance system was based upon primogeniture, in which one son, usually the eldest, inherited the house, and became successor of the ie. According to village custom, the eldest son was thus responsible for the care of aged parents, whereas the other sons, who did not inherit land or only a small fragment of the household property, were free of this responsibility. The younger sons could pursue their fortunes elsewhere, leaving the village to join the army or to migrate to the industrializing cities of Meiji Japan to become factory workers, craftsmen, shopkeepers, and service workers. By contrast to the strength of lineages in South China, the extended kinship system in Japanese villages was much weaker (Nakane, 1970). The village, made up of independent households, was more closely integrated with the State, and inter-village mobility was a common feature of rural life.

At the start of large-scale Japanese emigration to America in the late 1880s, Japan had completed two decades of rapid westernization and modernization under the Meiji State and was rapidly emerging as a major capitalist economy and state. After the Meiji Restoration (1868), universal education was introduced in villages, which succeeded in eliminating illiteracy among peasants. In rural schools, patriotism and the striving for national glory were pushed by the Meiji public educational system (Smethurst, 1974). It was in this modernizing cultural

12

context that young male peasants applied to government review boards to emigrate to America. The purpose of government screening was to ensure that the peasant men "sent" abroad were healthy and literate, and could well represent the Japanese nation (Ichihashi, 1932). In short, from the supply side, Japanese immigrants came to America with a higher level of human capital compared with early Chinese immigrants.

Japanese immigration to America began shortly after the passage of the Chinese Exclusion Act of 1882. On the demand side, Japanese laborers were brought to replace the departing Chinese laborers, in fact, in the very industries where Chinese previously were concentrated—railroad, agriculture, restaurants, and personal services (McWilliams, 1945). Their entry into the American labor market, when the anti-Chinese sentiment was still strong in California, resulted in the association of Japanese laborers with their predecessors. Like the Chinese laborers, Japanese were also declared ineligible for citizenship and were objects of economic and social discrimination (Ichihasi, 1932). After the first decade of large-scale immigration, the same social forces that had participated in the anti-Chinese movement organized the Anti-Asian League in 1905 to oppose Japanese immigration (Millis, 1915).

The labor market concentration of Japanese laborers was in agriculture, due to their rural origins, where they worked as contract laborers for white agriculturalists (Iwata, 1962). By 1909, more than 30,000, 75% of Japanese immigrants, worked in agriculture where they engaged in wage-cutting to gain a larger share of this labor market (McWilliams, 1945). Though they began at the bottom as contract laborers working under the supervision of Japanese labor contractors, the Japanese farm laborers soon began to strike out to work on their own, leasing land from white farmers and becoming tenant farmers (Iwata, 1962).

Light (1972) stressed the importance of rotating credit associations in Japanese-American ability to establish small businesses. Equally important, if not more so, was the early family formation by Japanese immigrants. Though Japanese sojourners came with the intention of returning to Japan, by the

13

second decade of sustained immigration, many began to send for "picture brides" to establish families in America. In sharp contrast to the Chinese sojourners, the sex ratio dropped from 2,369 males to 100 females in 1900 to 694 males to 100 females in 1910, and by 1920, it was 189 males to 100 females (Lyman, 1977). The more rapid formation of families was linked to the Japanese village and family culture, which through primogeniture, resulted in relatively weak ties to family and village for sons who were not successors to the ie. Without the economic interest of ensuring support from all sons, there were also weaker sanctions against women leaving village communities to join "picture" husbands in America, rather than, as in the Chinese case, remaining as virtual hostages in their parents-in-law's households.

Yanagisako (1975: 200) emphasized that "the building of families coincided with the movement from wage-labor to entrepreneurship." The formation of families allowed the *issei* to create in America a household mode of production, along similar lines to that of the ie corporate unit in Japan, which provided the issei farmer with the labor force required to operate an independent truck farm that utilized the labor of a husband-wife-children team. Moreover, it enabled issei males to make a rapid transition from the unskilled wage-labor market that they had entered to form a thriving ethnic enclave economy, which though dispersed in its settlement pattern nonetheless utilized ethnic solidarity to enhance competitiveness. This enabled Japanese immigrants to avoid being locked in secondary labor market jobs characterized by low wages, lack of internal mobility, temporary employment, and low return on human capital investment (Portes, 1981). The availability of unpaid household labor allowed issei truck farmers to compete effectively with white farmers, enabling them to gain a dominant share of the produce market. As Bonacich and Modell (1980) argued, household labor and ethnic solidarity facilitated the creation of vertical integration in the produce market, which created a monopoly-like control by Japanese farmers and distributors. Without the formation of nuclear families it would not have been possible for Japanese immigrants to establish independent truck farms that utilized the optimal division of labor and corporate household unit resulting in high per/unit land yields as in Japan.

Another aspect of the early family formation of Japanese was the emotional resources it provided the issei men, in addition to meeting their sexual needs (Kikumura, 1973). In the face of harsh and continuous racial and economic discrimination, the issei were nonetheless able to remain competitive and, against difficult obstacles, achieve impressive economic gains so that they became a dominant force in the produce industry (Broom and Riemer, 1949). The growth of a sizable second generation by 1920 accelerated the process of acculturation for Japanese as the nisei entered into American public schools and began to achieve the high educational attainment that now characterizes the Japanese-American second generation.

Thus in the early Japanese immigration, the weaker tie to family and village in Japan permitted the early formation of family life in America. This in turn resulted in a faster transition from sojourner to settler for Japanese immigrants in comparison to the Chinese sojourners on the mainland. Though Japanese immigrants confronted the same anti-Asian prejudice and discrimination as the Chinese, this did not generate a split-labor market conflict because by 1910 Japanese were leaving wage-labor rapidly and establishing ethnic enterprises in both rural and urban areas based upon a household mode of production.

Japanese success in truck farms provoked ethnic conflict with white farmers competing against the Japanese family farm. Unlike a split-labor market conflict, in which the threatened dominant working class seeks to exclude and drive out the cheaper competition, the conflict with white farmers was more like business competition between competing firms. Some white farmers favored Japanese tenant farmers for the higher prices they paid for their leases, while others suffered from their superior competitiveness. Thus while the competition and conflict generated anti-Japanese economic sanctions, chiefly in the passage of the 1913 Alien Lands Act, there were always white farmers, eager to profit from the higher leases and land prices paid, who helped Japanese tenants circumvent this discriminatory act (Iwata, 1962). Popular pressure against the continuation of Japanese immigration eventually resulted in the 1924 Immigration Act that excluded Japanese immigration. But the intensity of ethnic conflict and violence never approached that which was directed against Chinese laborers. After the Japanese exclusion act, Japanese small businesses continued to prosper in California until the forced evacuation of Japanese Americans to internment camps during World War II.

POSTWAR DEVELOPMENT AND CHINESE IMMIGRATION

The tendency to deal with culture as static and unchanging is widespread among both critics and proponents of cultural theories of ethnic stratification. Yet culture changes over time both in shaping and in reacting to socioeconomic change. Therefore, the supply side argument must be informed by historical events and their impacts on the nature of immigration.

The transition from sojourner to settler for Chinese males occurred over a period of 100 years, reflecting changes in village culture and economy and institutional contraints in America. The modern transformation of Chinese peasant culture began long before the completion of the Communist land revolution of 1949 (Yang, 1959). Not only did modern conceptions of marriage and family filter down from Hong Kong and Canton to villages in the Pearl River Delta, but the educational level of villagers improved following the introduction of modern schools in rural areas (Levy, 1971). There were two intertwined processes that resulted in the weakening of ties to the village for Chinese sojourners. The first was a gradual rural-urban migration whereby the dependents of sojourners in America left villages to reside in Toishan City, Canton, and Hong Kong. This rural-urban migration accelerated after the Communist victory in 1949. The second process was land reform and

16

collectivization in the 1950s, which dispossessed the families of sojourners, who were often landlords, of their property and economic base in the village economy (Yang, 1959). In many cases, the dependents of sojourning families were severely attacked as landlords in the Communist-led class struggle during both land reform and agricultural collectivization (Vogel, 1969). These village level changes in Kwangtung gradually resulted in weakening the ties to clan and village for Chinese sojourners in America.

Recent scholarship critical of cultural explanations has stressed that institutional constraints prevented Chinese males from bringing wives to America, thus delaying the emergence of Chinese families in America (Glenn, 1983). If institutional constraints were decisive, then there should have been larger numbers of Chinese women arriving in America after the first decades of emigration, as was the case of Japanese immigration. Instead, very few Chinese women, primarily prostitutes and wives of urban merchants, entered California prior to exclusion from 1850 to 1882. Moreover, the intergenerational succession of sojourners from 1882 to 1945, was almost exclusively a male phenomenon, whereby typically the son of a sojourner joined his father to work alongside him in America's Chinatown. When the father returned to China to retire, his son remained to succeed him, and continued the sojourning pattern into the next generation. Few daughters were involved in this intergenerational succession because by village custom women were expected to remain behind. Nonetheless, by 1920, there was a sizable second generation produced in America, by the original population of women, approximately 4,000 who entered America prior to 1882, and by women smuggled in, mainly prostitutes, after 1882. By 1950, the sex ratio of Chinese Americans, 100 years after the start of immigration, reached the same level Japanese Americans reached after only 30 years, 189 males for 100 females. This differential, we argue, largely stemmed from the cultural differences between Chinese and Japanese peasants.

In America, from 1920 to 1940, the growth of a second generation of American-born Chinese initiated a process of socioeconomic achievement in Chinatowns similar to that of the Japanese Americans. In Chinatowns, Chinese who remained in America and established families formed the basis of household production similar to that of the Japanese-American family enterprise. The American-born Chinese grew up in family enterprises, dividing their time between helping out in the family shop and getting ahead in school (Kingston, 1976; Nee and Nee, 1973). Like the nisei youth, the American-born Chinese were oriented to acculturation, though their social life was centered in Chinatowns, within a Chinese-American social world. Like the nisei, those who graduated from high school and college often returned to work in family enterprises because of the lack of opportunities for Chinese Americans in the primary labor market.

Changes in the demand structure for Chinese during and following World War II opened up new opportunity structures for Chinese Americans. During the war, when the United States was allied to Nationalist China, the law making Chinese ineligible for naturalization was finally lifted. Chinese Americans who joined the army often used the "War Brides" Act to marry and bring wives back from China, thus reducing further the uneven sex ratio.

The wartime industrial boom in California opened up jobs outside of the Chinatown enclave economy to Chinese Americans. It also stimulated the migration of southern blacks to California, shifting white anti-Asian sentiment to focus on the black migration. Chinese and Japanese formed a much smaller minority and, importantly, there had been no new immigration. As anti-Chinese sentiment declined in California, second-generation college-educated Chinese Americans increasingly sought professional and white collar jobs outside of Chinatown (Kwoh, 1947). This upwardly mobile second generation began the move out of Chinatown to mixed residential neighborhoods, and in the 1950s, Chinatown declined in population (Lee, 1960). The greater socioeconomic mobility of the second generation contrasted with the poverty of the elderly sojourners living out their days in Chinatown (Nee and Nee, 1973). The contrast in education, occupation, and income of these two

18

groups produced a bimodal socioeconomic distribution for Chinese Americans, which resulted in lower aggregate socio-economic standing.

The new Chinese immigration was characterized by a two-level immigrant stream, each responding to different demand structures. First, were the professional and white-collar immigrants, the "brain drain" immigration, from Taiwan and Hong Kong, who entered into the primary labor market and settled outside of Chinatown. The second was composed primarily of the urbanized wives, children, and kinsmen of the old Chinese sojourners who came from Hong Kong, ending finally their "split household" arrangements to reunite in America. These immigrants settled for the most part in Chinatown, and found jobs in the enclave economy, often working in small businesses run by kinsmen or by their fathers. Those who worked outside of Chinatown entered jobs in the secondary labor market. Both immigrant streams dramatically differed from the past in that both groups came with intact families for the purposes of permanent residence and eventual naturalization.

NATIVE-BORN JAPANESE
AND CHINESE

The post-World War II socioeconomic mobility of the nisei generation paralleled that of the second generation Chinese American because it was made possible by the same changes in the opportunity structure and the decline of anti-Asian sentiment in the Western states. When the nisei returned to the west coast after the War, the destruction of the Japanese-American economy meant that the nisei could not depend on working in their parents' businesses (Broom and Riemer, 1949). This, and the greater openness to Japanese Americans, resulted in a shift away from ethnic employment to employment in the primary labor market. As white collar and professional jobs opened to Japanese-Americans, they moved into white residential suburbs and assimilated into American society. The dispersed pattern of settlement for Japanese Americans reduced their visibility as a racial minority, because it promoted the rate of intermarriage (Kikumura and Kitano, 1973). The pattern of the postwar achievement of the native-born Chinese and Japanese population was similar, so that by 1960 the education, occupation, and income profiles of both groups were comparable (Hirschman and Wong, 1981).

CONCLUSION

We need to go beyond the "culture versus structure" debate to recognize the artificiality of an either/or framework on whether culture or structure dictates the trajectory of socioeconomic attainment. As we argue here, a "supply-demand" perspective allows us to deal with culture and structure as part of an integrated explanation for differential socioeconomic attainment. The cultural attributes of immigrant/minority groups we placed on the "supply-side," as we did the socioeconomic background and educational attainment prior to and after immigration. On the "demand-side" we grouped the structural constraints and opportunity structures created by the dynamics of capitalist economic development. We maintain that to explain the differential Chinese and Japanese socioeconomic achievement prior to and after World War II, both cultural and structural factors need to be taken into account.

The strong ties of Chinese and weaker ties of Japanese immigrants to family in the home village proved decisive in shaping the immigration and timing of family formation. Strong or weak family and village ties were rooted in the differences of village culture between Chinese and Japanese immigrants. The consequence of differences in immigration pattern and family formation resulted in different outcomes in the timing of socioeconomic achievement for Chinese and Japanese. Chinese remained sojourners, did not establish families (except for urban merchants), and were caught in an explosively violent anti-Chinese campaign fueled by a split-labor market ethnic conflict.

20

Japanese, on the other hand, made the transition from sojourner to settler within the first two decades of immigration, and left low-wage labor to establish small businesses based upon a household mode of production. The Japanese enclave economy was characterized by its concentration in small businesses based upon family labor, its dispersed pattern of settlement in truck farms in California, and by its ability to sustain competition with white firms. The Chinese enclave economy grew out of coercive expulsion from most labor markets, and small businesses were largely in noncompetitive sectors of the urban economy. The familyless Chinese sojourner, moreover, was more vulnerable to demoralization, whereas Japanese immigrants faced societal hostility with the emotional resources provided by a stable family life.

Though Japanese immigrants benefited from the growing international stature of a modernizing Japan, the underlying pattern of immigration and timing of family formation, rooted in strong or weak village ties, was decisive in the differential socioeconomic standing of Chinese and Japanese immigrants prior to World War II. Once Chinese Americans began to establish nuclear families in America and produce a sizable second generation, establishing household production similar to the Japanese, the socioeconomic attainment of the Chinese "family society" paralleled that of the Japanese, and sharply contrasted with the poverty and low socioeconomic standing of the aging "bachelor" sojourners.

Changes in institutional constraints, immigration laws, labor markets, and societal hostility, we argue, were rooted in the dynamics of capitalist economic development. Early capitalist development generated demand for cheap labor that could not be sufficiently filled by white labor. Both the early Chinese and Japanese immigration was in response to this demand for cheap labor. In an advanced capitalist economy, the demand for immigrant labor is more differentiated such that both skilled professional and technical labor filling empty positions in the primary labor market, and the traditional unskilled low-wage labor, combine to create bimodal immigrant streams. This has been reflected in the character of the new Asian immigration to the United States that followed the changes in immigration laws in the 1960s.

The high educational attainment of native-born Chinese and Japanese and the concentration of Chinese and Japanese population in strategic states such as California paved the way for the movement of the second generation into the expanding primary labor market in the post World War II advanced capitalist economy. However, the destruction of the Japanese enclave economy as a result of forced internment during World War II led to the dispersal of the Japanese-American population and an acceleration of their assimilation into American society. By contrast the persistence of the Chinatown enclave economy has restricted assimilation for those who live and work in the enclave economy, though the native-born Chinese Americans who entered the primary labor market experienced socioeconomic mobility similar to that of the Japanese Americans.

A supply-demand perspective provides a dynamic model for understanding differential socioeconomic achievement. In a sense, the historical process can be seen as playing the role of the marketplace in a "supply-demand" approach. Both the cultural attributes of immigrant/minority groups and the structural constraints and opportunity structures they face change over time. Indeed the process of cultural and structural change is interactive, as illustrated in the case of Chinese immigrants. There was no clear line of demarcation between cultural values and norms that resulted in a sojourning immigration pattern and structural arrangements characteristic of the Chinese peasant family and village. The destruction of the pre-Socialist socioeconomic structures of family and village life after land reform and collectivation resulted in changes in cultural attitude toward immigration. Thus the urbanized immigrants from Hong Kong who joined their sojourning kinsmen in America after 1950 came as nuclear families with weak village ties and with the intention of permanent residence. The new immigrants, moreover, were responding to a substantially different labor market of an advanced capitalist economy.

22

REFERENCES

Barth, G.
  1964 Bitter Strength: A History of Chinese in the United States, 1850-1870.
       Cambridge, MA: Harvard Univ. Press.
Bellah, R.
  1957 Tokugawa Religion: The Values of Pre-Industrial Japan. New York: Free
       Press.
Bonacich, E.
  1972 "A theory of ethnic antagonism: the split labor market." Amer. Soc. Rev. 37:
       547-559.
  1973 "A theory of middleman minorities." Amer. Soc. Rev. 38: 503-594.
Bonacich, E. and J. Modell
  1980 The Economic Basis of Ethnic Solidarity: Small Business in the Japanese
       American Community. Berkeley: Univ. of California Press.
Broom, L. and R. Riemer
  1949 Removal and Return: The Socio-Economic Effects of the War on Japanese
       Americans. Berkeley: Univ. of California Press.
Buraway, M.
  1976 "The functions and reproduction of migrant labor: comparative material from
       Southern Africa and United States." Amer. J. of Sociology 81: 1050-1087.
Castles, S. and G. Kosack
  1973 Immigrant Workers and Class Structure in Western Europe. London: Oxford
       Univ. Press.
Cheng, L. and E. Bonacich
  1984 Labor Migration Under Capitalism: Asian Workers in the United States
       Before World War II. Berkeley: Univ. of California Press.
Caudill, W. and G. DeVos
  1965 "Achievement, culture, and personality: the case of the Japanese-Americans."
       Amer. Anthropologist 58: 1102-1126.
Chen, T.
  1940 Emigrant Communities in South China: A Study of Overseas Migration and
       Its Influence on Standards of Living and Social Change. New York: Institute
       of Pacific Relations.
Chiswick, B.
  1977 "Sons of immigrants: are they at an earnings disadvantage?" Amer. Econ.
       Rev.: Pap. Proc. 67: 376-380.
  1978 "The effect of Americanization on the earnings of foreign born men." J. of
       Pol. Economy 86: 897-921.
  1980 "Immigrant earnings patterns by sex, race, and ethnic groupings." Monthly
       Labor Rev. 103: 22-25.
Duncan, O. D. and S. Lieberson
  1959 "Ethnic segregation and assimilation." Amer. Soc. Rev. 64: 364-374.
Fei, H. T.
  1939 Peasant Life in China: A Field Study of Country Life in the Yangtze Valley.
       London: Routledge & Kegan Paul.
  1953 China's Gentry: Essays in Rural-Urban Relations. Edited by (R. Redfield
       and M. Redfield, eds.) Chicago: Univ. of Chicago Press.

23

Freedman, M.
  1964 "The family in China, past and present," in A. Feuerwerker (ed.) Modern
       China. Englewood Cliffs, NJ: Prentice-Hall.
  1966 Chinese Lineage and Society: Fukien and Kwangtung. New York: Humanities
       Press.
Freedman, M. (ed.)
  1970 Family and Kinship in Chinese Society. Stanford, CA: Stanford Univ. Press.
Fukutake, T.
  1967 Japanese Rural Society. Ithaca, NY: Cornell Univ. Press.
Glenn, E. N.
  1983 "Split household, small producer and dual wage earner: an analysis of Chi-
       nese-American family strategies." J. of Marriage and Family.
Glick, C.
  1980 Sojourners and Settlers: Chinese Migrants in Hawaii. Honolulu: Univ. of
       Hawaii Press.
Hsu, F.
  1948 Under the Ancestors' Shadow: Chinese Culture and Personality. New York:
       Columbia Univ. Press.
Hirschman, C. and M. G. Wong
  1981 "Trends in socioeconomic achievement among immigrant and native-born
       Asian Americans, 1960-1976." Soc. Q. 22: 495-513.
  1984 "Socioeconomic gains of Asian Americans, Blacks, and Hispanics: 1960-
       1976." Amer. J. of Sociology 90: 584-607.
Johnson, C.
  1962 Peasant Nationalism and Communist Power: The Emergence of Revolutionary
       China. Stanford, CA: Stanford Univ. Press.
Ichihasi, Y.
  1932 Japanese in the United States. Stanford, CA: Stanford Univ. Press.
Iwata, M.
  1962 "The Japanese immigrants in California agriculture." Agricultural History
       36: 25-37.
Kikumura, A. and H. Kitano
  1973 "Interracial marriage: a picture of the Japanese Americans." J. of Social
       Issue 29: 67-81.
Kitano, H.
  1969 Japanese Americans: The Evolution of a Subculture. Englewood Cliffs, NJ:
       Prentice-Hall.
Kingston, M. H.
  1976 Woman Warrior. New York: Knopf.
Kwoh, B.
  1947 "The occupational status of American-born Chinese male college graduates."
       Amer. J. of Sociology 53: 192-200.
Lee, R. H.
  1960 The Chinese in the United States of America. Hong Kong: Univ. of Hong
       Kong Press.
Levy, M.
  1971 The Family Revolution in Modern China. Cambridge, MA: Harvard Univ.
       Press.

24

Li, P.
   1977 "Ethnic businesses among Chinese in the United States." J. of Ethnic Studies
          4, 3: 35-41.
Lieberson, S.
   1980 A Piece of the Pie: Blacks and White Immigrants Since 1880. Berkeley: Univ.
          of California Press.
Light, I.
   1972 Ethnic Enterprise in America. Berkeley: Univ. of California Press.
Lyman, S.
   1977 The Asian in North America. Santa Barbara, CA: Clio Press.
Melendy, B.
   1980 "Filipinos in the United States," in The Asian Americans: Historical Expe-
          rience. Santa Barbara: Clio.
McWilliams, C.
   1945 Prejudice—Japanese-Americans: Symbol of Racial Intolerance. Boston,
          MA: Little, Brown.
Millis, H. A.
   1915 Japanese Problem in the United States. New York: Macmillan.
Nakane, C.
   1970 Japanese Society. Berkeley: Univ. of California Press.
Nee, V. and B. Nee
   1973 Longtime Californ': A Study of an American Chinatown. New York:
          Pantheon.
Nee, V. and J. Sanders
forth-   "The road to parity: determinants of the socioeconomic achievements of
coming Asian Americans." Ethnic and Racial Studies.
Petersen, W.
   1966 "Success story, Japanese-American style," in M. Kurokawa (ed.) Minority
          Responses. Lanham, MD: University Press of America.
   1971 Japanese Americans. New York: Random House.
Portes, A.
   1981 "Modes of structural incorporation and present theories of labor immigra-
          tion," pp. 279-297 in M. Kritz et al. (eds.) Global Trends in Migration:
          Theory and Research on International Population Movements. New York:
          Center for Migration Study.
Rosen, B.
   1959 "Race, ethnicity, and the achievement syndrome." Amer. Soc. Rev. 24: 47-
          60.
Rosenblum, G.
   1973 Immigrant Workers: Their Impact on American Labor Radicalism. New
          York: Basic.
Saxton, A.
   1971 The Indispensable Enemy: Labor and the Anti-Chinese Movement in Cali-
          fornia. Berkeley: Univ. of California Press.
Schwartz, A.
   1971 "The culturally advantaged: a study of Japanese-American pupils." Sociology
          and Social Research 55: 341-353.
Siu, P.
   1952 "The sojourner." Amer. J. of Sociology 58: 34-44.

25

Smethurst, R.
    1974   A Social Basis for Prewar Japanese Militarism: The Army and the Rural
            Community. Berkeley: Univ. of California Press.
Sowell, T.
    1981   Ethnic America: A History. New York: Basic.
Sung, B.
    1967   The Story of the Chinese in America. New York: Collier.
Vogel, E.
    1969   Canton Under Communism. Cambridge, MA: Harvard Univ. Press.
Wakeman, F.
    1966   Strangers at the Gate: Social Disorder in South China, 1839-1861. Berkeley:
            Univ. of California Press.
Wilson, K. L. and A. Portes
    1980   "Immigrant enclaves: an analysis of the labor market experiences of Cubans
            in Miami." Amer. J. of Sociology 86: 295-319.
Wong, M. G.
    1982   "The cost of being Chinese, Japanese and Filipino in the United States: 1960,
            1970, 1976." Pacific Soc. Rev. 25: 59-78.
Yanagisako, S. J.
    1975   "Two processes of change in Japanese-American kinship." J. of Anthropo-
            logical Research 31: 196-224.
Yancey, W. L., E. P. Ericksen, and R. N. Juliani
    1976   "Emergent ethnicity: a review and reformulation." Amer. Soc. Rev. 41: 391-
            403.
Yang, C. K.
    1959   Chinese Communist Society: The Family and the Village. Cambridge:
            Massachusetts Institute of Technology Press.

*Victor Nee is an Associate Professor of Sociology at Cornell University and
the University of California at Santa Barbara. He is currently engaged in
comparative research on Asian-American and Cuban immigrant enclave
economies and on market socialism in China. He is currently a Visiting
Professor at Xiamen University in the People's Republic of China, where he will
conduct survey research on the impact of economic reforms on peasant households
from April to August 1985.*

*Herbert Y. Wong is Vice President of Research and Development for The John
Thomas Group, Inc., a management research and consulting firm in Laguna
Hills, California. He has been the Coordinator of Research for the Fielding
Institute, a fully accredited external degree program at the doctoral level in
Psychology and Human and Organization Development. He is presently
engaged in writing a book,* The Ambidextrous Manager, *which discusses the
need for a manager to incorporate both the subjective and objective elements
of a management environment for more effective decision making. His most
recent article is "Graduate Training and Initial Job Placement: A Fair
Science?" in* Sociological Inquiry. *His ongoing research projects include a
study on productivity and JOB/PERSON/MATCH in a Southern California
police department and in a regional office of IDS American Express.*

Household Structure and Family Ideologies: The Dynamics of Immigrant Economic Adaptation Among Vietnamese Refugees*

NAZLI KIBRIA, Boston University

Using materials from an ethnographic study of newly arrived Vietnamese refugees in Philadelphia, this article argues that household structure and family ideology play a critical role in the dynamics of immigrant economic adaptation. The study shows the Vietnamese refugee households that were more heterogeneous in age and gender composition to be more adept at "patchworking" or gathering together a wide variety of resources from diverse social and economic arenas. This "patchworking" strategy mitigates the instability and scarcity of available resources. The economic dynamics of the Vietnamese refugee households are also shaped by an ideology of family collectivism — a set of beliefs about family life that encourage the sharing of individual social and economic resources within the household. Cooperative household economic behavior is also fostered by beliefs that help to generate agreement among household members about household goals. These ideological dimensions of household life are, however, being shaped and in some cases challenged by the migration process.

What explains their [Indochinese refugees'] success? The values they come with — a dedication to family, education and thrift — are cited as the main reason by people who have observed the refugees (Hume 1985).

In recent years the popular media has often portrayed Vietnamese refugees as the latest "immigrant success story" — a group whose cultural predisposition for hard work, initiative and frugality has enabled them to climb out of poverty. These reports not only conceal the tremendous economic diversity of the Vietnamese American population (Gold and Kibria 1993; Gold 1992), but also suggest a particular model of immigrant economic achievement, one in which the cultural orientation of the group in question is critical to its success or failure. By contrast, scholarly analyses have increasingly rejected cultural models in favor of perspectives that focus on the role of external structural conditions in shaping immigrant economic adaptation (e.g., Lieberson 1980; Pedraza-Bailey 1985; Portes and Bach 1985; Portes and Rumbaut 1990; Steinberg 1981).

In this paper I suggest that a conceptual and empirical focus on the immigrant household and family[1] offers a fruitful avenue for exploring the ways in which cultural factors and external structural conditions shape immigrant economic life. There is growing interest in the family as a unit of analysis in migration studies (Grasmuck and Pessar 1990; Massey et al. 1987). Pedraza (1991) argues that the family provides a valuable intermediary level of analysis for migration scholars. That is, a focus on the family avoids the dichotomous extremes of

---

* I would like to thank Eun Mee Kim, Barrie Thorne and Diane Wolf for their comments on earlier drafts. Correspondences to: Department of Sociology, Boston University, Boston, MA 02215.

1. Whereas households are residential units, families may be defined as kinship groups in which the members do not necessarily live together. As in the case of a household in which members do not see themselves as kin, it is possible for the household and the family to be units that are entirely distinct. More commonly however, the household and family are vitally connected. As Rapp (1992:51) observes, "families organize households." That is, notions of family tend to define the membership of households as well as relations between household members.

micro- and macro-level approaches, which analyze migration as a process that is either individually or structurally determined. I suggest that the immigrant household and family are valuable dimensions to examine not only migration movements, but also the processes by which immigrants economically adapt to the "host" society. Analyses that focus on variations in household and family organization, both within and across immigrant groups, may be particularly useful in generating explanations for different patterns of economic adaptation.

The significance of household and family organization to immigrant economic life is suggested by an ethnographic study of newly arrived Vietnamese refugees in Philadelphia. The findings of my study indicate that household structure and family ideologies play an important role in the economic life of the group. Those Vietnamese American households that were more differentiated in their age and gender composition were more successful in attaining economic goals such as the purchase of a home or the establishment of a small business. Age and gender heterogeneity is advantageous for households because it widens their structure of opportunities. This facilitates attempts to "patchwork," or to bring together diverse resources into the household economy, a strategy that helps to mitigate the instability and scarcity of available resources.

While the household composition affects its collective ability to access resources, it is Vietnamese American ideologies of family life that shape the manner in which household members respond to available opportunities. The Vietnamese American households are organized around an ideology of family collectivism. This encourages cooperative economic behavior — or "patchworking" — by emphasizing the unity of household interests and the economic significance of kinship ties. Cooperative economic behavior is also facilitated for Vietnamese Americans by family ideologies that help to define collective goals, such as the education of the young, for household members.

Household Structure, Family Ideologies and Immigrant Economic Life

Family-centered studies of the economic behavior of immigrants often view the family as a strategic arena, a social site where individuals can collectively cope with the economic environment to survive and to reach their goals (Dinerman 1978; Massey et al. 1987; Wood 1981).[2] With its focus on the strategic and flexible character of economic behavior, this emphasis on family strategies appears to offer an opportunity for developing a dynamic and processual understanding of immigrant economic adaptation. I suggest, however, that its potential to do so has been constrained by its inattention to household structure and to family ideologies.

The Effects of Household Composition

One of the most basic ways in which households differ is in their composition — who is included within the boundaries of the household. The potential effects of composition on a household's pool of available resources have not been adequately explored in studies of immigrant economic adjustment. I suggest this is largely due to limited definitions of the resources or assets that are pertinent to the household economy. Wage labor is often seen as the sole economic resource of the household, and household composition has accordingly been assessed for its impact on the household's pool of wage labor (Angel and Tienda 1982; Massey et al. 1987; Perez 1986). But this exclusive concern with wage labor neglects other, equally valuable, types of contributions to the household economy. For example, women

2. For a review of the literature on family adaptive strategies, see Moen and Wethington 1992.

and children may contribute to the household economy by providing their unpaid labor to the family businesses that have been an important part of the economic experience of some immigrant groups (Aldrich and Waldinger 1990; Portes and Rumbaut 1990).

Besides wages to the household financial pot or labor to the family business, members may also contribute assets of other kinds to the household economy. As current discussions of immigrant economic life suggest, it is not just labor market conditions, but also such contextual factors as "the policies of the receiving government, and the characteristics of their own [immigrants'] ethnic communities" (Portes and Rumbaut 1990: 85) that are relevant to immigrant economic progress. Such assertions suggest that we define the structural environment as not simply the labor market, but also in terms of institutions that potentially provide a range of important social and economic resources for the household. State institutions and bureaucracies may provide facilities and services such as assistance with education, job training, legal protection, health care, and resettlement (Pedraza-Bailey 1985). Groups within the household that are clearly disadvantaged in the labor market, such as children, may even have a better ability than adults to bring in resources from state institutions (e.g., college tuition loans).

The immigrant household economy is also affected by its social embeddedness in ongoing social relations and networks. As suggested by the extensive literature on the adaptive role of social networks and ethnic community ties (e.g., Massey et al. 1987; Min 1988; Morawska 1985; Portes and Bach 1985), for the immigrant group, the ethnic community may be a crucial source of loans, jobs, and information. Once again, recognition of the important economic role played by the ethnic community enhances our ability to consider forms of contribution to the household economy that are hidden by focus on wage labor. For example, the work that immigrant women put into cultivating and sustaining the kinship and friendship ties that socially integrate a family into the ethnic community may be seen as an important form of labor, one that facilitates the access of the household economy to ethnic community resources (di Leonardo 1987; Ewen 1985; Seller 1981).

When the definition of household economy includes relevant resources and institutions, household composition must be considered as well. Instead of assuming that a household membership configuration that maximizes the capacity for wage labor (such as one that is dominated by adult men) is advantageous, it becomes important to consider household composition in light of its repercussions for a wider range of household assets. Resources that appear to have little value when viewed individually may prove to be critical in their economic impact on the household economy when combined with other types of assets.

The Impact of Family Ideologies

Another dimension of the household critical to understanding its economic dynamics are the beliefs about family life held by members (Grasmuck and Pessar 1991; Moen and Wethington 1992). These family beliefs or ideologies define norms and expectations about household activities and relations that affect the household economy. For example, beliefs about women's family roles have important implications for the household economy, since they shape women's labor force participation as well as the ability of female household members to control economic resources. In a study comparing the economic activities of single female factory workers in Java and Taiwan, Diane Wolf (1990, 1992) found that the Javanese women, in contrast to their Taiwanese counterparts, often did not contribute their earnings to the family economy. Instead, the Javanese women retained control over their pay, spending it independently of their families. Wolf attributes the Javanese pattern to the relatively high degree of autonomy accorded women in the Javanese kinship system. In this particular case, family ideology concerning women's roles weakened the ability of the household economy to effectively incorporate the financial resources of its young single female members.

One of the central ways in which family ideology impacts the household economy is through its role in defining normative patterns of economic exchange within the household. That is, family ideology helps to define the economic relationships of household members. It thus influences the extent to which individual household members view their own economic activities and resources as part of the collective household economy. A household economy in which members view their economic life in collectivist terms will differ in its goals and dynamics from one in which the orientation is individualistic. Analyses of immigrant entrepreneurship, for example, suggest that groups with an ideology that emphasizes a collectivist and familial orientation towards economic achievement are more likely to engage in small business than others (Aldrich and Waldinger 1990; Sibley Butler 1991). However, as Aldrich and Waldinger (1990) note, such economic orientations tend to be fluid and responsive to the changing social context, as evidenced by the often radical shifts in the extent of a group's orientation towards entrepreneurship over the course of a few generations.

In general, family ideology must be seen as not only varied across groups, but also as fluid and reactive, constantly shifting in response to changing social contexts. The changing character of family ideology is often downplayed in cultural analyses of immigrant economic adaptation, which tend to portray immigrant cultural traditions as "given" and static (Caplan, Whitmore, and Choy 1989; Glazer and Moynihan 1963; Petersen 1971). The fluidity of familial cultural traditions is highlighted by Geschwender's (1992) analysis of historical changes in women's labor force participation. He describes how women of various ethnicities in the United States entered the labor force out of economic necessity, in a departure from the behaviors prescribed by the "cult of domesticity." The entry of women into the labor force generated normative change among some ethnic groups, whereby women were expected to contribute to the household economy through employment. In brief, structural changes in the economy led to shifts in family ideology concerning women's employment outside the home.

Methods

During 1983-85, I studied newly arrived Vietnamese refugees in Philadelphia through participant-observation and in-depth interviews (Kibria 1993). I conducted 31 interviews, 15 with women and 16 with men in the ethnic community. The interviews, which were tape-recorded, focused on the respondents' past and current experiences of family life. I also asked my interviewees a series of questions about their employment experiences and household budgeting practices in the United States. Because my knowledge of Vietnamese was minimal, many, but not all, of the interviews took place with the help of Vietnamese language interpreters. I also interviewed 11 Vietnamese American community leaders and social service agency workers in the city about the organizations in which they were involved and the relationship of these organizations to the Vietnamese American population in the city.

I also conducted participant-observation in household and community settings. For more than two years, I regularly visited 12 households in the community. During these visits, I observed and talked informally with household members. I spent time as a participant-observer in the neighborhood of study, in an attempt to gain a better understanding of the informal community life of Vietnamese Americans in the area, and the relationship of community life to household dynamics. Eventually, I focused my time on three popular community gathering places — a restaurant, a grocery store, and a hairdressing shop — all neighborhood businesses run by Vietnamese Americans.

More than 80 percent of the study-participants were from urban middle-class backgrounds in Southern Vietnam. Those men who had been beyond school age in Vietnam had usually been involved in military or government service. Women had worked, often sporadically, in family businesses or in informal, small-scale trading. All had experienced economic and social dislocations following the 1975 political transition to Communist rule in Vietnam. Directly and indirectly, these dislocations were responsible for the decisions of the refugees to undertake the hazardous escape by sea out of Vietnam during the late 1970s and early 1980s. While most of the refugees had been resettled in Philadelphia by social service agencies, others had relocated there from other places in the United States to join with kin or friends, forming households with them. The households in the community tended to be extended in character, containing a variety of kinfolk and friends (cf. Gardner, Bryant, and Smith 1985; Gold 1992).

The Social Context

Critical to understanding the economic dynamics of the Vietnamese refugee households are the conditions they encountered in three social arenas: the labor market, government policies and services, and the Vietnamese ethnic community. These arenas were central axes in the structure of opportunities facing the group, and thus provided the structural parameters for their economic behavior. The discussion shows available resources to be limited and unstable in supply, and restricted in availability to certain segments of the community.

Labor Market

Labor market opportunities for Vietnamese Americans were limited, a reflection of both the conditions of the local economy and the job skills of the group. During the study the Philadelphia city economy was highly polarized, composed of a professional high-income sector and a service sector that provided mainly low-paid, semi-skilled or unskilled work. The increasingly limited range of job opportunities, combined with the effects of a nationwide recession, inflated unemployment and poverty rates in the city during the early 1980s (Philadelphia City Planning Commission 1984). Further restricting the group's employment opportunities was its minority ethnic status and lack of suitable job skills for the formal economy. It is not surprising then, that unemployment rates in the community were high; in mid-1984, roughly 35 percent of the adult men in the 12 study households were unemployed.

The jobs that were most easily accessible to the group were low-level service sector positions, such as cleaning and waitressing, which tended to be poorly paid, part-time, unstable, and devoid of benefits and opportunities for advancement.[3] Also available to the group were jobs in the informal economy, particularly in garment assembly, an industry in which the Vietnamese refugee women were far more likely to be involved than the men.

Government Policies and Services

The "political refugee" status of the Vietnamese Americans gave legal legitimacy to their presence in the United States, and also provided access to a federal refugee aid and resettlement system (Pedraza-Bailey 1985; Rumbaut 1989a). Voluntary social service agencies (VO-LAGS) played a leading role in finding housing for new refugee arrivals, and providing information on services available to refugees such as English language classes, job counseling, and income support. All refugees were eligible for cash assistance and medical benefits through the Refugee Cash Assistance and Refugee Medical Assistance programs. When eligibility (based on length of residence in the United States) for Refugee Cash assistance ran out,

---

3. Studies of Vietnamese refugee communities in other parts of the country reveal similar employment patterns (Gold 1992; Rumbaut 1989).

those meeting the family composition and income level requirements continued to receive assistance through programs available to U.S. citizens such as AFDC (Aid to Families with Dependent Children), SSI (Supplemental Security Income), Medicaid, Food Stamps and GA (General Assistance). While all of the Vietnamese refugees had some contact with this system of assistance, a few had more sustained contact with the programs than others. Given the eligibility requirements, it is not surprising that those who were elderly, disabled, under the age of 18, and single parents, were more likely to have a long-term relationship with the cash and medical assistance programs.

The cash and medical assistance available to Vietnamese immigrants by virtue of their refugee status has been identified as an important economic boost for the group. What has been less noted, perhaps because it is less visible, is the access provided by the system to valuable social relationships, or "social capital" (cf. Coleman 1988). For example, out of their initial contacts with the resettlement system, some of the refugees developed close relationships with individual social service agency workers or sponsors, relying on them as a source of information about jobs, bank loans, and educational opportunities. In one particular case, members of a church congregation that had collectively sponsored a refugee household helped them to obtain a bank loan that they needed to open a business. Furthermore, sponsors or social service agency officials often provided job referrals for refugees. For some of my respondents, the friends that they had gained through the refugee resettlement system represented their only relationships with persons outside the ethnic community and were thus highly valued as a source of help for dealing with the dominant society's institutions. In some cases these "outside" persons were identified by adults as important role models for their children, who could turn to them for help with homework and other academic matters. In short, the social relationships that households were able to acquire through the resettlement system enhanced the socioeconomic heterogeneity of its social networks.

Households with children under age eighteen had greater access to public education than other households did. Public schools provided the opportunity to gain educational credentials, to learn English, and to acquire other cultural skills important for getting by in the United States. Because of this, households with school-age children had an advantage in dealing with dominant society institutions, since their children could serve as reliable interpreters. In addition, much like the refugee assistance system, the schools were also an arena through which the immigrants were able to develop relationships with teachers and other school officials. Once again, these social relations could be an important source of information and assistance. A high school teacher in the community helped the families of his students fill out home loan mortgage forms, while another teacher provided much-needed information about the complex regulations of the public assistance bureaucracy.

Ethnic Community

Two dimensions of ethnic community life —economic enclaves and ethnic associations— are widely identified by social scientists as important resources for immigrants, at least in the initial process of settlement in the United States. Ethnic economic enclaves are important sources of jobs, training, and opportunities for advancement for immigrant groups (Portes and Bach 1985). Ethnic associations also provide assistance in the form of capital, information about jobs, business ventures, and various aspects of life in the "host" society.

For the Philadelphia Vietnamese community, both ethnic economic enclaves and formal ethnic organizations were under-developed, partly due to the recency of Vietnamese settlement in the area. Ethnic ties did, however, play an extremely important role in the group's economic experiences. The immigrants belonged to ethnic social networks that provided a range of important resources, including financial loans and information about jobs, housing, and welfare (cf. Gold 1992; Hein 1993). While these informal social networks were often based on kinship ties and shared neighborhoods, they were also organized around age, gender and social class background. In other words, the social networks of individuals reflected their status along these variables.

Patchworking and Household Composition

In the structure of opportunities that I have described, the resources potentially available from any one source were limited and unreliable. Available jobs tended to be low-paying and unstable. Payments from the Refugee Cash Assistance and other assistance programs were also restricted and viewed by the Vietnamese refugees as highly temporary and unstable assets that could be terminated abruptly. The immigrants saw social relations in the ethnic community as far more reliable sources of economic and social assistance than either the labor market or government assistance programs. But, given both the economically homogeneous and fairly transient character of the community, even these resources were viewed as inherently scarce and unstable.

Like other economically disadvantaged communities (Bolles 1983; Glenn 1991; Stack 1974), Vietnamese Americans responded to these economic conditions by pooling resources within their domestic groups. But the notion of "pooling," which suggests sharing resources, does not adequately convey the Vietnamese American practice of sharing diverse resources.[4] I suggest that this practice is better conveyed by the notion of "patchworking" because the term conjures up an image of jagged pieces of assorted material stitched together in sometimes haphazard fashion.

Patchworking — the bringing together and sharing of diverse resources — is a practice that helps the Vietnamese American households to protect themselves against economic instability, or fluctuations in the supply of resources. The importance of having access to multiple resources was suggested by the experiences of an informant named Binh, a man in his forties who came to the United States with his two teenage sons. After arriving, the family lived on the government benefits available to newly-arrived refugees. Binh also took English language classes while his sons attended high school. Binh described the household as being economically self-sufficient at this time. Although his sister and her husband lived in the city, Binh did not rely on them for assistance. In fact, priding himself in his self-sufficiency, he had forbidden his sons to either "give or take money or anything else from other people." After about two years, Binh began looking for work; however, his job search was cut short by a back injury. Despite what he described as debilitating back pain, he was told by social service agency workers that he was no longer eligible for government aid. At the same time, his oldest son, who had just turned nineteen, was also told that he could no longer receive public assistance. These events created a crisis during which the household relied heavily on Binh's sister for food and other household expenses. Binh said his beliefs regarding the viability of self-sufficiency and survival in the United States had radically changed as a result of this unfortunate period. He came to realize that relations with kin were virtually a necessity in the United States. He also recognized the dangers of having only one source of income.

In Binh's case, access to a diverse resource base provided some degree of stability in a risky economic context. In an environment in which the quantity of assets from any one arena was limited, it was also a strategy that enhanced the scope of a household's resource pool. In a household I observed, one member took courses in machine repair at a local technical institute, while another member worked for a sewing contractor at home, also taking care of the young children in the family, and collecting Refugee Cash Assistance payments.

---

4. The Vietnamese American practice that I observed of bringing diverse resources together extends the concept of income diversification, which has been noted by studies of developing societies to be a common strategy for dealing with risky economic contexts (Agarwal 1992; Perez-Aleman 1992).

Of the other two household members, one worked in an ethnic business run by friends and the other in a semi-skilled manufacturing job outside the city. Through these various activities, household members brought in wages from the formal and the informal economy, benefits from public assistance programs, and job skills and cultural capital from participation in training programs. Because a member worked in an ethnic business, the household also had access to a variety of ethnic community networks and resources.

The ability to access a wide range of resources was enhanced by a high degree of differentiation among household members. The structure of available resources was scarce, unstable, and restricted, since not all household members had equal access to jobs, welfare, or the ethnic community networks. For example, in many informal sector jobs, such as those in the garment industry, women were more favored as employees than men. Furthermore, age clearly affected access to government assistance programs. Households with children and elderly were more likely to have a sustained and long-term relationship with public assistance programs. Membership in social networks and access to the resources embedded in these networks was also determined by age and gender. Thus, a high degree of status differentiation among household members expanded the household's reach, allowing it to more effectively take advantage of available opportunities and to "patchwork" resources. The economic advantages of internally heterogeneous households were suggested to me by the words of a Vietnamese American man in his thirties who had come to the United States alone:

> After coming to America I realized that my college education from Vietnam doesn't mean anything here. I look around and I see that many of the Vietnamese who do well here are not the ones who have education. If you come here with your family, or maybe your relatives are already here, you're better off because you can live together and save money. The children can go to school and slowly they can help their parents. Maybe they can open a store together, or maybe two people can get jobs and support the family while the rest of the people go to school or the community college.

To further clarify the economic consequences of differentiation in household composition, I will next contrast the economic experiences of three specific households. These three households represent the range of diversity in terms of age and gender composition that I found in my sample. Different degrees of internal diversity resulted in different levels of access to such resources as public assistance and education, and to social networks in the community.

Household One: High Diversity

Household One contained members of varied age and gender. It consisted of seven people: a woman named Thanh[5] in her late fifties, her three adult sons, two daughters, and one son-in-law.

After arriving in the United States, all household members received government aid through refugee assistance programs. But about a year-and-a-half later, the four men in the household were cut off from these programs when social service workers judged them to be capable of economic self-sufficiency. The household economy continued, however, to draw resources from public assistance programs. After receiving Refugee Cash Assistance and Refugee Medical Assistance for more than two years, Thanh and her daughters were transferred into other aid programs. For Thanh and her youngest daughter (who was fourteen), age was a critical factor in their continued eligibility for government assistance. Due to her status as a low-income elderly person, Thanh was eligible for Supplemental Security Income. The youngest daughter could receive General Assistance because she was under age eighteen, attending school, and a member of a low-income household. Following the birth of her baby,

---

5. All names have been changed to maintain anonymity.

Thanh's older daughter became eligible for Aid to Families with Dependent Children, a program that targets low-income families with young children.

The diverse composition of Household One enabled it to have a sustained relationship with government aid programs. The household's age and gender diversity also gave it access to a wide range of community networks. About five years after arriving in the United States, the household opened a Vietnamese-Chinese restaurant. The household's wide-ranging networks were critical to its ability to open the business since small personal loans from friends and contacts provided the household start-up capital. The success with which the household was able to obtain these loans was related to its diversity. For example, Thanh was able to borrow money from her circle of friends, which was composed of elderly Vietnamese refugee men and women. Without Thanh, the household would not have had access to these financial resources. Similarly, Thanh's older daughter was able to prevail on her own group of woman friends for small loans. Thanh's three sons were also able to obtain funds from their friendship networks of young single men. In addition, Thanh's son-in-law, who was a member of the household, was able to tap into his own separate kinship networks in New York to obtain loans. In short, the household worked to obtain a large number of small personal loans to open the business. The age and gender diversity of the household contributed to the success of this strategy.

Household Two: Medium Diversity

Household Two represents the middle range in terms of age and diversity of the households in my study. The household consisted of six persons: a married couple named Hung and Lien, Hung's three younger brothers, and a male friend. Not only was the household numerically dominated by men, but it was also marked by age homogeneity. All of the household members were in their late teens or early twenties.

The household's homogeneous composition contributed to its somewhat weaker links to the public assistance system, compared to Household One. Two of Hung's younger brothers collected General Assistance payments, which they were eligible to receive because they were under age eighteen, and attending school. Hung and Lien had also attended school and received public assistance for about three years after arriving in the United States. But neither of them had been able to complete high school before turning eighteen. The household's access to public assistance did strengthen, however, after the birth of Hung and Lien's daughter. As a low-income mother, Lien became eligible for Aid to Families with Dependent Children.

Government assistance resources available to the household were crucial to its economic survival. All household members had trouble finding stable jobs. Hung and the two other young men who were not attending school worked sporadically, usually in janitorial jobs in restaurants. Lien often supplemented the household income by sewing garments at home or working as a waitress in one of the area's Chinese or Vietnamese restaurants. Further compounding the paucity of household economic resources was the fact that, unlike the first household, it was not connected to a set of diverse and wide-ranging social networks. The similar age of household members was a critical factor in the household's homogeneous networks. Household members' social circles tended to overlap a great deal since they all socialized with other Vietnamese refugees in the area who were young, unmarried, or newly married.

Household Three: Low Diversity

Household Three was extremely homogeneous in age and gender composition. It consisted of five unrelated men, all single and in their early twenties. All of the men had received

Refugee Cash Assistance and Refugee Medical Assistance after arriving in the United States for periods of one to two years. After this, the household was completely cut off from government aid programs. As young, able-bodied, single men, they were unable to meet the programs' core requirement: an inability to financially sustain oneself due to age, illness, or the burden of dependents. All five men had also arrived in the United States at an age (seventeen years or more) preventing them from taking full advantage of public education opportunities.

Like Household Two, the members of Household Three belonged to overlapping social circles. These social circles provided them with referrals and information about jobs as well as other aspects of life in the United States. However, as the young men discovered when they began to investigate the possibility of opening a car repair shop, their social contacts limited their financial capacity. They were unable to borrow enough money from friends and contacts for the venture. This inability reflected the limited range and diversity of the household's social networks, which were composed almost solely of young, single, recently arrived Vietnamese refugee men. Thus, unlike Household One, this household was unable to turn to a diverse set of acquaintants for financial loans.

Patchworking and Family Ideologies

While composition structured a household's access to societal resources, the manner in which these resources were utilized or "processed" was critically shaped by the family ideology of household members. Here I examine two ideological dimensions of Vietnamese refugee life that help to explain the "patchworking" strategy of households.

The Ideology of Family Collectivism

A tradition of defining kinship in an inclusive and fluid manner encouraged the members of the Vietnamese refugee households to view each other as kin, regardless of whether or not the relationships fulfilled formal kinship criteria (Kibria 1993; Luong 1984). Thus in the households that I observed, familial expectations of economic participation applied to all household members, both kin and non-kin. Underlying these economic expectations was an ideology of family collectivism, a set of beliefs about the nature and significance of family life. The ideology of family collectivism, which drew on Vietnamese kinship traditions, organized and undergirded the economic patchworking of households in several ways. It advanced the view that economic reliance on family ties was an appropriate and judicious response to the economic demands and opportunities of the migration process. It also helped to promote a collective, cooperative approach towards resources and activities among household members by stressing, and indeed, idealizing the unity of family interests.

Central to the ideology of family collectivism is the notion that the kin group is far more significant than the individual. This dimension of family collectivism drew strength from Confucian family traditions, including the practice of ancestor worship. Family altars that were used to perform rites to honor ancestors were a common sight in the Vietnamese American households that I visited. Ancestor worship affirmed the sacredness and essential unity of the kin group, as well as its permanence in comparison to the transience of the individual. It also highlighted obligation as a key feature of a member's relationship to the kin group. The central obligation of the family member was to place the needs and desires of the kin group over and above any personal ones.

Another component of the ideology of family collectivism is the belief that the family is an individual's most reliable source of support — the only institution that could be counted on for help under all circumstances. Among my informants there was a strong belief that kin ties were an economic safety net, a belief that had been cultivated by the long years of social turmoil in contemporary South Vietnam during which time kin ties had been a source of security for many Vietnamese. Respondents told me several traditional proverbs that stressed the durability and significance of kin over non-kin relations, such as: "A bitter relative is still a relative, a sweet stranger is still a stranger," and "If your father leaves you, you still have your uncle; if your mother leaves you, you can nurse on your aunt's milk."

In a variety of ways, these family beliefs encouraged individuals to maintain close economic ties to the households in which they lived and to participate in "patchworking." The ideology of family collectivism, for example, could be used as a sanction against rebellious household members who refuse to go along with the decisions made by others. One such situation involved a young man named Doan, who was living in a household with three older brothers, their wives and children. Doan's refusal to contribute money towards the collective household purchase of a family home gave rise to conflict with his older brothers. Doan was planning to use his extra income to sponsor his girlfriend (who was in a refugee camp in Thailand) to the United States. Drawing on notions embedded in the ideology of family collectivism, such as individual obligation to the family, Doan's older brothers interpreted his refusal as evidence of selfishness and lack of concern for the family, as well as lack of respect for his family elders. Doan justified his refusal by arguing that the purchase of a house would serve his brothers' interests far better than his own. Since his brothers were all married and had children (unlike him), it was far more important for them to secure housing that was stable and in a relatively prosperous neighborhood. Unable to resolve the dispute, Doan eventually moved out of the household and into a friend's home.

As this example suggests, households were not always successful in forcing deviant members to conform to established economic decisions. Migration had, in fact, created conditions that made non-compliance to the principles of family collectivism more likely than ever. According to traditional Vietnamese family patterns, authority in the family rested with men and the elderly. But migration to the United States had diminished the power of men and the elderly. This opened opportunities for traditionally less powerful groups to challenge their authority, thus increasing the potential for intra-household conflicts over economic decisions. Doan, for example, told me he probably would not have disagreed with his brothers' decision in Vietnam, because the elder status of his brothers had carried more authority there.

The challenge posed by migration to the authority of men over women was particularly striking. The economic power of men in the community had declined with migration, thus weakening the economic basis for male authority (Kibria 1990). In many households, men were periodically or chronically unemployed, with women contributing a major share of the household finances. This economic power shift challenged the traditional authority of men and generated household environments that were ripe for conflicts between men and women. It is not surprising then, that "patchworking" was often accompanied by dissension and negotiation between men and women, particularly over the ways in which money should be spent. But despite these conflicts, the wholesale defection of men and women from the household economy was rare, because most were dependent on it for economic survival and economic mobility. In this sense, the economic conditions of life in the United States, in their poverty and uncertainty, had reinforced traditional beliefs about the economic significance of kinship ties and how they fulfilled the function of an economic safety net. Thus the conditions of settlement in the United States were simultaneously strengthening and challenging the ability of the ideology of family collectivism to organize the economic life of the Vietnamese American households.

"Making it" Through the Education of the Young

For the Vietnamese Americans, cooperative household economic behavior is also promoted by widely shared goals that helped to generate consensus among members about collective economic investment. One of these goals is the schooling of the young. This is seen as an effective path by which the family as a whole can achieve mobility in the future, a view that encourages the household economy to invest resources in education. This perspective on education reflects the experiences of my informants in pre-1975 South Vietnam, a context in which academic credentials had been deeply valued among the middle class. Education could secure one a high-ranking place in the government bureaucracy or military, or in the professions. Historically, education was seen by the group as an effective method by which to achieve economic prosperity and stability (cf. Ogbu 1978). This understanding of education had been reinforced for the Vietnamese Americans by the comparatively greater opportunities in the United States for obtaining higher education.

A child's education was understood as a venture from which the household as a whole would reap rewards in the future. In the short run, the academic achievements of the young were a source of collective familial status and prestige in the ethnic community. In the informal social gatherings that I attended, it was not unusual for parents or other family elders to pass around and compare the report cards of school-aged children. In the long run, household members expected to gain not only status privileges, but also material rewards. In accordance with the prescriptions of the ideology of family collectivism, the young were expected to pay back their families after completing their education. In fact, many parents explicitly identified the children's education as an investment for their future and for the collective future of the kin group. Although not without ambivalence, these expectations of payback were also shared by many young Vietnamese Americans who often focused on fields that would allow them to more effectively meet family financial obligations. Thus a young Vietnamese American who was studying for a degree in pharmacy (although he would have preferred to study art) told me that he planned to buy a house for his sister and brother-in-law, with whom he was living, as soon as he completed college. Similarly, in a study of Southeast Asian refugee youth conducted by Rumbaut and Ima (forthcoming), a Vietnamese refugee said the children in his family were all expected to pay a money "tax" to their mother after completing college.

Expectation of future rewards to motivate households to invest in the schooling of the young was vividly highlighted to me by one case in which a young member was actually dissuaded by kin from continuing his education. Kim's mother and aunt discouraged him from taking courses in college, encouraging him instead to find a job that would help the household to amass the savings necessary to purchase a home. The household preferred to channel its educational aspirations into Kim's younger brother, who was seen as more likely to succeed academically, since he was proficient in English and was receiving much better grades.

The rewards of education are not the only means by which Vietnamese Americans collectively approach schooling. Researchers have noted how studying is organized in Vietnamese refugee households as a collective rather than individual task or activity. Children sit down together to study and assist each other with school-related problems (Caplan, Choy, and Whitmore 1992). Rumbaut and Ima (forthcoming) further describe the Vietnamese refugee family as a "mini-school system" with older siblings playing a major role in mentoring and tutoring their younger brothers and sisters.

The manner in which the Vietnamese immigrants view the education of the young helps to explain the well-publicized educational successes of Vietnamese refugee youth as a group (Caplan, Choy, and Whitmore 1992). Perhaps most importantly, the collectivist familial orientation to schooling that I have described results in a situation in which the stakes for doing well at school are extremely high; for the young, it is not only their own future that hinges on their ability to do well at school, but also that of the family. However, as with other ideological dimensions of Vietnamese American family life, these ideas about education are being challenged in the United States. Perhaps the most significant challenge stems from the diminishing strength of the ideology of family collectivism among young Vietnamese Americans, who are increasingly likely to favor an individualistic rather than collective familial approach to economic activities. For family elders, the cultural assimilation and potential defection of the young from the cooperative family economy raises questions about the education of the young as a collective goal. The "Americanization" of the young endangers the payback that kin hope to receive in the future from their investments in the education of the young.

Conclusions

In this paper I have argued that the organization of immigrant households and families is useful in examining the role of external structural conditions and cultural factors in shaping immigrant economic life. An ethnographic study of Vietnamese refugees suggests a number of specific ways in which the organization of households and families enter into the dynamics of immigrant economic life. A significant aspect of household structure that I encountered is the degree of age and gender diversity in household composition, which is found to impact the structure of household opportunities. Besides age and gender diversity, there are other variations in household structure — such as size, proportion of kin versus non-kin, lifecycle stage, and membership stability — that may be useful to explore in studies of immigrant economic adaptation (Angel and Tienda 1982; Moen and Wethington 1992; Perez 1986).

The consequences of diversity in household composition may also extend well beyond the access to resources that I have emphasized. Because age and gender are central bases of family inequality, a household that is age and gender diverse is also likely to be hierarchical in its internal relations. Such a household, in which some members have substantial authority over others, may organize its economic activities quite differently than a household that is homogeneous and thus more egalitarian in its relations between members. For example, hierarchical households may be better able to demand economic behavior from members that calls for self-sacrifice and is directed towards familial rather than individual goals.

Our understanding of the economic implications of age and gender diversity in households will also be enhanced by investigations into its consequences across varied social contexts. The economic advantages associated with membership diversity for the Vietnamese refugee households in my study were tied to the specific character of the structural environment that surrounded them. This was an environment in which all household members, regardless of age and gender, tended to have access to valued, although different, resources. It was not an environment in which a particular age and gender group (for example, young men) had *substantially* better acccess to societal resources than others. An important reason for this relative equality was the access of young and elderly persons to government aid and services (e.g., cash and medical assistance, public schooling). If such programs had not been available, it is possible that age and gender diversity in household composition would not have been a source of economic advantage.

This relationship between government programs and the economic advantages of age and gender diverse households also suggests that internal household differentiation may be an especially significant variable in the economic experiences of refugee immigrant groups. In the contemporary United States, immigrants who enter under the official classification of "refugee" have access to government assistance programs that are unavailable to non-refugee immigrants (Portes and Rumbaut 1990). To the extent that the benefits of household diversity stem from the availability of such programs, diverse households will be particularly advantageous for refugee groups. While they do not focus specifically on the linkages between household composition and government assistance programs, studies of Cuban refugees in the United States have noted the importance of both government aid programs and family structure to the economic adaptation of the group (Pedraza-Bailey 1985; Perez 1986).

While household organization is a useful dimension by which to explore the structural context of immigrant economic life, family ideologies provide an understanding of immigrants' responses to opportunities. Among the Vietnamese refugees of my study, the general response to the structural environment is to engage in cooperative and household-centered "patchworking." "Patchworking" behavior is supported by an ideology of family collectivism as well as beliefs concerning the relationship of the family economy to the education of the young. Structuralist analyses of immigrant economic adaptation tend to neglect such ideological factors, a neglect that weakens their ability to develop convincing explanations of how and why groups respond differently to similar circumstances. Studies that systematically compare the family ideologies of immigrant groups and their impact on economic behavior are needed in order to develop a fuller understanding of the dynamics of immigrant economic adaptation. Such studies must, however, avoid the static view of immigrant cultures that has often marked cultural analyses of immigrant economic adaptation (Caplan, Whitmore, and Choy 1989; Petersen 1971). My study reveals the family ideologies of the Vietnamese refugees to be responsive to shifting social conditions. It is clear that the Vietnamese American ideology of family collectivism is in a state of flux and being molded in often contradictory ways by the migration and resettlement process.

References

Agarwal, Bina
1992   "Gender relations and food security: Coping with seasonality, drought and famine in South Asia." In Unequal Burden: Economic Crises, Persistent Poverty and Women's Work, eds. Lourdes Beneria and Shelley Feldman, 181-219. Boulder, Colo.: Westview Press.

Aldrich, Howard E., and Roger Waldinger
1990   "Ethnicity and entrepreneurship." Annual Review of Sociology 16:111-35.

Angel, Ronald, and Marta Tienda
1982   "Determinants of extended family structure: Cultural pattern or economic need?" American Journal of Sociology 87:1360-1383.

Bolles, A. Lynn
1983   "Kitchens hit by priorities: Employed working-class Jamaican women confront the IMF." In Women, Men and the International Division of Labor, eds. June Nash and M. Patricia Fernandez-Kelly, 138-60. Albany, NY: State University of New York Press.

Caplan, Nathan, John Whitmore, and Marcella Choy
1989   The Boat People and Achievement in America: A Study of Family Life, Hard Work and Cultural Values. Ann Arbor, Mich.: University of Michigan Press.

Caplan, Nathan, Marcella Choy, and John Whitmore
1992   "Indochinese refugee families and academic achievement." Scientific American 266:36-42.

Coleman, James
1988   "Social capital in the creation of human capital." American Journal of Sociology 94:S95-S120.

di Leonardo, Micaela
    1987   "The female world of cards and holidays: Women, families, and the work of kinship."
        Signs 12:440-453.
Dinerman, Ina R.
    1978   "Patterns of adaptation among households of U.S.-bound migrants from Michoacan,
        Mexico." International Migration Review 12:485-501.
Ewen, Elizabeth
    1985   Immigrant Women in the Land of Dollars: Life and Culture on the Lower East Side,
        1890-1925. New York: Monthly Review Press.
Gardner, Robert W., Robey Bryant, and Peter Smith
    1985   "Asian Americans: Growth, change and diversity." Population Bulletin 40.
Geschwender, James A.
    1992   "Ethgender, women's waged labor, and economic mobility." Social Problems 39:1-16.
Glazer, Nathan, and Daniel P. Moynihan
    1963   Beyond the Melting Pot. Cambridge, Mass: MIT Press.
Glenn, Evelyn Nakano
    1991   "Racial ethnic women's labor: The intersection of race, class and gender oppression." In
        Gender, Family and Economy: The Triple Overlap , ed. Rae Lesser Blumberg, 173-201.
        Newbury Park, Calif.: Sage Publications.
Gold, Steven J.
    1992   Refugee Communities: A Comparative Field Study. Beverly Hills, Calif.: Sage
        Publications.
Gold, Steven J., and Nazli Kibria
    1993   "Vietnamese refugees and blocked mobility." Asian and Pacific Migration Journal 2:1-30.
Grasmuck, Sherri, and Patricia Pessar
    1991   Between Two Islands: Dominican International Migration. Berkeley, Calif.: University of
        California Press.
Hein, Jeremy
    1993   States and International Migrants: The Incorporation of Indochinese Refugees in the
        United States and France. Boulder, Colo.: Westview Press.
Hume, Ellen
    1985   "Vietnam's legacy: Indochinese refugees prosper in U.S., drawing on survival skills,
        special values." Wall Street Journal, March 21.
Kibria, Nazli
    1990   "Power, patriarchy and gender conflict in the Vietnamese immigrant community."
        Gender & Society 4:9-24.
    1993   Family Tightrope: The Changing Lives of Vietnamese Americans. Princeton, NJ:
        Princeton University Press.
Lieberson, Stanley
    1980   A Piece of the Pie. Berkeley, Calif.: University of California Press.
Luong, Hy Van
    1984   "'Brother' and 'uncle': An analysis of rules, structural contradictions and meaning in
        Vietnamese kinship." American Anthropologist 86(2):290-313.
Massey, Douglas, R. Alarcon, J. Durand, and H. Gonzalez
    1987   Return to Aztlan. Berkeley, Calif.: University of California Press.
Min, Pyong Gap
    1988   Ethnic Business Enterprise: Korean Small Business in Atlanta. Staten Island, NY: Center
        for Migration Studies.
Moen, Phyllis, and Elaine Wethington
    1992   "The concept of family adaptive strategies." Annual Review of Sociology 18:233-51.
Morawska, Ewa
    1985   For Bread With Butter. New York: Cambridge University Press.
Ogbu, John U.
    1978   Minority Education and Caste. New York: Academic Press.
Pedraza, Silvia
    1991   "Women and migration: The social consequences of gender." Annual Review of
        Sociology 17:303-25.

41

Pedraza-Bailey, Silvia
    1985   Political and Economic Migrants in America: Cubans and Mexicans. Austin, Texas: University of Texas Press.
Perez, Lisandro
    1986   "Immigrant economic adjustment and family organization: The Cuban success story re-examined." International Migration Review 20:1, 4-20.
Perez-Aleman, Paola
    1992   "Economic crisis and women in Nicaragua." In Unequal Burden: Economic Crises, Persistent Poverty and Women's Work, eds. Lourdes Beneria and Shelley Feldman, 239-259. Boulder, Colo.: Westview Press.
Petersen, William
    1971   Japanese Americans. New York: Random House.
Philadelphia City Planning Commission
    1984   Socioeconomic Characteristics for Philadelphia Census Tracts: 1980 and 1970. Technical Information Paper.
Portes, Alejandro, and Robert Bach
    1985   Latin Journey: Cuban and Mexican Immigrants in the U.S. Berkeley, Calif.: University of California Press.
Portes, Alejandro, and Ruben Rumbaut
    1990   Immigrant America: A Portrait. Berkeley, Calif.: University of California Press.
Rapp, Rayna
    1992   "Family and class in contemporary America." In Rethinking the Family: Some Feminist Questions, eds. Barrie Thorne and Marilyn Yalom, 49-70. Boston: Northeastern University Press.
Rumbaut, Ruben G.
    1989a   "The structure of refuge: Southeast Asian refugees in the U.S., 1975-85." International Review of Comparative Public Policy 1:97-129.
    1989b   "Portraits, patterns and predictors of the refugee adaptation process: Results and reflections from the IHARP Panel study." In Refugees as Immigrants, ed. David Haines, 138-183. New Jersey: Rowman and Allenheld.
Rumbaut, Ruben, and Kenji Ima
    Forth-   Between Two Worlds: Southeast Asian Youth in America. Boulder, Colo.: Westview
    coming   Press.
Seller, Maxine S.
    1981   "Community life." In Immigrant Women, ed. Maxine Seller, 157-166. Philadelphia, Penn.: Temple University Press.
Sibley Butler, John
    1991   Entrepreneurship and Self-Help Among Black Americans. Albany, NY: State University of New York Press.
Stack, Carol
    1974   All Our Kin: Strategies for Survival in a Black Community. New York: Harper and Row.
Steinberg, Stephen
    1981   The Ethnic Myth. Boston: Beacon Press.
Wood, Charles H.
    1981   "Structural changes and household strategies: A conceptual framework for the study of rural migration." Human Organization 40: 338-344.
Wolf, Diane L.
    1990   "Daughters, decisions and domination: An empirical and conceptual critique of household strategies." Development and Change 24:43-74.
    1992   Factory Daughters: Gender, Household Dynamics, and Rural Industrialization in Java. Berkeley and Los Angeles: University of California Press.

The principle of generation among the Japanese in Honolulu[†]

COLLEEN LEAHY JOHNSON

Department of Child and Family Studies,
Syracuse University, Syracuse, New York.

The concept of generation is used to analyze the differential meaning of ethnicity among the Japanese-Americans in Honolulu. By tracing changes in the family system within the context of historical events, a model is developed which explains the principle of second and third generation interest. Processes in Hawaii which favor ethnic boundary maintenance are also discussed.

THROUGHOUT THE COURSE of American history, the terminology used to depict immigrant groups has aptly paralleled the changing philosophies regarding their incorporation into the larger society. The most enduring tendency in the past has been to speak in terms of assimilation and acculturation, implying that the adaptational objective consists of the merging of minority groups into the host society through a linear, progressive shift over several generations. The ideology of *Anglo-conformity* implicitly stressed the superiority of English institutions, language and culture and encouraged the rejection of ancestral heritage and adoption of the Anglo-Saxon core culture. A more well-known and certainly more tolerant theme has been connected with the image of the *melting pot*. The goal in this case was the biological and cultural merger of various immigrant groups with their Anglo-Saxon hosts, resulting in an enriched and indigenous American culture. (Gordon, 1964).

While these ideologies retreat into the realm of merely historical interest, social and cultural pluralism has emerged as the popular ideology of today. This theme which espouses the desirability of an ethnic group's retention of their own way of life while participating

† Presented at the American Psychiatric Association, Honolulu, Hawaii, 1973. The article stems from research supported by the National Institute of Mental Health (MF-263-71). I wish to thank George Yamamoto, Andrew Lind and Frank Johnson who made comments on an earlier version of the paper.

Ethnic Groups
Vol. 1, 1976, pp. 13—35

43

in the larger society, is obviously more in accord with the bi-modal participation found among ethnic groups today. Nevertheless, when the empirical reality is examined next to any of these ideologies, a number of inconsistencies immediately become apparent. On one hand, the opportunity for merger with the core group clearly is arbitrary and selective, and has been compatible with American egalitarianism only as long as physical and cultural characteristics of the immigrant groups did not display significant disparity from the features idealized by the hosts. In attempting to extend the "melting pot" imagery to non-European groups, the metaphor languishes in the face of popular rejection. Likewise, pluralistic ideologies have been criticized for justifying the *status quo* and possibly blurring actual discriminatory practices.

Consequently, prejudice and discrimination have become significant variables to consider and certainly parallel popular interest. "The rise of the unmeltable ethnics" is possibly the ideology of the near future as heightened ethnic consciousness appears today in numerous forms, notably the militant ethnic power groups found on many university campuses. One opinion is that this new ethnic consciousness in the emergence of third generation interest groups rests in part on the buried resentment toward the dominant group for past injustices and unattained promises. (Goering, 1970; Novak, 1971).

While these ideologies have been given lip-service by layman and social scientists alike, the study of ethnicity has followed several directions. Some sociologists, on one hand, have concentrated on intergroup relations or "victimology" as they examine the effects of prejudice and discrimination. Although the unilinear assimilation model has been generally rejected, other social scientists have attempted to delineate conceptual differentials between behavioral, structural and cultural assimilation. (Gordon, 1964). Another area of interest has concentrated on bi-culturality both in value orientations and in bi-modal forms of social organization. (Lebra, 1972; Mayer, 1962).

Increasingly however, the unit of study is the ethnic group as an identifiable social form which possibly resembles neither the culture of origin nor the culture of adoption. (Glazer and Moynihan, 1963).

44

In these researches, the basic questions are addressed to the meaning and form of ethnicity. On one hand, it can be evidenced by a "sense of peoplehood" or a "consciousness of kind" arising out of common origins. On the other hand, ethnicity can be studied through the contemporary forms of social organization which structures the system of social relationships selectively along ethnic lines. Furthermore, ethnicity can carry a value component which sets up standards of evaluation which govern and interpret behavior. (Barth, 1969). Basically, it is necessary to determine the character of the boundaries of an ethnic group, whether such delimitations is expressed as a vague sense of peoplehood celebrated only on national holidays, or whether it involves a host of definitive norms premeating wide spheres of activity. (Gordon, 1964; Bender and Kagiwada, 1968).

While these interests focus on contemporary on-going social processes, the diachronic study of generational transition points to another fruitful area of inquiry. In the past few decades of ethnic research, some social scientists have focused their attention on the adaptation of the third generation. An essay written by M. L. Hansen in 1938 and delivered to the Augustana Historical Society (a group dedicated to the study of Swedish immigrants) has been retrieved and found to be relevant today. (Hansen, 1952). Known sometimes as "Hansen's Law", the principle of *third-generation interest* states that "what the immigrants' son wishes to forget, the grandson wishes to remember". In other words, by the time an ethnic group comprises three generations, there is a tendency to return to the fold of ethnic identification. In these instances, the second generation is found to border two cultures: the culture of one's parents and the culture introduced in the public schools and informal associations in the larger community. These individuals, often called the "marginal men", in the ambivalence and inconsistency of their statuses, tend to depreciate their parents' culture and explicitly seek Americanization. In contrast, the third generation, complacent in their Americanization, can now return to their ethnicity since it has been relatively untouched by conflict and stigma. (Nahirny and Fishman, 1965). Whether the "return" involves some vague ideological commitment or a crucial aspect of his or her identity naturally depends upon the individual and specific ethnic group.

In any case, it is apparent that each generation has faced different problems of adaptation, problems requiring various kinds of resolutions of the basic conflict between their ethnic heritage and the objective reality of everyday life. These resolutions have required selective retention, modification or revision of their ancestral culture in order to meet the needs of immediate situations. What form these resolutions have taken, has depended not only on a linear assimilation process but also upon the particular point in history and the individual's place in the generational progression. Consequently, there has been an interplay between the extrinsic factors, (i.e. the social, political and economic institutions as they have differentially acted upon each generation) and the intrinsic factors (i.e. the familial norms and values as they have changed over three generations).

Such a phenomenon can perhaps best be understood within a framework incorporating the concept of generation and examining it within the context of historical events. Generations, in this sense, are used not merely as age-sets but rather as a temporal construct which specify marked qualitative changes between units. (Berger, 1960; Foote, 1960). Rather than following a strictly chronological sequence, this paper follows Mannheim's position that occupants of a generation location share a generational "mentality" resulting from common experiences (Mannheim, 1960). Members of these units, in this paper, are defined by the generation distance in an ethnic group from the point of immigration, who are subject to the following experiences.

1) The unity of a generation lies in a shared location in the social system which predisposes those within the generation to a specific range of potential experience, a characteristic set of norms and values and a characteristic type of relevant behavior.

2) Each generation, upon reaching maturity, has an opportunity of selection from the transmitted heritage of their elders and new experiences and relationships of their contemporary situation.

3) The adoption of the new and disposal of the old can be either

implicit and unconscious or explicit, conscious and reflective. The implicit, unconscious aspect is, of course, the most enduring and, in the long run, the most influential determinant of behavior.

4) Not every generation redefines its experiences markedly enough to precipitate significant changes in norms or behavior in individuals or structural changes in the social system.

5) When the experiences, norms and behavior of the parent generation are in accord with those of the society, there is less likelihood that the younger generation will need to select markedly new modes of behavior. In this case, certain integrative principles activate cohesive inter-generational relationships. (Eisenstadt, 1956).

6) When the experiences, norms and behavior of the parent generation are in opposition to or non-accommodative with those of the wider society, the younger generation, by necessity, must select new modes of behavior to achieve full adult status. Consequently, legitimate change, or in modern parlence, a generation gap exists.

BACKGROUND[1]

The purpose of this paper is to describe such generational transitions among the Japanese-Americans in Honolulu. In attempting a definition of ethnicity as it has evolved over three generations, a conceptual model is presented which incorporates changes in the intrinsic system (familial norms and values) and the extrinsic system (extra-familial institutions). When these divergent factors are examined, some insights are presented which serve to explain heightened ethnic awareness and, hence, the principle of third generation interest as it applies to the Japanese-Americans in Honolulu. The degree of ethnicity, as discussed here, is determined by the extent the ethnic group functions in governing social relationships as well as defining modal norms and values.

The ascription of generational status is in itself a pervasive means of self-categorization among the Japanese-Americans. This is facilitated by linguistic categories which define the original

47

immigrants as the *issei,* their children, the second generation as the *nisei,* and their grandchildren, the third generation as the *sansei.*

The analysis is based on a comparison of sixty-one second generation families (*nisei*) and forty-three third generation families (*sansei*). These families were selected according to their socio-economic representativeness to the general Japanese community in Hawaii. Focused interviews were conducted which examined the family organization as contrasted to the individual's family of orientation. In addition, fifty informants were chosen for their general expertise on the Japanese-American culture, who discussed wide-ranging problem areas facing the adaptation of the Japanese-Americans. (Johnson, 1972).

If one is using a linear assimilation model, one can hypothesize a progressive shift on the part of the *sansei* in the following areas: acculturation or adoption of the value system of the host society; structural assimilation or large scale entrance into out-group institutions at the primary group level; marital assimilation or large scale intermarriage; and identificational assimilation or the development of a sense of peoplehood based on the host society.[2] (Gordon, 1964).

Among the sample families, acculturation was measured by examining values traditionally Japanese in origin versus ego-centered, individualistic value orientations characteristic of the American middle class. In contradiction to previous assumptions, a majority of the *sansei,* like the *nisei,* espouse collective values where obligations to the group take precedence over gratification of personal desires. Furthermore, concepts of filial piety and respect for elders were found to be strongly endorsed by the majority of the *sansei*[3]. Consequently, rather than suggesting linear assimilation, these findings indicate notable continuities between generations which suggest the persistence of ethnicity both in terms of ideologies as well as in norms governing day-to-day activities.

The extent to which ethnicity determines on-going social relationships was determined by examining each family's social network in regard to Japanese versus non-Japanese relationships and kinship versus non-kinship relationships. If there has been structural assimilation, one would expect to find increased contact outside the ethnic group with diminishing solidarity of the kinship group. Contrary to these expectations, it was found in a comparison between generations, that the *sansei*, like the *nisei*, show a marked preference for other Japanese in friendship selection[4]. Furthermore, the *sansei* indicate an even greater preference for relationships within the kinship unit over those of non-kin. (Johnson, 1974).

In regard to intermarriage, the Japanese have the lowest outgroup marriage rate of any ethnic group in Hawaii (15.7% for grooms; 25.4% for brides) (Lind, 1969: 108). Although this rate is four times as large as it was in 1949, amalgamation between ethnic and racial groups even at present rates would take many generations.

Likewise, the heightened ethnic consciousness in Hawaii today indicates that identificational assimilation has not taken place in Hawaii. With the positive endorsement of political leaders, ethnic associations proliferate and specifically espouse retention of all native heritages. Like other ethnic groups, the Japanese retain their ethnic identity (Meredith, 1970) not only as a sense of peoplehood but also as a social and political category. Although virtually all informants consider themselves first as Americans, any reference to themselves and others is generally qualified by specification of their ethnicity and frequently of their generation level.

Given these factors, it is quite evident that ethnicity is an important referent for the Japanese-Americans. However, an examination of changes in the extrinsic and intrinsic systems suggests that ethnic affiliation has a different meaning to the *nisei* than it does to the *sansei*. It is, therefore, appropriate to introduce the time perspective in the context of generation level in order to analyze these qualitative differences.

HISTORICAL EVENTS

Hawaii is unique among the fifty states in terms of its ethnic diversity and in the evolution of its political and economic institution. In the early 19th century, both the introduction of Western economic standards and the ardent Christian missionary activities decimated the indigenous Hawaiian population and its culture. Furthermore, the development of a plantation economy based on sugar cultivation required a larger working class than the Hawaiians could provide. After initial introduction of Chinese and Portuguese workers, the Caucasian leaders turned to Japan for a steady, cheap source of hardworking laborers. The numbers were sufficiently large that by 1900, only 14 years after the first arrivals, the Japanese made up 40% of the total population.

The plantation system is generally acknowledged to have provided the model for ethnic stratification for the Islands with the Caucasians as proprietors who controlled the workers with the heavy hand of despotic paternalism. (Lind, 1938). The policy of residential segregation by ethnic groups facilitated administration and also precluded the development of an inter-ethnic labor movement. The control of a small minority of Caucasians (7% in 1900) pervaded all institutions so that until World War II, Hawaii remained in Fuchs' words, "a plantation society with no significant middle-class, only one effective political party and sharp limitations on opportunity." (1961: 39).

In regard to the ideological attitude toward immigrant groups, the Caucasians, predominantly of missionary background, zealously sought to impose Anglicized culture over first the Hawaiians and later the Oriental populations at the expense of their traditional culture. (Hunter, 1971). At the same time, the Caucasians' control over political, economic and educational institutions essentially isolated the non-Caucasian population from intimate knowledge of the dominant culture.

The Japanese were in a distinctive situation in several respects. First, the conservation of Japanese traditions was facilitated by the high in-group attitudes of the immigrants. The immigrants were initially males who brought with them a traditional sanction against out-group marriage. Consequently, the parents often selected a "picture bride" from the native villages in Japan who joined her husband after living for some months with his family. This practice facilitated the transplantation of the Japanese family and its value system in Hawaii. Furthermore, the majority of these newly-founded families viewed themselves as sojourners in a foreign land who would eventually return to Japan once they had accumulated some wealth. Therefore, they attempted to maintain and transmit intact the Japanese culture and language to their Hawaii-born children. In the face of discrimination, they also maintained a loyalty to Japan usually in the form of a sacred attachment to their ancestral villages, as it was expressed in the continuity of their family. Learning English and adopting alien values and behaviors were clearly unnecessary and incompatible with retaining strong ties to their origins. The demoralizing effects of prejudice and discrimination only strengthened their allegiance to the homeland and to the ethnic associations which had been transplanted in Hawaii. These conservative goals, in an immediate sense, were somewhat realistic because of the Japanese plurality, the practices of ethnic segregation and the predominance of in-group marriages. In the long run, however, their children's exposure to Hawaiian-American culture in the school system posed a potential conflict situation.

Second, the Japanese were particularly victimized as targets of prejudice and discrimination. Stimulated by the militant expansionist policies of Japan in the 1930's and the fears of Japanese dominance in Hawaii, periodic, vitriolic attacks were mounted against the Japanese-Americans, attacks which failed to distinguish between the immigrants and their Hawaii-born children. (Hunter, 1971; Fuchs, 1961). On one hand, the assimilationists criticized the *nisei's* inability to become Americans. ("Once a Jap, always a Jap" was a frequent comment). In addition to verbal abuse, direct and indirect obstacles were erected by these same individuals, preventing Japanese-Americans from entering Caucasian-dominated institutions. Even barriers to educational advancement were imposed through failure to build high schools convenient to Japanese concentrations on plantations and in rural areas. These obstacles yielded during the 1930's to slow but progressive entrance by the *nisei* into trades, normal school, civil service and commercial enterprises. Although these gains were retarded by the events of the Pacific war, the Japanese in Hawaii generally fared better than those on the mainland who were so callously uprooted and degraded. Nevertheless, Japan's attack on Pearl Harbor directed greater suspicions and hostility toward the Japanese in Hawaii, which only decreased later in the war by their enthusiastic participation in the Army and in the local labor front.

The effect these events had on the adaptation of the *nisei* is quite apparent. Although their ages today range from 35 to 85 years, most individuals suffered the stigma and prejudice which was pronounced in the pre-war years. They also had to face the barriers toward advancement deliberately erected by the Caucasian elite to limit achievement and mobility. Furthermore, they were products of enculturative agents who spoke little English and had scant knowledge of Hawaiian-American culture.

Following the war, these conditions dramatically changed. There was an erosion in the concentration of wealth and power in the hands of the Caucasians both by the war-time events, the G.I. Bill, and the rapid increase in voting potential of the *nisei*. Furthermore, there was a full circle in the attitude of the larger community from negative evaluation of Japanese as threatening aliens, to a positive evaluation as patriotic citizens.

The *sansei* generally are products of the post-war era. In the sample, they are generally under forty, have more education, higher income and occupational status. To be *sansei* is not to be identified with the humble plantation worker or domestic servant. Rather, it means belonging to the same ethnic group which includes many of Hawaii's political and professional leaders. It means that there are few invectives in the mass media which criticize their "alien" customs and allegiances. Instead, pluralistic philosophies emanate, praising Hawaii as a favored setting for preserving ancestral heritages in an atmosphere of tolerance.

Although this abbreviated history does not do justice to the complex series of events in Hawaii, certain features can be integrated with the progression of intrinsic events taking place in the family and culture of the Japanese. By using the grossest categories of generation, we can postulate that the cultural inventory of the *nisei* included the effects of limited opportunity, hardship and a stigmatized ethnic identity. On the other hand, the *sansei* by and large escaped these handicaps because much of their later socialization took place when prejudice abated, opportunities expanded considerably, and the stigma attached to their ethnic group diminished.

Although not all *nisei* experienced these handicaps and certainly not all *sansei* found life all that easy, these generational categories are an appropriate framework to analyze the events taking place in the Japanese family.

INTRINSIC EVENTS

Because of low wages in the pre-war years, the goal of return to Japan was unattainable for most *issei*. Thus, the problem of generational continuity between themselves and their *nisei* offspring became magnified. It must be remembered that most immigrants from Europe considered migration as a permanent, irreversible move to a new land, so they by necessity viewed their children's assimilation as a positive mode of adaptation and acted to shape this adjustment. (Inkeles, 1955). In contrast, the second generation Japanese-Americans generally had no such assurance of parental approval as they made adaptive adjustments to the new environment. Instead, such adjustment in the children threatened the parents' cherished dream of returning to Japan. Furthermore, by the time the *nisei* reached adolescence, the problem was magnified by the emergence of two linguistic sub-groups in the family segregated along generation lines. Consequently, the *nisei* faced the problem of somehow resolving their parents' norms and values—traditionally Japanese and communicated through the Japanese language—with the demands of a Caucasian-dominated society in Hawaii. Since the parental norms were largely non-accommodative to the larger society, selective acculturation and assimilation were required.

Furthermore, the principle compatible value, that of achievement through hardwork and education, was blocked by the considerable discrimination during the pre-war years. In any case, although the *nisei* could readily accept the American middle-class achievement orientation, the attendant demands for self-reliance, autonomy and individualism directly contradicted the collective values of the Japanese family. (Lebra, 1972). Finding themselves bound by parental norms of obligation, filial piety, deference and reticence, they faced self-imposed obstacles to enacting their instrumental roles in the outside world. For example, one of the cardinal tenets under the concept of filial piety was that of respect for elders. However, to be respectful, as translated into everyday behavior, meant to be quiet and to defer or to avoid imposing on others. (One frequent comment described being respectful as meaning to "shut up"). Nevertheless, to succeed in school or in competition for jobs, one had to speak up and assume a verbal assertiveness which called attention to oneself.

In the face of these contradictory expectations from the home, the public school and the job, the *nisei* often chose explicit, self-conscious Americanization. But to translate this new-found identity into concrete behaviors involved a direct confrontation with the basic norms involved in their enculturation. Resolution of these tensions ranged from a withdrawal from competition in the wider community to an adoption of a bi-cultural mode of participation, where one form of behavior operated for primary relationships in the family and kinship circles, and another form was reserved for secondary, instrumental relationships. This compartmentalization with multiple and incongruous criteria for ethnic membership could only promote role strain and a dilemma in ethnic identification for many *nisei*.

Even with the post-war expansion of opportunities, the *nisei* still inherited a set of parental norms which were in opposition to the dominant society. The more acculturation they underwent, the more they encountered direct conflict with their own enculturation within their family. With this generation it is appropriate to speak in terms of an assimilation model since revisions in their culture were required. In looking over student papers and autobiographies of the era, there is frequent reference to themselves as marginal men and women. (Social Process in Hawaii 1935 — 1963). In this sample, some *nisei* respondents commented on their identity with ambivalence: "I don't know what I am. I'm not Japanese like my parents or American like my children." The general tone implied that being a *nisei* included the qualities of conflict and hardship due to having a limited range of available opportunities and distinctive cultural and psychological conflicts. In interviews conducted by this investigator, several informants went so far as to label themselves "the sucker generation", caught first between the demands for filial piety by their Japanese parents and then later the individualistic demands of their American children.

However, the marked changes taking place in the political and economic institutions were paralleled by some selective revision by the *nisei* as parents in the structure and values of the Japanese family. (Masuoka, 1941; Johnson, 1972). In general, in their families of procreation the nuclear family has replaced the patrifocal, extended family, while the hierarchical structure of the elders over the young and males over females is somewhat modified. Primogeniture generally has been replaced by equal inheritance. Kinship affiliation has shifted from the patrifocal to a bilateral form where both the husband and wife's family are of equal importance. Of even more significance, the overwhelming demands of filial piety, although still significant, have been diluted and replaced by more symmetry. Obligation and reciprocity now tends to flow both ways. Esteem in one's old age is still implicit but also must be earned by making concessions to children's individual needs and allowing them alternatives to arbitrary parental commands. Furthermore, obligation to parents has come to be shared by all offspring rather than falling only on the eldest son. Rather than an onerous, duty-bound circle of kin, the second generation has evolved a solidary, close-knit kinship group where *some* individual options can be asserted without destroying the secure, predictable environment that kin can provide.

As noted above, the experiences of the *sansei* differ significantly, and here it is appropriate to speak in terms of ethnic-boundary maintenance. Not only have the old prejudices abated but the ideologies of "Anglo-conformity" or the "melting pot" have largely been forgotten as the ethnic group has emerged as a legitimate social form positively recognized by the power structure. In regard to their family system, the *sansei* have been beneficiaries of the modifications made by their *nisei* parents. In growing up in a more flexible unit, they can exercise more options without jeopardizing the parent-child relationship. With less discrepancy between parent and child in language and values, fewer areas of conflict are posed as the *sansei* moved outside the ethnic group.

A GENERATIONAL MODEL OF ETHNICITY

These differential processes of adaptation by the *nisei* and *sansei* can best be understood by the following model. The *nisei* in their generational location possessed a body of experiences which included the effects of a negative evaluation by the dominant group as threatening aliens with strange customs and behaviors. The accumulative cultural inventory was a body of contradictions: the implicit inventory included the heritage from their parents which was Japanese in content and language while the explicit inventory, particularly in their education and peer group experiences by and large pressured them to be American and repress their parents' culture.

In the fulfillment of their adult role demands, particularly in occupational roles, status conflict and identity confusion were inevitable. Any modifications made created marginality both in social distance from their parents and in the barriers to full acceptance by the dominant group. Any success in the non-Japanese sphere was only vicariously reinforced by outsiders, for the *nisei* were excluded from entrance to primary Caucasian groups. Consequently, status ambiguity in instrumental roles and generational discontinuity with the *issei* resulted. Although the *nisei* have been bicultural in their activities, their identity and their value system, the familial and the instrumental are in basic contradiction and have created an *ethnic ambivalence*. Such a situation has demanded that the *nisei* act as agents of change, upon the assumption of their adult roles.

As we have discussed, the *sansei* generally matured in an atmosphere of greater tolerance as less stigma was directed toward their ethnic group. Furthermore, their implicit cultural inventory derived from their parents was more accommodative particularly because, first, it was transmitted in the same language as they used outside the family and, second, the content included more options in modes of adaptation. Furthermore, the explicit inventory, in their school experiences and peer group relations, was more compatible with familial sources. Thus, in meeting adult role demands, they are not required to make radical revisions, for there is a congruence between parental expectations and those of the dominant group. In

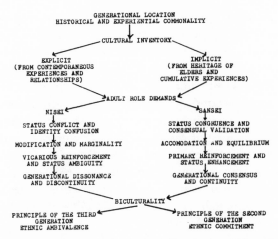

FIGURE 1.   Ethnic Attitudes and Generational Experience

other words, their identity is consensually validated in both their familial and instrumental role performances. Since reinforcement comes from these two major spheres, their status is enhanced at the same time that they can preserve continuity with their parents and the ethnic group.

Like the *nisei*, the *sansei* are also bicultural, but their bimodal participation and their identity are compatible with the expectations of both groups. A *sansei* can succeed in the larger society while still preserving kinship and ethnic solidarity. Since a positive evaluation comes from both the ethnic and instrumental spheres, *ethnic commitment* can operate without sanctions.

CONCLUSION

If one accepts this model, one can conclude that the principle of the second generation is that of ethnic ambivalence, while the principle of the third generation is that of ethnic commitment. I have concluded that this ethnic identity is not merely the "objectification of ethnic culture" where traditional physical objects are taken out of context and used as symbols of ethnic identity. (Gans, 1956). It is not an identification with abstract values and ideology symbolizing the essence of their ancestry. (Nahirny and Fishman, 1965: 319). On the contrary, the *sansei's* ethnicity finds its expression in the operation of bounded, ethnically-dominated social groupings where kinship loyalties have increased rather than decreased in the progression from second to the third generation. Furthermore, ethnicity is found in a value orientation where collective values more reminiscent of Japan outweigh the lonely pursuit of ego-centred interests so typical of the American middle class.

Certain processes operating in Hawaii can be identified as facilitating this ethnic commitment. Although some factors are unique to the Japanese in Hawaii, others can be relevant to the third generation of most ethnic groups.

1   The internal differentiation of the ethnic group

The Japanese-Americans, in being the largest plurality until the last decade, have been able to maintain a complex ethnic social organization which has become internally differentiated to include social class and acculturative variations. For example, an upwardly-mobile family who has moved into an ethnically-mixed occupational arena does not have to leave the Japanese community to form friendships with those who share their goals and interests. Ethnic relationships are readily accessible in all spheres of activity and available to accommodate to the wide range of Japanese versus Americanized behaviors.

2   Evaluational congruency

With the decrease in constraints imposed by prejudice and discrimination, there is a congruency between the ethnic group's self-evaluation and that accorded it by the society at large. When such a change occurs, group membership can be comfortably maintained without loss of self-esteem. (Bender and Kagiwada, 1968: 370; Yinger, 1961: 254). One need not escape the group to resolve conflicts in identity. The ethnic group itself can provide a diversity of role models typifying successful resolution of acculturation dilemmas, while individuals can still retain desirable ethnic life styles. Furthermore, integration with larger society can take place through occupational placement and even at the behavioral level with the adoption of new styles of behavior, while the boundaries around primary relationships remain ethnically determined.

3 Accommodative generational transmission

The process of generational transmission of the *issei* as parents differed markedly from those of the *nisei* as parents. The *issei*, typical of most immigrant parents, were ineffective agents of transmission of an ethnicity adaptive to the *nisei* adult role expectations. Because of their allegiance to a Japanese way of life and their self-imposed sojourner status, any revisions they made in socialization norms to meet Hawaiian requirements could only operate to separate them from their heritage and even jeopardize the hoped for return to Japan. Consequently, those *issei* who clung to their Japanese ways created a wide gap between themselves and their children and transmitted a cultural heritage, at least in part, non-accommodative to the Hawaiian setting. In any case, the heritage had to be communicated through the Japanese language to children who were rapidly becoming more facile with English. Hence, the discontinuities in norms was further accentuated by a distinct attenuation of cross-generation communication.

On the other hand, the *nisei* as parents can be effective agents for transmitting a cultural inventory adaptable to the Hawaiian society —most importantly an inventory that could be expressed in the same language of their children. The data from my larger study suggests that this inventory is the result of the *nisei's* selective modification and revision of their *issei* parents' heritage. In brief, the principle modifications have involved the introduction of flexibility into the obligatory ties that bind the Japanese family together. Rather than rigidity in a hierarchy of obligations to kin, fluidity has been introduced, which has allowed for the element of choice, the variable of affection over duty, and a greater symmetry in the flow of reciprocity. Stress on deference, modesty and reticence, although prominent, also has diminished or at least has been compartmentalized and reserved for certain ethnic relationships.

4 Retention of a collective value orientation

At the same time, most *nisei* chose to preserve the security-based network of relationships which have sacrificed ego-centered pursuits in favor of interdependency. Overall, unlike most ethnic groups who came to America, the Japanese have been able to resist the incursion of the ideology of individualism which can operate to fragment traditional bonds of familial solidarity. This fragmentation frequently appears when external constraints to open competition are lifted by the dominant group. (Yinger 1961). However, the flexibility introduced in fulfilling familial role demands has not impeded the *sansei's* assumption of adult occupational roles in the larger community. Familial role expectations have been segregated from the secondary, instumental roles outside the core ethnic relationships. In other words, ethnic identity can become dormant or at least inconspicuous in specific situations calling for universalist criteria.

5 The ethnic group as an integrative institution

Another process of change between second and third generation involves the mechanisms used to maintain an equilibrium between those forces which detach members from their group and those that serve to integrate or connect the group. Stated simply, the ethnic group boundaries are to be maintained, while economic and political success are simultaneously pursued in the larger system. Neither total social regression into the ethnic group nor total rejection of the ethnic group is desirable. Oscar Handlin aptly described this age-old American process:

The distinctive qualities of family life in the United States made the need for anchorage to a group particularly acute there. Whether in the seventeenth or the nineteenth century the extended family quickly shrank after immigration to the conjugal pair and its offspring. Detached from the community and often physically and socially isolated, the American family was thrown back upon its own resources; and uncertainty as to the roles of its members frequently produced severe internal tensions. Such conditions increased the desire for identification with a group that would provide the family with roots in the past, locate it in the larger society, and supply it both with a pattern of approved standards of behavior and with moral sanctions to aid in maintaining internal discipline. (Handlin, 224-225).

In the United States in general, one view sees the search for roots in the past by the third generation as being fulfilled merely by affiliation with one of the three major religious categories: Catholic, Protestant or Jewish rather than an ethnic criteria. (Herberg, 1955). In any case, the search for roots can be merely ideological in form or in the case of the Japanese, it can take place within the matrix of an actively-functioning social group. Whatever the case may be, the farther one moves from his or her original origins, the greater one needs to establish some link with the past. This past can have more recent roots, as I suggest it does with the *sansei*. The roots lie within the Japanese-American community in Hawaii where one can establish the pride of the locally-born, a "local" who belongs to a dominant ethnic group.

6   Minimization of group differences

For an ethnic group to provide such sources of identity and to demand loyalty from its members, it has to reach some compromise with its rivals, the dominant group. Practically speaking, it has to become more like its rivals in order to compete for the loyalty of its potential members. (Handlin, 1961: 227). By diminishing the range of differences between the ethnic group and the dominant group (as the *nisei* have done) loyalties to the ethnic group can operate without stimulating a host of conflicts between themselves and competing loyalties to the larger community. This minimization of group differences is a result of a two-fold process: the partial acculturation of the *nisei* to the dominant group, and the ability of the Japanese to exert a partial acculturation in terms of evaluative criteria upon the larger community. This has been accomplished by the movement of the Japanese into strategic positions particularly in education.[5]

Although at the present time there is no ultimate measure of a two-way process of acculturation, one can hypothesize a reciprocal action between the Caucasian and Japanese sub-cultures. Namely, I am tentatively suggesting that the Japanese-Americans have been able to exert enough influence on the Hawaiian society so that at least a small degree of bimodal acculturation has taken place through the nature of their influence. In their ascent into the middle class, they have moved into important positions where they can exert a degree of influence over the extra-familial agencies of socialization in the overall society. For example, large numbers occupying positions in public education, state government and public service occupations can espouse norms of the ethnic group which act to modify official American philosophies of education. For the *sansei*, this means that these norms from the schools are more likely to coincide with those of their family. In contrast to the pre-war period, the contemporary situation provides continuities between the home and the outside world, instead of the discontinuities and conflicts experienced by the *nisei* in the 1920s and 1930s.

In conclusion, we can posit "a principle of third generation interest" for the Japanese-Americans which can be summarized as: "What the *nisei* rejected explicitly, the *sansei* can accept with commitment." The *sansei's* acceptance of ethnicity thus is not rooted in their Japanese heritage of the past, but rather in a viable, functioning group of today. They have not "returned" to the culture their parents left or to a "vague nostalgia and undefined ideology of a far-off land". (Glazer, 172). Instead, identity is lodged in group membership which provides self-esteem rather than stigma. The decline in prejudice and imposed constraints have initiated a change from a defensive solidarity to that of a positive ethnic cohesiveness not only providing roots to the past but also a security-based system of social relationships.

This point of equilibrium which typifies the *sansei* has been accomplished by a generational transfer from the *nisei* parents of a cultural inventory which is accommodative for life in Hawaii today. Confident in their Americanization and subject to an enculturation which is continuous with adult role requirements, the *sansei* can use the ethnic group as a reference group for defining norms and standards of evaluation which are appropriate to their adult role requirements. This source of identity provides institutional affiliation, a cultural heritage, an identity and sense of peoplehood, and a predictable system of social relationships.

Notes

1. The two largest ethnic groups in Hawaii are Caucasians and Japanese each of whom make up approximately one-third of the population. Other ethnic groups in sufficient numbers are Hawaiians, Filipino, Chinese, Korean and Puerto Ricans. In this paper, the Japanese-Americans are referred to simply as Japanese both for economy's sake and to replicate the term they use to describe themselves.

2. Gordon also includes the absence of prejudice, discrimination and power conflict among his variables. These factors have by and large come to pass in Hawaii as is noted in the following discussion. However the recent influx of businessmen and tourists from Japan has stimulated in the mass media and in informal discussions some fears of a new kind of threat to residents of Hawaii. Older informants have expressed concern that there are parallels to the anti-Japanese attitudes of the pre-war years.

3. In response to the question "What is the greatest advantage in the Japanese family system?", 75% of the *nisei* and 58% of the *sansei* chose respect for elders as their first point. Mothers were also asked "What is the most ideal personality characteristic you would like to see in your child?", 49% of the *nisei* and 42% of the *sansei* chose first such collective values as respect, humility and compassion.

4.

	Social Networks	
Personnel	Generation	
	Nisei —n = 61	*Sansei* —n = 43
Mostly Japanese friends	82%	72%
Ethnically mixed friendships	18%	28%
Kin dominant	38%	58%
Divide time equally	28%	23%
Friend dominant	34%	19%

5. While there are no records kept of the ethnicity of the teachers in the public schools, the investigator made a spot check of the State Department of Education Directory and found that well over half of all principals and assistant principals are Japanese.

References

Barth, F. (1969). *Ethnic Groups and Boundaries,* Boston: Little Brown.

Bender, E. J. and G. Kagiwada (1968). Hansen's Law of "Third generation return and the study of American religo-ethnic groups". *Phylon,* **29,** 360-370.

Berger, B. (1960). "How long is a generation?" *British Journal of Sociology,* **11,** 20-23.

Eisenstadt, S. N. (1956). *From Generation to Generation.* Glencoe: Free Press.

Foote, N. (1960). "The old generation and the new." *In* the *Nation's Children.* Vol. 3. *Problems and Prospects.* E. Ginzberg, Ed. New York: Columbia University Press.

Fuchs, L. (1961). *Hawaii Pono: A Social History.* New York: Harcourt, Brace and World.

Gans, H. J. (1956). "American Jewry: present and future." *Commentary,* **21,** 555-563.

Glazer, N. (1964). "Ethnic groups in America: from national culture to ideology." *In Freedom and Control in Modern Society.* M. Berger, Ed. New York: Octagon, pp. 158-173.

Glazer, N. and D. Moynihan (1963). *Beyond the Melting Pot.* Cambridge, Mass.: M.I.T.

Goering, J. (1970). "The emergence of ethnic interests: A case of serendipity." *Social Forces,* **49,** 379-384.

Gordon, M. (1964). *Assimilation in American Life.* New York: Oxford University Press.

Handlin, O. (1961). "Historical perspectives on the American ethnic group." *Daedalus,* Spring, pp. 220-232.

Hansen, M. L. (1952). "The third generation in America." *Commentary,* **14,** 492-500.

Department of Education (1971-1972). *Educational Directory Personnel Roster,* Honolulu.

Herbert, W. (1955). *Protestant, Catholic, Jew.* New York: Doubleday.

Hunter, L. (1971). *Buddhism in Hawaii.* Honolulu: University Press of Hawaii.

Inkeles, A. (1955). "Social change and social character: The role of parental mediation." *Journal of Social Issues,* **11,** 12-23.

Johnson, C. (1972). The Japanese-American Family and Community: Generational Continuities in Ethnic Affiliation. Dissertation, Syracuse University.

Johnson, C. (1973). "Alternatives to alienation: A Japanese:American example." *In Alienation: Concept, Term and Meaning,* F. Johnson, Ed. New York: Seminar Press.

Johnson, C. (1974). "Gift-giving and reciprocity among the Japanese-Americans in Hawaii." *American Ethnologist,* **1,** 295-308.

Lebra, T. (1972). Acculturation Dilemma: The Function of Japanese Moral Values for Americanization. Council on Anthropology and Education Newsletter. Fall 6-13.

Lind, A. (1938). *An Island Community: Ecological Succession in Hawaii.* Chicago: University of Chicago Press.

Lind, A. (1967). *Hawaii's People,* 3rd. ed. Honolulu: University Press of Hawaii.

Mannheim, K. (1970). "The problem of generation." *Psychoanalytic Review,* **57,** 378-404.

Masuoka, J. (1941). "The life cycle of an immigrant institution in Hawaii: The family." *Social Forces,* **23,** 60-64.

Matsumoto, G., G. Meredith and M. Masuda (1970). "Ethnic identification: Honolulu, and Seattle Japanese-Americans." *Journal of Cross-Cultural Psychology,* **1,** 63-76.

Mayer, P. (1962). "Migrancy and the study of Africans in towns." *American Anthropologist,* **64,** 576-592.

Nahirny, V. and J. Fishman (1965). "American immigrant groups: Ethnic identification and the problem of generations." *Sociological Review,* 13, 311-320.

Novak, M. (1971). *The Rise of the Unmeltable Ethnics.* New York: MacMillan.

Sociology Club of the University of Hawaii (1935-1963) *Social Process in Hawaii.*

Yinger, J. M. (1961). "Social forces involved in group identification and withdrawal." *Daedalus,* Spring, 247-262.

Interdependence, Reciprocity and Indebtedness: An Analysis of Japanese American Kinship Relations*

COLLEEN LEAHY JOHNSON**
Syracuse University

This paper presents an analysis of the qualitative aspects of kinship interaction among Japanese Americans in Honolulu. Based on semistructured interviews with 104 families, the findings indicate an increase in kinship solidarity with the third generation. Explanations of these findings utilize theories of exchange and reciprocity. When exchange processes operate to encourage indebtedness and take place in an interdependent network of kin relationships, an obligatory pattern of interaction results. Since this pattern differs from the option model of the modified extended family, it is suggested that research on kinship should go beyond measures of contact and aid to a study of mechanisms which reinforce the solidarity of some extended family structures.

For the past fifteen years, the debate concerning the structure of the modern family has concentrated on the "kin family network" (Sussman and Burchinal, 1962) or the "modified extended family" (Litwak, 1959). Documentation of the presence of extensive kinship contact and mutual aid has questioned the notion of the isolated nuclear family form which had dominated family sociology for some years (Parsons, 1949). To borrow Gibson's (1972) metaphor, the isolated nuclear family was officially "buried" with the publication of a collection of articles in 1965 (Shanas and Streib, 1965). Today, the concept of the modified extended family provides the model which portrays the nuclear family participating actively in kinship affairs while still retaining some autonomy (Litwak, 1959). In this case, kinship ties can be used optionally on an intermittent basis or activated in time of need. Furthermore, the ties have been shown to function despite geographical or social mobility.

Although there is extensive understanding of the types of aid, the degree of social contact, and the personnel involved (Adams, 1968, 1971), several problems still demand further clarification. First, there is some controversy concerning how much kin contact and aid determines the degree of isolation of the family (Gibson, 1972). Second, few researchers have attempted to identify the underlying kinship norms and the mechanisms used to reaffirm the individual's attachment to the kinship unit. In other words, there is a need to show how optional or obligatory these relationships are and why. Third, the problems are most noticeably apparent when one examines the varying significance of kinship among racial and ethnic subgroups in the United States. For example, stemming from their research on Black families, Hays and Mindel (1973) express the need for pluralistic perspectives of family structure to account for ethnic and minority groups. However, future studies also would benefit from the development of theories to explain the integrative mechanisms which bind, in varying degrees, the nuclear family to the kin network.

*This article stems from research conducted in Honolulu, Hawaii, 1970-1971. The research was supported by the National Institute of Mental Health (MF-263-71).

**Department of Child and Family Studies, College for Human Development, Syracuse University, Syracuse, New York 13210.

PURPOSE

The purpose of this paper is twofold. First, it will analyze the maintenance of primary kinship relations over two generations of Japanese Americans in Honolulu. In addition to documenting the usual measures of social contact, it will describe the mechanisms used to perpetuate kinship solidarity through patterns of *reciprocity, indebtedness,* and *dependence.*

Second, the paper will attempt to explain how the operation of these patterns leads to the development of a level of integration within the kinship system such that it can be described as an obligatory system rather than an optional system. In order to develop this theory, it will be necessary to review aspects of exchange theory which are relevant to the kinship processes described below.

Within exchange theory, the concept of reciprocity has proved useful in understanding how "the principle of give and take" defines, regulates, and harmonizes social relationships.[1] In contrast to economic exchange, reciprocity typifies a type of exchange which is ideally nonexploitive and accompanied by sociability. One premise, put forth by Gouldner (1959:249), assumes that the persistence and stability of any structure is enhanced if there is mutual dependence and reciprocal interchange, while a decrease in these characteristics is linked to tension and disruption. Furthermore, social relationships are conceptualized in terms of both reciprocity and dependence and by a fundamental ambivalence between one's need to interrelate and be dependent and the need to express oneself and be autonomous (van der Veen, 1971:379). In other words, there is tension between egoism and altruism, group interests and personal interests, or the need to give versus the desire to hold. Van der Veen suggests that the normative content of

any culture shapes socially acceptable resolutions of this ambivalence, such that one component can be accentuated or denied, or the components can be compartmentalized.

If we accept the premise that the level of dependence and the utilization of reciprocity norms affect group integration, it is a most appropriate area to investigate in kinship research. It would be productive to go beyond the usual measures of social contact and mutual aid, and examine processes of exchange and the type of indebtedness incurred. For example, if A gives a gift or service to B and B returns the debt within a prescribed period and in a more or less equivalent form, the relationship is more symmetrical and less binding emotionally (Sahlins, 1965). However, if B, the initial recipient, is unable to repay the debt under these conditions, he or she ideally must be continuously vigilant for the opportunity of repayment, if the culture stresses reciprocal interchange. In such a situation, one is never free psychologically from the obligation which creates what Gouldner (1960) identifies as a "shadow of indebtedness." In some kinship systems, as in other social groups, there appear to be mechanisms which inhibit repayment, thus maintaining indebtedness and consequently, greater interdependence.

Such a pattern of reciprocity probably is qualitatively different from that found in modern kinship systems, because the indebtedness creates an obligatory, rather than optional, relationship. Although reciprocity functions within the modified extended family in the United States (Adams, 1968), this aid takes place within a normative framework which idealizes self-expression and autonomy in contrast to interdependence. If this is indeed the case, then one would expect to find mechanisms which are utilized to suppress the development of dependence. One possible mechanism would be a system of reciprocity which encourages debt repayment and avoids indebtedness.

Few family researchers have dealt analytically with the exchange processes of American kinship systems, although the theory has been used sporadically in the analysis of family power and courtship (Edwards, 1969). While he does not explore the theoretical implications, Litwak (1965) probably best summarizes the nature of exchange in the American modified extended family, which

---

[1] The concepts of reciprocity and exchange are used interchangeably in this paper. Reciprocity, as used here, follows Lebra's (1975) definition. It is considered a subset of exchange centering on the social and emotional embeddedness of giving and receiving rather than the economic aspects of acquisitiveness and maximization of gain. However, when referring to the less emotionally-laden processes of actually giving and receiving, "exchange" has been used to follow the more common usage.

prevents a reversion to the dependency of the classical extended family. These exchange components include partial and competitive aid, concerns with immediate and equivalent reciprocity, limitations to normative occasions for exchange, exchange over social and geographical distance, and the fact that initiative for the aid must come from the donor. (In other words, if one asks for the aid, the indebtedness assumes an obligatory quality at odds with kinship norms.) One might add another prominent feature of mutual aid—real assistance at time of great need. For example, in the early married years, this type of aid often comes disguised as a gift in order to preserve the idea of the autonomy of the newly formed family (Sussman, 1965).

Sussman (1970) has identified contemporary kinship as an opportunity model dominated by concerns for "pay off" or "what's in it for me." In other words, altruistic giving, which is characteristic of the generalized reciprocity of primitive societies, is not seen as existing in modern kinship. Egoism, independence and concern for self-gain are considered functional in that they fulfill the requisites for goal achievement in occupational placement (Litwak, 1965). Options can be exercised in using kinship ties depending upon how facilitative they are in achieving instrumental goals. At the same time, these ties do not impede mobility by such rules as nepotism or particularistic criteria for status placement.

A study of three Western industrial societies has revealed that such an option model has not necessarily produced isolation of aged parents from their children, but has produced what has been termed "intimacy at a distance" (Shanas, Townsend, Wedderburn, Friis, Milhaj and Stehovwer, 1968). The integrity of marriage and the independent household is respected to the extent that social distance is scrupulously observed (even though four-fifths of the sample of elderly have seen one child within the past week). Shanas and her colleagues (1968:173) go on to observe that, "once weakened, family relationships are difficult to renew or repair; they need to be regularly reinforced—like conditioned reflexes."

The mechanisms for reinforcement of kinship ties are examined in this paper insofar as they apply specifically to the Japanese Americans in Hawaii. It is proposed that one important point of differentiation between the two systems lies in the utilization of the exchange relationship to create permanent debtor-creditor relationships. It also is suggested that this type of exchange serves to regulate and sustain obligatory interdependent kinship ties.

METHODS

The research on which this report is based is a comparison of 61 second generation (*nisei*) and 43 third generation (*sansei*) families.[2] The sample, although nonprobablistic, was selected to be representative of the educational and occupational levels of the Japanese American population in Honolulu. Other criteria for selecting the families were that both parents were Japanese, the families were intact with some children still at home, and the families were "normal" in terms of absence of social and psychological deviance. Schools, churches, community centers and public housing at diverse socioeconomic levels provided the sources of the sample families. In addition, approximately 50 informants, many of whom were males, provided, in varying detail, descriptive accounts of their families, particularly in regard to the qualitative aspects of kin relatedness and the processes of exchange. Two geneologies were recorded which traced the expansion of the kinship group and the changes in relationships over generations.

Focused interviews for the 104 families were conducted with the wives. These interviews usually were from two to four hours long. In addition to specific questions about numbers of kin and amount of contact and mutual aid, open-ended questions were used to probe for normative and attitudinal dimensions. These discussions were guided by questions about goals in childrearing,

[2]The Japanese language provides a terminology for emigrants and their descendants which is still widely used as a category of ascription. *Issei* is the emigrant or the first generation; *nisei*, their children or the second generation; and *sansei*, their grandchildren or the third generation. Respondents placed themselves objectively by generation level in their distance from Japan. They also used the terms subjectively to explain their behavior and this generation term occasionally differed from the objective assignment.

advantages and disadvantages in the Japanese family system, and changes between generations. In approximately one-half of the interviews, detailed descriptions of patterns of reciprocity were recorded, the processes of which were later amplified and cross-checked with key informants.

FINDINGS

By definition, the Japanese American family is a nuclear type in that the family is economically independent and resides in a separate residential unit (Parsons, 1949). Only 14 percent of the sample live in a three-generation household, while an additional 18 percent have relatives living in the immediate neighborhood. Economic cooperation in family business enterprises is present in 11 percent of the families.

By most measures, the Japanese Americans in Honolulu aptly portray an ethnic group which retains a solidary kinship unit. For example, the numbers of relatives of the sample families on Oahu (the island on which Honolulu is located) are strikingly large for both generations, but of particular interest is the expansion of the kinship unit with the *sansei*. The mean number of relatives for the *nisei* is 26 and for the *sansei*, 42. The insularity of island living, which in this case has permitted extensive social mobility, but limited geographical mobility, has provided a large number of accessible kin.

In regard to the degree of kinship contact, each respondent was asked to estimate how much of their free time was spent with kin. Among the *nisei*, 38 percent spend more time with kin, 28 percent divide their time equally between relatives and friends, and 34 percent spend more time with friends. An increase was reported by the *sansei* with 58 percent spending more time with kin, 23 percent dividing their time equally, and 19 percent spending more time with friends.

Through an exploration of the kinds of contact, a natural division appeared between the ceremonial occasions for meeting (New Year's, weddings, funerals) when most relatives were included, and the informal occasions which included the modified extended family; *i.e.*, primary relatives in each spouse's family of orientation (Table 1). Over half of the families in each generation attended these ceremonial occasions at least six times a year with the large extended

family. However, evidence suggests that the kinship unit, particularly the modified extended family, has increased in significance for the third generation. When examined in terms of informal social contact, 64 percent of the *nisei* and 88 percent of the *sansei* see parents, siblings and other intimates once a week or more.

Turning to the mutual aid patterns found in these families, less than 10 percent of the families reported little or no contact with, or mutual aid in, their kinship group. The pattern for the large majority involves extensive aid, services, emotional support and occasionally money among what they call members of the "immediate family." These relatives can include parents, siblings and their families of procreation and, in some cases, aunts, uncles and cousins. Since there are no explicit rules which state that all siblings, aunts or uncles must be included in frequent exchanges, the patterns of aid can be focused on selected relatives with whom one has the most social contact.

The increased kinship solidarity contradicts the assumption that kinship solidarity diminishes with social mobility (Adams, 1971). When a comparison is made between the generations in this sample, it shows that the *sansei* are predominantly middle class: 74 percent have some college education as compared to 49 percent of the *nisei*; and 60 percent of the *sansei* are in managerial or professional occupations in comparison to 36 percent of the *nisei*. The interaction between social class, ethnicity and generation level rarely has been examined systematically, so it is difficult to compare and to document the popular assumption that solidarity is undermined as increasing assimilation takes place. In this sample, structural assimilation is

TABLE 1. KINSHIP GET-TOGETHERS

	Nisei N=61 (Percentage)	Sansei N=43 (Percentage)
Formal-Extended Family		
6 or more times/yr.	52	57
Less than 6 times/yr.	25	25
Rarely	13	– –
None	10	18
Informal-Modified Extended Family		
1/wk. or more	64	88
1/mo. or more	11	4
Less than 1/mo.	20	2
Relatives absent	5	4

found in occupational, educational, residential and some associational relations. Although 10 percent of the *sansei* move in ethnically mixed friendship networks, kinship is even more of a determinant of social relationships than it is with the *nisei*.

There is some evidence, however, that some immigrant groups bring a value system to this country which is compatible with maintaining kinship solidarity and perhaps resistant to change through assimilation. For example, some values of Japanese culture still can be discerned among descendants in Hawaii. The value orientations relevant here include social embeddedness in the group (sociocentricity), obligation to parents and all superiors (*on*), the regulation of debts and their repayment (reciprocity), and dependence (Benedict, 1946; Lebra, 1974; Nakane, 1970).

Sociocentricity

The precedence given to primary group interests over individualistic interests was expressed most notably in the mother's responses to childrearing topics. In open-ended responses to questions on the desired behavior of children, the majority of the mothers (65 percent) chose those behaviors related to concern for others, humility, and compassion, while only 15 percent chose egocentric behaviors such as independence and personal freedom. The pervasive theme in the interviews was the need for careful consideration in maneuvering in the primary group and the need for suppression of "selfish" interests.

Obligation to Parents (On)

Obligation to parents was described by most respondents as a salient and limiting factor in family activities. (It is interesting to note that this concept generally is not indexed in family texts.) Although some respondents complained of the constraints imposed by this value, 75 percent of the *nisei* and 58 percent of the *sansei* identified respect for elders as one advantage of the Japanese family.

The Japanese culture has provided the base in the institutionalization of behaviors related to the concept of *on* (obligation passively incurred by superiors). Filial piety placed the parents in a strategic position over their children in that it was phrased in terms of a noncontingent debt of obedience (Benedict,

1946; Lebra, 1969). Although such a unilateral debt of obedience could not transcend completely the transplantation of the family to the immigrant setting in Hawaii, it was more than casually implemented by the immigrants (*issei*) in their *nisei* children (Masuoka, 1941). This principle, as described by respondents, ranged normatively from such a moral commitment as "Parents gave us life; why shouldn't we feel that way," or, "It's repayment for all they did—I'm thankful for it," to a more resigned attitude of, "We're raised that way, it comes naturally to us." This relationship will be described in greater detail below.

Regulation of Debts and Repayments

Gift-giving and systems of reciprocity in Japan have long interested social scientists because of their elaborate and semi-official regulation. The material exchanges in Hawaii and Japan have been described elsewhere (Johnson, 1974; Befu, 1966-1967, 1968). Of interest here is the respondents' descriptions of the world of debts and credits in which they live. One must be continually concerned with what one has received—both material and nonmaterial—and how and when one should repay it. In other words, there is constant reflection and concern about the regulation of one's indebtedness and how such debts and credits affect one's relationships with others.

Dependence

Dependence has been identified as a key concept in understanding the Japanese personality (Doi, 1973). This topic has not been researched directly with the Japanese Americans in Hawaii. However, one study of needs among college students found that Japanese American students showed a lower need for independence than their Caucasian counterparts (Arkoff, 1959). This research finds such dependence in several areas of family life. As noted above, independence as a goal in childrearing generally was rejected. Instead, an interdependence is expressed in various ways. Young people are expected to live at home until marriage, unless they attend college on the mainland or enter the military service. Furthermore, aged parents, who can no longer live alone, usually move in with one offspring rather than to a nursing home or housing for senior citizens.

A social embeddedness is apparent in the

ages of individuals integrated into the kinship group. All age levels usually are incorporated into family and kinship activities. Most mothers are hesitant to hire babysitters at night for exclusively-adult gatherings. In fact, they tend to avoid Western or *haole* style entertaining which is limited to adults, and prefer Japanese gatherings where children are invariably invited.[3] Older family members generally also are incorporated into these social gatherings, so that the net results are age-integrated rather than age-segregated social networks.

RECIPROCITY AND EXCHANGE SYSTEMS

A value orientation which affirms socio-centricity, obligation, reciprocity, and dependence has provided some guidelines for the regulation of exchange relationships among kin. The data indicate that these values and exchange patterns create a system of relationships which is more obligatory than the optional system in the modified extended family. Interestingly enough, the persistence of these values and obligations exists within a framework of important structural changes in the family which more closely resembles the bilateral American system.

Traditionally, Japan has had the stem family structure in which descent and inheritance passed from the father to the eldest son. The eldest son, as sole inheritor, remained in the family home with his wife and offspring, while younger sons formed branch houses. With the father's increasing age and debility, the son gradually assumed the headship and, along with his wife, the primary responsibility for care and support of his parents. This patrilineal system continued to operate among most *issei* (immigrants) in Hawaii and their *nisei* sons. However, with the changed circumstances of the *nisei* as middle-aged parents, the system has become much less prevalent. Most respondents plan to divide their wealth among all their *sansei* offspring. Consequently, it usually is expected that all

offspring bear eventual responsibility for any assistance their parents might need in their old age. The implications for this change are deemed important for the present kinship system, in that obligations are diffused over the entire sibling group.

Parent-Child Exchange

We have seen that the normative emphasis on filial piety was an important part of the cultural heritage the *issei* instilled in their children. This norm, as operationalized among the *nisei,* took numerous forms: delay of marriage if the family required support; giving up a job on the mainland; financial support; incorporation of the elders into the family of procreation; and generally respectful and obedient behaviors.

Changes in the Japanese parent-child relationship with the *nisei* as parents of mature offspring have produced changes in the nature of reciprocity. First, since most older *nisei* have social security or pensions, it is more common to find nonmaterial aid from offspring to parent rather than monetary support. Second, since the principle of primogeniture has changed to equal inheritance, all children share not only the inheritance but also the responsibility for the care of the aged parents. Third, from the parents' point of view, as reported by the informants and *nisei* respondents, they have modified the noncontingent expectations of filial piety by introducing more symmetry into the relationship. They must earn the respect by being more flexible with their children. Hence, for the *sansei*, obligations to parents can be fulfilled more easily because they are less burdensome and are not concentrated on one offspring. Furthermore, since money is less often given, assistance does not usually diminish the family income. The principle which operates here has been described as the "law of extended credit" (Ekeh, 1974). Individuals in a system of relationships are linked together in such a fashion that if one member cannot reciprocate a debt (in this case to a parent), others can fulfill the obligation for the time being.

It is proposed that such changes in the parent-child relationship have not led to the option model of kinship, because obligation to parents, although somewhat modified, remains explicitly stated. One pattern of responses among the *sansei* was:

[3]Caucasians of northern and western European origin are termed *haoles.* Although the term is Hawaiian for foreigner, it is most often used to distinguish the lighter skinned population from those of Polynesian and Oriental origin.

> I owe a great debt to my parents for having raised me. Although this debt can never be fully repaid, it is easier now than it was with my parents. We do not have the duty-bound obligation that our parents had. Instead we want to help out and see them frequently.

Apparently, the expressive content of the relationship receives more emphasis as the instrumental content diminishes and as the family surrenders its corporate functions.

In most comments on the nature of interdependence between parent and child, the general consensus is that this relationship transcends ordinary considerations of *quid pro quo* or utilitarian advantage (Sussman, 1965). Explanations revolve around internalization of moral norms which are diffuse and unspecified. Yet, as in all relationships, a propensity toward symmetry operates. Nevertheless, these processes can operate differently, in a qualitative sense, among various populations in terms of goals and means. In the case of the Japanese Americans, the means, as described above, capitalize on dependence rather than independence in the socialization process. In regard to goals, if Japanese parents sacrifice and struggle while raising their children, they expect, not only success, but the rewards of dutiful children and an interdependence in the relationship. Most Japanese parents anticipate receiving respect, obedience and noncontingent support in their old age. Even with social security, emotional support must replace material support.

The literature on aging indicates that the comparable American system of expectations, at least in the middle class, contains quite different norms which center on independence. "I want to be independent in my old age and never be a burden to my children." "I would like to have my children nearby as long as it doesn't interfere with their career" (Clark and Anderson, 1967). In other words, by American standards, mutual dependence is optional and contingent upon fulfillment of occupational demands first.

In contrast, by Japanese American standards, mutual dependence generally takes precedence over other demands and is compatible with the prevailing norms. Although it can be viewed as obligatory, the option for family ties over autonomy is preferred as a natural consequence of the socialization process. Although some offspring do move to the mainland to pursue occupational success, this choice is available only if at least one sibling remains in Hawaii to tend to the parents' needs. It is not uncommon to find individuals who gave up promising careers to return to Hawaii to fulfill filial duties when no one else was available.

Therefore, it can be assumed that obligation to parents, although qualitatively different than other forms of indebtedness, can lay the foundation for other relationships. Not only does it prepare an individual for a sociocentric orientation in primary ties, but it provides the normative pressures for other reciprocal relationships.

Sibling Exchange

The change in the parent-adult child relationship has parallel changes in the sibling relationship. Among the *sansei*, all siblings share in fulfilling obligations to parents, preventing the burden from falling on one individual. With the removal of monetary support, the relationship becomes more specialized in its social and expressive content.

Although the norm of reciprocity is explicity structured into most areas of social life, Sahlins (1965) has suggested that its usage varies according to the degree of intimacy and sociability in the relationship. First, balanced reciprocity, more common in less intimate relationships, is one of symmetry and equal exchange within a prescribed time period. Among the Japanese Americans, this type of reciprocity has been institutionalized into a system of gift giving (*kosai*). Since this phenomenon is reported elsewhere (Johnson, 1974), it will suffice to comment here on the function of *kosai* in maintaining kinship contact without necessarily involving high sociability. Gifts of money are exchanged at certain points in the life cycle, but since the return of the gift is specified in terms of equivalence and is time-bound to defined occasions, indebtedness can be discharged temporarily.

In contrast, generalized reciprocity among intimates, which is discussed below, is typified by high sociability and a mutual interdependence in terms of aid, hospitality, gifts and emotional support which flow freely without thought of immediate or equivalent return (Sahlins, 1965). What distinguishes generalized reciprocity among intimates from balanced reciprocity, or *kosai*, among more distant relationships is the quality of the indebtedness. For one thing, among primary relations the social quality of the exchange far outweighs the material characteristics of the gift or service. This type of exchange, identified by Malinowski (1926) as the "pure gift," is described by the Japanese Americans as "giving from the heart." Ideally, a donor gives to a close relative or friend on the basis of love and respect, rather than because of normatively defined obligations. In actuality, however, the donor expects an undefined repayment in the future, while the recipient must be continually vigilant for the opportune time to discharge the debt. Since the distinctive principle is that such an exchange does not stipulate a time-bound, equivalent return, a shadow of indebtedness is created which can be perpetual in nature, because the debt is not discharged specifically.

This pattern of reciprocity is particularly prominent among siblings, and most of the following discussion describes this relationship. However, relationships with other kin and friends can also be typified by the same type of exchange, if they have an intimate relationship with ego.

Nisei exchange. The pattern of support among *nisei* siblings in the prewar years, which was reported by several families, offers a particularly clear example of how these processes operate. Since the immigrant parents had limited incomes, they sometimes concentrated their resources on one child. Because of severe economic constraints, the older children, irrespective of sex, left school after eighth grade to take jobs as laborers or domestics. Most of their wages were given to their parents, who in turn allocated part of the money to send one or more younger children through high school and possibly universities or professional schools. Such a pattern of economic expediency resulted in a wide range of achieved social class levels among members of the sibling group. The eldest son remained an unskilled plantation worker, while the youngest son became occupationally mobile.

As resources were pooled through the income of the older children, they were redistributed among the younger children. Ordinarily, in sibling groups such as this, one would expect a breach of solidarity because of the discrepancy of social class. However, such a social distance did not usually result, in part because the debts to older siblings by the younger sons were not repaid in money. Instead, the recipients would discharge their indebtedness through countless favors, services and gifts throughout their lives. Their homes and pocketbooks were continually open, particularly to any niece or nephew, who needed assistance to continue his or her education. Obviously, this transfer of obligations would begin a fresh cycle of reciprocity, for the recipient carried the indebtedness throughout his or her life. The original donor, the older sibling, received as rewards, not only countless forms of assistance but also the compensatory mechanisms of respect and esteem through self-sacrifice and generosity.

Although the level of education generally increased with decreasing age within a *nisei* sibling group, the eldest son was favored by traditional rules of inheritance. He would receive any property or capital and, in turn, was expected to assume major responsibility for the care of aged parents. If a family invested in real estate and retained the Japanese inheritance rules, a conflict among siblings could occur, since the property probably was obtained through the hard work of every family member. With inflated land values in Hawaii today, the inheritor could well be a wealthy man to the exclusion of the other siblings.

However, as with the different educational and occupational levels, no bitterness and resentment arise as long as generalized reciprocity operates with its high sociability and generosity. As long as the well-to-do sibling continues the reciprocal interchange and long-term debt discharge, status differentials are minimized. Hence, the system acts as a mechanism for *status equalization* among siblings.

As an example of how this system works, a couple of comfortable means performed the following services in the husband's capacity of oldest son and the most affluent member of the family. As head of the family, all members came to him for advice and assistance. He inherited his father's estate after housing his parents for some years. He used part of his inheritance to buy a house large enough to accommodate the extended family. In turn, he and his wife took in his brother and his family for one year. They paid the college tuition of several younger siblings on both sides of the family. They sent her sister to receive training to become a nurse and took care of his mother's sister. In addition, they assisted three sisters financially who had lost their husbands and bought wedding gowns for three nieces.

Their recompense is intangible by American standards, yet it serves important social functions. Obviously, they enjoy high status as generous benefactors. In addition, for most *nisei*, the greatest ambivalence is expressed between American middle-class materialism and Japanese simplicity of life style. If *issei* parents are still alive, they tend to bemoan what money is doing to their children and grandchildren, recalling the virtues of struggle and hardship. Since materialistic acquisition calls too much attention to oneself, one means to detract from it is an active system of reciprocity. The redistribution of wealth among immediate kin, as in the above example, makes one's affluence less conspicuous, detracts from another's envy and assures one's rank in the kinship group.

Nevertheless, the fact that debts involving large sums of money were not repaid in kind led to a particularly enduring kind of indebtedness, which the recipient could not discharge. Hence, the debtor-creditor relationship persisted and usually was accompanied by high sociability. In a discussion of this problem of debt discharge, one respondent said with resignation, "The Japanese family doesn't want your money. They only want your soul."

However, such a system of asymmetrical reciprocity can be vulnerable, if self-interest supercedes group interest or if the sociability level is reduced. Because such a delicate unspoken balance is maintained between giving and taking, there are no mechanisms to handle deviance. A favor which is given has no clear stipulation of return, so an individual cannot completely discharge his debt to the other. Consequently, the recipient must always be attuned to the appropriate moment to return the debt. On the other hand, the donor may, at a later date, expect a repayment in an undefined form which does not come. Because of the diffuse nature of the obligation and the unclear rules for the repayment, resentments and minor hurts can smolder for years until they explode into an open rupture. In such a system, expectations

of reciprocity which are not met are fertile ground for a breakup of the kinship group. Situations of this sort are the source of common talk among the Japanese in Honolulu. An extreme example, which was documented in the course of the research, involved two sisters living in houses on the same lot, who allegedly had not spoken for thirty years. After a few years of this social distance, a fence was constructed between the houses, and the breach was considered incapable of mending.

Sansei exchange. Nevertheless, the expectations of mutuality, which are built into the system of give and take, usually operate more smoothly if large amounts of money are not exchanged. The *sansei* generally avoid money as a medium of exchange, preferring instead to maintain kin relationships on a social and emotional level. As one respondent commented, "We don't dish out money—only lots of advice." In general, the third generation, as children, did not have to sacrifice their own educational attainment in favor of a sibling, and they are not subject to inequitable primogenitary inheritance. This change in the kinship system involves both the displacement of the instrumental and monetary functions to extrafamilial institutions, greater equalization among siblings, and an increase in the expressive and sociability functions. Such a reorganization of reciprocity possibly could account for the increased kinship solidarity among the third generation.

Patterns of reciprocity have not decreased in numbers as nonmonetary aid and services continue to be exchanged. Furthermore, money still is exchanged in the *kosai* exchange, but, as mentioned above, expectations of return have been defined. Consequently, the indebtedness is not as strong.

The potential for conflict which stemmed from inequitable distribution of resources has been reduced somewhat in recent years. However, the removal of corporate functions, particularly in the economic area, apparently has not lessened family ties or the strength of the indebtedness. As instrumental functions have been surrendered to other institutions, there is greater concentration on expressive functions.

Irrespective of the items exchanged, this system is regulated by the "law of extended credit" (Ekeh, 1974:55) by which the debts might be distributed among several relatives rather than merely within a dyadic relationship. The following is an example of how generalized exchange operates in a *sansei* family in which such reciprocity extends collaterally to cousins:

> My husband (a stonemason) has been going to a cousin's every Sunday to help him build a stone fence. It's a $1500 job, if it had been hired out, he estimated. John expects no repayment but does it because he likes his cousin. It has to be someone close for him to help so much. But he also helped his cousin's friend put in a tile shower. He says he's helping his cousin by helping the friend. If we do this, then we can get help from others. Like another cousin is a mechanic, so we can take our car to him to get it fixed free.

In most cases, the system of debts and credits remains, but in a less determinant form. As Gouldner suggests, reciprocity does not require uniform performance from individuals whose behavior it regulates. Its very indeterminacy facilitates perpetuation of the indebtedness. If A performs countless favors for B, B's mental ledger records these on the debit side. As he attempts repayment, he possibly is still acting as both a recipient and a donor as A continues his generosity. B is thus in a cyclical system of give and take, in which he finds his debts accumulating irrespective of his efforts at repayment.

For example, informal entertaining among intimates is one visible source of kinship solidarity. Reciprocal hospitality through the frequent exchange of dinners between related nuclear families generally does not discharge the debt as it would among most Americans because of the guests' lavish contributions to the dinner. They might bring an expensive delicacy like *sashimi* (Japanese raw fish), the cost of which might outstrip all other expenses for the meal. In totalling the debts and credits, the hostess, in the end, might be uncertain as to whether or not she has actually discharged the debt or whether or not she or her sister should actually be hostess on the next occasion.

Another frequent exchange of aid involves babysitting services. In one case, the woman who works fulltime leaves her children in the care of her sister. The sister refuses to accept payment even though her own husband holds down two jobs to maintain their standard of living. The means of repayment by the working mother are extremely diffuse and involve countless favors, services and gifts. The more the recipient of babysitting services attempts to discharge the debt, the more her sister becomes obligated and even more resistant to accepting monetary reimbursement. Her solution is to increase her endeavors on behalf of her working sister and her children, while her sister must, in turn, attempt reciprocity in a spiralling system of exchange.

The subtlety of this reciprocity is apparent, for money is avoided just as are cold calculations of return or self-maximization. It does not necessarily mean that self-serving interests are absent; it merely implies the presence of norms which suppress their expression.

The manner in which most Americans resolve such a dilemma is similar to resolving any role strain by withdrawal, forgetfulness, deception or compartmentalization. When we examine American kinship reciprocity, we find that the norms facilitate these strategies. The system is optional; it frequently functions over geographical distance; and, in the normative hierarchy, personal interest should precede kinship interest. Thus, one is less likely to be enclosed in a system of perpetual indebtedness, just as one has less expectations of social and emotional support from kin.

CONCLUSION

This paper has reported on the maintenance of kinship relations among second and third generation Japanese Americans. Interviews with 104 families found an increase in kinship contact and sociability among third generation families despite social mobility and increasing assimilation into extrafamilial institutions. Interpretations of these findings centered on the conclusion that the Japanese American kinship system operates on a more obligatory basis than the optional basis reported for the American kinship system.

Mechanisms which maintain this solidarity have been identified as having their source in a value system derivative of Japan which emphasizes sociocentricity, obligation to parents, reciprocity and dependence. As these values are translated into the regulation of kin relationships, it was observed that the obligatory nature of the tie between parent and child has laid the ground rules for the binding nature of other forms of reciprocity. It is concluded that an enveloping dependency on socialization, age integration in family activities, and an emphasis on sociocentric values can prepare an individual for a social embeddedness within the primary group throughout life.

Interestingly enough, the cohesiveness of this tie has persisted and even increased despite structural changes in the family from a patrilineal to the bilateral American form and despite considerable social mobility. The effect of this structural change has been largely a redistribution of indebtedness to parents among the entire sibling group rather than being centered on the eldest son. Hence, the second factor that probably contributed to the high kin solidarity, is not only the inheritance rules which are more equitable, but a set of filial obligations which becomes shared and less burdensome. Sibling solidarity is possibly increased through these processes.

The third and closely related factor is the transfer of corporate functions to nonfamilial institutions. In other words, exchange of large sums of money is rarer among the *sansei*, leaving the kinship group as a unit for sociability within a reciprocal system which does not threaten the family budget.

Lastly, this paper has discussed how the actual processes of exchange are regulated by the norm of generosity which is both diffuse and lacking in specificity in terms of equivalence of return within a specific time period. Thus, despite repeated attempts to discharge debts to kin, members of such a kinship system all too often accumulate debts at a rate which keeps them in a debtor rather than in a creditor status. It was concluded that this indeterminancy in debt repayment acts as a mechanism to inhibit repayment and actually strengthens indebtedness. Gouldner (1960: 175) discusses how this process works through the use of reciprocity:

> We should also expect to find mechanisms which induce people to remain socially indebted to each other and which inhibit repayment. This suggests another function performed by the requirement of only rough equivalence of repayment that may be involved in reciprocity. For it induces a certain amount of ambiguity as to whether indebtedness has been repaid and, over time, generates uncertainty about who is in whose debt.

When reciprocal interchange is pervaded by unconstrained generosity and when the norms do not define the time or amount of repayment, such an uncertainty as to who is the debtor and who is the creditor is inevitable. The more diffuse the reciprocity, the more nebulous are the forms of repayment. Furthermore, the frequency with which aid flows from one individual to the other makes a careful accounting of debts and credits quite difficult. Before one debt can be repaid, more gifts, most likely, have been received, so that the recipient can easily be placed in the role of continual debtor. This diffuseness probably accounts for the persistence and even increase in kinship solidarity among the *sansei*, even though the monetary aspects of the exchange have diminished.

A more obvious explanation for the strength of these mechanisms which inhibit repayment involves the strong adherence to the norms of reciprocity and generosity. When cold calculations of self-gain are sanctioned, it becomes unthinkable, at least on the overt level, to exploit others or display resentment. However, the paradox inherent in reciprocity is that it is eventually self-serving, for its very definition implies repayment. The egoism in altruism, as suggested by Gouldner (1960), was also identified by numerous respondents: however burdensome the obligations are today, one will eventually receive rewards. The underlying philosophy is couched in the terms of "I help others, so they will help me in the future."

Whether the debts are of day-to-day thoughtfulness or of a more substantial nature, both donor and recipient are aware of the obligation and plan to meet each other's expectations in the daily round of give and take. Since there is no specification of the discharge of the debt, there is a perpetual awareness of what is owed to others and what is due to oneself. Most importantly, due to the diffuse quality of generalized exchange, which acts as a mechanism to restrain repayment, social relationships are maintained in a highly *gemeinschaft* quality. Since one rarely is free from this perpetual indebtedness to some primary relatives, family solidarity obviously is strengthened (irrespective of the negative evaluations some individuals might assign to these burdens).

In conclusion, it appears necessary at this

point to go beyond measures of kinship contacts to an examination of the qualitative aspects of kin interaction and the identification of processes used to regulate the relationship. With these kinds of data, theoretical understanding of the processes of family solidarity possibly lies in the investigation of patterns of reciprocity and the underlying value consensus which enforces them.

REFERENCES

Adams, Bert
1968 Kinship in an Urban Setting. Chicago: Markham.
1971 "Isolation, function and beyond: American kinship in the 1960's." Pp. 163-186 in Carlfred B. Broderick (Ed.), A Decade of Family Research and Action. Minneapolis: National Council on Family Relations.

Arkoff, A.
1959 "Need patterns in two generations of Japanese Americans in Hawaii." Journal of Social Psychology 50 (August):75-79.

Befu, Harumi
1966- "Gift-giving and social reciprocity in Japan"
1967 France-Asie 21 (Winter):161-177.
1968 "Gift-giving in a modernizing Japan." Monumento Nipponica 23 (3-4):445-456.

Benedict, Ruth
1946 Chrysanthemum and the Sword. Cambridge, Massachusetts: Riverside.

Clark, Margaret, and Barbara Anderson
1967 Culture and Aging. Springfield, Illinois: Charles C. Thomas.

Doi, Takeo
1973 The Anatomy of Dependence. Tokyo: Kodansha International Limited.

Edwards, John
1969 "Familial behavior as social exchange." Journal of Marriage and the Family 31 (August): 518-526.

Ekeh, Peter
1974 Social Exchange Theory. Cambridge, Massachusetts: Harvard University Press.

Gibson, Geoffrey
1972 "Kin family networks: Overheralded structure in past conceptualizations of family functioning." Journal of Marriage and the Family 34 (February):13-23.

Gouldner, Alvin
1959 "Reciprocity and autonomy in functional theory." Pp. 241-270 in L. Gross (Ed.), Symposium in Sociological Theory. Evanston: Row Peterson.
1960 "The norm of reciprocity: A preliminary statement." American Sociological Review 25 (April):161-179.

Hays, William, and Charles Mindel
1973 "Extended kinship relations in Black and White families." Journal of Marriage and the Family 35 (February):51-57.

Johnson, Colleen
1974 "Gift-giving and reciprocity among Japanese-Americans." American Ethnologist 1 (May): 295-308.

Lebra, Takie
1969 "Reciprocity and the asymmetrical principle: An analytic appraisal of the Japanese concept of 'on'." Psychologia 12 (December):129-138.
1974 "Intergenerational continuity and discontinuity in moral values among Japanese." Pp. 90-117 in T. Lebra and W. Lebra, Japanese Culture and Behavior. Honolulu:East-West Center.
1965 Social Structure and the Family: Generational ican Anthropologist 77 (September):550-565.

Levy-Strauss, Claude
1969 The Elementary Structures of Kinship. Boston: Beacon Press.

Libby, Roger, and John Carlson
1973 "Exchange as concept, conceptual framework or theory? A case of Goode's application of exchange to the family." Journal of Comparative Family Studies 4 (Autumn):160-170.

Litwak, Eugene
1959 "The use of the extended family group in the achievement of goals." Social Problems 7 (Winter):177-187.
1965 "Extended kin relations in an industrial democratic society." Pp. 290-325 in Ethel Shanas and Gordon Streib (Eds.), Social Structure and the Family: Generational Relations. Englewood Cliffs, New Jersey:Prentice-Hall.

Malinowski, Bronislaw
1926 Crime and Custom in Savage Society. London: Routledge and Kegan Paul.

Masuoka, Jitsuichi
1944 "The life cycle of an immigrant institution in Hawaii: The family." Social Forces 23 (October):60-64.

Nakane, Chie
1970 Japanese Society. Berkeley:University of California.

Parsons, Talcott
1949 "The social structure of the family." Pp. 173-201 in Ruth Anshen (Ed.), The Family: Its Functions and Destiny. New York:Harper and Row.

Sahlins, Marshall
1965 "On the sociology of primitive exchange." Pp. 139-185 in Michael Banton (Ed.), The Relevance of Models for Social Anthropology. London:Tavistock.

Shanas, Ethel, and Gordon Streib
1965 Social Structure and the Family: Generational Relations. Englewood Cliffs, New Jersey: Prentice-Hall.

Shanas, Ethel, Peter Townsend, Dorothy Wedderburn, Henning Friis, Poul Milhaj, and Jan Stehouwer
1968 Old People in Three Industrial Societies. New York:Atherton.

Sussman, Marvin
1965 "Relations of adult children to their parents in the United States." Pp. 62-92 in Ethel Shanas and Gordon Streib (Eds.), Social Structure and the Family: Generational Relations. Englewood Cliffs, New Jersey:Prentice-Hall.

78

1970   "The urban kin networks in the formulation of family theory." Pp. 481-508 in Reuben Hill and Rene Konig (Eds.), Families in East and West. Paris:Mouton.

Sussman, Marvin, and Lee Burchinal
1962   "Kin family networks: Unheralded structure in current conceptualization of family functioning." Marriage and Family Living 24 (August): 231-240.

van der Veen, Klaus
1971   "Ambivalence, social structure and dominant kinship." Pp. 377-408 in Francis L. K. Hsu (Ed.), Kinship and Culture. Chicago:Aldine.

Incorporation into Networks Among Sikhs in Los Angeles

Anne K. Fleuret

Department of Anthropology

California State University, Los Angeles

ABSTRACT: Anthropologists engaged in field research in urban areas are faced with methodological problems quite different from those of the student of traditional societies. In this paper the problem of geographical dispersal of the population under study is taken up. Various techniques of incorporation into the social networks of group members are discussed, with reference to the Sikh community of Los Angeles. These include neighborhood, kinship, common employment, and others. The most profitable means of incorporation is pointed out, and its significance detailed.

In any urban setting there are likely to exist bounded groupings of persons whose internal organization will be of interest to the anthropological fieldworker. Membership in such groups may be defined in terms of any one or a combination of such variables as ethnicity, religion, language, occupation, sex, age, or other criteria. If such a group tends to cluster into a residential community or neighborhood the task of the fieldworker is facilitated because of the proximity and geographical identity of his informants. In such a situation, as in an African village or other more traditional sites for anthropological investigation, living in the neighborhood may in itself be sufficient to ensure the inclusion of the fieldworker in the day-to-day social activities of his informants. Rapport is enhanced by the ability of the anthropologist to communicate with informants in their own symbolic terms and on their own home ground.

However, not all the communities or groups of persons of interest to anthropologists cluster conveniently in this way. Many recent immigrant ethnic minorities in the Los Angeles area are territorially dispersed. The Sikh population of the city is a case in point. The Sikhs are a very small and very recently arrived minority in the Los Angeles area, numbering about five hundred. They are immigrants from the Punjab region of India who practice a distinctive mono-theistic and syncretic religion but who have nevertheless retained the structural form of the Hindu Jati system. In theory if not in practice all Sikhs reject the consumption of tobacco and symbolize common membership in a military brotherhood by keeping unshorn hair (including men's beards) and wearing steel bangles. Those who have retained these symbols are thus physically extremely distinctive. Even though sizeable groups of Sikhs have lived in the Imperial Valley, in Stockton, and in the Marysville-Yuba City area since the turn of the century, these earlier established Sikh groups are predominantly agriculturalists and semi-rural in residence. The Los Angeles group conversely is composed almost exclusively of highly educated professionals (such as dentists, teachers, and engineers) and a proportion of college and university students, mostly male. Due to the varying demands of occupation and employment, residence in the Los Angeles area is widely dispersed, from the Sun Valley-Pacoima area in the north to Long Beach and Orange County in the south. Even a few strays who live in Lompoc, Oxnard and Bakersfield consider themselves attached to the Los Angeles group.

Despite this wide territorial/geographical dispersal, however, Los Angeles Sikhs do have a central focus for communal activities. This is the Sikh Temple, located in the Hollywood area. Religious services are held regularly every Sunday, and the first and third Sundays are further distinguished by the preparation and serving of *langar*, a communal meal. So in some ways Sikh life in Los Angeles does have a geographical focus. The problem is, since the community essentially gathers together only once a week, how does the "outsider" maintain contact with informants once the gathering has dispersed?

The fieldworker is thus posed with the problem of how to establish himself as a functioning member of the Sikh group, in order to gain rapport and conduct successful fieldwork. It is essential for him to in some way become incorporated into the social network(s) of one or more Sikh informants, to become a functioning part of their social universe, so that rapport can be established and data can be collected.

The usage of the term network derives from that of Barnes (1954) and Bott (1957, 1971). According to Barnes, "Each person is, as it were, in touch with a number of people, some of whom are directly in touch with each other and some of whom are not. . . .I find it convenient to talk of a social field of this kind as a *network*. The image I have is of a set of points some of which are joined by lines. The points of the image are people, or sometimes groups, and the lines indicate which people interact with each other" (1954:43).

Bott adds to this the idea of connectedness. "By connectedness I mean the extent to which the people known by a family [or informant] know and meet one another independently of the family [or informant]" (1971:59). She distinguishes close-knit and loose-knit networks, close-knit ones having a high degree of connectedness and loose-knit ones having a low incidence of such relationships. It is obviously to the advantage of the outsider to endeavor to introduce himself into a network through an informant where his subsequent dealings with members of that network do not have to be consistently arranged through one key individual.

Epstein (1961), through the collection and analysis of the social contacts of one of his African informants over the course of several days, has indicated broadly a number of the social institutions through which an individual can widen the range of his social contacts and incorporate previous outsiders or unknowns into his social network. Among these are neighborhood and locality; kinship; ethnicity (in this case membership in the same indigenous African ethnic group); "social" (such as attendance at sports events or drinking parties); and a range of persons with whom the informant interacts regularly and intensely who did not fall into any of the previous categories. In Epstein's case study, and in the case of those families in Bott's study who had very close-knit networks and highly segregated conjugal roles, the most important single category of persons with whom the informant(s) regularly interacted consisted of *kin*.

In the case of Sikhs in Los Angeles similar institutions can be isolated as potential arenas for incorporation into networks. Neighborhood, as indicated, is of minor concern because of the dispersal of the Sikh group; but kinship, voluntary associations, occupation, and education are all potential sources of inclusion. In addition, among the Sikhs, there are additionally two highly specialized avenues that can be utilized to join their networks. These are conversion to the Sikh religion, and membership (without necessarily undergoing conversion) in the Sikh Temple.

It remains to assess the utility of these various institutional approaches to the urban "outsider" fieldworker and to try to establish which of them yields the greatest amount of rapport and the widest range of contacts in a fieldwork situation.

Neighborhood, or geographical contact, as previously indicated, is likely to be the least fruitful means of approach for joining Sikh networks. Since there is no residential clustering of Sikhs, and since visiting of homes seems to be limited and spontaneous, mere physical proximity to a Sikh family is not a guarantee of expanding contacts in the community. On only one occasion, to my knowledge, did living nearby significantly contribute to the expansion of an outsider's Sikh social contacts; this occurred when a set of brothers, all students, persuaded on older married couple living in the same apartment building to visit the Sikh Temple on a major religious holiday. But because such contacts are so subject to chance, living in the same neighborhood is not a valuable means of gaining access to incorporation into Sikh networks.

Common occupation or employment is a second means to effect such inclusion, but once again a rather risky one. The high degree of specialization and professional employment among Sikhs means that the "outsider" must also be highly trained and highly skilled. While Jagtar Singh, a machinist, does invite Hermann, a fellow employee, and his wife to dinner at his home, and while Gurmukh, an accountant, dates several fellow employees, common occupation or jobs in the same place seems once again too uncertain a path to lead to the necessary social contacts.

Education is a somewhat more valuable means to acquire contacts, whether in a student-to-student or teacher-to-student relationship. The educational institution provides an atmosphere of common interest, and certain colleges and universities are well known as the place to go in order to expand social horizons. Also, a large educational institution such as UCLA or USC usually has a number of Sikh students. Nevertheless the school remains unsatisfactory because the network of a Sikh student is most likely composed primarily of non-Sikhs in the first place. Thus it is not a realistic place to make contact with numbers of potential informants.

Voluntary associations of various types, including clubs, civic organizations, and professional groups, can provide access to Sikh networks. Common membership in such organizations has introduced a number of outsiders to extended social contacts with Sikhs. Dr. K., president of the Sikh Study Circle, has been responsible for bringing in many visitors whom he has contacted in this way. The problems with this approach from the point of view of the fieldworker are twofold. First the necessary membership in the voluntary association must be established. This is impossible for fieldworkers who cannot afford, or do not have the necessary qualifications for, such membership. Secondly, people incorporated into the Sikh network in this way have very often been labelled as distinguished guests. This label generates social distance between outsider and potential informant.

While both Bott and Epstein conclude that informants' networks and contacts are composed primarily of kinsmen, this is not true of Sikhs in Los Angeles. Most of the families of Sikhs were recruited to the Los Angeles area not by pre-established kin ties, but by professional and geographical factors. There is a wide range of job possibilities in precisely those fields in which Sikhs specialize, and the climate of California, especially the Central Valley but Los Angeles also, is said to be very similar to that of the Punjab. Furthermore, there are many more men than women. Many of the men came to the United States originally as post-secondary students and have remained in the country after completing their degrees. For example, Ajmer received an engineering degree from Ohio State 12 years ago and now works for the Los Angeles County Road Department. Dalip received a physics degree from California Polytechnic State University, Pomona and works now for Jet Propulsion Laboratory. Gurmukh earned an accounting degree in Toronto and fled the snow to come to California and work for Kaiser Foundation Medical Services. Ajmer is married to an American. Dalip and Gurmukh are single. None has any Sikh relatives in the United States.

However, it is possible for an outsider to be incorporated into Sikh kin networks in two ways--by ties of affinity, and by fictive ties. Kin ties are the strongest and most enduring kinds of social links that an individual can establish, but at the same time they are full of pitfalls. Marriage to a Sikh, especially a non-Sikh woman to a Sikh man, places immediate constraints on behavior and communication. While these constraints are much less restrictive in Los Angeles than in Amritsar or Dar es Salaam, they nevertheless exist. Among more conservative Sikhs there is strict conjugal role segregation with women's activities being conducted in the home, and with a wife's social contacts with male non-kin being sharply restricted and regarded with suspicion. Thus ties of affinity, while very inclusive and not subject to termination, as Sikhs view divorce negatively, are nevertheless too restrictive of behavior and too demanding to be successfully employed as a means of incorporation.

Ties of fictive kinship, especially the extension of classificatory kin terms are also a possibility. However, it becomes clear after observation that the uses of such terms (for example, being called "sister" by same generation females, or being asked by females in the first ascending generation to call them "auntie") are a consequence, not a cause, of inclusion in networks.

Conversion is, in its way, just as inclusive as kinship, especially since devout Sikhs place strong emphasis on the physical symbols of the religion such as unshorn hair. One of the fundamental tenets of the faith is that anyone is free to worship in the Temple, God's House. Although Sikhs do not actively proselytize, conversion, in the Punjab, is an ongoing process. Many Hindu families will raise one or two children as Sikhs. Several members of the Los Angeles Temple were raised in this way.

Because of this, when a large group of American Sikhs under the leadership of a Punjabi Sikh "Yogi" joined the Los Angeles Temple and began to participate in religious services, they were, at first, welcomed. However, after a time the welcome began to wear thin. There were a number of reasons for this. Perhaps the primary reason was because of the strong identification of Sikhism with the Punjab cultural region of India. Not only do Sikhs have expectations of certain types of religious behavior, but of accompanying forms of cultural behavior as well. The American converts were able to adapt fairly well to the religious expectations of fellow Sikhs, but they consistently misused important cultural categories. For example, white is a color for garments that among Punjabis is reserved for widows and extremely holy or religious men, yet among the converts several young married women frequently wore white. Most of the converts were unable to speak the Punjabi language or read the Gurmukhi script in which the Sikh holy book is written. They were unable to play musical instruments, to sing *shabaats* (hymns) or popular songs, to cook, or even to peel garlic in the proper manner. After a time conflict began to arise between Punjabi and non-Punjabi Sikhs. This conflict was rooted in cultural differences, blamed on an unequal distribution of rights and duties in terms of *sewa* (service) to the Temple, and culminated in the withdrawal of the converts from the Sikh Temple. They have since established their own *"ashram"* under the guidance of their Yogi but no longer participate in religious services at the Temple.

Conversion also places restrictions on comportment and makes certain types of demands that would inconvenience the fieldworker. There are certain types of dietary restrictions, especially for women. The ban of tobacco would doubtless inconvenience many. Behavioral restrictions of the same order as those imposed by ties of affinity prevail. A woman who recently braved public opinion in the Temple to question the Board of Directors on aspects of the financial affairs of the Temple was referred to for weeks afterward as "that bold one." And, as shown, the inability to properly manipulate cultural categories, categories taken for granted among Sikhs, would handicap efforts to establish rapport.

So, in the end, membership, the last potential network-expanding technique, is the best. As previously mentioned, Sikh tradition encourages the inclusion of all, Sikh and non-Sikh alike, in Temple activities. But mere attendance is not enough. An outsider must legitimize himself by becoming a dues-paying member of the formal Sikh organization and by making regular contributions to the finances of the Temple. These contributions are not kept secret; rather, the contributor and the amount are publicly announced at the end of every religious ceremony. Defaulters are conspicuous by the absence of their names from this listing.

Membership permits an outsider to fully participate in all the affairs of the Temple, to vote in elections for officers, even to run for office, to serve on committees. The present membership and building fund committee has two representatives who are members but not converts. At the same time, however, membership does not place the same types of formal restrictions on behavior that conversion and kinship do; the participant is permitted to retain many personal freedoms he would otherwise have to do without. Since he is not a convert to Sikhism, nor a Sikh by marriage, both implicit and explicit expectations of certain types of cultural and personal behavior are absent. Membership in the Temple is the best technique by far for acquiring and expanding personal relationships with Sikh informants--relationships that can ensure the outsider's incorporation into close-knit networks and establish rapport with the community under study.

REFERENCES CITED

Barnes, J.A.
    1954   Class and committees in a Norwegian island parish. Human
                 Relations 7:39-58.

Bott, E.
    1957   Family and social network. London: Tavistock.

Epstein, A.L.
    1961   The network and urban social organization. Rhodes Living-
                 stone Journal 29:29-61.

Mitchell, J.C. (ed).
    1969   Social networks in urban situations. Manchester University
                 Press.

FILIPINO HOMETOWN ASSOCIATIONS IN HAWAII[1]

Jonathan Y. Okamura
University College London

Hometown associations have proliferated among Filipino immigrants in Hawaii since the arrival of increasing numbers of Filipinos after the liberalization of United States immigration laws in 1965. These organizations either have been started anew or represent revivals of previously inactive groups. Awareness of their growing numbers seems to have given rise to a desire on the part of immigrants who share a common specific locality of origin to establish and to maintain ties with one another through formal organization. From a review of various lists of Filipino voluntary associations compiled by the Oahu Filipino Community Council (a federation of Filipino organizations on Oahu), the Filipino 75th Anniversary Commemoration Commission,[2] and the Philippine Consulate General in Hawaii, it seems that there were 62 Filipino hometown and provincial organizations on the island of Oahu in 1981. These associations comprise a little more than half of the total number of voluntary organizations represented on these lists. Yet, despite the significant increase in the number of hometown associations since 1965, most of these organizations are not especially active and are no longer necessary to meet the mutual aid functions for which they were originally established during the plantation period of labor recruitment. This paper seeks to determine the factors that account for the continued existence and establishment of hometown associations and the purposes they presently serve.

BASES OF MEMBERSHIP

The bases of membership of Filipino regional, that is, hometown or provincial, organizations reflect the nature of both the historical and present processes of immigration to Hawaii. The more intensive plantation labor recruitment during the 1920s in the Ilocos region in northern Luzon[3] and the continued predominance of Ilokanos among Filipino immigrants to Hawaii are evident in the greater number of Ilokano associations. That is, 39 associations, or almost two-thirds of the total number of regional organizations, base their memberships on communities in the Ilocos region. Because of the substantial numbers of Ilokano immigrants in Hawaii, 34 of these associations represent hometowns, while the remainder are provincial or wider regional organizations. There are also nine associations whose memberships are drawn from Pangasinan province, which is adjacent to the Ilocos region, and eight of these are hometown associations.

The earlier arrival and the lesser numbers of plantation workers from the Visayas region are reflected in the few organizations which represent that area. Significantly, these are not hometown but provincial associations for Bohol, Siquijor, Samar and Leyte, and the Visayas in general.

In the past, there was only one association that drew its membership from the Tagalog area around Manila, but it later changed its name so that non-Tagalogs could also join. However, since the post-1965 immigration of Filipinos to Hawaii there are several organizations that represent provinces in the central Luzon area including Bulacan, Tarlac, Cavite, Batangas, and Nueva Ecija.

The basis of membership in Filipino regional organizations is common locale of origin, either a town or a province, in the Philippines. Associations also extend membership to the spouses of members if they are not from the community in question and to local, Hawaii-born Filipinos whose parents are from that community. However, few local Filipinos join hometown associations or participate in their activities. Most associations are not very restrictive about membership and, in some cases, have provisions for honorary membership to persons, usually officers of other associations, who would otherwise be ineligible to join. However, in one association an individual who is not from the town or related to someone from the town can only become a member by first being declared an adopted son or daughter of the town by resolution of the municipal council in the Philippines.

Annual membership dues in Filipino hometown associations are generally between $2 to $5 per person. Some associations, aware that their members have more pressing economic obligations, charge only an initial membership fee. It is not uncommon for hometown associations to have fairly large memberships, between 200 to 400 persons, although active members comprise a minority of the total membership. In some hometown associations the leaders emphasize that their activities, especially the larger social gatherings, are open to all persons from the town, whether or not they are association members.

ENTITLEMENTS AND BENEFITS OF MEMBERSHIP

Filipino hometown associations provide various benefits for their members. In most cases, it is stated in its constitution and by-laws that one of the objectives of the organization is to provide assistance to members in times of illness, emergency, or death. In the event of the latter, members may be assessed a specified amount, generally between $2 and $5, or the association contributes a prescribed sum of money to the family of the deceased. Such death benefits are not inconsiderable, and the deceased's family may receive anywhere from $200 to $500, depending on the size of the membership of the association. In one especially large organization, the deceased's beneficiaries could receive up to $850. This money is often presented to the family at the wake for the deceased by the association's president who may also deliver a short eulogy. In addition, some associations donate a floral wreath in its name, and one organization also pays for the announcement of the death on a Filipino radio station. Association members are expected to attend the services for a deceased member.

Some hometown associations provide small monetary amounts to members when they are hospitalized or when a member takes a trip to the Philippines. Several associations award scholarships to the children of members.

In addition to these benefits which are specified as entitlements of membership, members may receive additional benefits through informal interaction with other association members. Friendships may develop, and contacts can be made with persons who may be sources of information on jobs and housing or who can provide introductions to persons who are able to furnish such assistance.

Most hometown associations hold at least one large social gathering during the year, usually a dinner and dance or a potluck picnic. Some organizations appear to compete implicitly with one another for prestige in terms of where they hold their social affairs, and for these associations Waikiki hotel banquet rooms have become the standard. These social functions are generally for the installation of new officers, the coronation of the association's beauty queen, to commemorate the anniversary of the founding of the organization or, less frequently, to honor municipal officials or other distinguished guests from their hometown. The proceedings at these affairs are very similar; the keynote address, one of several speeches, is delivered by a Filipino politician or government official, and officers are inducted by an official from the Philippine Consulate. In some of the more traditional associations, the Philippine national anthem along with the Star Spangled Banner are sung at the beginning of the program.

The souvenir programs for these social affairs are also very similar in format and are modeled after the program booklets which are prepared for town fiestas in the Philippines. Their contents include congratulatory messages from the president of the Philippines (fabricated in some instances), the provincial governor of Ilocos Norte or Ilocos Sur, the governor of Hawaii, the mayor of Honolulu, and the consul-general of the Philippine Consulate in Hawaii. These messages seem intended to enhance the prestige of the association. Also included in the souvenir program are advertisements and congratulatory remarks from Filipino travel, real estate, and insurance agents, restaurant owners, and other businessmen, many of whom are association leaders, and from other Filipino voluntary organizations. These advertisements are a significant source of funds for associations and establish reciprocal relationships with other voluntary organizations that can be expected to make similar appeals for advertising when they hold their annual social gatherings.

In only a few cases are these social functions of hometown associations held to coincide with their town fiesta in the Philippines or include aspects of a typical fiesta. One association does hold an annual *Fiesta ti Kailokuan,* or fiesta from the Ilocos, that comprises some of the more traditional elements of the town fiesta. It includes the presentation of a standardized drama or *comedia Ilokana,* song and dance numbers, and the coronation of the fiesta queen. The latter follows Philippine tradition as the queen, dressed in a formal gown with a long train, promenades with an escort to her throne where she is presented with a sash, crown, and trophy by different Filipino politicians and community leaders.

Almirol (1978:82) maintains that in California, Filipino voluntary associations "provide a social framework for interpersonal relations within the ethnic community." This generalization as it stands is also valid in Hawaii, especially since many hometown associations draw their memberships from Honolulu and widely scattered plantation towns, and members may not have the opportunity to see each other regularly. It must be noted, however, that most hometown associations in Hawaii do not have regular and frequent activities that bring their members together. In most organizations, meetings are supposed to be held every three months but usually are held irregularly, and the majority of members do not attend anyway. The infrequency of meetings is essentially because associations have few ongoing activities that require discussion or participation by members. Most members of Filipino associations seem content to limit their participation to the purchase of fund-raising tickets, to the payment of dues and death benefits, and to attendance at the annual banquet or Christmas party. It is a commonly heard expression among Filipino immigrants that they are "too busy" with work, family, and other social obligations, and this factor may also account for their lack of participation or nonmembership in hometown associations. It might also be pointed out that there are other, perhaps more frequent, social occasions within the immigrant Filipino community for "townmates" (immigrants from the same hometown in the Philippines) to renew their ties with one another and with other immigrants. Whenever a family celebrates a rite of passage, such as a baptism, wedding, birthday, or graduation, townmates are generally invited, whether or not they are members of a common hometown association.

Nonetheless, although large social gatherings such as installation or anniversary banquets or potluck picnics are generally held only once a year, association members still appreciate these opportunities to see each other and to renew their relationships. Similarly, while meetings do not attract most of the members of an organization, for those who do attend regularly they are occasions for convivial fellowship before and after association matters are discussed. Meetings are commonly held at the homes of members rather than at more formal settings, and refreshments are served afterwards. On special occasions such as the election of officers that attract more than the usual number of members, the association may pay for a pig to be prepared for everyone's enjoyment.

TIES WITH THE HOMETOWN

Most Filipino regional associations in Hawaii have made monetary or other charitable contributions to their home communities in the Philippines, and this activity is often stated as one of the primary objectives in the constitution and by-laws of organizations. In the recent past, associations have donated money to their hometowns for the construction of health centers, a water tank, an electric power plant, for repairs to the municipal building and town plaza, to assist schools, churches, and hospitals, and for walkie-talkies and uniforms for the town police. For the more costly projects, plaques are commonly erected in the hometown which note the name of the contributing association. Besides these enduring kinds of projects, monetary and material assistance are sent to home communities on occasions of natural disasters such as floods or fires. It should be noted that in the great majority of cases these contributions are not regular organization activities but were given either at the request of the hometown or at the inclination of the association. Only a few organizations have annual fund-raising projects, such as popularity beauty queen contests, banquets, or the sale of foodstuffs, to raise money for their hometowns.

Once a hometown association has donated money or material goods to its home community, it can expect to be besieged with continued requests for assistance. In one case, the administrators of an elementary school in the Philippines sent a copy of a resolution which expressed their gratitude to the association of their townspeople in Hawaii for its contribution towards the purchase of playground equipment. Accompanying the resolution was yet another which formally requested their donation of a typewriter. The latter was a rather modest request because previously the association had been asked to purchase a station wagon for the municipal government. These contributions seem to have enhanced the perception on the part of people in the home communities that the United States is a veritable land of plenty where even immigrants have easy access to material wealth.

Donations to their hometown are a means for former residents in Hawaii to demonstrate their continuing concern for their home communities and to signify to townspeople that they have attained a measure of economic success as immigrants in their adopted country. In return for their charitable contributions, association members are accorded social prestige as civic minded and prosperous individuals by their home communities. Such recognition can be enjoyed at a distance; for example, chairs that were donated to a public school in the Philippines each bore the name of the individual donors in Hawaii. The relation between the home community and the hometown association would seem to be of greater benefit to the former than to the latter since the hometown gains substantially more in tangible terms than do association members. Certainly, it is more common for the home community to request assistance than for the association to offer it. Also, while townspeople in Hawaii do have a desire to assist in the development of their hometowns, they are sometimes suspicious if money sent to the town is actually spent on the project for which it was intended. Municipal officials and association officers are the usual objects of these suspicions.

Some of the more active associations organize *balikbayan* (returnee from abroad) trips to the Philippines for their members, usually to coincide with the fiesta of their hometown. These organizations also commonly sponsor popularity beauty queen contests in conjunction with their trips home so that the association's queen, along with her attendant princesses, can be crowned during the town fiesta. Proceeds from the popularity contest are sometimes presented as a contribution to the hometown during the fiesta. Popularity queen contests are generally decided on the basis of the sale of raffle tickets, the prize sometimes a trip to the Philippines, and the winner is the young woman who has sold the most tickets.

A few of the hometown associations that organize popularity queen contests have revived the social box dance as another means to raise funds. In the past, this practice was commonly observed on the plantations in Hawaii among Filipino laborers and is still held in the Philippines. At a box dance, each of the queen contestants brings three wrapped boxes which usually contain some food item or alcoholic beverage. During the evening's proceedings, the master of ceremonies announces that the next dance is for the box of a particular candidate "to the damage of $25." The young men present then begin bidding at that amount for the privilege of dancing with the young lady and also for the box. As a higher bid is made, a young man steps forward to dance, and the winner of the box is the gentleman who has made the highest bid by the end of the song. The money he is thus obliged to pay is contributed to the monetary tally of the candidate in question.

During the plantation era, social box dances were occasions for eligible young men to distinguish themselves in order to gain the attention of a young woman or her parents. The winning bid for a box was then about $10, while at present it may be $50 to $100. However, during the "last canvassing" when the final tally will be made and the queen declared, winning bids may be in excess of $1,000, although this money is not from a single individual but from close relatives and friends of a candidate who pool their resources. Besides money that is received from the winning bids, supporters of a contestant also place envelopes of money collected from the sale of raffle tickets into a ballot box. At the end of the evening's proceedings, a final tally is made of the money raised by each candidate, and the young lady who has raised the most money is declared the association's queen. Social box dances and popularity queen contests in general have the potential to raise substantial amounts of money for an association, depending on the number of candidates, and gross proceeds of $15,000 to $20,000 from such events are not uncommon.

The officers and other members of a hometown association can expect to be treated as special and honored guests of their hometown when they return for its town fiesta. For example, in the case of one such association that has organized annual trips to their hometown since 1975, the party in their rented bus is met at the municipal boundary by townspeople, and they proceed in a motorcade to the town. Upon their arrival, they are honored guests along with other *balikbayans* at a lavish party hosted by the town mayor at which they are individually recognized. During the town fiesta, one of the evenings is sponsored by the hometown association and is highlighted by the coronation of its queen and princesses and by the presentation to the town by the association president of a monetary contribution, $1,000 in recent years.

Voluntary Associations as Adaptive Mechanisms

Much of the social anthropological literature on voluntary associations has focused on their role as adaptive mechanisms in situations of social and cultural change (see Kerri 1976 for a review). Functional analysis has resulted in a decided emphasis on the positive aspects of voluntary associations such that all manner of activity in these associations is viewed as being of eufunctional significance for their members. Nonetheless, the literature from Africa in particular (Banton

1956; Little 1957, 1965; Parkin 1966) has clearly demonstrated the part that voluntary associations play in the adjustment of migrants from rural areas to towns and cities. However, this adaptive role of voluntary associations is not as appropriate to an understanding of Filipino immigrants and their hometown associations in Hawaii.

For example, Little (1957:593) maintains that in West Africa voluntary associations facilitate adjustment for the urban migrant by serving as a substitute for the extended family and thus satisfying many of the same needs as this traditional grouping. This support and assistance are provided in the form of companionship, legal counsel and protection, and sickness and funeral benefits (Little 1957:593). In the past, Filipino laborers on the plantations were provided with such familial aid and support by joining a *saranay* or mutual aid society. These associations were formed among townmates or the wider Filipino planta-tion community to provide various social and security benefits. For their one dollar monthly dues, members were entitled to attend picnics, dances, and social gatherings hosted by another member. In the event of illness or death of a member, the club made a contribution to his family through assessments on its members (Alcantara 1981:58). Hospitalization and death benefits were also provided through another form of mutual aid society, the *inanama,* although since its members did not assemble it lacked the social functions of the *saranay* (Alcantara 1981:58). Mutual assistance was also available through membership in a *kumpang (amung* in Ilokano) or rotating credit association in which a number of men contributed a prescribed amount of money each month and received in turn the entire sum that was collected.

At present, hometown associations no longer perform a surrogate role of the extended family for Filipino immigrants in Hawaii because of the fairly extensive kinship ties of most immigrants since the 1965 changes in United States immigration laws. It is on his kin that the newly arrived immigrant depends for assistance in finding his first job and for his initial accommodation, which is usually provided at no expense (Okamura 1983:163-164). Even after he has been settled in Hawaii, he continues to rely on his kin for advice and assistance, for example, in petitioning other members of his family, learning to drive a car, or buying a house. It might be noted that certain kinds of security provisions, such as health and unemployment insurance, retirement benefits, and welfare assistance, are provided through one's employer or by the state government, thus also lessening the dependence of immigrants on hometown associations.

In the absence of close relatives, it is true that the recently arrived immigrant may turn to townmates for assistance, but the basis for expecting aid is not common membership in a hometown association but the townmate relationship itself. In the immigrant setting in Hawaii, townmates look upon each other as quasi-kin and are considered as potential sources of assistance. Thus, in the event of the death of a townmate, one would not refrain from the customary paying of respects at his wake or funeral and a monetary contribution to his family simply because the deceased, although a townmate, was not a member of the hometown association. A distinction must be maintained between townmates and members of a common hometown association. Although both relationships derive from common origin in the same town, many of the familial functions that Little (1957) assigned to voluntary associations in West Africa are observed by immigrant Filipino townmates in Hawaii whether or not they share mutual membership in a hometown association.

Little (1957:593-594) also contends that in West Africa voluntary associations serve as substitutes for traditional agencies of social control and for the resolution of private disputes. In the past on the plantations, the association president may have admonished members not to bring shame to their fellow members by unsociable behavior (Alcantara 1981:58). At present, however, hometown associations do not have that degree of authority over their members. At the individual level, sanctions against improper behavior originate in the family and extend to the larger Filipino community through informal neighborhood gossip networks. Similarly, domestic disputes can be settled within the family and need not be taken to association leaders.

What should be clear at this point is that Filipino hometown associations in Hawaii do not facilitate the adjustment of immigrants by serving as surrogates for the extended family. The essential reason for this is because the social circumstances of Filipino immigrants at present differ considerably from the plantation period of labor recruitment. Furthermore, Filipino immigrants have a more viable adaptive mechanism, the presence of real kinsmen, to assist them in their adjustment to the wider Hawaii society.

Little (1957:593) also implies that in West Africa voluntary associations facilitate adaptation for rural immigrants into the towns by functioning as acculturative mechanisms insofar as they instill new standards of dress, etiquette, hygiene, and punctuality. In particular, he notes that the "traditional-modernized" association acts as a "cultural bridge which conveys . . . the tribal individual from one kind of sociological universe to another" (Little 1957:593). He also remarks that by encouraging the migrant to socialize with persons from outside his lineage and tribe, the association assists him in adjusting to the more cosmopolitan atmosphere of urban life (Little 1957:593).

Filipino hometown associations in Hawaii do not serve this acculturative role for immigrants because they do not exert that degree of influence or control over their members. Filipino immigrants experience acculturation processes more through their daily work situation, where they usually must speak English, interact with non-Filipinos, observe interpersonal norms of behavior appropriate to such relationships and become acquainted with aspects of local culture in Hawaii, than through their membership in hometown associations. While members may be exposed to such association practices as parliamentary procedures, organizing fund-raising and social activities, and seeking office, these are not activities that are of instrumental use in an immigrant's daily life. Furthermore, hometown associations tend to maintain certain cultural traditions and social relations rather than serve as instruments of social or cultural change. That is, Ilokano is the common medium at meetings, links with the home community are continued, hometown traditions are perpetuated, and social ties with townmates are reinforced. While hometown associations cannot be said to encapsulate an immigrant in a network of social relationships solely with other immigrants, they also do not promote interactions with other ethnic groups since non-Filipinos are rarely present at association activities and affairs except for politicians seeking Filipino votes.

Despite the inapplicability of some of Little's (1957) notions of voluntary organizations as adaptive mechanisms to the case of Filipino hometown associations in Hawaii, one of his West African findings is quite appropriate. He observes that voluntary associations serve an adaptive role through the new criteria of social achievement they set up and through the opportunity they offer for the "ambitions of the rising class of young men . . . who have been to school" (Little 1957:592). A similar observation is made by Banton (1956:365) who notes that Temne companies in Freetown allocate new leadership roles in a context where the traditional authority structure based on age is inappropriate with urban life and where prestige lies in acquiring western technology and culture. Since the post-1965 immigration of Filipinos to Hawaii, the leadership positions in many hometown associations have passed from oldtimer plantation recruits or longtime members of an organization in general to these more recent immigrants. However, the presidency is an exception to this trend since it often continues to be held by an oldtimer out of the members' sense of respect for his longtime contributions to the association. In other cases, post-1965 immigrants have started a regional association if there was none before or it had become inactive.

While it would be incorrect to depict these newer association leaders as young in an absolute sense, they are relatively younger by at least a generation from the oldtimers. They also differ from their predecessors in being far better educated; in many cases they were college graduates and professionals in the Philippines before immigrating to Hawaii. They also hold more prestigious occupations than the oldtimers in management, administrative, or clerical work. While the younger leaders have a greater command of English than the oldtimers, this ability is not necessarily an advantage in the internal affairs of the association since those are generally conducted in Ilokano.

SCHISM IN HOMETOWN ASSOCIATIONS

The proliferation of voluntary associations in Hawaii is commonly perceived by Filipinos as evidence of divisiveness and disunity within their community. For the 1930s Cariaga (1974:85) also noted the same observation being made of the Filipino community; "It is often said that one of the unfortunate features of life among Hawaii Filipinos is their lack of leadership and of unity. Disputes occur between factions and their leaders. Often organizations with the same objectives compete, as it would seem, unnecessarily." However, the increase in the number of Filipino voluntary associations is not necessarily the result of disharmony but is a reflection of the numerical growth of the Filipino community since the 1965 changes in United States immigration laws and of the diversity of interests of Filipinos. Furthermore, organizational divisiveness within the Filipino community is not manifest between associations as much as it may be within the same association. Most organizations, through their officers, are supportive of the activities of other associations (Okamura 1981). Association officers sell fund-raising tickets for each other, pay for advertisements in souvenir banquet programs, donate trophies and door prizes and are invited to attend each other's social affairs. While they must pay for their own tickets to these social functions because they are fund-raising activities, they can expect that other leaders will reciprocate and attend their social affairs. Also, many association officers occupy positions in several organizations since they were invited to join as honorary members. Furthermore, in only a few cases does more than one hometown association represent a particular group of townspeople. While it is true that Filipino regional associations have proliferated since the post-1965 immigration to Hawaii, they have not done so necessarily as a result of segmentary schisms from other organizations or because they represent rival associations to ones already in existence.

Internal discord was characteristic of Filipino hometown associations in the past. Alcantara (1981:147) notes that retired plantation workers generally considered these clubs, as they called them, to have been status-oriented, divisive, proliferative, and short-lived. He maintains that associations were used by their officers as avenues for status competition since holding office in a club, particularly the presidency, was a means to distinguish oneself from the general rank and file of common laborers (Alcantara 1981:150). Not surprisingly, the most common complaint against officers was that they used the association for their personal self-glorification. Meetings were conducted in English rather than a Philippine language and were occasions for the demonstration of oratorical skills through interminable argumentation over such matters as the interpretation of charter rules (Alcantara 1981:150). Alcantara (1981:150) contends that such discord and divisiveness were inherent in Filipino voluntary associations because they were organized by various *partidos,* or alliances of kinsmen and friends, that sought ways to assert their relative prestige rather than by individuals who desired membership benefits. Thus, the defeated faction in an election would lose interest in association affairs and withdraw its support or might start another club.

At present, hometown associations can be credited with bringing together all the various groupings of first generation Filipinos in Hawaii, that is, former plantation laborer oldtimers, 1946 plantation recruits and other post-war immigrants, and post-1965 newcomer arrivals. However, cleavage appears to be present between the oldtimers, or longtime members of an association in general, and the more recent immigrants. The former resent the latter "taking over" the association and "telling us what to do." After they had been in charge of the organization's affairs for many years, the oldtimers do not appreciate the changes that the newer members would like to introduce. In one association, the oldtimers resisted the attempts to start a scholarship fund because there had been no provision for such when their children were younger. On their part, the post-1965 immigrants complain that the oldtimers "want to do the same old things," prefer to have social activities rather than civic projects and engage in endless arguments over trivial matters.

Yet despite such internal cleavages within Filipino hometown associations between the younger and the older members, the more active members from among the latter are often accorded positions as advisers or as members of the board of directors. While these positions are somewhat honorific in nature, oldtimers are often asked to offer their opinions (if they have not already taken an active part in the meeting up to that point) during discussions of association matters. Kinship norms such as respect for elders continue to be observed in hometown associations despite a general emphasis on achievement criteria of status for election to office.

Factionalism continues to be the organizational basis of divisiveness within Filipino hometown associations in Hawaii. Opposing factions tend to coalesce over differences with the officers of an association, most commonly over their disbursement of association funds. Members are often suspicious that the officers have used the organization's assets for their personal benefit rather than for their intended purposes. During meetings, the treasurer's report is inevitably followed with questions as to the reasons for particular expenditures by the club or its officers and whether receipts are available to prove that such monies were actually spent.

LEADERSHIP IN HOMETOWN ASSOCIATIONS

The primary function of Filipino hometown associations in Hawaii is no longer to provide mutual aid as was the case during the plantation period essentially because most immigrants have close kinsmen who can be depended upon for moral and material support in times of need. Although many associations continue to provide death benefits, such security provisions would seem to be of absolute necessity only for the destitute and elderly without any relatives. Furthermore, as stated above, retirement plans, medical insurance, and unemployment benefits are available through employers or from the state government, and life insurance policies can be purchased on one's own.

The question thus arises why do Filipino hometown associations continue to exist since they no longer serve the functions for which they were originally established. Necessary for an adequate understanding of this question are two perhaps contradictory processes. First, the arrival of substantial numbers of Filipino immigrants in Hawaii since 1965 has led to an increase in the number of regional organizations, either through the revival of inactive ones or the establishment of new ones. Second, most of these associations have few regular activities for their members, and the majority of members do not take an active participatory role in them. Thus, despite the widespread proliferation of Filipino regional organizations, they seem to exist in somewhat dormant form. Selznick's (1952:96) description of a typical voluntary association as "skeletal in the sense that they are manned by a small core of individuals—the administration, the local sub-leaders, a few faithful meeting-goers—and around whom fluctuates a loosely bound mass of dues-payers" is a fairly accurate description of most Filipino hometown associations in Hawaii. Nonetheless, hometown associations evidence a remarkable capacity for perdurance despite their general periods of inactivity.

The more general question as to factors that lead to the emergence of voluntary associations has been addressed by a number of anthropologists. While Kerri (1976:34) claims not to have the answer to the question that he poses for himself, "What causes individuals and/or groups to resort to the use of common interest associations as mechanisms for dealing with adaptive problems?," he does note that the introduction of common interest associations has been in some cases the result of efforts "to deal with problems for which existing pathways had been found ineffective." From a similar adaptive perspective, Little (1957:594) contends that the two factors that are primarily instrumental in the "growth" of African voluntary associations are the existence of an urban population which is predominantly "immigrant, unstable, and socially heterogeneous," and the "adaptability of traditional institutions" to urban settings. On the other hand, Banton (1956:367) argues from the viewpoint of the cultural background of the immigrant group and maintains that "the more devolution of authority there is in tribal societies the more rapidly do contractual associations like companies emerge" in the urban area.

Of these generalizations, Kerri's is perhaps the most relevant to an explanation of the initial emergence of Filipino voluntary associations in Hawaii during the period of labor recruitment since they were clearly started to mitigate the insecurities of the harsh living and working conditions on the plantations. For the most part, these mutual aid associations represented adaptations of traditional barrio practices to the social setting in which immigrant workers found themselves.

Filipino voluntary associations seem to have proliferated during the plantation period. Cariaga (1974:84) noted that "A widely reported fact is that Filipino organizations 'spring up like mushrooms and die away as quickly', giving rise to the apt aphorism of a Filipino pastor of Honolulu who remarked that 'The inauguration of an organization, with all its pomp and ceremony, serves likewise as its funeral ceremony'." Cariaga implicitly accounted for the emergence of these associations in terms of leadership within the Filipino community. He noted that the usual leaders in the barrios whence came the plantation workers, that is, the elders and the *caciques,* or landowners, did not migrate to Hawaii. Thus, in this fluid situation in which everyone shared peasant origins and a common socio-economic status as unskilled laborers, until a new basis for leadership could be firmly established, "Every migrant Filipino is likely to feel himself about as fine and worthy of being the head of any current enterprise as his fellows. When a society is formed, there are plentiful candidates for the position of officers, but not many ordinary members" (Cariaga 1974:87).

At present, community leadership is also relevant to an understanding of the question that was initially posed as to why Filipino hometown associations continue to exist and to be newly established if they are no longer necessary to meet the mutual aid purposes for which they were originally intended. The essential factor in the continued existence of most Filipino hometown associations are their officers, particularly the president, and a few of the more active members who maintain the continuity of the organization, if in name only. If it were not for their leaders, associations would fall, as many have, into various states of inactivity. Leaders are the members who attend meetings faithfully, organize fund-raising projects, banquets, dances, picnics, and other activities for members, and represent the organization at gatherings of other Filipino associations. Officers assume this greater participatory role not only because it is their expected duty but also because they have the most to gain from such activity. While leaders may have attained a measure of economic success through their occupations, they and other members of hometown associations are generally denied social recognition and leadership positions in the wider Hawaii society. Therefore, should they wish to assert claims to superior status within the Filipino community, they may do so by serving as officers in a voluntary association.

Association officers and other members who desire prestige can seek distinction in commonplace settings such as at association meetings. They do so through ways that are intended to impress the general rank and file of members, for example, by demonstrating their knowledge of parliamentary procedures, using flamboyant expressions in English, engaging in drawn out arguments over trivial points, and generally by speaking out much more than most of the other members. Officers address the assembled group as *gaygayyem ken kabkabsat* (friends and siblings), an expression commonly used by politicians in the Ilocos region. Members address officers with the honorific title *apo* (sir) or *apo presidente*, as the case may be.

The hometown association itself confers recognition through its multitude of elective and appointive offices open to members. For example, there are often two vice-presidents, not only a secretary, treasurer, and auditor, but also assistants for these offices, several sergeants at arms, and numerous advisers and members of the board of directors. Recognition awards for outstanding achievement and service to the association are presented to members at the annual banquet. In addition, the Philippine Consulate General in Honolulu bestows "Presidential Gold Medal" awards and trophies, supposedly from the president of the Philippines, to the leaders of its favored organizations.

Officers of hometown associations are also accorded recognition in their home communities in the Philippines. Their annual messages of greetings to townspeople are included in the town fiesta souvenir booklet along with those sent by more illustrious dignitaries such as the president of the Philippines and the governor of the province. The list of officers of the association is also included in the fiesta booklet. Should an association organize a trip to their hometown, the leaders can expect to be treated as honored guests of the town. Municipal officials fete them at lavish parties, and they "rub shoulders" with the social elites of the town.

Association officers also gain prestige and recognition in their home communities as resourceful leaders for organizing monetary contributions to the hometown. These donations are an indication of the significance of achievement of status in hometown associations. In this striving among officers and members to attain status, there seems to be an orientation to the Philippines rather than to Hawaii for validation of their claims. Association officers organize fund-raising projects such as popularity queen contests not only because of the considerable amounts of money that can be raised, but also because through their presence in the hometown for the presentation of the contribution to the town and the coronation of the queen and princesses the officers can thereby assume a greater role in the town fiesta proceedings.

Social recognition and prestige are the rewards for association leaders in keeping the organization functioning. Officers speak of the sacrifices they must make in money and time spent away from their families in order to organize association activities. Yet there are tangible rewards for association leaders who through their positions come into contact with a wide segment of the Filipino community in Hawaii. Many of these leaders are in the insurance, real estate, and travel business, occupations that depend on "good public relations" with the community as Almirol (n.d.: 24) noted for Filipino leaders in California. Filipino community leaders in Hawaii are especially noticeable in the travel agency business, either as owners or as sales representatives. Their contacts with association members and the larger Filipino community prove beneficial when those persons decide to visit their hometowns or to petition their relatives to Hawaii. These contacts prove even more rewarding if the association regularly sponsors *balikbayan* trips to the hometown or beauty queen contests with travel arrangements for the queen, princesses, and their accompanying families handled by the leader's agency.

Thus, through the organizing efforts of their leaders, Filipino hometown associations in Hawaii provide a corporate representation of townmates and thereby afford an organized means for the maintenance of social relations, not necessarily interpersonal relationships, with one another. By collective reinforcement of the townmate relationship through formal membership, hometown associations foster a sense of group identity and loyalty for members as immigrants who share a common locality of origin. Thus, the hometown association becomes the focus for the mobilization of townmates when their support and participation are required. Association members and townmates alike are appealed to through the hometown association on such occasions as to honor a distinguished visitor from their town, to recognize the achievements and contributions of a townmate, to render assistance to a townmate in times of need, to contribute aid to the hometown, or when the United Filipino Council of Hawaii (a statewide federation of Filipino voluntary organizations) or the Philippine Consulate requests the participation of the larger Filipino community for a special event. While these activities represent some of the functions of hometown associations, any one of them cannot be said to be the primary purpose of associations in general because organizations vary in the extent to which they sponsor these various activities. That is, not all hometown associations serve these purposes on a regular basis because many associations are not especially active. However, what is common to all hometown associations once they have been established, even though they are relatively inactive and have been for some time, is that they provide a formal means for the organization of the above functions as the need arises or as members decide to implement them. As stated earlier, Filipino hometown associations are quite tenacious despite lack of interest and participation by their general membership. Thus, in their corporate form (Smith 1975:177), they represent the potential for mobilization of townmates for association activities.

CONCLUSION

While the proliferation of Filipino hometown associations since the post-1965 immigration to Hawaii would appear to indicate their significance for immigrants, the general low level of participation by members in association activities and the infrequency of these occasions would denote otherwise. Nonetheless, hometown associations afford various benefits for their members. They provide members with moral and material support in times of need, in particular, death benefits. The occasional social gatherings and meetings are opportunities for members to renew their relationships with one another. Organized donations to their hometowns are a means for members to contribute in a substantial way to the development of their home communities and thereby to gain recognition and prestige as civic minded and economically successful individuals. Since leadership positions in the wider Hawaii society are generally denied to Filipino immigrants, those persons who would like to assert their claims to superior status within the Filipino community can do so by holding office in a hometown association. In particular, associations provide an avenue for the ambitions of the younger, educated post-1965 immigrants who would like to establish themselves as leaders in the Filipino community.

Despite these varied functions, hometown associations do not serve as adaptive mechanisms for Filipino immigrants, except in a very general sense, as they did during the plantation labor recruitment period because the post-1965 immigrants have kinsmen to assist them in their adjustment process. Also, because hometown associations do not exert a significant degree of influence over their members and tend to maintain certain cultural traditions, they do not foster the acculturative adjustment of Filipino immigrants to Hawaii society through familiarization with local norms of interpersonal behavior or the use of English. However, although hometown associations serve various functions, it cannot be claimed that these activities are their primary purposes in general since most associations do not implement these enterprises on a regular basis because of their common inactivity. Thus, Filipino hometown associations in Hawaii provide a corporate mode for townmates to maintain their social relations with one another and thereby foster their potential mobilization for association activities.

NOTES

1. I would like to thank M. G. Smith for his comments of an earlier draft of this paper.
2. This was an appointed state body whose task was to coordinate activities planned to mark the anniversary of Filipino immigration to Hawaii in 1981.
3. The Ilocos provinces include Ilocos Norte, Ilocos Sur, La Union, and Abra.

BIBLIOGRAPHY

Alcantara, R. R.   1981.   Sakada: Filipino Adaptation in Hawaii. Washington, D.C.
Almirol, E. B.   1978.   Filipino Voluntary Associations: Balancing Social Pressures and Ethnic Images. Ethnic Groups 2:65-92.
——— n.d. Filipino Ethnicity and Voluntary Associations. Unpublished ms.
Banton, M.   1956.   Adaptation and Integration in the Social System of Temne Immigrants in Freetown. Africa 26:354-368.
Cariaga, R. R.   1974 (1936).   The Filipinos in Hawaii, A Survey of Their Economic and Social Conditions. Master's thesis, University of Hawaii. Reprinted by R and E Research Associates, San Francisco.
Kerri, J. N.   1976.   Studying Voluntary Associations as Adaptive Mechanisms: A Review of Anthropological Perspectives. Current Anthropology 17:23-47.
Little, K.   1957.   The Role of Voluntary Associations in West African Urbanization. American Anthropologist 59:579-596.
———   1965.   West African Urbanization: A Study of Voluntary Associations in Social Change. London.
Okamura, J. Y.   1981.   Filipino Voluntary Associations and the Filipino Community in Hawaii. Paper presented at the Second International Philippine Studies Conference, Honolulu.
———   1983.   Immigrant Filipino Ethnicity in Honolulu, Hawaii. Unpublished Ph.D. dissertation, University of London.
Parkin, D.   1966.   Urban Voluntary Associations as Institutions of Adaptation. Man 1:90-95.
Selznick, P.   1952.   The Organizational Weapon. New York.
Smith, M. G.   1975.   Corporations and Society: The Social Anthropology of Collective Action. Chicago.

ELENA S. H. YU is a Visiting Scientist at the National Center for Health Statistics, Department of Health and Human Services. Her areas of interests are family sociology, social medicine, and Asian-American studies. Dr. Yu's latest publication is a monograph entitled *Fertility and Kinship in the Philippines* (University of Notre Dame Press, 1980).

FILIPINO MIGRATION AND COMMUNITY ORGANIZATIONS IN THE UNITED STATES[1]

ELENA S. H. YU

INTRODUCTION

Of the major Asian populations in the United States, the Filipinos are growing the most rapidly, through both natural birth and immigration. By 1980, they are expected to comprise one-fourth of the Asians in this country. Yet, an exhaustive search of the social scientific literature reveals a dearth of empirical studies on this ethnic group. Aside from a few papers on Filipino migration statistics (Keely, 1973; 1975; Pernia, 1976; Pido, 1977; Card, n.d.), the rest of the articles that one finds in a few edited books on Asian Americans (Gee, 1976; Sue and Wagner, 1973; Tachiki et al., 1971; Hundley, 1976) still draw heavily from works which are based on data collected by the early pioneer researchers (notably Bogardus, 1929a; 1929b; 1929c and Catapusan, 1934).[2] How sociologists came to ignore the Filipinos after the research impetus of Bogardus and others, is a perplexing question but perhaps not too surprising in light of the public's general benightedness — American sociologists included — about who the Filipinos really are. In fact, even though they have been in this country since the beginning of this century, most Americans did not recognize them until the late 20s and even then, only a few were aware of their existence (Lasker, 1931:3).

Originally classified as non-Aliens, but still barred from citizenship, the Filipinos were accorded the status of "nationals" — a terminology in consonance with the nature of American sovereignty in the Philippine Islands. It is also a manipulation which happened to be convenient to the American labor unions as well as to the Hawaiian Sugar Planation Association and its subsidiaries, for it allowed them the liberty of recruiting Filipino plantation and farm workers as substitute laborers for the "yellow race" (Chinese and Japanese mainly) who had been excluded through the harshest exclusionist policies ever legislated in this land. It was not until July 2, 1946 (or a little over thirty years ago), that Congress enacted legislation making Filipinos *racially* eligible for U.S. citizenship. But what the legislative branch of the government granted on July 2, the executive branch took away two days later. On July 4, 1946, the Philippines was granted its independence. From then on, the Filipinos were no longer American nationals, but Philippine citizens who must come under the restrictive immigration policy of 100-a-year quota to the United States, along with Japan, China, Korea, and other countries of the "Eastern Hemisphere." This quota system was in effect until the late sixties.

The expected decline in the Filipino population in this country was given attention by at least one scholar (Burma, 1954:155) who predicted their declining number on the basis of their high male/female sex ratio and perceived high frequency of mixed marriage. Furthermore, misclassified as "Spanish-speaking," "Spanish surnamed," and sometimes subsumed under "Oriental and others," if not simply as "Others," the Filipino identity disappeared from the hard data which positivist sociologists lean on so heavily for their analysis.

Sociological oversight, however, does not explain why Little Manilas have, by and large, remained small and invisible, while other Asian-American communities such as Chinatowns and Little Tokyos have become conspicuous and permanent landmarks. Neither does it explain why Filipino communities have remained invisible when there are at least 2,685 Filipino organizations throughout the United States and at least 483 of them may be found in the State of California.[3] Nor does sociological oversight explain why among the "Asiatic" immigrants, both the Chinese and the Japanese, have developed their own ethnic enterprise despite mounting prejudice and discriminatory legislations, whereas Filipino ethnic enterprise appears to have been on the upsurge only recently.

The purpose of this paper is to provide at least some partial answers to the questions raised above. The author will argue that the formation of viable Asian ethnic communities is the net result of various criss-crossing factors, among the more important of which are: the historical circumstances under which an Asian population was lured to America, its subsequent adaptation in the host society, and the specific kinship system upon which the group has historically constructed its complex system of social organization. For the Filipinos, certain crucial elements which made for a viable insular ethnic community in the early days of immigration were missing. With the understanding that additional research is necessary to refine her argument, the author offers some tentative observations and hypotheses concerning the interrelationship between waves of Filipino migration, and kinship system on the one hand, and community organizations on the other hand.

103

WAVES OF FILIPINO MIGRATION

The different waves of Filipinos who came to the United States can be meaningfully described by their occupations. If we disregard the fact that as early as 1765, Filipino seamen who escaped from the Spanish galleon trade between Mexico and Manila had settled along the coast of Louisiana (Espina, 1974:118), we may — at the risk of oversimplification — speak of four distinct waves of Filipino immigrants: The *Pensionados* and students, the plantation laborers and farm workers, the "Army and Navy" men, and the professionals.

A. *The Pensionados and Students*

The first Filipinos to arrive in this country were the *Pensionados.* They were a group of 100 young, talented, and promising Filipinos handpicked and financed by the Philippine government for education in the United States, and were under contract to return to their homeland for public service upon completion of their training. After the first 100 *Pensionados* departed for their studies in October, 1903, other students followed in subsequent years. Usually assigned as "houseboys" to the home of faculty members or other neighboring families (Lasker, 1931:3), these students were well-liked and quickly adapted to the American way of life. By 1910, all of the first 100 *Pensionados* had returned to their homeland to become provincial and national leaders in years to come. The success of these *Pensionados* fired the ambition of their relatives and townfolks, who became more convinced that an American education was the key to personal progress and the fastest means towards the attainment of an *illustrado* (or elite) status. The majority of students who came afterwards, called "fountain-pen boys," were between seventh grade and the first year in high school. Unlike the original group, many of the latter students were not on government subsidy. According to Brown and Roucek (1937:521), only five percent did not have to work. Certainly, many Filipino students had to struggle all year round to earn a living as itinerant workers in the fish canneries of Alaska down through the farmlands of Southern California, moving to the city during the winter to work as culinary helpers, domestic workers, or gardeners.

By 1930, the Filipinos were the third largest foreign student population on American campuses, next to the Chinese (many of whom came under the Boxer Indemnity Fund) and the Canadians (cf. Lasker, 1931:142). The economic depression and a strong anti-Filipino exclusionist movement slowed the flow of student migration until after the Second World War, when a different governmental relationship between the United States and the Philippines, along with other changes in American immigration laws, triggered a new wave of Filipino immigrants.

104

B. The Plantation/Farm Laborers

Three years after the *Pensionados* came to this country, on December 20, 1906 to be precise, a new wave of Filipino migration began with the arrival of 15 laborers bound for the sugar plantations in Hawaii. Although the number fell far short of the 300 families that the Hawaiian Sugar Planters' Association had hoped to recruit, this was to be the beginning of a mass importation of Filipino laborers in years to come. With the passage of the first Chinese Exclusionist Act of 1882, and the Scott Act of 1888, followed by the Gentlemen's Agreement of 1907 which quickly slowed the flow of both Japanese and Korean contract workers to the United States, the American economic system needed a substitute source of labor supply — one that could be exempted from the exclusionist legislations but which would be equally cheap. Naturally, the Filipinos were the most logical choice because the Philippine Islands became an American possession in 1898, and they were racially distinguishable from the "yellow race" despite some oriental admixture.

When the Exclusion Act of 1924 restricting Japanese immigration was finalized, the importation of Filipino laborers also reached a record peak. By 1925, the flow of labor supply from the Philippines was stable enough for active recruitment to be discontinued. Oversupply of laborers in Hawaii was quickly adjusted by regulating the sale of steamship tickets in Manila and by secondary migration to California where "stoop" laborers were in demand as the Japanese farm hands who immigrated earlier began to enter leases in their own names and daringly cultivated farmlands considered to be marginally productive by White settlers. To ensure profits, the Japanese farmers relied heavily on labor-intensive interplanting techniques (cf. Modell, 1977:95). Thus Filipino laborers were in demand by both the White farm owners and the fledgling Japanese farmers. When some of the laborers' three-year contracts with the Hawaiian sugar plantations came to an end, new Filipino laborers were brought into the United States again for replenishment, resulting in another peak immigration during 1927 and 1928. The flow of migrant workers began to ebb as the cycle of economic depression came into full swing. But even before the economic conditions worsened, the Filipinos as a whole were at the bottom of the American wage scale, especially in California where they constituted 40 percent of the farm laborers (Wallovits, 1966:28), and 80 percent of the asparagus cutters (Bloch, 1930:66).

C. The "Army and Navy" Men

Of the different "Asiatics" who have migrated to the United States for more than a hundred years, the Filipinos were the only ones who

105

have served in large numbers in the American Armed Forces without possessing an American citizenship. In fact, as soon as the American military forces had "pacified" the Philippine Islands at the turn of the century (and there are some writers who would dispute that, cf. Francisco, 1973), Filipinos were hired to work for the Navy. From a total of nine persons in 1903, the number of "Manila Men" in the Navy grew steadily, such that when the United States entered the First World War in 1917, another six thousand volunteers were recruited. In addition, a Philippine Militia, some 25,000 strong, was trained by American officers and mustered into the United States Army (Malcolm, 1951).

When the Second World War broke out, a rule which barred recruitment outside of the Philippines prohibited some 80,000 or more Filipino volunteers in the United States from serving in the American Armed Forces until an amendment was introduced (cf. Santos, 1942). The First Filipino Infantry Battalion was formed with more than 5,000 recruits. Finally, when the Korean War escalated, a surge in recruitment resulted in an increase of more than 5,000 Filipinos in the U.S. Navy betweeen 1953 and 1958. By 1970, an estimated 22,000 or more Filipinos had entered the U.S. Navy since World War II (Ingram, 1970). The Bases Agreement between the Philippines and the United States continues to allow Filipinos to be recruited into the U.S. Navy.

D. The Professionals

The influx of Filipino professionals to the United States forms part of a larger development in the U.S. immigration policy. From 1949 through 1965, Europe contributed the largest proportion of professionals to this country, such that between the years 1961 and 1965 alone, 50 percent of the immigrant professionals came from Europe. Adoption of the Immigration Act of 1965 ended a 44-year policy which systematically discriminated against the immigration of people whose ancestry of birth was from the Asian Pacific triangle (Keely, 1973). In a matter of less than a decade, Asia quickly outpaced Europe as the major supplier of professionals to the United States. Thus, between 1969 and 1972, more than half (55.9%) of all the immigrants who reported their occupation as "professionals," had originated from Asia while only 19.6 percent came from Europe, and another 14.5 percent migrated from other parts of North America. Barring a reversal in American immigration policy, this changing trend is expected to continue (Keely, 1975).

If one examines the immigrants coming from the Philippines, one finds that on the average, 30 percent are professional, technical, and kindred workers. For the most part, these professionals are physicians,

106

surgeons, pharmacists, dentists, and nurses. Between 1965 and 1966, the number of Filipino immigrant physicians and surgeons alone almost quadrupled from 66 to 259. By 1970, seven hundred and sixty-nine physicians and surgeons from the Philippines were admitted to the United States (cf. National Science Foundation 1972:29). In contrast to an average of 11.2 percent of professional workers among all immigrant groups in 1970, the Philippines had 29.7 percent (Keely, 1973). The consequences of this new influx of Filipinos will be explored in the following section of this paper.

THE EFFECTS OF MIGRATION PATTERN

A major difference in ethnic adaptation between the Filipinos and the other Asian immigrants is that while the Chinese, the Japanese, and the Koreans have formed highly visible settlements across the country, the Filipino community has historically remained on the low end of visibility except to the most zealous vigilantes at the height of anti-Filipino sentiments during 1928-1935. Here and there, one finds the last surviving city blocks — in San Francisco, Stockton, Fresno, Salinas, and Los Angeles — that were once the hub of Filipino life in this country, but as DeWitt (1976:21) puts it, even then "these urban ghettos were little more than stopover points on the way to seasonal farm labor employment." Except for Stockton, which has succeeded in 1972 in building an impressive Filipino Center through federal funding, Little Manila does not present the image of a bustling ethnic commercial district wherever they are located.

Evidently, the peculiar pattern of Filipino immigration to the United States plays a large part in their ethnic adaptation. First of all, the plantation and farm workers were highly mobile by virtue of the nature of their work. Consider for example the following itinerary: Oakland, Eureka, Yreka, Ukiah, Napa, Redding, Red Bluff, Chico, Marysville, Sacramento, Delano, Stockton, Salinas, Tracy, Paso Robles, Modesto, Fresno, Visalia, San Jose, Santa Barbara, San Bernardino, Santa Ana, Santa Rosa, San Luis Obispo, San Pedro, San Diego, El Centro, Los Angeles, San Francisco, etc. To survive on their meager income and still have enough left to remit to their relatives back in the old country, the farm workers must work fast enough at each stop in order to keep pace with the ripening harvests in the next location. Consequently, they did not form permanent ethnic settlements.

The Army and Navy men, on the other hand, work for the American military institution which, for obvious reasons, is a total institution. Although they tend to be clustered in kitchen-help services, their life in the Armed Forces is sufficiently regimented to disallow the formation of voluntary Filipino organizations so long as they are

107

employed. Once discharged, they are scattered although some have chosen to live near the naval bases.

Against these two groups of compatriots, the professionals form a distinctive contrast in that while not exactly isolated from the White civilian population, the nature of their work also facilitates dispersal. Duplication of specialties within a confined geographical boundary often proves economically disadvantageous to Filipino professionals, and a prestigious location in a high-income White neighborhood offers obvious social and financial gains. Trained in Western rather than Eastern science and technology, they can hardly be said to offer culturally derived consumer needs even though their ethnic background may be a source of comfort to some Filipino clients.

Hence, the characteristic waves of Filipino immigration to the United States has had far reaching consequences on the "invisibility" of their community. Unlike the early Chinese settlers who were forced to conduct their trades within confined areas because of discriminatory practices perpetrated by the majority population, and because the goods they sell catered to specific ethnic consumer demands, the Filipinos — though similarly restricted by housing and other legal discriminations before the Second World War — were highly mobile and scattered for occupational reasons. The fact that historically they arrived after the Chinese and the Japanese who had already gained a foothold in the Oriental retail trade, especially in grocery and food processing, also means that the unique Filipino culinary needs were partially served by earlier Asian immigrants. By cleverly expanding the ethnic variety of products they carried, the Chinese and Japanese surreptitiously pre-empted the ability of Filipino proprietors to meet unique consumer demands.

The influx of professionals after 1965 merely increased the disparity among the Filipinos since these recent arrivals are socially, economically, and educationally different from the rest of the immigrants. As privileged elite or aspiring middle-class residents in the old country, they had no compelling reason to mingle with those from a humble origin. As professionals trying to "make it" in the new country, they have even less reason to associate with the old farmhands. The result is a dispersed and divided community.

Last but not least, the conspicuous absence of a mercantile class among the early Filipino immigrants deserves some emphasis here, for it is, after all, the hustle and bustle of merchants in Chinatowns and Little Tokyos that make these Oriental communities so visible.

THE ABSENCE OF A MERCHANT CLASS

The notable lack of Filipino merchants among the early immigrants is the result of 450 years of colonization which inadvertently suppresssed the emergence of native capitalism in the Philippines. Since 1565, the peculiar mode of Spanish control over the Philippine Islands led to the development of a three-tier economy (Wickerberg, 1965): (1) a "Western" economy managed solely for and by the Spaniards whose main objective was to trade Mexican silver for Chinese luxury goods. This was the basis for the famous Galleon Trade that plied between Manila and Acapulco; (2) a "native" subsistence economy which remained largely as it was during the pre-Conquest era because Spain had no interest in developing it. The Galleon Trade was the primary source of income for the Spanish settlers in the Philippines, and (3) a "Chinese" economy which mediated between the other two systems. Besides maritime trading and artisanry with the local population, Chinese merchants who had been trading in the Philippines since the 11th century acted as middlemen, taking Chinese imports to the villagers in exchange for their local crafts and products for the Spaniards. Such style of colonial administration produced enduring consequences in the Philippines, for the agricultural development of the country was haphazard, if not largely neglected, while the Chinese gradually acquired a virtual monopoly of the retail trade.

Furthermore, the establishment of "free trade" with the United States since 1909 allowed the Philippines to export raw agricultural goods, in exchange for American manufactured and processed imports (McHale, 1952). Consequently, power production and manufacturing in the islands were retarded since the move to grant the Philippines independence (which started as early as 1909 but was not effectively articulated until the Tydings-McDuffie Act was signed in 1934) had stymied any long-term business interests the Americans might have had in the Philippines.

Within the small circle of affluent Filipinos, wealth was amassed less often through mercantile trade than through the acquisition of large tracts of land. This was enhanced by the widespread practice of *prenda* since the Spanish conquest. Through *prenda,* the impoverished peasant contracts a "temporary sale" of his land or other property for the minimal amount of money he needs to sustain his family during an emergency. And if he should be unable to pay back the money he borrowed, he automatically loses the title to his land. Consequently, the rich have always been able to acquire large tracts of land, and the poor become poorer.

Until the 60s, when various aspects of the Philippine economy were steadily nationalized, the existence of a large Filipino merchant class was overshadowed by American and European businessmen and by Chinese middlemen. Under these kinds of socio-historical conditions, it comes as no surprise that less than one percent of the early Filipino immigrants were businessmen (cf. Bloch, 1930:14).

Interestingly enough, in 1938 there were 16 Filipino restaurants and cafes, 12 barber shops and 11 newspaper businesses in Los Angeles (Aquino, 1952). Why there were that many restaurants when the Filipino population in Los Angeles City was only 4,503, according to the 1940 Census, is not altogether clearly explained. By 1952, there were more barber shops than restaurants and cafes. It appears that the preference for barber shops was due to the fact that this kind of enterprise required very little education, and did not command large capital. This trend is now changing, however. Filipino newspapers, published in English, remain a popular enterprise although the number has dwindled over the last forty years. As of this writing, there are five Filipino newspapers being published in Los Angeles: *The Philippine News-Los Angeles edition,* the *Philippine-American Times,* the *Asian-American News*, the *Balitaan,* and the *Philippine Catholic Magazine.*

Grocery stores appear to be gaining some popularity among the Filipinos, as they always have with the Chinese and the Japanese merchants. One cannot help but notice that while there was only one Filipino grocery store in Los Angeles in 1933, there were six of them by 1952. As of 1972, Filipinos owned 323 businesses in the SMSA of Los Angeles and Long Beach, 29 percent of which is in retail trade, while the largest percentage (35.6%) is in Selected Services (see Table 1). Impressive though it may be, Filipinos do not compare well with their fellow Asian businessmen except in selected services. In the same table, one notes that 53.8 percent of the Chinese and 54.3 percent of the Koreans are owners of retail trade businesses, compared to only 29.1 percent of the Filipinos. However, the possibility exists that this may be due to the numerically smaller Filipino population *vis-a-vis* the Chinese population in the SMSA of Los Angeles and Long Beach, even though the area has the second largest concentration of Filipinos in the continental United States. To rule out this possibility, the author examined the SMSA of Honolulu, Hawaii, where there are more Filipinos (66,653) than Chinese (48,897), according to the 1970 Census reports. Here, one finds that more Chinese (31.8%) are owners of retail trade businesses than Filipinos (19.9%), and that more Filipinos (46%) are owners of Selected Services businesses than Chinese (34%). In the San Diego SMSA, which has the third largest Filipino population in the continental United States, most of the Filipino-owned businesses are in the retail trade (38.2 percent) but the Chinese who are much smaller in number, own 57.8 percent retail businesses by comparison. (Table not shown due to space limitation; cf. U.S. Department of Commerce, 1975.)

110

TABLE 1

MINORITY-OWNED BUSINESSES IN LOS ANGELES-LONG BEACH, CALIFORNIA, SMSA, 1972, BY INDUSTRY DIVISION, IN PERCENTAGE[a]

Ownership	All Industries Number (Percent)	Constr. %	Mnfct. %	Trans-port %	Whole-Sale Trade %	Retail Trade %	Finance Ins. Rl Est. %	Selected Srves[b] %	Other[c] Indust. %	Indust. not Classif. %
Chinese	1,378 (100.0)	1.2	4.2	0.4	4.0	53.8	4.4	25.5	1.0	5.4
Japanese	5,304 (100.0)	1.6	1.9	0.7	1.6	20.8	4.3	16.4	49.1	3.6
Korean	398 (100.0)	1.3	4.5	1.3	6.0	54.3	3.0	20.1	3.8	5.8
Filipino	323 (100.0)	2.5	0.6	1.2	0.9	29.1	9.0	35.6	11.5	9.6
Asian-Indian	121 (100.0)	---	3.3	---	8.3	40.5	2.5	36.4	0.8	8.3
Other Minor.	368 (100.0)	4.6	3.8	1.6	4.6	33.7	10.9	31.5	3.3	6.0
Not Specif	3,829 (100.0)	2.8	3.2	1.3	2.8	36.4	5.8	27.1	13.4	7.2
Total	11,721 (100.0)	2.0	2.7	0.9	2.6	31.7	5.1	22.3	27.3	5.4

a Computed from Bureau of the Census Special Report: Minority-Owned Businesses. Asian Americans, American Indians, and others, U.S. Department of Commerce, February 1975, Table 4, pp. 108-110.

b This includes hotel and other lodging places; personal services (laundry, dry-cleaning, etc.); photographic studios; beauty shops; funeral service; business service; services to buildings (window cleaning; exterminating; etc.); personnel supply services; automotive repairs; recreation services; health services, and kindred.

c This includes landscape services; fishing and hunting, and others.

111

Clearly, then, there are some marked differences in the socioeconomic attainment and adaptation of the Filipinos and the Chinese, both of which show a high percentage of foreign-born in their respective populations (53 percent for the Filipinos and 47 percent for the Chinese as of the 1970 Census, compared to only 5% for the total U.S. population). No doubt, the low visibility of the Filipino community in this country is due in part to the paucity of retail businesses within a geographic boundary. Indeed, Table 2 shows that under the managerial and administrative occupations, the Filipinos (2.5%) are almost as under-represented as the Blacks (2.2%), while the Chinese (8.9%) and the Japanese (8.2%) come relatively closer to approximating the White distribution (11.4%).

Light (1972) examined the ethnic enterprises of Chinese, Japanese, and Blacks and concluded that the rotating credit system[4] plays a crucial role for Oriental immigrants in the early days of their adjustment to the United States. It was through the rotating credit system that the Oriental immigrants were able to circumvent the structural obstacles of raising investment capital for business ventures, while Blacks were doubly handicapped by the fact that they had no such rotating credit system and that there was a lack of trained Black bankers to establish stable banking institutions as an alternative to White financial establishments which discriminated against them. How applicable this argument is with the Filipino immigrants remains to be seen.

The rotating credit practice has certainly not been noted by earlier researchers on the Filipinos in America and is not mentioned in current publications either. However, the author's own informal inquiries yielded evidence that such a rotating credit system of the type described by Light (1972) is known to the Filipinos and is very much in vogue at present. They call it *"Paluwagan,"* which means "to loosen up, to ease, or to broaden," as opposed to the word *"mahirap,"* which means "poor." *Paluwagan* is also referred to as "12 o'clock." Until additional data can be collected in a more systematic manner, it appears that the Filipino immigrants who are engaging in *Paluwagan* first heard about it or participated in it while in Manila working at white-collar jobs. Some suggested that this actually originated with the bank tellers. However, it was and still is established more for "fun" and "sociability" than for business ventures because, in the words of one informant, "it requires a much larger sum of individual contribution to have enough to start a business with." It is said to be especially popular among housewives to help finance the cost of drapes and other home-decorating materials as they move to the suburbs, and for unattached males to get together and have a wholesome social life without going to

Table 2

PERCENT DISTRIBUTION OF EMPLOYED PERSONS: MAJOR OCCUPATIONAL GROUPS, BY RACE, 1970[a]

Major Occupational Groups	Filipino	Chinese	Japanese	Blacks	White
Professional, technical and kindred workers	23.6%	26.5%	19.0%	8.3%	14.8%
Managers and administrators except farm	2.5	8.9	8.2	2.2	11.4
Sales Workers	2.7	4.3	6.4	2.2	6.7
Clerical and kindred workers	17.2	16.8	20.2	13.8	18.0
Craftsmen, foremen, and kindred workers	8.3	5.4	11.8	9.1	13.5
Operators, including transport	12.9	14.8	11.7	23.6	17.0
Laborers, except farm	5.2	2.3	5.9	9.3	4.1
Farmers, farm managers, farm laborers, and foremen	7.8	0.6	3.8	3.1	4.0
Service Workers, except private household	18.7	19.6	11.0	20.0	9.4
Private household workers	1.1	0.8	1.8	8.3	1.3

[a]Source: U. S. Census Bureau, Subject Reports (1970).

113

a lot of expenses. Families may engage in them to pay for the cost of a large party that they plan to give, or to cover other festivities, such as weddings.

From the descriptions and information which the author has been able to gather so far, it appears that *Paluwagan* may be a "modern" and "urban" practice, and therefore, unknown to the early immigrants. If so, this would indirectly lend further support to Light's argument, although the detrimental effects of four hundred and fifty years of colonization on Filipino small business and entrepreneurship cannot be overemphasized.

COMMUNITY ORGANIZATIONS AND VISIBILITY

If occupational heterogeneity, geographic mobility, and the belated development of the merchant class had rendered their community invisible to outsiders, the proliferation of Filipino clubs and voluntary organizations should have attracted considerable attention to their presence. And, indeed, they were quite visible before the Second World War — so much so that it was reported in the media as a "Filipino problem." That was, of course, a different era in American history, one still unenlightened by the Civil Rights Movement that was to surge in the 60s.

The relatively homogeneous Filipino populations prior to the Second World War and their painful realizations that the American ideals of equality they had learned in Philippine village schools in fact applied only to Whites, led them to a keen sense of brotherhood among the oppressed. Sparked by some leading Filipino writers in the English language (such as Carlos Bulosan and Manuel Buaken) who had personally suffered the brutalities endured by the farm workers, this sense of brotherhood among the oppressed was quickly translated into actions. Filipino organizations were formed and strikes were organized. But even before Filipino literary writers emerged from the American farm laboring class, their Brown brothers in the Hawaiian plantations had struck successfully as early as 1920. The leader was Pablo Manlapit — the first Filipino to pass the bar examination in Hawaii, who also established the Filipino Labor Union. The six-months-long strike under his leadership was followed by another strike in April 1924, which affected twenty-three Hawaiian sugar plantations (Melendy, 1977).

However, of the many Filipino organizations that were formed before the Second World War, only one may be said to have achieved the status of a "national" organization, though it is really more of a cult than a community organization.

Few people now remember the Filipino Federation of America, Incorporated. But in Los Angeles and Stockton today, the last vestige

114

of this organization still remains. It was founded in December 1925 by Hilario Camino Moncado, a Cebuano who claimed to be part of the holy trilogy with Christ and Jose Rizal (Thompson, 1941). Large masses of laborers were proud of Moncado because he symbolized the material success that they were unable to achieve in this country. Even though he was initially eyed with suspicion by the establishment, by 1939 he was greeted in Hawaii by the mayor, the senators, representatives, and aspirants to political office. Because he advocated peaceful co-existence between the Filipinos and the Americans, his members were often used as strike-breakers against other Filipinos who sought to unionize the laborers.

Since the 40s, the F.F.A. has lost its role as a "national organization." The "Filipino problem" has been replaced by the "Mexican time bomb." In Post-war America, no other Filipino organization was to attain the degree of visibility that the F.F.A. had. An attempt was made in 1969 to establish the Filipino-American Political Association, FAPA (now spelled with a P and called PAPA), as a national organization to work on human rights issues. But in the opinion of some community leaders, the so-called local chapters of PAPA do not always see themselves as part of the national organization. During gubernatorial or presidential elections in the United States, a united front surfaces. Otherwise, local "chapters" are not active. The rest are social clubs and local associations which tend to use similar names from city to city, even though they are not linked into a network of associations.

The large influx of Filipinos in recent years, who are less concerned with the laborer's situation than with establishing themselves in suburbia, have generated a certain amount of misgivings among the oldtimers (cf. Galedo et al., 1970; Munoz, 1971:94-95). Although attempts have been made to "do something" for the elderly, the process has been a laborious one. In the late forties, Filipinos in Delano contributed and constructed the Filipino Recreation Center at 1457 Glenwood (Delano Centennial Board, 1974:56). In 1975, a 59-unit housing complex called Agbayani Village, located in Kern County, Delano, was also completed through volunteer labor. But between 1968 and 1972, the Filipinos in Stockton encountered one stumbling block after another in their efforts to establish a Filipino Center. The internal problems were as ominous as the external oppositions from government bureaucracy. Although these problems were mentioned in an unpublished report written by Galedo, Cabanera and Tom (1970), they deserve some emphasis here, because they seem to be representative of the kinds of difficulties the Filipino communities face in different cities.

A. The Case of Stockton

Stockton, not listed in the 1970 Census among the cities with at least 5,000 Filipinos, had 47 Filipino associations in that same year, out of which thirteen groups were "each looking out for the welfare of its members" (Galedo et al., 1970:13). The precise kind of assistance extended to others was not clear, nor were the conditions under which such assistance was offered. However, attention was given to the fact that during the 20s and the 30s, three Filipino organizations (the Daguhoy Lodge of the *Legionarios del Trabajo,* the *Caballeros Dimas Alang,* and the Filipino Federation of America) each contributed towards their respective central fund to defray hospital and funeral expenses for their unmarried members in the area. Although these organizations still exist today, they have essentially the same membership as they had when they were formed, minus those that passed away. Over time, new organizations have been formed, increasing in number with each passing year. Each raises funds to build its own meeting place. Both the *Legionarios del Trabajo* and the F.F.A. have their respective buildings, but not all organizations which solicited "building funds" were able to fulfill their plans (Galedo et al. 1970:26) reported that:

> "The funds which had been raised somehow never produced a center, and the money often mysteriously disappeared. When the ledgers were turned over to a newly-elected treasurer of one particular organization, he found that the stubs recording the expenses of the organization had been torn out."

This problem is apparently not unique to Stockton alone. It was observed by Lasker as early as 1931 (Lasker, 1931:125; cf. also Menor, 1949:50). It still is a sensitive issue in many community organizations across the country (See the *Philippine News,* week of February 10-16, 1979, for an article on a controversy concerning the disbursement of funds in FACLA or the Filipino-American Community of Los Angeles).

To the proliferation of organizations and independent fund-raising activities is added an understood differentiation of functions rigidly defined by their respective by-laws. Fraternal or regional organizations owed their fealty to their own members *first,* and to the general Filipino population in Stockton *last.* The larger Filipino communities distributed in other parts of the United States do not seem to exist insofar as these local organizations are concerned (Galedo et al., 1970).

The social conscience of some middle-class Filipinos in the Stockton area, however, was stirred when a Filipino census-taker brought to their attention the destitution, isolation, and trepidation of the Filipino elderly living in the inner city. With the help of other active community members, a small nucleus of Filipino-Americans including the census-taker pushed a dormant plan previously conceived in 1968 to provide decent housing for their elderly population (Galedo et al., 1970). Eventually, the Filipino Organizations of San Joaquin County — representing a coalition of several Filipino associations— was formed to work very specifically for a Filipino Community Center (Galedo et al., 1970:14). But this does not mean the project was unanimously supported by the Filipino-American community. In fact, the issue was apparently so controversial that the leader of one of the Filipino organizations resigned when the members voted to support the concept of a Filipino Center.

Seven years have passed and the Filipinos in Stockton are proud of their Filipino Center, built in August 1972 — a ten-story building with 128 apartment units, annexed to a two-story commercial building offering *inter-alia:* culinary, medical, and travel services (Neitz, 1979:1). They have reason to be proud. This is the first and the largest federally financed Filipino Center in the United States which is owned by a local coalition of Filipino organizations called the Association of Filipino Organizations, Inc.

Ironically, in San Diego, where there are more Filipinos than in Delano or Stockton, there exists no Filipino Community Center. Chicago, with far less Filipino population than San Diego, boasts of a Rizal Center. And, although San Francisco was among the first to have a Filipino Senior Citizens Center, it does not have a modern Filipino Community Center such as that found in Stockton (cf. San Diego *Taliba,* January 16-31, 1979). It appears, then, that the smaller the number of Filipino-Americans, the more likely are the voluntary organizations to work cooperatively to build a center for their community, instead of for their own organization.

B. *The Case of San Diego*

According to the 1970 Census Report PC(2)-1G, the Filipino population in San Diego's Standard Metropolitan Statistical Area (SMSA) was 15,069. A newspaper article in 1971 (Herrera, 1971:B-1) quoted a total population size of 32,000 without citing any sources. At a recent formal gathering, some community leaders claimed a figure of 80,000. The difficulty of ascertaining the precise population size of any asian minorities, and the advantage of having large numbers are all too obvious.

Like Honolulu, San Francisco, Los Angeles, and many other cities, the Filipinos in San Diego have formed numerous associations. No one really knows how many associations there are in the area. Estimates

117

range from 40 to 90 organizations. Most are social clubs more than anything else. Each had their own fund-raising activities and almost all of them relied heavily on beauty pageants as a primary fund-raising device: Miss Philippines of San Diego County, Mrs. Philippines, May Queen of Flowers, Ms. Cavite, Ms. Sampaguita, and so forth. These organizations would have remained unconcerned about broad social issues, if not for three Filipina beauty contestants who read off what was then considered an anti-establishment *manifesto* from the stage of a beauty pageant at the El Cortez Hotel on July 3, 1971. Their "radical movement" was well planned. The three beauties had the manifestos hidden in their bosom. What better way to air their views than in the middle of a question-and-answer quiz during the beauty contest?

The newspaper reported that one of the three contestants was wearing the black eagle insignia of the United Farm Workers on her sleeve. In brief, their message was to urge the community to redirect attention from pageants and socials to issues of injustice, poverty, the war in Vietnam (a national issue at that time), the plight of the Filipino-American farm workers, and equality. This small incident, nevertheless, was a turning point for the Filipinos in San Diego—just as a year before, a little incident stirred the conscience of some middle-class Filipinos in Stockton.

As an initial step towards coordinating activities in San Diego, the presidents of 17 Filipino-American associations formed the Presidents' Circle. In October 1972, they incorporated themselves under the new name: Council of Pilipino-American Organizations. COPAO now has 28 member organizations, and has just elected its first woman chairperson. A review of the local newspapers since 1970 reveals the progress the Filipinos in San Diego have made so far. A student group at San Diego State College (now San Diego State University) called *"Matapang"* (or fierce) received funding in 1971 for a summer recreation project called *Project Bayanihan,* offering Tagalog language courses, Karate, Filipino folk dancing, a nursery class for children, and family picnics. In 1972, *Operation Samahan* (meaning "working together") was funded to offer needed services to the Filipino-American elderly who were prviously being attended by a few volunteer physicians and other community members working together in their spare time in a Filipino-American barbershop. The success of *Operation Samahan* is evidenced by its continuous and increased funding since 1972. However, a move was made in 1975, to make each component of the project totally independent from the other — a splintering which some community members would like to define as "decentralization," in order not to highlight the interpersonal distrust and tensions which apparently led up to the schisms. There is thus the *Operation Samahan* project whose fiscal agent is the COPAO, and which irregularly publishes a newsletter, the *Pahayagan.* It also offers social services (counseling, crisis intervention, etc.) to the community, and shares the same building with the *Operation Samahan Senior Citizen,* which is independently managed by the Filipino senior citizens. They became their own fiscal agent. The third group, now calling itself the *Operation Samahan Health Clinic,* sets up their own office elsewhere. There is now a fourth project which also uses a similar name: the *Samahan Women's Program,* which is also a social service program.

Ever since 1970, various community leaders have planned on building a community center for Filipino-Americans and establishing a Filipino research center. The plan has not yet materialized, although some organizations have conducted fund-raising campaigns for their own proposed building—a situation that parallels the developments of other Filipinos in other cities. As of this writing, the Filipino-American Veterans Association has its own one-story building which houses their meeting hall as well as the offices of two military-veterans associations: the American Legion Leyte Post and the Fleet-Reserve Association Branch 84. Another organization called PASACAT (or the Pilipino-American Society and Cultural Arts Troupe), also owns a one-story building with 2,000 square feet in National City. These are the only two Filipino associations in the community known to have corporate property ownership.

The cases of Stockton, San Diego, and other Filipino communities in this country provide a fascinating opportunity for analyzing ethnic adaptation in its natural setting — a rare opportunity which sociologists have yet to rediscover. The tendency of Filipino associations to divide and multiply themselves was noted as early as 1931, in the most exhaustive study of their immigration at that time (Lasker, 1931). Community leaders everywhere are now beginning to realize the weakness of this irresistible tendency towards atomization. In a speech given by Mr. Alex Esclamado, publisher and editor of the *Philippine News* (Jan. 27, 1979), the leadership crisis of the Filipinos was articulated as follows:

> . . . Our major problem is that we have so many leaders who refuse to subrogate their individual ambitions to the collective good. . . (Whenever we have an election of officers), the loser cannot admit the fact that there's a better man (than him). The loser often establishes another organization so that he can become a President as well. (Audience laughed in agreement.). . . Another social cancer that we have is that we can't stand to see a Filipino go up. If someone goes up, we want to pull him down. (Even

119

louder laughter and applause from the audience.) How can
the Filipino go up if our own kind always pulls him down?"

Even though a movement has been initiated since the late sixties to
unify the various organizations under some umbrella associations, it has
achieved only partial success. For example the umbrella organization,
Filipino-American Council of San Francisco, has only 31 out of more
than 200 organizations in that area (see *Philippine News,* week of
January 27-February 2, 1979).

The question arises as to whether this lack of solidarity and the
constant emergence of new associations among the Filipinos is due to
personality or to certain inherent structural uniformities of the Filipino
society that manifest themselves in a recurrent manner across time and
space. Without minimizing the effects of alienation on immigrants and
the role of individual selfish motivations which precipitate schisms, the
author will argue below that the recurrence of mushrooming organizations actually reflects a system of social organization that can be
expected to emerge from the bilateral kinship structure of the Filipinos.

KINSHIP AND COMMUNITY ORGANIZATIONS
Unlike the first-generation Japanese immigrants who formed
associations on the basis of prefectural (*Ken*) identity, and the Chinese
who organized along patrilineal kinship lines (called clans or surname
associations), as well as on the basis of territorial boundaries (called
district associations), the Filipinos — past and present — form groups on
the basis of interest, notwithstanding their regional groupings based on
provincial boundaries. It is within this ethnic group more than within
the other two Asian groups that one finds the absence of basic unifying
associations which command unwavering fealty from all their members.

This critical difference between Filipino associations offers some
fascinating opportunities for comparative research into kinship as a
system of social organization. Both the Chinese clan and district
associations are formed on the basis of unalterable ascriptive criteria.
The patrilineage from which one inherits one's surname and property as
well as the geographic origin from which one traces one's ancestral
roots have always formed the basis of Chinese social organizations
overseas: in the Philippines, in the United States, and in Latin America
(e.g. see Crissman, 1976; Lee, 1936; Light, 1972; Weiss, 1974).

In contrast, Filipino kinship is bilateral. That is to say, there is no
common ancestral point of origin. Instead, genealogical reckoning is
traced through both the male and the female line simultaneously. All
those persons who are consanguineally related to an individual
constitute his/her kindred. Since kindred is not a discrete unit but a

relational concept, there is no concrete territorial manifestation of kindred groupings other than the household in which the individual and some immediate members of his/her family reside. This is distinct from Chinese kinship where a huge lineage will sometimes overlap perfectly with the village boundary, and where the ancestral hall contains the list of (male) lineage members, and requires upkeep — therefore, "corporate" management. A built-in unitary, hierarchical structure in the Chinese kinship system legitimizes the authority of the senior head of household toward the maintenance of the ancestral hall, ancestral land, and the supervision of all lineage members.

Theoretically, bilateral kindred relations may be traced lineally and collaterally *ad infinitum.* In reality, however, the range of an individual's kindred is limited although a sharp line is almost never drawn. The individual has considerable latitude in selecting from among his/her consanguineal kin those members whom he/she recognizes as his/her kindred. Thus, a central feature of bilateral kindred is its optative characteristic. Viewed contrastively with the compulsory nature of Chinese kinship, this optative feature of Filipino kinship dilutes the sense of moral obligations towards kinsmen outside of the nuclear family unit. In the Philippines, fictive kinship through *compadrazgo* (or coparenthood) is often employed to strengthen existing kindred ties. In other words, one seeks out one's own kinsmen to serve as godparents for one's own children, so that in addition to an already existing consanguineal relationship there is also a spiritual bond (Friends, of course, are also commonly asked to serve as co-parents. For a more thorough discussion of the significance of *compadrazgo* relationships in the Filipino kinship system, see Yu and Liu, 1980).

In the context of Filipino kinship, each household is a nucleus of its own, with the head of household serving as the spokesman for that household only. Since both male and female children have equal inheritance rights, whatever assets earned by that head of household are equally divided among all children from one generation to the next. There is no built-in unitary kinship structure to subsume all the consanguineally-related households in a given area under any kind of hierarchical order, nor to corporately manage property over generations. In other words, the relationship between one household and another is theoretically egalitarian and universalistic.

In the process of migration, Filipino ethnic adaptation followed a different path from that of the Chinese not only because the Filipinos were highly migratory and lacked a merchant class, but also because their kinship structure required no rigid model from which to pattern their new life in the host society. Through their previous practice of *compadrazgo,* the Hawaiian plantation workers were able to develop a

121

fictive-kinship network by "stretching" the number of sponsors from two to sixty-five, in some cases (Cariaga, 1936a and 1936b). But because of overt racial discrimination in pre-war America, this practice remained endogamous. The effectiveness of this fictive kinship network is also severely limited by the extremely small number of married Filipinos and, therefore, American-born Filipino babies.

Obviously, then, each organization can only claim the fealty of a small membership drawn mostly from friendship circles. Each organization lasts for as long as the leaders are active and alive. Unless they specifically incorporate themselves, many of these atomized organizations will die a natural death. Instead of being drawn into their parents' organizations, the younger Filipinos form their own youth organizations based on their specific interests. The concept of historical continuity and lineage perpetuity is not a built-in feature in Filipino organizations, just as it is also absent in their bilateral kinship system. The idea of a "lineage association" or "district associat'on" which has a *moral corporate* existence because it is a person's primary duty to serve one's ancestors and kinsmen, dead or alive — is foreign to the Filipinos.

Put differently, the Filipino organization is time-bound and place-bound. Membership is contemporaneous and collateral. Participation is voluntary and individualistic. Its function is social rather than moral. Leadership is attained by means of elections rather than pre-determined by ascriptive criteria. Positions of authority are acquired not by seniority but by personal qualities such as oratorical ability. Each leader formulates his own agenda; the organization by-laws may exist, but they do not dictate an agenda which every incumbent must follow. New organizations mushroom whenever the inclusion of larger numbers of a dialect or interest group previously under-represented leads to schisms. Consequently, there is a lack of cohesion within the community as a whole, which in turn contributes to the community's lack of visibility in the larger society.

CONCLUSION

In the seventy-some years that the Filipinos have settled in the United States, they have become the third largest Asian minority in this country. Yet, for various reasons, they have somehow remained an "invisible" community. In this paper, the author traced some of the historical and social structural factors which contribute to their lack of visibility.

From the first one hundred *Pensionados* to the boatload of contract laborers, followed by thousands of Armed Forces volunteers, up to the last planeful of professionals, the Filipino identity remains confusing to Americans—and some may add, to the Filipinos themselves. They are from the orient, but not Orientals. They speak Spanish, but are not Spanish-speaking people. They were not American citizens, nor were they defined as aliens. They are a family-oriented people, but the larger kinship network is not a unifying force in overseas settlements. They form countless organizations, but remain unorganized.

In the first forty years of their immigration, the Filipinos were largely without women, elderly, or family. The absence of a merchant class among the early immigrants and the demands of migratory labor kept the young, male Filipinos on the road all year round. As a result, they did not form permanent ethnic settlements, such as those established by the Chinese and the Japanese. Their communities were concentrated in Hawaii and on the West Coast, hardly visible to most Americans elsewhere. When legal restrictions on interracial marriage were removed after the war, they married outside of their group in high frequency. Today, they are said to have the highest rate of intermarriage with other groups as compared to other Asian immigrants.

Their bilateral kinship structure exerted no compulsion for them to form closed associations based on purely ascriptive ties and particularistic standards, as did the Chinese and the Japanese. Instead, they form groups based on diverse interests. Regional origin is required for membership in some organizations but the choice of membership rests with the individual. Free from any social structural constraints to lend support to any leadership that pleases them, the Filipinos are thus able to play one leader against another. Leaders respond to "constituency" demands in order to sustain their power base. This reduces the ability of any single leader to claims of being the community representative or spokesman, much less to mold the community's relationship with the host society, as Chinatown leaders have successfully done. The aforementioned factors, together with the notable absence of a strong merchant class, have greatly reduced their visibility as an ethnic group in the United States.

NOTES

1. In preparing this article, the author benefited from her conversations and interviews with a number of Filipino community leaders, including Grace Blazskowski, Peope Balista, Ray Aragon, Delfin Labao, Romy Santos, and others. Thanks are also due to William T. Liu for his critical comments and to Larry Hong for his editorial assistance on an earlier draft of this paper.

2. Other writers include Lasker (1931), Corpus (1937-38), Feria (1946), Foster (1932), Gonzales (1929), Lord and Lee (1936), Rojo (1937).

3. Figures supplied by Mr. Alex Esclamado, publisher and editor of the *Philippine News,* in a speech he gave at the Convention Center, San Diego,

January 27, 1979, on the occasion of the Installation of Officers of the Council of Pilipino-American Associations and Cavite Association of Southern California, Inc.

4.   In its simplest form, a rotating credit system works as follows: A group of trusted (and trusting) individuals agree to contribute a fixed and equal amount on a periodic basis. At each meeting, one of the participants receives the total sum collected on that day. He is free to use it any way he wants. At the next meeting, another person takes his turn to use the money. Everyone has one chance to receive the same amount of money, hence the word "rotating." There are other variants of this system. For a concise discussion on the significance of rotating credit systems in Chinese, Japanese, and the Black ethnic enterprise see Light (1971).

REFERENCES

AQUINO, VALENTIN R.
   1952   *The Filipino Community in Los Angeles.* M.A. Thesis, University of Southern California.

BLOCH, LOUIS
   1930   *Facts about Filipino Immigration into California.* Special Bulletin No. 3. State of California, Department of Industrial Relations. San Francisco: California.

BOGARDUS, EMORY S.
   1929a   "American attitudes towards Filipinos." *Sociology and Social Research* XIV (September-October); 59-69.

   1929b   "The Filipino immigrant problem." *Sociology and Social Research* XIII (May-June):472-79.

   1929c   "Foreign migration within United States territory: the situation of the Filipino peoples." *Proceedings of the National Conference of Social Work*:573-79.

BROWN, FRANCIS J. and JOSEPH S. ROUCEK
   1937   *Our Racial and National Minorities.* New York: Prentice Hall.

BURMA, JOHN
   1954   *Spanish-Speaking Groups in the United States.* Durham, North Carolina: Duke University Press.

CARD, JOSEFINA JAYME
   n.d.   "Demographic and social-psychological determinants of high-level migration from the Philippines to the United States." *Carnegie-Mellon University, Department of Psychology Report No. 72-8.* Mimeo, unpublished.

CARIAGA, ROMAN R.
   1936a   *The Filipinos in Hawaii: A Survey of the Economic and Social Conditions.* Thesis, University of Hawaii.

1936b   "Some Filipino traits transplanted." *Social Process in Hawaii,*
Volume II (May):20-23.

CATAPUSAN, BENICIO T.
1934   "The Filipino labor cycle in the United States." *Sociology and Social Research* XIX (Sep-Oct):61-63.

CORPUS, SEVERINO F.
1937-38   "Second generation Filipinos in Los Angeles." *Sociology and Social Research* XXII (Sep-Aug):446-51.

CRISSMAN, LAWRENCE W.
1967   "The segmentary structure of urban overseas Chinese communities." *Man* 2:185-204.

DELANO CENTENNIAL BOARD
1974   *Where the Railroad Ended. . . . A History of Delano, 1873-1973.* Visalia, California: Vosten's/American Year Book Company.

DEPARTMENT OF COMMERCE, U.S.
1973   *U.S. Census Subject Reports (PC(2)-1G: Japanese, Chinese, and Filipinos in the United States.* Washington: U.S. Government Printing Office.

DEPARTMENT OF COMMERCE, U.S.
1975   *Minority-Owned Businesses: Asian Americans, American Indians, and Others.* Bureau of the Census Special Report. Washington: U.S. Government Printing Office.

DeWITT, HOWARD
1976   *Anti-Filipino Movements in California: A History, Bibliography, and Study Guide.* San Francisco: R and E Research Associates.

ESPINA, MARINA K.
1974   "Filipinos in New Orleans." *Proceedings of the Louisiana Academy of Sciences* 37 (December):117-121.

FERIA, R. T.
1946   "War and the status of Filipino immigrants." *Sociology and Social Research* XXXI (September-October):48-53.

FOSTER, NELLIE
1932   "Legal status of Filipino intermarriage in California." *Sociology and Social Research* XVI (May-June):441-54.

FRANCISCO, LUZVIMINDA
1973   "The first Vietnam: The Philippine-American War — 1899-1902." *Bulletin of Concerned Asian Scholars,* December: 2-16.

GALEDO, LILLIAN, LAURENA CABANERO and BRIAN TOM
    1970   "Roadblock to community building: a case study of the Stockton Filipino Community Center Project." *Asian-American Research Project, Working Paper No. 4, November.* Mimeo. Davis, California: University of California, Davis, Asian American Studies Division.

GEE, EMMA
    1976   *Counterpoint: Perspectives on Asian America.* (Ed.) Los Angeles; Asian American Studies Center, University of California, Los Angeles.

GONZALES, D. V.
    1929   "Social adjustments of Filipinos in America." *Sociology and Social Research* XIV (Nov-Dec):166-73.

HERRERA, BARBARA
    1971   "Goals, heritage clash as Filipinos ponder wider role in community." *Evening Tribune,* San Diego, August 19, p. B-1.

HUNDLEY, NORRIS JR.
    1976   *The Asian American: The Historical Experience.* (Ed.) Santa Barbara: American Bibliographical Center — Clio Press, Inc.

INGRAM, TIMOTHY
    1970   "The floating plantation." *The Washington Monthly,* October Issue:17-20.

KEELY, CHARLES B.
    1973   "Philippine migration: internal movements and emigration to the United States." *International Migration Review* 7 (Summer):177-187.

    1975   "Effects of U.S. immigration law on manpower characteristics of immigrants." *Demography* 12 (May) 179:191.

LASKER, BRUNO
    1931   *Filipino Immigration.* N.Y.: New York Times and the Arno Press. Reprinted 1969.

LEE, BUNG CHONG
    1936   "The Chinese store as a social institution" *Social Process in Hawaii* II (May):35-39.

LIGHT, IVAN
    1972   *Ethnic Enterprise in America.* Berkeley: University of California Press.

LORD, VIRGINIA and ALICE W. LEE
    1936   "The Taxi Dance Hall in Honolulu." *Social Process* II:46-49.

MALCOLM, GEORGE A.
1951   *The First Malayan Republic.* Boston: Christopher Publishing House.

MCHALE, THOMAS R.
1952   "Economic development in the Philippines." *Journal of East Asiatic Studies* 1 (3):110.

MELENDY, H. BRETT
1977   *Asians in America: Filipinos, Koreans, and East Indians.* Boston: Twayne Publishers.

MENOR, BENJAMIN
1949   "Filipino plantation adjustments." *Social Process* XIII:48-51.

MODELL, JOHN
1977   *The Economics and Politics of Racial Accomodation: The Japanese of Los Angeles, 1900-1942.* Urbana: University of Illinois Press.

MUNOZ, ALFREDO N.
1971   *The Filipinos in America.* Los Angeles: Mountain View Publishers.

NATIONAL SCIENCE FOUNDATION
1972   *Scientists, Engineers, and Physicians from Abroad.* Washington, D.C.

NEITZ, TAMARA J.
1979   "The Filipino community's gift to Stockton: a center for everyone." *Stockton News,* January 31, p. 1.

PERNIA, ERNESTO M.
1976   "The question of the brain drain from the Philippines." *International Migration Review* 10:63-72.

PIDO, ANTONIO J. A.
1977   "Brain drain Philippines." *Society* 14 (September 10):50-53.

ROJO, TRINIDAD A.
1937   "Social maladjustments among Filipinos in the United States." *Sociology and Social Research* XXI (May-June):447-57.

SANTOS, BIENVENIDO
1942   "The Filipinos in war." *Far Eastern Survey* XI (November 30): 249-50.

SUE, STANELY and NATHANIEL WAGNER
1973   *Asian-Americans: Psychological Perspectives.* Ben Lomond, California: Science and Behavior Books, Inc.

TACHIKI, AMY et al.
    1971   *Roots: An Asian American Reader.* University of California Press.

THOMPSON, DAVID
    1941   "The Filipino Federation of America, Incorporated: a study in the natural history of a social institution." *Social Process* VII: 24-35.

WALLOVITS, SONIA
    1966   *Filipinos in California.* M. A. Thesis, University of Southern California.

WEISS, MELFORD S.
    1974   *Valley City: A Chinese Community in America.* Cambridge, Mass.: Schenkman Publishing.

WICKERBERG, EDGAR
    1965   *The Chinese in Philippine Life, 1850-1898.* New Haven, Connecticut: Yale University Press.

YU, ELENA and WILLIAM T. LIU
    1980   *Kinship and Fertility in the Philippines: A Cultural–Demographic Analysis.* Notre Dame, Indiana: University of Notre Dame Press.

Amerasia 16:1 (1990): 35-54

Korean Rotating Credit Associations in Los Angeles

Ivan Light, Im Jung Kwuon, and Deng Zhong

Rotating credit associations (RCAs) are informal social groups whose participants agree to make periodic financial contributions to a fund which is "given in whole or in part to each contributor in rotation."[1] Familiar in many developing countries, and a frequent subject of anthropological inquiry,[2] RCAs have also attracted sociological attention for two reasons. First, RCAs facilitate the entrepreneurship of immigrant and ethnic minorities in developed market economies, thus becoming a factor in social mobility.[3] Second, depending on naked social trust, RCAs are theoretically interesting economic organizations.

The provision of investment capital is the more studied issue.[4] Obtaining loan capital poses an obstacle for all small business ventures, but the problem is especially severe for immigrant or ethnic minority entrepreneurs, who lack credit ratings, collateral, or are the victims of ethno-racial discrimination. RCAs reduce the severity of this financial obstacle. First, RCAs encourage saving. Second, RCAs make the whole group's savings available to member households for consumption or investment, preventing capital escape. Third, RCAs circumvent the slow, unfriendly, and bureaucratic channels of banks and insurance companies, the mainstream financial institutions of market societies.[5]

Ivan Light is professor, department of sociology, University of California, Los Angeles. Im Jung Kwuon and Deng Zhong are graduate students in sociology, University of California, Los Angeles.

The authors acknowledge with thanks small research grants from the Asian American Studies Center and the Student Research Program at UCLA. However, only the authors are responsible for errors or fact or opinion found in this article.

Finally, RCAs are educational institutions in which the more skilled teach money-handling to coethnics.[6] For these reasons, RCAs represent cultural resources that support the consumption, home purchase, and commercial enterprise of groups endowed with the tradition.[7]

RCAs in Social Theory

Although entrepreneurship research has been the most active source of sociological interest in RCAs, the RCAs are also of theoretical importance outside entrepreneurship studies. Utilizing social trust to solve the problem of business trust, RCAs reduce the transaction costs of non-bureaucratic credit. Minimizing transaction costs, RCAs also avoid the overhead costs that result from bureaucratic internalization of market transactions. This reduction renders RCAs effective credit agencies that compete with banks and insurance companies, the modern and bureacratized solution to the problem of social trust in credit.[8]

Three positions characterize the theoretical literature: functionalism, transaction cost analysis, and embeddedness theory. Functionalists claim that modernization promotes the autonomy of economic behavior from social roles and social networks.[9] In a seminal functionalist work, Geertz defines modernization as a "process of social structural differentiation and reintegration" in the course of which actors learn to distinguish social contexts in which economic calculation is legitimate from those in which it is not.[10] Because RCAs are particularistic, Geertz predicts their disappearance in the course of modernization. According to Geertz, RCAs are "self-liquidating, being replaced ultimately by banks, cooperatives, and other economically more rational types of credit institutions."[11]

Like other functionalists,[12] Geertz believes that differentiation causes modernization without explaining how differentiation actually proceeds. This formula leaves unanswered the role of conflict, of elites, and of law in effecting the change as well as the evenness of differentiation. Also, when specifying that differentiation will "ultimately" prevail, Geertz provides no time frame for the process, rendering it unclear when the prediction will be disconfirmed.

Functionalism's success turns on several still unanswered questions of fact. First, functionalists claim that RCAs cannot compete effectively with financial bureaucracies. For example, Reitz maintains that RCAs cannot assemble sums of money sufficiently large to permit the capitalization of viable firms in an advanced market economy.[13] Second, Graves and Graves treat RCAs as an "adaptation to poverty" rather than a means of escape from it.[14] This interpretation identifies RCAs as benighted products of economic backwardness, and condemns them to extinction as advancing economies liquidate pockets of poverty. Finally, it might be alleged that RCAs are only useful among marginal social groups locked out of bureaucratic credit institutions by temporary barriers (such as racial discrimination, ignorance, foreign origin) that must in time disappear.

Transaction Cost Analysis of RCAs

Transaction cost analysis adopts a viewpoint partially compatible with that of functionalism.[15] From a transactional perspective, RCAs are of interest because of their reliance on naked social trust. An essential condition of business, social trust does not go naked in advanced market economies. Instead, it depends upon law, contracts, collateral, credit agencies, banks, and escrow and insurance companies. These formal organizations permit lenders to trust strangers with their money. When debtors prove untrustworthy, lenders recover by foreclosure, law suits, or insurance. With this security available, lenders can provide funds to strangers they do not trust, and credit exists in financial markets.

Because the problem of social trust is so serious, Western market economies have abandoned market-coordinated provision of credit to giant financial bureaucracies. Williamson dismisses economistic apriorism according to which actors are omniscient and self-interested. Instead, he substitutes "bounded rationality" for omniscience, and "opportunism" for self-interest.[17] Williamson nonetheless excludes from analysis "the social context in which transactions are embedded" even while acknowledging that "customs, mores, habits, and so on" do "have a bearing" upon transaction cost economizing.[18] Of course, the more important their bearing, the less satisfactory a theory that excludes social factors from analysis. These premises are compatible with functionalism's exclusion of social factors from economic behavior in modern societies.[19]

Embeddedness Theory

Derived from social anthropology, embeddedness theory claims that "structures of social relations" always influence economic behavior to the extent that overlooking their influence is a grave error.[20] Here, embeddedness theory departs from transaction cost analysis which never considers social relationships. Embeddedness theory departs from functionalism in its stress upon the continuing influence of social relationships upon economic action even in fully modern societies. Embeddedness theory concedes that the fusion of business and social roles recedes with modernization. Whereas functionalists (and most Marxists) accept the economists' utilitarian vision in advanced market economies, rejecting only their account of economic action in premodern societies, embeddedness theory rejects the economists' asocial version of economic behavior in modern, modernizing, and premodern societies.[21]

Comparative Research on RCAs

RCAs pose no theoretical anomaly in backward economies so long as they exist without competition from bureaucratic institutions of credit. But in differentiated economies, the spectacle of archaic RCAs surviving competition with banks and insurance companies poses a theoretical anomaly. At this point, entrepreneurship research becomes of more general theoretical relevance because, as a matter of empirical fact, Afro-Asian immigrants in the United States have long utilized rotating credit associations to support their independent business and they continue to do so.[22] According to Moon, RCAs also contributed to the entrepreneur-ship of Korean immigrants in the United States between 1903 and 1918.[23] In Britain and France, historical studies are missing, but current research demonstrates that Afro-Asian immigrants currently utilize rotating credit associations for business capitalization.[24] However, it has proven difficult to document just how big a role the RCAs play and have played in immigrant entrepreneurship whether in Europe or North America. Granted, RCAs proliferate, but how important is the credit they provide to the immigrant communities that use them?

On this issue, the entrepreneurship literature raises two key questions: what proportion of entrepreneurs used rotating credit associations, and how much of their start-up capital did RCAs provide? If RCAs were of negligible importance, then one can dismiss their influence on entrepreneurship because, whatever inter-group differences in entrepreneurship exist, RCAs did not cause them. The same two questions have a different salience in the theoretical literature. If the RCA plays a negligible role in the immigrant entrepreneurs' capitalization, then evidence supports the arguments of those who expect RCAs to fail in competition with modern financial bureaucracies. Conversely, to the extent that immigrant RCAs play an important role in business capitalization, transaction cost theory is confounded, embeddedness theory strengthened, and functionalist theory is handed back the still unsolved problem of how and how fast differentiation actually proceeds.

Kye: a Korean RCA

The rotating credit association has a centuries-long history in Korea. Its first known usage is described in a census volume of 1663. Koreans call their RCA *kye* (pronounced keh). The word means "contract" or "bond," but it is often translated voluntary association.[25] The earliest kyes were non-monetary associations for mutual aid among subsistence-farming peasants. Mutual aid kyes continue to exist, and Chun identifies funerals, weddings, and seasonal ceremonies as occasions for the formation of mutual aid kyes.[26] Money kyes became more important with the commercialization of Korean agriculture and society. Money kyes are more common in cities than in the villages. Moreover, rural money kyes are commonly interest-free whereas urban money kyes have evolved complex methods for the payment of interest to the fund. Janelli and Yim declare money kyes "an extremely popular form of savings and investment in South Korean cities."[27]

Kennedy declares that money kyes became more popular in urban areas after the Korean War. He also maintains that the money kyes "successfully competed with other sectors of the money market," a claim he confirmed by Bank of Korea publications dated 1969.[28] Because kyes diverted funds from the banking system, Korean banks regard and regarded them as economic competitors, and studied their practices and extent in hope of emulating their market appeal. Nonetheless, more recent survey evidence suggest that kyes probably peaked in popularity around 1969. In that year's survey of South Korea, the Bank of Korea found that 72 percent of adult respondents were kye members. Another survey found that member households invested about 26 percent of their monthly income in kyes.[29] Subsequent bank surveys of urban Korean households recorded declines in kye participation. In 1976, the Bank of Korea found that 42.5 percent of urban households were kye members, and in 1986 only 34.1 percent were still kye members.[30]

Yi declares kye "the only way the poor have" of acquiring lump sums of money as well as "the most frequent and profitable investment activity of the poor."[31] In the mid-1970s, "middle and upper income savers" were especially attracted to kyes, utilizing their cash withdrawals for "such costs as childrens' educational expenses."[32] Contrary to what functionalists would expect, Korea's peasantry included fewer money kye participants than did Korea's intelligensia. If money kyes were simply disappearing, one would expect rural and backward population segments to retain the practice longer than progressive urban segments as, for example, peasants retain folk music and costume longer than do urban non-manual workers.

Nearly all Korean kye participants were and are women.[33] This fact has encouraged the claim that kye participants do not understand interest rates. However, in their study of women kye participants in Seoul, Janelli and Yim demonstrate that bidders structured their offers

133

in full knowledge of the interest rate advantage of different turns. Although the women did not use mathematical interest formulas, they used "common sense" and "crude mathematical intuition" to reach a judgement that was roughly correct. When the women adjusted their interest bids to accommodate social relationships, they knew the accomodation's cost.[34]

Another fallacy maintains that kyes involve only "pin money," and that the kyes' functions were and are social, not economic. Compatible with a functionalist view of kyes, this fallacy rests upon Western assumptions about family roles. Although Korea is a patriarchal society, women customarily manage family finances in Korea.[35] Korean women utilize RCAs to save and to invest whatever income their households save or invest, routinely a great deal as South Korea's saving rate was second only to Japan's in East Asia.[36] Naturally, most of the money returned to households from kyes is utilized for consumption. But, especially in South Korea, where a third of workers are self-employed, the line between household income and enterprise income is frequently indistinct.

Kyes in the United States

Koreans were among the most entrepreneurial of America's immigrants in the 1970s and the 1980s. In view of the ubiquity and importance of kyes in South Korea, the hypothesis naturally arises that Korean entrepreneurs in the United States utilized kyes to support their numerous firms, a position enthusiastically endorsed in the popular media.[37] Reviewing research on Korean RCAs in Los Angeles and elsewhere in the United States, Light and Bonacich reported that kye was a frequent practice among Korean Americans, that kyes raised substantial sums of money, and that this money often supported the capitalization, expansion, or cash flow of Korean-owned business firms.[38] Indeed, kyes were so widespread in Los Angeles' Korean-American community that Korean banks developed kye-like savings plans in order to compete with them.[39]

At the same time, a number of puzzling methodological issues surfaced. Contrasting the results of three ethnographic and four survey research studies of Korean kyes, Light and Bonacich found discrepancies in the extent of kye participation reported. Although both methods yielded evidence of kye participation, ethnographic research yielded much larger estimates of the probable extent of kye participation than did survey research. For example, in the most generous survey result, Kim and Hurh interviewed ninety-four Korean business owners on Chicago's South Side. Thirty-four percent of respondents indicated that they had "accumulated some of their own capital through the rotating credit system."[40] However, using ethnographic methods, Kunae Kim found 82 percent participation in kye among seventy-seven Los Angeles Koreans she studied.[41]

Conceivably, more Korean-Americans used the kye for consumption, housing, or business than used it for business alone. Although probably fair, this conclusion does not resolve the methodological puzzle. Ethnographic researchers also reported problems of respondent rapport and candor which have implications for the survey results too. In evaluating the discrepancy between ethnographic and survey results, one must pay some attention to methodological issues.[42]

According to the ethnographers, Korean-American respondents were reluctant to discuss kye participation at all. In fact, finding respondent suspicion and hostility unbearable, one Korean-American ethnographer prematurely terminated his research assignment rather than face it.[43] Assessing the problem of respondent candor, Kunae Kim concluded that survey research "could not elicit intimate and honest response regarding the kye from respondents."[44]

Why should Korean-Americans be so reluctant to discuss kyes?[45] First, many Koreans regard kyes as archaic survivals of a backward society. Second, many Korean-Americans erroneously believe that kyes are illegal in the United States, a belief supported by poorly researched articles in the American press. Third, few kye participants report interest income to the U.S. tax authorities any more than they had reported it to Korean authorities.[46] Therefore, their interest income unlawfully escaped taxation in both countries. Fourth, interest rates prevailing in kyes typically excede statutory maxima. Interest rates earned by kye members in the United States generally exceed 30 percent a year, an amount much in excess of what the federal usury statute permits.[47] As recipients of usurious, tax-evading interest income, kye users did "not wish to identify themselves" to policemen or tax authorities in Korea, and one supposes that immigrant kye users had the same reluctance.[48]

Question wording has posed another methodological problem. Survey questionnaires have asked respondents whether they ever participated in a kye. In most cases, respondents were men but their wife, sister, mother or other female relative was the kye participant. In such cases, a male respondent properly answers "No" to this question. He never participated; his wife did. However, a "No" answer causes underestimation of true household participation rates.

Finally, surveys did not distinguish between an RCA's savings function and its credit function.[49] Therefore, when kye participants invested in a business funds they had saved in a completed kye, they might subsequently identify the money's source as "own savings," thus obscuring kye's role in assembling those savings.

Community support and participation is probably essential to successful surveys of RCA utilization. Woodrum, Rhodes, and Feagin conducted the most successful survey study of participation in rotating credit associations. Thanks to the Japanese American Research Project, a research effort paid for and promoted by Japanese community organizations, the authors had a list of every surviving Issei who had migrated to the United States before 1924. From this list of 18,000 Issei, the authors took a systematic sample of 1,024 with a 99 percent response rate. Among their aged respondents, 38.1 percent reported participation in ko, the Japanese rotating credit association.[50]

These Japanese-American results provide a basis for comparing available Korean-American results. In the absence of the massive, twenty year effort undertaken by the Japanese American Research Project, available Korean-American results derive exclusively from low budget efforts that suffered serious problems of sample randomness and respondent candor. H. C. Kim obtained a non-exhaustive list of Korean-American business firms in four cities from which he sampled 300. However, only fifty-two firms responded to his mailed questionnaire survey, a response rate of 17 percent. Of those who did respond, only two percent of had obtained all their capital from kye, but Kim's question left undisclosed the proportion who had use kye to obtain any of their business capital.[51]

Young interviewed forty Korean-American owners of produce stores in New York City, approximately 5 percent of all Korean-American produce merchants in the city.[52] These stores he had obtained from a comprehensive list of all produce stores in New York City. However, Young selected respondents on the basis of location in four clusters rather than randomly. Although Young declared that his respondents were "cooperative," he did not indicate what refusal rate his research encountered. Among his forty respondents, only one acknowledged that kye had provided "most of his start-up capital," but twenty-one knew of other Koreans who had participated. When respondents attribute familiarity to others like themselves, but disavow personal involvement, analysts have to suspect that respondents did not provide candid answers.

Light and Bonacich completed a telephone survey of Korean entrepreneurs listed in a Korean yellow pages directory of Los Angeles.[53] Of more than 1,000 listees, only 325 valid telephone contacts were obtained, a result attributed to inaccuracies and outdated information in the telephone directory. Although the survey was conducted in the Korean language, of 325 listees validly contacted, only 63 percent agreed to participate in the survey. Of 213 entrepreneur respondents, only one percent acknowledged making any use of kye in financing their business firms.

In a study of Korean merchants in black neighborhoods, Kim and Hurh obtained a list of Korean merchants on Chicago's South Side from the Korean Chamber of Commerce of Chicago. This list did not include all Korean merchants on the South Side, and it excluded all Korean merchants outside the South Side black belt, the majority of Chicago area Korean merchants. Kim and Hurh were able to interview only 75 percent of the original list. Others refused or could not be located. However, they found several unlisted Korean stores in the neighborhood, bringing to ninety-four the number of entrepreneurs they finally interviewed. Their survey disclosed that 34 percent of store owners acknowledged accumulating "some of their capital" through kye. Of those who did thus utilize kye, most indicated they had utilized kye capital for their first business. Only six had used kye as a method of capital accumulation in their current business.[54]

With the exception of Kim and Hurh, the survey results uniformly portray negligible kye use among Korean entrepreneurs. True, Hurh and Kim's results show levels of kye utilization higher than those reported in the other surveys comparable with levels reported among aged Japanese-Americans. However, none of the survey studies reported levels of kye utilization consistent with those suggested in the ethnographic literature.

Methods of Research

Although ethnographers dismiss survey research because of the candor issue, such dismissal excludes any hope of exact measurement of kye use. It would certainly be desirable to obtain the exact results that only survey research can yield. To this end, when an opportunity presented itself, we designed a survey of kye utilization intended to minimize the objections to previous survey research while retaining the advantages of the survey method.

Rather than sampling the Korean community or some business neighborhood, as others have done already, we located an important Korean trade association in a manufacturing industry. This trade association forms our sampling universe. In June 1987 the Korean American Garment Industry Association had 368 entrepreneur members in Los Angeles. Each entrepreneur owned and operated one or more garment manufacturing factories. Entrepreneur members represented about 50 percent of the Korean entrepreneurs in the Los Angeles garment industry, and approximately 11 percent of the entire garment entrepreneur population of Southern California. The average entrepreneur member employed forty workers in his factories.

The research team explained our scientific purpose to the director of the KAGIA, and, thanks to a family friendship connection, elicited his cooperation in a study of kye utilization among the KAGIA membership. Declining to release his Association's membership list for sampling, the director agreed to mail our questionnaire to the entire KAGIA membership along with the Association's monthly newsletter.

We developed a self-administered questionnaire of ten items along with an explanatory letter of introduction. Bailey recommends the mailed survey when respondents must be assured anonymity because a topic is sensitive. Our letter explained the scientific importance of our research, indicating also that RCAs were not illegal. The questionnaire and letter were translated into Korean, pretested, revised, and mailed to the entire KAGIA membership along with the Association's April, 1987 newsletter. At our request, the Association's director included a communication in Korean, vouching for the bona fides of the research, and urging members to return the survey questionnaire in the postage paid envelope provided. We hoped this endorsement would increase the respondents' willingness to participate.

By June 1, 1987, we had received seventy-four completed questionnaires. Therefore, we included a follow-up questionnaire in the June 1987 KAGIA newsletter. By September 1, 1987, we had received 110 replies in all, a response rate of 29.9 percent of the total KAGIA membership. Although this response rate is low, there are three mitigating circumstances.[58] First, we did not have access to a master list of Association members, and could not identify first-wave non-respondents for additional follow-ups. Second, our research addressed a sensitive subject of which respondents were already known to resist discussion. Finally, our results are based on 29.9 percent of the sampling *universe*, not 29.9 percent of a sample thereof.

Results of the Self-Administered Survey

Twenty-two of our respondents were female, and eighty-eight were male. The KAGIA Director reported that only eight of the Association's members were female. However, the Director also indicated that in some cases, women operate factories whose nominal owner is their husband or son. In other cases, wives have secretarial and accounting responsibilities that apparently included filling out our questionnaire. In any event, we found no statistically significant differences between male and female respondents in respect to factory size, or household participation in kye, whether in the United States or in Korea.

Asked whether, when still living in Korea, any member of their household had participated in a kye, 54.5 percent responded "Yes," and 43.6 percent "No." Other responses were uninterpretable. Asked whether, since moving to the United States, any member of their household had participated in a kye, 77.3 percent answered "Yes," and 20.9 percent "No." Of sixty entrepreneurs whose households had not utilized kye in Korea, forty-four had used it in the USA. Conversely, of forty-seven whose households had utilized kye in Korea, only seven became non-users in the United States. We found no statistically significant difference in mean employment size of factory between entrepreneurs who had and who had not used kye in the United States.

Our respondents used kye more in the United States than they had used it in Korea. The change resulted from two causes. First, entrepreneurs use kye more frequently than non-entrepreneurs. Therefore, an increase in entrepreneurship pursuant to immigration would increase kye usage among immigrants. Only one-fifth of Korean American entrepreneurs had been self-employed in Korea prior to emigration.[59] Assuming that the same increase in self-employment occurred among the garment owners we surveyed, their increased kye use in this country probably reflected their choice of self-employment in this country.

Second, immigrant entrepreneurs utilized kye because they encountered gaps in the American financial system. Small business owners typically fall outside the service market of mainstream financial institutions. However, when kyes fill gaps in financial service they compete effectively with mainstream financial institutions that still cannot serve adequately and often *cannot offer service at all* to certain communities. Additionally, the immigrant entrepreneurs' increased utilization of the Korean RCA in the United States is mute evidence that the institution facilitated their social mobility rather than their accommodation to inferior status. Therefore, functionalist explanations do not fit this evidence.

Asked whether any of the funds invested as start-up equity capital had originated in a kye when they started their garment factory, 36.3 percent answered "Yes," and 58.2 percent answered "No." Other responses were uninterpretable. Even if we assume that those forty respondents who indicated kye use were, as a result of self-selection, the only Korean entrepreneurs who had used the institution, all 258 non-respondents being non-users as well, we still have an 11 percent rate of kye utilization among the garment entrepreneurs. As that 11 percent must represent the lowest possible estimate of kye use in that population, we are on safe ground in concluding that between 11 and 36 percent of the Korean manufacturers utilized kye funds for business capitalization.

Money derived from concluded kyes represents personal saving; money derived from a continuing kye (against the future necessity to repay) represents credit. Of those who had obtained investment capital from kye participation, 55 percent indicated that they had invested money saved from an already concluded kye in their business; 40 percent indicated that money borrowed from a continuing kye, an unpaid loan, was invested as start-up equity; and 5 percent indicated that they had utilized both completed and continuing kyes. This result may explain why other survey studies reported much lower levels of kye utilization among Korean entrepreneurs. Those studies did not distinguish kye's savings function from its credit function. They asked only about kye's credit use. When credit use is distinguished from savings use, it becomes apparent that the credit use was less important than the previously ignored savings use.

Entrepreneurs were more reluctant to indicate what percentage of their start-up equity had actually been generated by kyes, whether as savings or as loans. Of those thirty-nine who had already indicated that their own firm had utilized equity capital originating in a kye, only twenty-six specified the exact percentage of start-up capital they had obtained in this manner. However, among those twenty-six kye users who did respond, kye's mean contribution to total equity was 62.1 percent. Concluded kyes and continuing kyes made unequal contributions to this total. Among those who used kyes for business investment, and indicated its percentage contribution to their initial capitalization, concluded kyes generated 40.6 percent of start-up capital, and continuing kyes generated another 21.5 percent. As the concluded kyes represented a form of personal saving, the results indicate that the frequently encountered category "own savings" probably glosses over the utilization of rotating credit associations as a method of saving, thus underestimating the contribution of RCAs to entrepreneurship.

We asked kye users which persons in their household were or had been the actual participants in a U.S. kye. Among male entrepreneurs, two-thirds reported that their wife had been the kye participant. As kye participants in Korea are almost exclusively women, a male participation rate of one-third represents masculinization of the institution in the United States. The increased proportion of male users in the United States is hard to reconcile with the hypothesis that kyes became less important in Los Angeles than they had been in Seoul. If the "pin money" theory has any truth, then masculinization of American kyes presumably indicates an increased importance of kyes in this country, a conclusion incompatible with the functionalist view of a declining institution.

Among all respondents, male and female, 57 percent indicated that another household member had participated in the kye, utilizing household funds. If a survey asked respondents only whether they had participated in a kye, 43 percent of those from kye-using household would truthfully have answered No to this question. As other surveys have asked exactly that question, their results probably underestimated kye use.

Of those entrepreneurs who had personally participated in a kye, 59.6 percent owned bigger than average garment factories. Of those whose household had been represented by another member, usually a wife, only 38.1 percent owned bigger than average factories. This difference was statistically significant at the .05 level. The result implies that owners of bigger factories more frequently assumed personal responsibility for overseeing their household's kye participation than did owners of smaller factories, who delegated this function to their wives. Therefore, masculinization of kyes in the United States is compatible with the claim that kye use generally increased in this country in response to increased entrepreneurship among the Korean immigrants.

Discussion

Obtaining information about kye participation is difficult. Nonetheless, we have shown that future research on entrepreneurial utilization of RCAs must consider their thrift as well as their credit role, and the participation of women, especially of wives. If these distinctions are not made, estimates of RCA use will be too small. Additionally, researchers should distinguish household participation in RCAs and investment of RCA proceeds in a business. If this distinction is ignored, estimates of entrepreneurial use of RCAs will be too large.

Between two-thirds and nine tenths of Korean entrepreneurs made no business use of kye, whether for credit or savings. The kye's role in the Korean garment industry was nonetheless significant. Among kye users and non-users combined, but excluding inconclusive responses, mean utilization of kye for start-up capital amounted to 18.1 percent of total capitalization. Among the kye-using minority, kyes produced almost two-thirds of total start-up capital. As the sums involved were not small, we can reject the claim that RCAs cannot raise capital sums sufficiently large to organize viable firms in advanced market economies. As the kye users were Algeresque garment entrepreneurs, we can also reject the claim that RCAs organize adaptation to poverty rather than an escape route from it.

Running on naked social trust, kyes filled some of the financial needs of these Korean entrepreneurs in Los Angeles, and, in so doing, permitted more Koreans to finance business firms than would have been able to achieve this goal without recourse to kyes. Conceivably, these extra entrepreneurs represent an appreciable share of the Koreans' numerical margin of entrepreneurial superiority. To this extent, the Korean kyes underscore the useful influence of RCAs upon entrepreneurship. Admittedly, only a minority of manufacturing entrepreneurs in Los Angeles opted for kyes. This split is what one would expect from a functionalist view although small business owners rarely borrow from banks either.[60]

Since the Korean entrepreneurs used kyes more in the United States than in Korea, we can rule out ignorance of financial alternatives as the cause of their enhanced utilization of RCAs in this country. Clearly, the Korean immigrant community institutionalized social trust to an extent that kyes continued to offer some Korean entrepreneurs a useful tool for saving and borrowing. Conceivably, acculturation of Korean immigrants will erode their community solidarity, thus depriving their descendants of access to the traditional kye. If so, kye's obsolescence would occur because acculturation destroyed the social solidarity that the institution required—thus eliminating kye's transaction cost advantage. Although compatible with the functionalist prognosis, such an ending would not signal the expected outperformance of kye in a straight economic competition.

On the other side, so long as social trust persists, kye enjoys a permanent transaction cost advantage relative to bureaucratic institutions.[61] In turn, this transaction cost advantage supports the premodern social trust that makes kyes possible. Like ethnic business generally, kyes encourage the ethnic solidarity they require.[62] In short, social trust reciprocally shapes credit institutions and is shaped by them, being helped to persist where credit institutions require a high level of social solidarity in the user population, and damaged where general social (not economic) life undermines the requisite solidarity. This result supports the claim that bureaucratized financial institutions accelerated the atomization of the population rather than having, as previously thought, served the otherwise intractable needs of already atomized people.[63]

From a theoretical point of view, Korean RCAs shake one theory, refute another, and support two. First, RCAs are fully compatible with embeddedness theory and with cultural explanations of entrepreneurship which represent, indeed, the principal source of empirical support for embeddedness theory.

Second, Korean RCAs are impossible to accommodate to Williamson's transaction cost analysis since the trusting relations of the participants fall into the sphere of social mores that Williamson excludes from analysis altogether. Worse, the transaction cost approach cannot explain the evolution of financial institutions in Korea since kyes were and are critical parts of that evolution. Therefore, transaction cost must prove of limited value in explaining the evolution of financial institutions anywhere since relations of social trust are so basic to this whole subject.

Finally, the kye evidence suggests some modifications to functionalism. Geertz correctly predicted the shift from mutual aid to money kyes in Korea as well as the apparent reduction in kye participation there since 1969. On the other hand, the survival of kyes is the product of two structural features Geertz overlooked. First, the kyes operate in hard to reach populations (such as immigrant communities) that bureaucratic institutions of finance never reach. Since there is no guarantee that banks will ever penetrate all the recalcitrant financial markets, kyes could in principle survive forever.

Second, both in Korea and in Los Angeles, kyes benefitted from the rich possibilities for tax evasion they afforded. Ironically, modernization bequeathed this favorable tax status to kyes, thus encouraging their persistence. Until and unless modernization strips kyes of their tax advantages, kyes shall enjoy a tax-free investment status. There is no guarantee that modernization will ever strip kyes of this advantaged tax status. Indeed, the modernization of societies generally renders ascriptively based trust of enhanced value in all forms of illegal business transactions.[64]

Third, the survival of kyes depends upon the economic role of women. It is a historical irony that, having assigned to women the dirty work of minding the family's money, Korean culture has put in their hands a key tool of modernization. So long as Korean women control saving, but remain feminine in outlook, Korean households will manage money in RCAs. In that sense, the functionalists' much-vaunted full financial differentiation waits upon a homogenization of gender roles that is still very far in the future for Koreans.[65]

Notes

1.   Shirley Ardener, "The Comparative Study of Rotating Credit Associations, *Journal of the Royal Anthropological Institute* 94, pt. 2, (1964): 213; David Y. H. Wu, "To Kill Three Birds with One Stone: The Rotating Credit Associations of the Papua New Guinea Chinese," *American Ethnologist* 1 (1974):565-584.

2.   Carlos G. Velez I, *Bonds of Mutual Trust: The Cultural Systems of Rotating Credit Associations among Mexicans and Chicanos* (New Brunswick: Rutgers University, 1981); Dan Soen and Patrice de Comarond, "Savings Associations among the Bamileke: Traditional and Modern Cooperation in Southwest Cameroon," *American Anthropologist* 74 (1972):1170-1179; Clifford Geertz, "The Rotating Credit Association: A 'Middle Rung' in Development," *Economic Development and Cultural Change* 10 (1962):241-263; Marvin P. Miracle, Diane S. Miracle and Laurie Cohen, "Informal Savings Mobilization in Africa," *Economic Development and Cultural Change* 28 (1980):701-724.

3.   Ivan H. Light, *Ethnic Enterrpise in America* (Berkeley and Los Angeles: University of California, 1972); Eric Woodrum, Colbert Rhodes, and Joe R. Feagin, "Japanese American Economic Behavior," *Social Forces* 58 (1980): 1235-1254; Janet Chan, and Yuet-Wah Cheung, "Ethnic Resources and Business Enterprise: A Study of Chinese Businesses in Toronto," *Human Organization* 44 (1985): 149; Roger D. Waldinger, *Through the Eye of the Needle* (New York and London: New York University, 1986):5-6.

4.   Ivan Light, "Immigrant and Ethnic Enterprise in North America," *Ethnic and Racial Studies* 7 (1984):195-199; Frank Fratoe, "A Sociological Analysis of Minority Business," *Review of Black Political Economy* 15 (1986): 5-29.

5.   _____, "Numbers Gambling Among Blacks: A Financial Institution," *American Sociological Review* 42 (1977):892-904.

6.   Soen and de Comarond, 1178; Geertz, 260; Maurice Friedman, "The Handling of Money: A Note on the Background to the Economic Sophistication of Overseas Chinese," *Man* 59 (1959):64-65.

7.   James S. Coleman writes that RCAs cannot operate in disorganized groups that lack mutual trust. He evidently supposes that RCAs can operate wherever the requisite trust is present. Admittedly, mutual trust is a necessary condition of RCA operation. However, trust is not also a sufficient condition of RCA use. RCAs embody what Swidler calls a "culturally-shaped skill." Cultural skills do not easily cross cultural boundaries. For example, black Americans have never utulized RCAs even though black West African cultural tradition still utilized by black West Indians in the United States. See: James S. Coleman, "Social Capital in the Creation of Human Capital," *American Journal of Sociology* 94: Supplement S95-S120; Ann Swidler, "Culture in Action: Symbols and Strategies," *American Sociological Review* 51 (1986):275; Aubrey W. Bonnett, "Structured Adaptation of Black Migrants from the Caribbean: An Examination of an Indigenous Banking System in Brooklyn," *Phylon* 42 (1981):3465-355; Light, *Ethnic Enterprise*, ch. 2).

8. Modern financial institutions also experience fraud. As recent events in the savings and loan industry underscore, embezzlement is frequent even in insured, mainstream financial associations. "What has caused the $50 billion or more in savings and loan losses is incompetent, if not criminal, management. Fraud is a major culprit. So are insider borrowing, self-dealing, and loan policies that encourage larceny." See: James Ring Adams, "Post Election Bailout: Congress and the Thrift Industry Must Bear the Blame," *Barron's* 68 (7 November 1988):9ff; Robert Rosenblatt and Paul Houston, "Massive Fraud Blamed for 40% of S & L Failures," *Los Angeles Times*, July 19, 1990.

9. Jeffrey C. Alexander, *Action and Its Environments* (New York: Columbia University, 1989), ch. 2; Neil Smelser, *Social Change in the Industrial Revolution* (Chicago: University of Chicago, 1959):2-3; Marion J. Levy, *Modernization and the Structure of Societies* 1 (Princeton, New Jersey: Princeton University, 1966):38-46, 60-66, 71-74.

10. Geertz, 263; see also John Derby, "The Role of Tanomoshi in Hawaiian Banking," *Social Process in Hawaii* 30 (1983):66-84.

11. Jeffrey G. Reitz, *The Survival of Ethnic Groups* (Toronto: McGraw Hill, 1980):242; see also Hyung-Chan Kim, "Ethnic Enterprises among Koreans in America," in Hyung-Chan Kim ed., *The Korean Diaspora* (Santa Barbara, California: ABC-Clio, 1977):104-105.

12. Nancy B. Graves and Theodore D. Graves. "Adaptive Strategies in Urban Migration," *Annual Review of Anthropology* 3 (1974):134.

13. For a review of transaction cost analysis, see: Mayer N. Zald, "Review Essay: The New Institutional Economics," *American Journal of Sociology* 93 (1987):701-708.

14. Stewart Macaulay, "Non-Contractual Relations in Business: A Preliminary Study," *American Sociological Review* 28 (1963):55-69; Light, *Ethnic Enterprise*, chs. 2, 3.

15. Lynne G. Zucker, "Production of Trust: Institutional Scources of Economic Structure, 1840-1920," *Research in Organizational Behavior* 8 (1986):83; Bernard Barber, *The Logic and Limits of Trust* (New Brunswick: Rutgers University, 1983); Michael Hechter, *Principles of Group Solidarity* (Berkeley and Los Angeles: University of California, 1987):107-111.

16. Oliver Williamson, *Markets and Hierarchies* (New York: Free Press, 1975): 26-30; Oliver Williamson, "Transaction and Cost Economics: The Governance of Contractual Relations," *The Journal of Law and Economics* 22 (1979):233-261; Oliver Williamson, *The Economic Institutions of Capitalism* (New York: The Free Press, 1985).

17. Williamson, *Economic Institutions*, 51.

18. Williamson, *Economic Institutions*, 22, 44; Williamson, *Markets and Hierarchies*, 107-109.

19. In contrast, sociological approaches invoke "moral communities" within which trustworthiness is a reasonable assumption. Trustworthiness shifts the transaction cost advantage to the RCA. See: Abner Cohen, "Cultural Strategies in the Organization of Trading Diasporas," in

Claude Meillassoux, ed., *The Development of Indigenous Trade and Markets in West Africa* (London: Oxford University Press, 1971):267.

20. Mark Granovetter, "Economic Action, Social Structure, and Embeddedness." *American Journal of Sociology* 91 (1985):482, 503; Karl Polanyi, *The Livelihood of Man* (New York: Academic Press, 1977): ch. 4.

21. The theoretical case centers on the cheapness of ascription; the empirical documentation centers on the utility of ethnicity in business. On the cheapness of ascription see: Leon Mayhew, "Ascription in Modern Societies," *Sociological Inquiry* 38 (1968):105-120; Harold L. Wilensky and Anne T. Lawrence, "Job Assignment in Modern Societies: A Reexamination of the Ascription-Achievement Hypothesis," in Amos H. Hawley, ed., *Societal Growth* (New York: Free Press, 1979): 202-248. On the continuing utility of ethnicity in business and commerce, a vast literature now exists. See: Edna Bonacich and John Modell, *The Economic Basis of Ethnic Solidarity* (Berkeley: University of California, 1980), chs. 1, 2.

22. Light, *Ethnic Enterprise*, ch. 2. See also: Nguyen Van Vinh, "Savings and Mutual Lending Societies (Ho)," unpublished paper dated 1949, Yale University Library; Woodrum, Rhodes, and Feagin, "Japanese American Economic Behavior," *Social Forces* 58 (1980):1235-1254; Bonnett, 346-355; Michel S. Laguerre, *American Odyssey: Haitians in New York City* (Ithaca, New York: Cornell University, 1984); Ivan Light and Edna Bonacich, *Immigrant Entrepreneurs: Koreans in Los Angeles, 1965-1982* (Berkeley and Los Angeles, California: University of California, 1988); James Leung, "Asian Immigrants Tapping Underground Banks for Cash," *San Francisco Chronicle*, May 2, 1988: I, 1; Christine Gorman, "Do-It-Yourself Financing," *Time*, July 25, 1988:62.

23. Hyung June Moon, "The Korean Immigrants in America," Ph.D. dissertation, University of Nevada, Reno, 1976, 192.

24. Hassan Boukbakri, "La Restauration Tunisienne à Paris," in Gildas Simon, ed., *Marchands Ambulants et Commercants Etrangers*, (Poitiers: Centre Universitaire d'Etudes Mediterraneenes de l'Universite de Poitiers, 1984):90; Michelle Guillon and Isabelle Taboada-Leonetti, *Le Triangle de Choisy: Un Quartier Chinois a Paris* (Paris: Editions L'Harmattan, 1986):114; Pnina Werbner, "Enclave Economies and Family Firms: Pakistani Traders in a British City," in Jeremy Eades, ed., *Migrants, Workers and the Social Order* (London: Tavistock Publications, 1987):226.

25. Kennedy, "The Korean Kye," 198.

26. Kyung-Soo Chun, *Reciprocity and Korean Society: An Ethnography of Hasami* (Seoul, Korea: National University Press, 1984):139.

27. Roger L. Janelli and Dawnhee Yim, "Interest Rates and Rationality: Rotating Credit Associations among Seoul Women," *Journal of Korean Studies* 6 (1988):165.

28. Kennedy, "The Korean Kye," 206.

29. Nine Vreeland, *Area Handbook for South Korea*, 2nd ed. (Washington, D.C., U.S. Government Printing Office, 1975):241; Kennedy, "The Korean Kye," 206.

30. Janelli and Yim, ftn. 2.

31. Kyn-Tae Yi, *Modern Transformation of Korea*, translated by Sung Tong-Mahn, (Seoul, Korea: Sejong Publishing Company, 1970):70.

32. Vreeland, 240.

33. Nathan Benn, "The South Koreans," *National Geographic* 174 (1988):245; Susan Chira, "It's Clubby, It's Thrifty, and It Can Cover the Bills," *New York Times*, November 19, 1987, Sect. 1, p. 1.

34. Janelli and Yim, 185.

35. Gerard F. Kennedy, "The Korean Fiscal Kye (Rotating Credit Association)," Ph.D. dissertation (University of Hawaii, 1973):155; *Idem.*, "The Korean *Kye*," 210-211. Benn, 245; Nancy Rivera Brooks, "Women Business Owners Thriving in the Southland," *Los Angeles Times*, October 24, 1988; on American family roles in financial record-keeping, see Scott Coltrane, "Demographic Trends in the Division of Household Labor," paper presented at the 60th Annual Meeting of the Pacific Sociological Association, Reno, Nevada, April 15, 1989.

36. Vreeland, 240.

37. Marlys Harris, "How the Koreans Won the Greengrocer Wars," *Money* 12 (March 1983):190-198; Merrill Goozner, "Age-Old Tradition Bankrolls Koreans," *Chicago Tribune*, July 19, 1987; Gorman, 62; Douglas Frantz, "Hanmi Bank Uses Ancient Asian Lending Practice to Help Koreans," *Los Angeles Times*, October 5, 1988; Brooks, Section 4:1; Mark Arax, "Pooled Cash of Loan Clubs Key to Asian Immigrant Entrepreneurs," *Los Angeles Times*, October 30, 1988.

38. Light and Bonacich, ch. 10.

39. Frantz, Section 4:1.

40. Light and Bonacich, 57. Kwang Chung Kim and Won Moo Hurh, "Ethnic Resources Utilization of Korean Immigrant Entrepreneurs in the Chicago Minority Area," *International Migration Review* 19 (1985):82-111; In-Jin Yoon, "Korean Immigrant Businesses in Chicago," paper presented at the Annual Meeting of the American Sociological Association, San Francisco, August 13, 1989.

41. Kunae Kim, "Rotating Credit Associations among the Korean Immigrants in Los Angeles," M.A. thesis, Department of Anthropology, University of California at Los Angeles, 1982. These are our calculations from Kim's discussion.

42. Ethnographic research on kyes in Korea encountered the same reticence. "Like people everywhere, Koreans do not like to have their personal affairs, especially their fiscal affairs, the subject of direction investigation." Kennedy, "The Korean Kye," 207. Therefore, Kennedy advised kye researchers to abandon the "ideal" of randomly sampling kye users.

43. Edward Chang, "Korean Rotating Credit Associations in Los Angeles," (1983). Unpublished paper in Library of the Asian American Studies Center, University of California at Los Angeles.

44. Kunae Kim, 13. Bleek Wolf declares it "a truism" that "survey research cannot handle delicate issues." See his "Lying Informants: A Fieldwork Experience from Ghana," *Population and Development Review* 13 (1979):14;

also see: Steven Nachman, "Lies My Informants Told Me," *Journal of Anthropological Research* 40, 1984:536-555; Arlene Dallalfar, "Iranian Immigrant Women in Los Angeles: The Reconstruction of Work, Ethnicity, and Community," Ph.D. dissertation, University of California at Los Angeles, 1989, esp. 73-74.

45. Light and Bonacich, ch. 10.

46. Kennedy, "The Korean Kye," 206-207; Frantz, Section 4:1.

47. Carlson, 10. See also: Colin D. Campbell and Chang Shick Ahn, "Kyes and Mujins: Financial Intermediaries in South Korea," *Economic Development and Cultural Change* 11 (1962):62.

48. Vreeland, 239.

49. Chan and Cheung, 149.

50. Woodrum, Rhodes, and Feagin, 71. This statistic recalculated from their Table 8, 1245.

51. H. C. Kim, "Ethnic Enterprises," 97, 104, 107.

52. Philip K. Y. Young, "Family Labor, Sacrifice and Competition: Korean Greengrocers in New York City," *Amerasia Journal* 10:2 (1983):53-71.

53. Light and Bonacich, 411.

54. Kim and Hurh, 92-93.

55. Light and Bonacich, 309.

56. Kenneth Bailey, *Methods of Social Research*, 2nd edition (New York: Free Press, 1982):156.

57. Thomas A. Heberlein, and Robert Baumgartner, "Factors Affecting Response Rates to Mailed Questionnaires," *American Sociological Review* 43 (1978):449.

58. Bailey, 177-178.

59. Light and Bonacich, 286-289.

60. Light, *Ethnic Enterprise*, ch. 2.

61. Thomas Cope and Donald V. Kurtz, "Default and the Tanda: A Model Regarding Recruitment for Rotating Credit Associations," *Ethnology* 19 (1978):215.

62. Bonacich, and Modell, 33-36.

63. Light, *Ethnic Enterprise*, ch. 8; Viviana A. Rotman Zelizer, *Morals and Markets* (New York and London: Columbia University Press, 1979), ch. 8; William G. Ouchi, "Markets, Bureaucracies, and Clans," *Administrative Science Quarterly* 25 (1980):129-141.

64. The Mafia is an example. The Mafia is a family business that modernization has not eliminated and may even have encouraged. See: Francis A. J. Ianni, *A Family Business* (New York: Russell Sage Foundation, 1972). Yet the Mafia is resolutely ascriptive and particularistic in its operations.

65. Karl Schoenberger, "Korea: It's Suffer, not Suffragette," *Los Angeles Times*, October 16, 1989.

THE CHINESE AMERICAN CITIZENS ALLIANCE:
AN EFFORT IN ASSIMILATION, 1895-1965

Sue Fawn Chung

AUTHOR'S NOTE: This essay is based on the research done for my senior honors thesis for the history department at the University of California, Los Angeles, June, 1965, written under the guidance of Prof. Roger Daniels. A travel grant from the university permitted me to do research in San Francisco at that time.

In San Francisco in 1895 a small group of American citizens of Chinese ancestry established the United Parlor of the Native Sons of the Golden State (NSGS), which later was renamed the Chinese American Citizens Alliance (CACA). The group's purpose was to improve the position of Chinese Americans and to work toward political, economic, social, and cultural integration—assimilation. Sociologists Raymond Teske, Jr., and Bardin Nelson, in an excellent summary of scholarship on acculturation and assimilation written before 1973, have defined assimilation as a dynamic process that may be treated as an individual or group process involving direct contact, changes in values, a change in reference group, and internal change—all in the direction of the majority society and, most importantly, requiring acceptance by the host society.[1] In the late nineteenth and early twentieth centuries, the members of the NSGS/CACA were not the only Chinese Americans working towards assimilation, but their efforts as a group in working with the majority society—particularly in the area of politics, in adopting many American values and ideas, in celebrating American, rather than Chinese, holidays, and in encouraging other Chinese Americans to

150

assimilate—were broader and have been well documented in their publications. They were aided in their efforts by changes in the political, social, and economic milieu of American society. By the early 1960s they essentially had achieved their goal of assimilation. This study, based primarily on oral interviews and CACA documents published before 1966, is a history of the NSGS/CACA and the efforts of its members to assimilate during the seventy years after the founding of the organization.

The members of the NSGS/CACA probably were responding to criticism from the majority society, including sympathetic observers like Reverend Otis Gibson of the Methodist Episcopal Church in San Francisco, who felt that the Chinese were too slow in assimilating in the late nineteenth century.[2] Sociologist Rose Hum Lee, a leading authority on the subject of Chinese Americans, proposed in 1960 that only complete and unreserved acculturation, assimilation, and integration could bring a final solution to the problems of the Chinese Americans.[3] By the 1960s, when this goal was approximately achieved by NSGS/CACA, the members would discover that this was not the final solution to the problems of the Chinese Americans.

BACKGROUND

From the arrival of the first Chinese in San Francisco in February 1848, the majority of nineteenth-century Chinese immigrants experienced minimal communication with the host society because most of them were unfamiliar with the language, laws, and customs of the United States. These sojourners,[4] who maintained a homeland orientation because their main objective was to return home however long they worked and lived abroad, were visibly and culturally different from the majority society and remained aloof from that society. They formed organizations to satisfy their immediate economic and social needs. Stanford Lyman, in *Chinese Americans*, has traced the homeland forerunners of these community organizations and their manifestations in the United States.[5] By the late nineteenth century community organizations had developed in the major Chinatowns in the United States and their representative was the Chinese Six Companies, more formally called the Chinese Consolidated Benevolent Association (CCBA), which eventually included not only the leaders of the district associations (*huiguan*) but also other

151

Chinatown organizations.[6] The CCBA fostered strong ties with the immigrants' homeland, often by working closely with the official representatives of the Chinese government and some times, during these early years, by hiring a scholar from China to serve as president of the CCBA.[7]

Some Chinese Americans—American citizens either by birth or naturalization or, in most cases, by being the foreign-born progeny of a male American citizen (and categorized by the United States government as native-born)—felt that the effectiveness and homeland orientation of the CCBA and some of the other Chinatown organizations had limited value. They felt a growing commitment to the United States and found that their numbers were increasing. In 1870, 1 percent of the total Chinese in the United States were native-born, but by 1900 this figure had increased to 11 percent (see table 1). Their numbers reached 52 percent by 1940. From the 1870s until the 1950s, these Chinese Americans born and raised in this country were often ridiculed by the predominant foreign-born Chinese, who called them *tusheng*, or its modern version, ABC (American-born Chinese), or "brainless" (because of their lack of knowledge and appreciation of traditional Chinese culture) or other derogatory appellations.[8] For decades this angered many Chinese Americans. In the 1890s some of the Chinese Americans desired to publicly separate themselves from foreign-born Chinese both within the Chinatown communities and before the majority community.

The passage of the 1892 Geary Act, which extended the Chinese Exclusion Act of 1882 for another ten years and required certification of residence for Chinese living in the United States, prompted these Chinese Americans into action when they realized that the act violated their rights as American citizens. The CCBA and the Chinese minister to the United States could only make written protests to the United States government about the provisions of the act since they basically represented noncitizen immigrants and were themselves noncitizens. In 1892 a group of Chinese Americans in New York formed a Chinese Civil Rights League in order to appear before the House Committee on Foreign Affairs, assist in the preparation of a test case before the Supreme Court, make the Chinatown communities more aware of the gravity of the consequences of the act, and work towards the protection of the civil rights of Chinese Americans.[9] The league members felt that they could be more effective than the CCBA.

TABLE 1
Nativity of Chinese Males in the United States, 1850-1980

Year	Chinese in U.S.	Native Born	Foreign Born	Chinese Males	%	Native Born	Foreign Born
1850	758	- -*	- -	- -	- -	- -	- -
1860	34,933	- -	- -	33,149	95%	- -	-
1870	63,199	1%	99%	58,633	93%	1%	99%
1880	105,465	2%	98%	100,686	95%	1%	99%
1890	107,488	- -	- -	103,620	96%	- -	- -
1900	89,863	11%	89%	86,341	96%	8%	92%
1910	71,531	21%	79%	66,836	93%	18%	82%
1920	61,639	30%	70%	53,891	87%	25%	75%
1930	74,954	41%	59%	59,902	80%	35%	65%
1940	77,504	52%	48%	57,389	74%	45%	55%
1950	117,629	54%	46%	77,008	65%	47%	53%
1960	237,292	61%	39%	135,549	57%	56%	44%
1970	433,469	53%	47%	227,163	52%	53%	47%
1980	812,178	37%	63%	410,936	51%	- -	- -

Source: U. S. Bureau of the Census, Census of the Population, 1850-1980 (title varies; figures are approximate rather than accurate). Census figures before 1960 do not include Alaska and Hawaii.

*No separate figures are available.

The Chinese Americans were defeated when the Supreme Court upheld the constitutionality of the Geary Act on May 15, 1893, in the case of *Fong Yue Ting v. United States*.[10] The failure of the CCBA, the activities of the Chinese Civil Rights League, and the increasing anti-Chinese sentiment, especially as expressed in discriminatory legislation, prompted a group of Chinese Americans in San Francisco to think about establishing an organization to defend their rights as citizens.

FORMATIVE YEARS

On May 4, 1895, a small group of Chinese Americans, encouraged by an unidentified Caucasian attorney, met at 753 Clay Street in San Francisco's Chinatown to discuss the founding of a fraternal organization for the purposes of fighting for their rights as American citizens, improving and elevating their position as Chinese Americans so that the foreign-born Chinese

would respect them, and accelerating the process of assimilation
into the American society.[11] Modeling themselves after the
patriotic Caucasian Native Sons of the Golden West, they called
their organization the United Parlor of the Native Sons of the
Golden State (NSGS), the parent organization of the Chinese
American Citizens Alliance (CACA).[12] They elected seven men
as their officers: Chun Dick, president; Sue Lock, vice-president;
Ng Gunn, secretary; Li Tai Wing, treasurer; Leong Sing, marshal;
and Leong Chung and Lan J. Foy, inside and outside sentinel.
On May 10, 1895, they filed the articles of incorporation for
their organization with the county clerk of the city and county
of San Francisco.

The organization underwent several changes from its inception in 1895 to its crystalization in 1928.[13] At first, the NSGS
stated its purpose as social and friendly intercourse, mental improvement, and mutual benefit. These aims were not unlike
those of the other organizations in Chinatown, but the NSGS was
not oriented toward China as a homeland and all of its members
were Chinese Americans by birth in the United States, by birth
in China as sons of American citizens, or by naturalization. In
the beginning the leadership of the organization was in the hands
of businessmen, professionals, or white-collar workers, and by
the 1930s, as more Chinese Americans were able to obtain a
college degree or some college education, the membership and
leadership reflected this achievement.[14] The number of founding members is unknown, but in San Francisco in 1900 there
were 4,767 native-born Chinese in a Chinese population of
13,954, a fairly substantial source of membership for NSGS.
When the first president, Chun Dick, who came from a wealthy
San Francisco mercantile family, moved to New York, the organization seemed to fall apart. Then in 1904, when Congress re-
enacted and continued all exclusion legislation indefinitely and
unconditionally, the NSGS was reorganized under its original
charter under the leadership of Walter U. Lum, Joseph K. Lum,
and Ng Gunn, one of the original founders. The organization
gained new momentum.

One of the early concerns of the founders was to establish
roots in the United States through property ownership. In order
to carry out this purpose, the NSGS, like the Native Sons of the
Golden West, proposed in its charter to sell, rent, lease, mortgage, improve, and otherwise dispose of and deal in real estate

and personal property. This separated the members from many Chinese sojourners, who often preferred to invest their money in China. However, this goal was difficult to accomplish due to discriminatory real estate legislation and local real estate practices. The leaders of the organization established themselves as role models when in 1914 they began planning for the construction of a permanent headquarters, the Grand Lodge at 1044 Stockton Street, San Francisco, which was completed on August 10, 1921, at the cost of $135,000.[15] The funds were obtained through a bank loan and a building fund of forty dollars levied upon each member. By the early 1950s the loan was paid off and the organization became full owner of the property.[16]

The articles of incorporation also permitted the organization "to establish subordinate lodges, parlors, or branches with such members, officers, authorities, and powers as the society may determine . . ." In 1912 local lodges were founded in San Francisco (incorporated May 15, 1912), Los Angeles (same date), and Oakland (June 21, 1912), and the original parlor became the Grand Lodge. When Fresno formed a chapter on January 18, 1914, and was followed by San Diego, the organization became statewide.[17] Chinese Americans outside California became enthusiastic and wanted to affiliate with the organization, but they were not "native sons of the Golden State." In order to expand outside of California and include these others, the name of the organization had to be changed.

At the third annual convention, held in Los Angeles in 1915, the NSGS decided to adopt a new name—Chinese American Citizens Alliance. Local lodges were formed in Chicago (March 28, 1917), Detroit, Boston, Pittsburgh, and Portland (February 24, 1921). (Table 2 shows the Chinese population in these cities.) Some attempts were made to bring New York into the organization, but by 1915 New York had established its own independent Chinese-American Citizens Alliance with a different Chinese name and the two organizations never got together.[18] Since the organization had expanded to ten lodges by 1927, the old articles of incorporation and constitution were considered too vague. In addition, the similarity to the Native Sons of the Golden West was no longer desirable, partially because the NSGW refused to recognize the NSGS and allow the latter into an umbrella structure and partially because the social-political milieu was changing, resulting in a growing, albeit slow, tolerance and recognition of Chinese Americans.

Therefore, in 1927 changes in the nature of the CACA were made, and at a special convention held in San Francisco from November 15 to December 4, 1928, new articles of incorporation, a new constitution, and a new name were adopted; these were filed in San Francisco on December 14, 1928.

The new articles of incorporation were more specific and sophisticated; the purpose of the organization now included the following:

> to unite citizens of the United States of Chinese descent into closer bonds, to elevate the moral standard among its members, to disseminate among them true ideas of personal and public morality as well as principles of political rights and liberties and the duties of true citizenship; to promote the general welfare and happiness of its members and the Chinese communities in America; to quicken the spirit of American patriotism and to encourage and promote education; to use every effort to have its members perform their duties as American citizens; to insure and protect the legal rights of its members and to secure equal economic and political opportunities for them; to promote social intercourse and friendly feeling among the members . . .
>
> To establish, maintain, manage, and control newspapers and other enterprises in conjunction with and for the purpose of carrying out the objects of this corporation, provided, however, that such newspapers or enterprises shall not be conducted or operated in any way for any gain or profit, but solely for the purpose of better carrying out the objects of this corporation.
>
> To organize auxiliaries [such as the Mandarins, and Bears, younger groups], to affiliate with other associations, and make rules for the regulation of the same.[19]

The cardinal principles, however, were derived from the original articles:

> To fully enjoy and defend our American citizenship; to cultivate the mind through the exchange of knowledge;

to effect a higher character among the members; and to
fully observe and practice the principles of Brotherly
Love and mutual help. It is imperative that no member
shall have sectional, clannish, tong, or party prejudices
against one another, or to use such influences to oppress
fellow members.[20]

Thus, the CACA members made a commitment to the process of
assimilation through their stated goals. As each decade passed,
they made some headway and gained some recognition from the
majority society for their efforts.

MEMBERS

Unlike the foreign-born Chinese, many members of the
CACA usually were born and raised in the United States and had
little knowledge of China and traditional Chinese customs.[21]
The people in the Chinatowns had preserved many of the old
world traits, but not in their complete form. Some of the adaptations bore little resemblance to anything found in China, while
others preserved older traditions that had been forgotten in China with the passage of time.[22] These adaptations of traditions
were passed on from the first generation to the second generation, who would select some of the customs and practices that
were considered useful for the next generation. In this way a
process of filtration continued.

At the same time, due to the high visibility of the Chinese in
the United States and the discrimination they experienced, the
Chinese Americans were very aware of their racial difference
and heritage.[23] This was described by Kit King Louis in 1932:

While the American-born Chinese are in grammar
schools, they are proud of their citizenship. As they
advance in the schools and have more contact with the
American community, they begin to feel discrimination
against them and race-consciousness develops. They
wake up from an illusion; many feel disappointed and
pass through a period of emotional disturbance. Some
find satisfaction in returning to their own group . . . and

some maintain the attitude that they should organize themselves to struggle for citizenship rights.[24]

The major obstacle to Chinese Americans' efforts to assimilate before the 1950s and 1960s was blatant discrimination on the part of the host society. Anti-Chinese sentiment gradually lessened with the passage of national exclusionary acts. However, discriminatory practices often limited Chinese American efforts to be a part of the majority society. For example, Mary Roberts Coolidge, writing in 1909, related the story of a Chinese newspaper editor. A prominent member of a Presbyterian church, he tried to find housing òutside of Chinatown, and when he finally found a Frenchman who was willing to rent him a flat, one of the tenants—a black family—strenuously objected, with the result that the newspaper editor and his family settled in Chinatown instead.[25] Other acts of social, political, and economic prejudice complicated the assimilation process, and the Chinese Americans knew that they had to be a part of the Chinatown community until the barriers of prejudice and discrimination broke down.

Thus, throughout the early twentieth century, CACA members realized the importance of knowing the Chinese language since opportunities in the majority community were limited. Although the monthly meetings of the lodges were conducted in English, the minutes were kept in Chinese. Eventually, fluency in Chinese, especially written Chinese, became increasingly rare among the members. In 1953 the Grand Lodge passed a resolution to keep all proceedings in English and Chinese, and in 1957 it passed a resolution to do all bookkeeping and correspondence in English as a result of the predominant use of English.

Until the 1970s membership in the CACA was always restricted to American male citizens of Chinese ancestry who were twenty-one years of age or older, of good character, and capable of self-support.[26] A prospective member had to be sponsored by two members of good standing and his application was reviewed by a screening committee, which made a recommendation to the lodge members at the next monthly meeting. By their opposition three members in good standing could exclude the applicant from that lodge or any other local lodge for a period of two years thereafter. According to Y. C. Hong, grand president of CACA from 1949 to 1953, "An invitation to join the Alliance is and has always been regarded as recognition of one's intellectual achievement, ability, and dedication to help better the lives of his fellow men as well as become better Americans."[27] Thus, a large number of CACA members were professional men, especially lawyers, medical doctors, dentists, newsmen, and businessmen. This upper strata, or elite, of Chinese society also could easily assimilate into American society if the barriers of discrimination were lowered. However, since this was not the case, many found that they had to work within the Chinese community and gained satisfaction from this work.[28] At the same time they wanted to work for changes and improve the position of Chinese Americans.

Membership reached new heights during the depression years. One factor was the changing American attitude; the host society gradually accepted the Chinese and Chinese Americans, as reflected, for example, in fiction.[29] Another factor was the increasing number of Chinese American males eligible for membership. From 8 percent in 1900, their numbers increased to 18 percent in 1910, 25 percent in 1920, 35 percent in 1930, and 45 percent in 1940. By the 1930s, in some cities, the CACA members represented a majority of the native-born Chinese American population (see table 2).

TABLE 2
Total Chinese and Native-Born Population, 1930,
Compared with CACA Membership, 1927-1931

City	1930 Total Chinese	Native Born	CACA Members 1927	1929	1931
Boston	1,595	636	83	108	116
Chicago	2,757	833	565	574	574
Detroit	710	273	95	73	73
Fresno	747	—	181	176	176
Los Angeles	3,009	1,421	721	746	766
Oakland	3,084	1,682	400	403	405
Pittsburgh	296	100	125	126	126
Portland	1,416	786	191	199	200
San Diego	509	214	130	128	133
San Francisco	16,303	7,754	2,213	2,266	2,287
CACA Membership Totals:			4,704	4,799	4,856

Source: U. S. Bureau of the Census, Census of the Population, 1930 (Washington, D.C.: Government Printing Office, 1932-33); and CACA Convention Proceedings, 1927-31.

The organization was slow in giving women equal membership. When American women acquired the right to vote in 1920, CACA members at the national conventions often considered establishing auxiliaries for wives of members in order to encourage participation by native-born women, who had outnumbered foreign-born Chinese women since 1900,[30] but no formal organization materialized. Some lodges, including the Los Angeles and San Francisco lodges, established unofficial women's auxiliaries with their own officers. In response to claims that the CACA membership might be more effective if, like the Japanese American Citizens League, men and women could join and participate on an equal basis, the CACA admitted women in the 1970s. Significant in this regard is that some members were so progressive that they would even raise the issue of female participation —a concept alien to most traditional Asian males.

The system of membership and the ideals the organization adopted were patterned after American models. Members wanted to express their Americanism and assimilate into the majority society. They accomplished this through their numerous political, economic, and social activities, which met the needs of many Chinese Americans at that time.

POLITICAL ACTIVITIES

CACA members exercised their rights as citizens to try to redress many of the discriminatory policies and acts, especially in regards to immigration, levied against the Chinese in the United States. The members appealed to government agencies or supported worthwhile court cases in order to ensure the legal rights of their members and other Chinese in the United States. They also worked to aid other Chinese Americans to become better citizens and to exercise their franchise intelligently—goals expressed in the preamble of the CACA constitution.

One of the early political activities that brought the CACA prestige was its success in 1913 in blocking the proposal by California State Senator Anthony Caminetti (representing the Tenth District of Alpine, Amador, Calaveras, El Dorado, and Mono from 1907 to 1913) to disenfranchise Chinese

Americans.[31] After this victory the members participated in trying to solve a multitude of other political problems.

The CACA also successfully fought against the National Origins Quota Act of 1924, Sections 4 and 13.[32] At the 1925 convention the Grand Council decided to present the members' grievances to Congress and appointed as their representative Y. C. Hong, who was born in San Francisco in 1899, worked for the Immigration Service from 1918 to 1928, and received his law degree from the University of Southern California in 1925. On behalf of the CACA Hong wrote a letter to Congress charging that the act was contrary to American values and that the United States government was not fulfilling its responsibility of protecting and helping American citizens. He pleaded for revisions. Several representatives, including Hong and Peter Soo Hoo of the Los Angeles lodge, Kenneth Fung, Peter Lum, and Walter U. Lum of the San Francisco lodge, Wu Lai Sun of the Portland lodge, and George Fong of the Detroit lodge, testified several times before the Senate Subcommittee of the Committee on Immigration. Their activities were supported by the Chinese American Citizens Alliance of New York and other Chinese American community organizations.

Hong wrote a pamphlet entitled "A Plea for Relief Together with a Supplement Containing Some Arguments in Support Thereof," and stated on February 6, 1928 at the Senate Subcommittee hearing: "The right of a man to have his wife with him in this country . . . is a fundamental right recognized, not, only in civilized society, but even among savages . . . But this right is denied to us who are American citizens."[33] He pointed out that 80 percent of the Chinese population in the United States was male and therefore the only ways in which a Chinese American male could marry were to marry a white woman, which was prohibited in many states, to marry a foreigner outside the race who could enter under the nonquota immigrants, or to go to China and marry a woman whom he might not see but once every ten years.[34] (Note—some Chinese males chose to marry blacks, Hawaiians, Mexicans, or Native Americans.)

A compromise was finally reached and on June 13, 1930, the 1924 act was amended to permit alien wives married before May 26, 1924, to enter the United States. Victory was attained on August 9, 1946, when Chinese wives of American citizens were granted nonquota status. However, when the Judd Bill (H.R.

161

199), which was passed by the House of Representatives on March 1, 1949, eliminated the nonquota status of Chinese wives, the CACA successfully persuaded United States Senators to kill the bill in the Senate. The nonquota privilege was extended to husbands of American citizens in the McCarran-Walter Immigration Act of 1952. The CACA tenaciously fought against other discriminatory legislation in a similar manner.

The CACA also aided American citizens who appealed to them for assistance with immigration problems. Chin Bow arrived in Seattle, Washington, on July 9, 1924, at the age of ten. His grandfather was born in the United States, and his father, although born in China, gained his American citizenship through his father.[35] In 1922 his father came to the United States and established residency. Chin Bow followed, but was not permitted to enter because he was an alien. When his case was taken to the United States District court in Seattle, he won, but Commissioner Weedin of the Immigration Service appealed the decision in the United States Ninth Circuit Court of Appeals in San Francisco. Chin Bow's father turned to the CACA for help and the Grand Lodge assisted him in hiring an attorney and contributing $250 to defray legal fees. The decision was in favor of Chin Bow. Finally the case went to the Supreme Court and the Grand Lodge gave more legal and financial assistance. However, this time, on June 6, 1927, the Supreme Court reversed the decisions of the lower courts and declared that Chin Bow was not a citizen because his father had not resided in the United States before his birth. The CACA participated in numerous other cases similar to this one.

The CACA was involved in other national legislation. Although some members worked toward the repeal of the Chinese Exclusion Acts, which was signed into law by President Franklin D. Roosevelt on December 17, 1943, Fred Riggs, who studied the repeal process, felt that most of the credit for the demise of the 1882 Act was due to the activities of the Citizens Committee to Repeal Chinese Exclusion, a Caucasian group.[36] Political pressures that arose because China had become an ally to the United States during World War II and speculation that China would be a great marketplace for American goods and a source of raw materials contributed to the passage of the Repeal Act of 1943.

Members of the CACA were very active during the hearings regarding the revisions of the McCarran-Walter Act of 1952.[37] This act provided for the right of naturalization and property ownership for Asians, accorded a nonquota status to wives of Asians who were permanent residents, and retained the national origins quota system of 1924. At first the CACA criticized the absence of judicial review of consular discretion and decision and the arbitrary administration of the law by the American consular officials in Hong Kong. In 1955 the Grand Council voted to send representatives to Washington, D.C., to participate in the hearings for revisions of the act in November of that year. Then in 1957 the CACA published and widely distributed a pamphlet, "Current Report by San Francisco Lodge on Changes in Immigration and Nationality Act," which described in detail their position and recommendations. Their vigilance in this matter continued. In July 1962 Samuel E. Yee, grand secretary of the CACA, was the leading witness at the hearings of the Senate Subcommittee to Investigate Problems Connected with Refugees and Escapees in Washington, D.C., and he was assisted by two other CACA members, Earl Sun Louie, a prominent Republican, and Ngai Ho Hong, a prominent Democrat, both of San Francisco.[38] At the 1963 convention the Grand Council supported the amendment of Section 249 of the McCarran-Walter Act, which had a bearing upon the granting of permanent resident status to Chinese aliens as well as other foreigners. The Grand Council also supported President John F. Kennedy's proposal on immigration and H.R. 7903 on amending and revising the Immigration and Nationality act. Not only did the CACA send representatives and lobbyists to Washington, D.C., but it also asked members to urge other Chinese Americans to support this position through letters to congressional representatives and to create a greater interest in these matters in their communities.

The CACA has also encouraged its members and other Chinese Americans to vote. Members must vote or they are fined.[39] In the 1944 election, for example, the Los Angeles lodge had 270 members who were eligible to vote and these members persuaded 700 other Chinese Americans to register to vote at the lodge.[40] The lodges also sponsored informative programs about candidates and election issues. Samuel E. Yee, grand secretary and former president of the San Francisco lodge, who also served as deputy city attorney of the city and county of San Francisco, claimed,

163

"Our survey that is made by the San Francisco Lodge each year shows that our recommendations and endorsements invariably are followed by the general electorate among Chinese American voters."[41] After World War II the CACA recommendations were followed even more closely by older Chinese Americans who were not as fluent in English as the younger generation.

The organization took some positions on foreign policy issues, especially those concerning China, but this was never a major focus of the group. In 1947, for example, the CACA was effective in persuading many Chinese in the United States not to participate in the election of representatives to members of the Legislative Yuan of the Chinese Nationalist government. This request had been made by the Chinese Nationalists because their government recognized dual citizenship and some Chinese responded by voting at the headquarters of the CCBA in different cities. The San Francisco lodge consulted its attorney in Washington, D.C., about the legality of the election, since the United States did not recognize dual citizenship, and once the legal issues were resolved, the CACA issued a formal announcement advising non-participation in the election. As a result of these efforts, no representatives were sent to the Legislative Yuan from the United States. (Two representatives were, however, elected the following year.)[42] The CACA also was supportive of American foreign policy towards China in general and, for example, supported the Eisenhower administration's stance against the People's Republic of China and its totalitarian political ideology, which "directly opposed . . . the principles and aims of [the CACA]."[43] However, after diplomatic relations were restored between the United States and the People's Republic of China (PRC) in 1979, CACA has often invited both PRC and Taiwan officials to its functions.

CACA members participated in other types of local, state, and national political activities. By the 1960s a few members had run for local offices, and some, like Samuel E. Yee, deputy city attorney of San Francisco, or Judge Delbert Wong of Los Angeles, held government positions by appointment. These prominent members enhanced the activities of the organization not only in political activities but also in economic and social activities. They demonstrated that Chinese Americans could be assimilated into the American society and make positive contributions.

ECONOMIC AND SOCIAL ACTIVITIES

The CACA provided some economic and social benefits to its members through a death benefit/insurance program and social activities. More importantly, it aided the wider Chinese community in its creation of a Chinese American newspaper, educational programs, and fight against defamation in an effort to fulfill its goal "to promote the general welfare and happiness of its members and the Chinese communities." Although the local lodges had a more varied program of activities, the Grand Lodge served as the leader and basic model, so its activities are stressed in this study.

The organization had several programs for the welfare of its members. In 1920, because of the numerous discriminatory practices of American insurance companies, the leaders of the CACA instituted an insurance, or death benefit, program, which had been in the planning stages for years. Basically the program paid widows and children of subscribing members a death benefit of from five hundred to one thousand dollars. Between 1921 and 1925 there were 2,909 participants in the insurance program. The CACA eventually got into a financial crisis because of this program, and by 1947 the Grand Council decided to discontinue the program as American insurance regulations had been liberalized.

Social programs also benefited members. Before the 1950s Chinese Americans were not able to attend many of the social affairs of the majority community. In response to this void, the CACA sponsored its own social functions, including athletic tournaments, picnics, get-together dinners, and dances. These events often celebrated American, not Chinese, holidays, showing a change in the basic orientation of the membership. Thus, for example, two of the main social events of the year were the San Francisco lodge's New Year's Eve dance and the Los Angeles lodge's Valentine's Day dance.

The leaders also felt that it was important to establish lines of communication to the community. At the eighth biennial convention held in Oakland in August 1921, the United Publishing Company, Inc., was proposed as the organization's official organ and means of publishing books, pamphlets, and stationery. The company opened for business in San Francisco on November 1, 1921, and changed its name to the Chinese Times Publishing Company in 1926. After a shaky beginning the membership decided to increase the company's capitalization so that a daily newspaper could be published. On July 5, 1924, the *Chinese Times* made its debut as the first successful Chinese daily newspaper owned, edited, and published by American citizens of Chinese ancestry. Most other Chinese daily newspapers in San Francisco and New York were supported by the Chinese government's political party, the Kuomintang, or other groups with ties to China. The leaders felt that a bilingual publication would have been ideal, but they did not have the capital or writing talent to support an English press along with their Chinese press and were fearful that an English-language newspaper would go the way of the short-lived English-language weekly, *The Oriental and Occidental Press*, which began on June 9, 1900, in San Francisco and was directed at the majority community as well.[44] Like other Chinese dailies, the *Chinese Times* was not limited to the San Franciso or California areas in its circulation, but was circulated throughout the United States. By 1929 it claimed the largest circulation among the Chinese newspapers in San Francisco.[45] A comparison of the circulation figures, although probably exaggerated, demonstrates this (see table 3). When the *Chinese World* began its English section on December 1, 1949, and the *Young China* followed suit in 1961, the *Chinese Times* considered the bilingual possibilities, but decided to remain a Chinese-language newspaper in order to continue to fulfill its original aim of being "dedicated to the service and betterment of the Chinese community in America" and its purpose of "arousing its readers to their civic duty."[46] By the 1950s Chinese Americans who were fluent in English were making up their own minds about political issues and current events based upon the majority community newspapers. The group that still needed help consisted of Chinese Americans who felt more comfortable with Chinese than English and new immigrants who wanted to learn more about their new environment. However, under the management of S. K. Lai, president of the board of directors from 1965 to 1978, the *Chinese Times* remained one of the highest circulating Chinese dailies and in 1977 expanded its operations and moved to larger quarters on Sacramento Street.

TABLE 3
Circulation Figures for Three San Francisco Chinese Dailies

	1925	1926	1927	1928	1929	1930	1964
Chinese Times	3,870	6,268	6,268	7,105	7,953	7,953	9,650
Chinese World	7,562	7,562	7,562	7,200	7,000	7,557	7,200
Young China	6,800	6,800	6,800	6,800	5,510	7,490	6,345

Source: Ayer's Directory of Newspapers and Periodicals, rev. ed., 1965.

The CACA, a majority of whose members had attended or graduated from college after the 1930s, became known as a promoter of equal educational opportunities and educational endeavors. As early as 1915 the organization donated gifts for the reconstructed Oriental School in San Francisco's Chinatown.[47] When the new Oriental School could not house the growing number of Chinese students in the early 1920s, the organization pushed for an expansion of the facilities and eventually an annex was constructed.[48] The NSGS also worked toward renaming the school in order to eliminate the racial overtones and proposed that the Oriental School be called the Harding School, but the San Francisco Board of Education rejected that name in favor of Commodore Stockton in 1924.[49] In 1925, when the board of education created an integrated secondary school, Francisco Junior High School, in the North Beach area adjacent to Chinatown, the NSGS appealed to the board to allow the students of Commodore Stockton to attend the seventh and eighth grades there. They were supported by the Northern Federation of Civic Organizations, a group of clubs located in the northern part of San Francisco. The board yielded despite protests from white parents and organizations such as the Northern Federation of Civic and Improvement Clubs.[50] Attorney Kenneth Fung, an officer of the NSGS/CACA, was very active in the fight for desegregation in the 1920s and early 1930s. He told the school board in 1934: "Segregation does not make for good American citizenship. Our children, born here, should be given American training comparable with that of other American students and should not be subjected to a humiliation which would only breed discontent. This would start a prejudice against our children."[51]

In addition to fighting for equal educational opportunities, the CACA also offered English-language classes and practical Chinese-language classes for their members and the general Chinese community. The English classes were a major means of helping the Chinese-speaking person make the adjustment to his new environment. The CACA hoped to promote and enhance "the study of Americanism and patriotism" through oratorial contests in the late 1950s and other similar programs. The Chinese classes enabled Chinese Americans to communicate with the foreign-born segment of the community. Walter U. Lum of San Francisco, assisted financially by Joe Shoong of the Oakland lodge, Tom Chan of the Chicago lodge, and Y. C. Hong of the Los Angeles lodge, even worked out a basic course of study that gave the student a vocabulary of three to four thousand Chinese characters. This course was taught in a manner very different from the traditional Chinese language training and was closer to a Western approach to Chinese training.[52] Although the programs lasted for several years, many of the lodges had to abandon them due to declining community support, dwindling funds, and comparable courses offered by other organizations and individuals.

The CACA was also concerned about the image of the Chinese in America. When Charles R. Shepherd's *Ways of Ah Sin* was published in 1923, the Judiciary Committee of the NSGS decided to take a stand against this type of sensational anti-Chinese literature, which had been produced since the late nineteenth century. (For example, P. W. Donner's *Last Days of the Republic* (1880) included pictures of a Chinese as governor of California and a group of Chinese drinking tea, subtitled "Chinese Mandarins in Washington," thus hinting at the possible takeover of the United States by the Chinese. Robert Woltor's *Short and Truthful History of the Taking of California and Oregon by the Chinese in the Year A.D. 1899* (1882) had similar themes.) The committee at the 1923 convention asked for a condemnation of Shepherd's book because it created prejudice and ill feelings between the races and presented erroneous and defamatory statements about the Chinese. They unsuccessfully called for a suppression of the book and brought the attention of federal and state officials and postal authorities to the book's contents and obscenities. The CACA has continued to work toward fostering a more positive image of the Chinese in the United States, condemning books, television programs, and movies that portray Chinese in an unfavorable and untruthful manner.

In other programs the CACA organized a Chinese Medical Relief Committee in 1937 in response to the Sino-Japanese War (1937–45), sponsored the "Miss Chinatown" beauty contests between 1948 and 1956, established a Chinatown community health information program, promoted good citizenship through the "I Am An American Day" from 1952 to 1959, and supported educational activities, such as the Asian American Studies Center at UCLA in the late 1960s. When the Mandarins, a junior affiliate, sponsored a softball league, basketball team, and other youth activities in Los Angeles in the late 1940s, the *Chinese World* commented, "They are constantly striving to better the lot of the Chinese youth in the Los Angeles area."[53] CACA activities for the promotion of the general welfare and happiness of their members and the Chinese communities in the United States have been quietly recognized.

Since the inception of the NSGS/CACA, the members have worked toward achieving assimilation. They have made direct contact with the wider community, changed their values, no longer looked to China as their main reference point for actions and attitudes, and made numerous internal changes. They have worked in many areas, but the most outstanding achievements have been in the realm of politics. However, as Teske and Nelson have pointed out, assimilation, unlike acculturation, requires that the host society accept and have a positive orientation toward the minority groups.[54] When the NSGS/CACA first gained prominence in San Francisco in the 1910s, the host community still discriminated against Chinese Americans. Discrimination did not really begin to break down until the 1920s, when the 1924 act gave the majority society a feeling of security against any future Asian "immigration invasion." In the 1920s Chinese artifacts, designs, and games like *mah-jong* became popular. In the 1930s the majority community sympathized with China during the Sino-Japanese War begun in 1931 in Manchuria. Friendship between China and the United States was established during World War II. These events contributed to a more friendly attitude toward the Chinese in the United States. This spurred Chinese Americans to respond, resulting in the growth of the organization during the 1920s to 1940s. Their successes in immigration matters that affected the Chinese American community became a hallmark of their political activities. Finally, whether or not they were members of the CACA, more Chinese Americans had, like other second and third generation Americans, adopted the attitudes necessary for assimilation.

Since World War II, there has been a greater acceptance of Chinese Americans in political and social, educational, and economic arenas, as well as greater social interaction with the majority community. Instead of stimulating growth in the CACA, this greater integration has led to a slow decline in its membership and activities. For example, in 1935 the Los Angeles lodge reported a total membership of 826, but in 1963, when there were more Chinese Americans in the Los Angeles area, the membership totaled only 233, with 22 of those men members for forty or more years.

Several complicated factors led to the decline in membership and prestige. The once progressive organization of the twenties, thirties, and forties became viewed as a conservative organization, especially with its continued promotion of the Chinese language. Once the Walter-McCarran Act was passed, Chinese Americans did not feel so committed to the cause of immigration since entire families were in the United States. Some members did not agree with the predominantly conservative Republican orientation of the CACA and decided to become involved with Democratic groups, such as the Chinese American Democratic Club (founded in 1954) in San Francisco or even an integrated Democratic club, which was possible in the sixties. The civil rights movement of the early sixties allowed the Chinese Americans to integrate in many areas and interact on a more or less equal basis. The postwar generation had more experience in the majority community and did not feel the need to rely solely upon a predominantly Chinese American milieu. Thus, integration into the majority society helped lead to the decline of the CACA.

This decline involves complex factors, such as the different character of the post-sixties Chinese immigrants, the emergence of new Chinese American organizations, such as Chinese for Affirmative Action and the Chinese American Democratic Club, which meet the changing needs of the community and the changing American society more fully. Also, the number of Chinese immigrants has increased due to new immigration laws, leading to a decline in the percentage of native-born Chinese Americans (see table 1), and thus diminishing the need for an organization such as the CACA. The CACA needed new blood to keep the organization alive. These new members have largely been recent Chinese immigrants who gained citizenship in the late fifties and early sixties and still feel that they are "marginal men"—people living in two cultures, Chinese and Western. Since 1955 the organization has been criticized because of its failure to gain a wider constituency and its involvement with local, rather than national, issues.[55] Nevertheless, because the CACA has made many contributions to the improvement of the Chinese community in the United States, raised the political consciousness of Chinese Americans, and provided a springboard for assimilation, it has survived.

NOTES

1. Raymond H. C. Teske, Jr., and Bardin H. Nelson, "Acculturation and Assimilation: A Clarification," American Ethnologist 1, no. 2 (May 1974): 351–68.
2. Otis Gibson, The Chinese in America (Cincinnati: Hitchcock and Walden, 1877), 369.
3. Rose Hum Lee, The Chinese in the United States of America (Hong Kong: Hong Kong University Press, 1960), 430.
4. Paul C. P. Siu, "The Sojourner," American Journal of Sociology, 58, no. 1 (July 1952): 34–44; Georg Simmel, "The Stranger," in The Sociology of Georg Simmel, trans. and ed. Kurt Wolff (Glencoe, Ill.: The Free Press, 1950); and Robert E. Park, Race and Culture, vol. 1, ed. Everett Cherrington Hughes et al. (Glencoe, Ill.: The Free Press, 1950).
5. Stanford M. Lyman, Chinese Americans (New York: Random House, 1974), chap. 2–3. See also his dissertation, "The Structure of Chinese Society in Nineteenth-Century America" (PhD diss., University of California, Berkeley, 1961).
6. William Hoy, The Chinese Six Companies: A Short, General Historical Resumé of its Origin, Function, and Importance in the Life of the California Chinese (San Francisco: Chinese Consolidated Benevolent Association, 1942); Gunther Barth, Bitter Strength: A History of the Chinese in the United States, 1850–1870 (Cambridge: Harvard University Press, 1963), 77–128; Stanford L. Lyman, The Asian in North America (Santa Barbara, Calif.: Clio Press, 1977); Betty Lee Sung, The Story of the Chinese in America (New York: Collier Books, 1967), 135–37; and Shih-shan Henry Tsai, The Chinese Experience in America (Bloomington: University of Indiana Press, 1986), chap. 2.
7. Ching-hwang Yen, Coolies and Mandarins: China's Protection of Overseas Chinese During the Late Ch'ing Period (1851–1911) (Singapore: Singapore University Press, 1985), chap. 7; Him Mark Lai, "Historical Development of the Chinese Consolidated Benevolent Association/Huiguan System," Chinese America: History and Perspectives 1987 (San Francisco: Chinese Historical Society of America, 1987).
8. Interview with Y. C. Hong, grand president of the CACA (1949– 1953) in 1965; tape deposited with the Oral History Project, University of California, Los Angeles.
9. Elmer C. Sandmeyer, The Anti-Chinese Movement in California (Urbana: University of Illinois Press, 1939), 104; Walter Fong, "The Chinese Six Companies," Overland Monthly, ser. 2, 23 (May 1894): 525; and Lyman, "The Structure of Chinese Society in Nineteenth-Century America," 409–12.
10. Fong Yue Ting v. United States, 149 U.S. 698.

11. Y. C. Hong, A Brief History of the Chinese American Citizens Alliance
(San Francisco: Chinese American Citizens Alliance, 1955), 1. See also Lim
P. Lee, "The Political Rights of the American Citizens of Chinese Ancestry,"
Chinese Digest 2 (October 1936): 11; and idem, "The Chinese American Citizens
Alliance, Its Activities and History," Chinese Digest 2 (October 1936): 11, 15.

12. The Native Sons of the Golden West, which had been prominent in anti-
Chinese activities, objected to the similarity of their names but could not do
anything about it.

13. Much of the information about the organization was acquired through the
following documents of the CACA, some of which are only available in Chinese
and others in English or English and Chinese: Application for Permit to the
Commissioner or Corporations of the State of California, Sacramento, California,
by the Chinese Times Publishing Company, 1926; Articles of Incorporation of
the Chinese American Citizens Alliance, December 1928; Articles of
Incorporation of the United Parlor of the Native Sons of the Golden State, May
1895; Report on Changing the Alien Wives Act, 1925–1930; Proceedings of the
Biennial Convention of the Chinese American Citizens Alliance, Grand Lodge,
1923, 1925, 1927, 1929, 1931, 1935, 1939, 1951, 1953, 1955, 1957, 1959, 1961,
and 1963; Constitution of the Chinese American Citizens Alliance, revised, 1955;
National Biennial Convention Book, various dates; Statutes of the San Francisco
Lodge, 1949; miscellaneous pamphlets and publications.

14. The professional standing of the members is reflected in the professions
of the men who held the grand presidency. Some of their names, terms of
office, lodge affiliations, and occupations are as follows:
Walter U. Lum (1912, 1914, 1915–17, 1923–29, 1933–35), San Francisco,
newspaperman.
Leong Kow (1917–23), San Francisco, newspaperman and immigration
interpreter.
S. K. Lai (1929–31, 1935–47), San Francisco, accountant for the Southern
Pacific Railroad and president of the Chinese Times.
Harry T. Yip (1931–33), Los Angeles, assistant to the president of the
National Dollar Stores, Inc.
Kenneth Y. Fung (1947–49), San Francisco, attorney.
Y. C. Hong (1949–53), Los Angeles, attorney.
Henry Lem (1953–59, 1961–63), San Francisco, newspaperman.
George Chew (1959–61), Oakland, Department of Motor Vehicles.
Wilbur Woo (1963–65), Los Angeles, produce businessman and banker.

15. Julius Su Tow, The Real Chinese in America (New York: Academy Press,
1923), 113.

16. Samuel E. Yee, grand secretary of the CACA, interview with author, 1964. Tape on deposit with the Oral History Project, University of California, Los Angeles.

17. Incorporation dates are omitted from local lodges that became inactive before 1961. See Gustave K. Lee, "The Purpose and Aim," in the Twenty-Sixth Biennial National Convention (San Francisco: Chinese American Citizens Alliance, 1961), 9.

18. Tow, The Real Chinese in America, 113; and N. C. Chen, ed., Meiguo huaqiao nianjian (Handbook of the Chinese in America) (New York: People's Foreign Relations Association of China, 1946), 574. The Chinese American Citizens Alliance's Chinese name is Meizhou tongyuan zong hui; the one in New York is called Huaren tusheng hui.

19. Articles of Incorporation of the CACA, December 1928.

20. Nowland C. Hong, president, Los Angeles lodge, CACA, to East/West, February 17, 1971, reprinted in "Chink!" A Documentary History of Anti-Chinese Prejudice in America, ed. Cheng-Tsu Wu (New York: World Publishing Company, 1972), 256.

21. Winifred Raushenbush, "The Great Wall of Chinatown," Survey 9, no. 2 (May 1926): 154–55; the author speaks specifically about the members of the CACA in this regard.

22. An example of this can be seen in the use of kinship terminology. See Elizabeth Cheng, "Some Features of the Kinship Terminology Used in New York Chinatown," Southwestern Journal of Anthropology 8 (Spring 1952): 97–107.

23. On the cultural dualism of Chinese Americans, see Ching-chao Wu, "Chinatowns: A Study of Symbiosis and Assimilation" (PhD diss., University of Chicago, 1928), 287; see Ng Bickleen Fong, Chinese in New Zealand: A Study in Assimilation (Hong Kong: Hong Kong University Press, 1959), on generational differences and interactions between Chinese and Caucasians.

24. Kit King Louis, "Problems of Second Generation Chinese," Sociology and Social Research 16 (January-February 1932): 256. See also his article, "Program for Second Generation Chinese," Sociology and Social Research 16 (May-June 1932): 455–62.

25. Mary Roberts Coolidge, Chinese Immigration (New York: Henry Holt and Company, 1909), 438–39.

26. Some males under age twenty-one were able to affiliate with the organization beginning in the 1930s. Why this practice began and when it stopped is not known.

27. Y. C. Hong, "Milestones of the Chinese American Citizens Alliance," in

the Twenty-Seventh Biennial National Convention (Los Angeles: Chinese American Citizens Alliance, 1963), 16.

28. See Fong, Chinese in New Zealand, 7–8; and Kian-moon Kwan, "Assimilation of the Chinese in the United States: An Exploratory Study in California" (PhD diss., University of California, Berkeley, 1958), 139–41.

29. See, for example, Sue Fawn Chung, "From Fu Manchu, Evil Genius, to James Lee Wong, Popular Hero: A Study of the Chinese-American in Popular Periodical Fiction from 1920 to 1940," Journal of Popular Culture 10, no.4 (Winter 1976): 534–47.

30. In 1900, 52 percent (2,353) of the 4,522 Chinese women in the United States were born in this country; by 1910, 64 percent (3,014 out of 4,675) were native; by 1920 the figure rose to 67 percent (5,214 out of 7,749) and remained at that percentage in 1930 (10,175 out of 15,152); and by 1940 their numbers reached a high of 72 percent (25,944 out of 40,621). (United States Bureau of the Census, Census of the Population, (title differs slightly for some decades) [Washington, D.C., 1900, 1910, 1920, 1930, 1940]).

31. Jack Chen, The Chinese in America (San Francisco: Harper & Row, 1980), 201; and Tsai, The Chinese Experience in America, 97. I do not have records of the CACA activities before 1924. This proposal cannot be located in the California Legislature, Senate Journal, 40th Session (1913) or any of the earlier sessions. In June 1913 Caminetti was appointed commissioner of the U.S. Immigration and Naturalization Service, but when he tried to interfere with the prosecution of his son Drew in a white slavery case later that month, his political career declined. See report by Stephens of Texas in the Congressional Record, 63rd Congress, 1st Session (June 17– August 2, 1913), vol. 50, 2532–33; and the San Francisco Chronicle, June-August 1913.

32. For more details on the act, see Helen Chen, "Chinese Immigration into the United States: An Analysis of Changes in Immigration Policies," in The Chinese American Experience, ed. Genny Lim (San Francisco: Chinese Historical Society of America and Chinese Culture Foundation of San Francisco, 1981), 44–45.

33. U.S. Congress, Senate Committee on Immigration, Hearing on S. 2771: Admission as Nonquota Immigrants of Certain Alien Wives and Children of United States Citizens (Washington, D.C.: Government Printing Office, 1928), 4–15. See also U.S. Congress, House of Representatives Committee on Immigration and Naturalization, Hearings on H.R. 6974: Wives of American Citizens of Oriental Race (Washington, D.C.: Government Printing Office, 1928).

34. Y. C. Hong, "A Plea for Relief Together with a Supplement Containing Some Arguments in Support Thereof" (San Francisco: Chinese American Citizens Alliance, 1928).

35. Weedin v. Chin Bow, 274 U.S. 657 and 47 S.Ct. 772 (1926).

36. Kim Fong Tom, "The Participation of the Chinese in the Community Life of Los Angeles" (Master's thesis, University of Southern California, 1944), 68–70. The author mentions the CACA's work in passing, but Fred W. Riggs attributes this repeal to the Caucasian group, Citizens Committee to Repeal Chinese Exclusion, in Pressures on Congress: A Study of the Repeal of Chinese Exclusion (New York: King Crown's Press, 1950), 43, 118. CACA convention proceedings and other materials were not available for the war years.

37. Chen, "Chinese Immigration," 45.

38. Young China, July 13, 1962, details this event.

39. Charles Kasreal Ferguson, "Political Problems and Activities of the Oriental Residents in Los Angeles and Vicinity" (Master's thesis, University of California, Los Angeles, 1942), 77.

40. Tom, "Participation of the Chinese in Los Angeles," 68–69.

41. Samuel Yee, interviews with author, 1964–65. Tape deposited with the Oral History Project, University of California, Los Angeles.

42. This is discussed further in Wen-hui Chung Chen, "Changing Socio-Cultural Patterns of the Chinese Community in Los Angeles" (PhD diss., University of Southern California, 1952).

43. This was reiterated in a resolution passed as late as 1961 at the CACA annual convention.

44. Yuk Ow, A Selected List of Published and Unpublished Materials Written by the California Chinese with Brief Biographical Sketches of the Authors and Comments on the Works, Bancroft Library, University of California, Berkeley, manuscript.

45. Chen, Chinese of America, 201.

46. Application for permit from the State Corporation Department of the State of California.

47. San Francisco Call and Post, January 21, 1915. See also Victor Low, The Unimpressible Race: A Century of Educational Struggle by the Chinese in San Francisco (San Francisco: East/West Publishing Company, 1982).

48. Low, The Unimpressible Race, 113.

49. Ibid., 115.

50. Ibid., 116–19.

51. San Francisco News, November 21, 1934. See also Low, The Unimpressible Race, 130.

52. Hong, "Milestone," 15.

53. Chinese World, February 3, 1950.

54. Teske and Nelson, "Acculturation and Assimilation," 359.

55. For a discussion of criticism of the CACA's local focus, see Kung-Lee Wang, "The Changing Chinese Americans: Trends in Political Awareness and Involvement Since 1950," in The Chinese American Experience, ed. Genny Lim

(San Francisco: Chinese Historical Society of America and Chinese Culture
Foundation of San Francisco, 1981), 304. For a discussion of the CACA's
failure to gain a wider constituency, see Chen, <u>Chinese of America,</u> 201.

The author is indebted to the following CACA officers (all now deceased)
who generously gave their time and memorabilia and granted formal (*) or
informal interviews: Walter K. Chung, president of CACA Mandarins, 1948–49;
Albert L. Hing, first president of the CACA Mandarins, 1946–47; Y. C. Hong,*
grand president of the CACA, 1949–53; William Lem, past president of the
Oakland Lodge; and Samuel E. Yee,* grand secretary of the CACA, 1964–65. I
also want to thank Albert C. Lim, past president of the Chinese Consolidated
Benevolent Association, Thomas Chinn, historian, and H. K. Wong,* civic
leader and historian (now deceased), all of San Francisco, for their enlightening
interviews. Formal interviews were taped and these tapes were deposited with
the oral history department at UCLA.

THE HMONG REFUGEE COMMUNITY IN SAN DIEGO: THEORETICAL AND PRACTICAL IMPLICATIONS OF ITS CONTINUING ETHNIC SOLIDARITY[1]

GEORGE M. SCOTT, JR.
University of California
San Diego

The Hmong refugees in San Diego have retained their traditional sense of ethnicity despite strong assimilative forces that threaten to weaken it. These forces are both external and internal in origin, the former being concentrated in the actions of local social service providers and the latter existing as a rational, purposive strategy applied by the Hmong community leaders. The leaders, however, also join with their people in desiring the maintenance of ethnic solidarity. An explanation for this assimilation-contra-assimilation paradox is sought by examining factors in Hmong culture, both past and present, in the light of various theoretical approaches common in the literature on ethnicity. An approach that addresses the interaction of primordial sentiments, structural conditions, and interest-based ethnic movements is best suited for this purpose, and an attempt is made to apply this understanding to the concerns of refugee policy makers and social service providers.

In the spring of 1976, the first few families of Lao Hmong refugees arrived in San Diego from the resettlement camps in Thailand. Taking into account their traditional existence[2] — slash-and-burn cultivation in the mountains of northern Laos and a subsistence economy supplemented by a cash crop of opium; a largely kinship-based social and political organization; tribal autonomy, both political and economic; a world view characterized by animism, shamanism, and ancestor worship; and a language only recently written (by missionary-linguists)— of the various Southeast Asian refugee groups the Hmong are culturally the most disparate from the receiving society.

How long and to what extent will the Hmong be able to maintain their ethnic and cultural identity in the face of powerful assimilative forces that threaten to weaken it, if not sweep it away? After six years, at least in San Diego, this sense of identity has survived — in fact it has increased — even though there are concerted efforts, originating from both outside *and* within the Hmong community, that press in the opposite direction. The empirical and theoretical understanding of this paradox, along with its implications for refugee policy makers and social service providers, is the aim of this essay.

Given the wide and obvious cultural disparity, it is no surprise that the original Hmong families in San Diego preferred to live close together. Indeed, the resettlement policy established prior to their arrival was designed to allow for this preference.[3] Nor was it unexpected that this first cluster of Hmong families attracted others, both those moving on their own from other parts of the country, and those arriving from overseas.

It was also assumed by the policy makers and service providers that this process of continuing additive clustering would be temporary. In time, families and individuals would begin to move into the mainstream of American society — as had happened with the local Vietnamese, Lao, and Cambodian refugee populations. After about one year, the original cluster did overflow into a second area, but this dispersal was spatial rather than social. Kin and friendship ties were actively maintained between the two clusters, and they form one community. In fact, the more its population grows, the more clearly is the community's distinctiveness manifested.

For policy makers and service providers this is more than an intellectual challenge, because it impedes economic participation in the larger society. In the words of a local refugee resettlement worker:

> In 1976, we fought tooth and nail to get these people to go to work, and we were successful. But now that a lot more of them are here, they have their own community. . . So now there's more unemployment. They've withdrawn into themselves — into their community — and it's harder for the agencies to reach them with the message, "Go to work!"

Indeed, changes in the rate of unemployment within the San Diego Hmong community over the last six years support this: from about 40% in 1976, it rose to 84% in 1979 and dropped back to 77% in 1981, where it stands today.[4] Moreover, of those employed, all but a very few remain in the minimum wage, semi-skilled occupations for which they received entry-level training from one of the local refugee vocational programs, even though these occupations were selected because they held relatively high potential for advancement (e.g., electronics assembly). One result is, of course, that the vast majority (about 95%) of the local Hmong refugee population is supported in varying degrees by various forms of public assistance.

There is, however, a small group of men who act as their community's representatives to the outside world. Relatively young, Western-educated, literate in English, and gainfully employed (the few who have progressed beyond the minimum wage level), they seem to embody all the qualities required for successful adjustment to American society: assertiveness, initiative, attentiveness, and public image consciousness. They appear to the untrained eye like additional members of the large, generalized (and stereotyped) San Diego population of successful, enterprising "Asian-Americans." In fact, these youthful, "Americanized" men comprise the formal leadership of the local chapter of the semi-national Hmong mutual-aid association, "Lao Family Community, Inc.," and one of their duties is to extoll continually the virtues of learning English, achieving a marketable skill, and finding gainful employment — in a word, becoming self-supporting — virtues that they themselves so successfully exemplify.[5]

This message is communicated both informally, on an interpersonal basis, and formally, during neighborhood and community-wide meetings. The language used ranges from sympathetic encouragement to angry admonition, depending on circumstances and persons. In addition, the leaders make it a point to reward notable achievements: graduates at all levels and types of education (both academic and vocational) are feted once a year in the spring; newly-wed couples in which both partners achieved English proficiency and employment before marriage are honored with a special, formal reception; and anyone who finds an especially good job is praised at the next community-wide meeting. Thus, the exhortation of "Go to work!" coming from outside the community is more than adequately joined from within.

Moreover, Lao Family (as it is commonly referred to) evidences a degree of organization, systemization, and efficiency displayed by none of the other Southeast Asian refugee associations, with the possible exception of that formed by professional and middle class Vietnamese. Yet the level of sophistication of the Hmong association is even more surprising when viewed against its own constituency, which is far from achieving proficiency in English or even a minimal vocational skill, let alone middle class status.[6]

There is a further complication. While the leaders of Lao Family espouse ideals of assimilation, they also encourage community solidarity and ethnic identity. They want their people to adopt the necessary language, vocational, behavioral, and other skills required for participation in the American economy, but they want them to achieve this accommodation as a group, and as *Hmong*. They praise the successful by saying, "Your success brings honor not only to yourself and your family, but all your people" and " Do not forget who you are" and "Remember we should all stay together." The service providers, on the other hand, perceive a contradiction in this and are skeptical. As an ESL (English as a Second Language) teacher put it:

I know they [the Lao Family officers] tell their people to stick together — not that they really need to, mind you — and I think that's good. I mean, right now they really need each other, or at least they did earlier. But look, I'm sorry, sooner or later they'll have to learn to act more individually or they just aren't going to get anywhere. They want the good life, don't we all, but they just can't have it both ways.

This at first sight seems plausible[7] but rather than addressing the probable outcome of the leaders' goal, we will focus on the goal itself, or, more specifically, on its apparently self-contradictory nature. Why, then, should those who seem able to make a success of assimilation, and who also advocate it for those less assured of success, nevertheless insist on the maintenance of Hmong identity, both for themselves and for the others? (And, of course, why do the others appear to concur?)

The Concept of Assimilation

In order to frame this question more directly in anthropological and sociological terms, we shall first have to explore briefly the concept of assimilation. The two definitions of this concept commonly accepted today are "a process of boundary reduction that can occur when members of two or more societies or of smaller cultural groups meet" (Yinger 1981:249) and "a process in which persons of diverse ethnic and racial backgrounds come to interact . . . in the life of the larger community" (Simpson 1968:438).

As a complete phenomenon, assimilation is usually considered to consist of four sub-processes (Yinger 1981).[8] First, there is *integration*, or " the process of structural assimilation of persons from two or more formerly separate sub-societies into a set of shared interactions, [which] occur in situations that vary from the relatively impersonal contacts within economic and political institutions to the personal contacts within neighborhoods, friendship circles, and marriage" (p. 254). Secondly, *acculturation* (cultural assimilation)[9] refers to "the process of change toward greater cultural [i.e., cognitive, behavioral, and material] similarity brought about by contact between two or more groups . . . [which is] more extensive among the members of smaller and weaker groups, or among those who have migrated into or been brought into another society" (p. 251). The third sub-process is *identification* (psychological assimilation), which refers to the process by which members of different societies develop a single, shared identity. The direction of change can vary from equal contributions from all sides to a one-way shift of one group toward the identity of another. The former tends to occur in situations of relative political, economic, and numerical parity, and the latter, when recent immigrant or otherwise weak groups are in the presence of a dominant society (pp. 252-253). Finally, there is *amalgamation*, or biological assimilation, which can result from either intermarriage or sexual exploitation, the latter, of course, not necessarily resulting in the assimilation of the offspring into the exploiters' society (p. 255).

Although these sub-processes can be presented separately for purposes of analysis, in reality they are interdependent. Changes in one, whether toward facilitation or hindrance, tend to produce like changes in the others. Moreover, neither the order nor rate of occurrence of the sub-process is fixed; depending on the type of inter-group contact, they may begin together or in various different orders and proceed pari passu or at differing rates (Yinger 1981:256). The former situation is rare, however, occurring primarily when the cultural differences between the two groups in contact are minimal yet the differential in political and economic dominance between them is sufficient for assimilation to be desired. In most cases, as Gordon (1964:77) and Teske and Nelson (1974:365) have noted, it is more likely that some degree of acculturation will precede the other sub-processes, because the cultural differences are usually wide enough to require the assimilating group to adopt at least some of the cognitive, linguistic, and behavioral skills of the dominant society in order to achieve occupational integration, not to mention integration into more personal areas, as well as identification and amalgamation.

Finally, a group may remain arrested indefinitely at a stage of acculturation without moving on to the other areas of assimilation, because its path has been blocked by the discriminatory practices of the dominant society (Gordon 1964:77-78; Teske and Nelson 1974:359-360; Yinger 1981: 251). The converse may also occur: a group may desire integration with only the requisite amount of acculturation, and if allowed to proceed without discrimination, may travel far into (at least) the occupational structure of the core society (Teske and Nelson 1974:364; Yinger 1981:254).

What the Hmong primarily desire is integration, with just enough acculturation to make this possible, and no identification or amalgamation.[10] This simultaneous desire for assimilation *and* "contra-assimilation"[11] is not unusual — as Yinger (1981) points out, it is the essence of ethnic group relations in today's world — but it does require explanation. There are three questions to be addressed — one empirical, another theoretical, and the third practical. First, we should identify the particular features of Hmong history and traditional culture that will account for their behavior in San Diego. Second, to what extent do these features support existing theoretical formulations? Third, how may the answers to these questions be of use to the social service providers and policy makers concerned with the Hmong's resettlement?

Primordial Sentiments and Social Circumstances

Following Glazer and Moynihan (1975: 19-20), we can distinguish two basic approaches to the problem: the "primordialist" and the "circumstantialist." The first explains the persistence of ethnic attachments by their affective significance; the second views ethnic attachments as a product of social circumstances, both internal and external to the group. Some scholars in the second category confine their attention to structural conditions (e.g., Hechter 1975, 1978; Horowitz 1975; Yancey et al. 1976), while others also examine the rational, strategic selection of ethnicity as a means of attaining political and economic goals (e.g., Bell 1975; Cohen 1969, 1974a, 1974b; Despres 1975; Doornbos 1972; Fisher 1978; Halsey 1978; Hechter 1974; Nagata 1974; Parkin 1974; Patterson 1975; Young 1976).

The circumstantialist approach tends to disregard primordialist features, especially in complex, urbanized societies. The primordialists are usually more inclusive and give some explanatory weight to structural conditions. Yet they tend to treat these two determinants separately, with the result that the primordial sentiments, along with their affective charge, and the structural conditions both appear as constants, explaining the variable of ethnicity, but having little, if anything, to do with one another (see, for example, Gambino 1974; Gordon 1964; Greeley 1974; Issacs 1975; Novak 1972). A few attempts have been made, most notably by Epstein (1978), Johnston and Yoels (1977), and, even though he is critical of the primordialist approach, Doornbos (1972), to treat the primordial sentiments and structural conditions themselves as variables and to ask how they influence one another in affecting the ultimate variable of ethnicity.

Let us begin with the primordialist approach. The key definitional element is affective salience. Shils (1975), focusing on kinship, put it this way: "The attachment to another member of one's kinship group is not just a function of interaction. . . . It is because a certain *ineffable significance* is attributed to the tie of blood" (p. 122; emphasis added). Geertz (1973) expanded the definition beyond kinship and other primary groups to include larger-scale groups based on common territory, language, religion, and social practices. These " 'givens' of social existence, " he wrote, ". . . are seen to have an *ineffable*, and at times *overpowering, coerciveness in and of themselves*. One is bound to one's kinsman, one's neighbor, one's fellow believer, ipso facto. . . . by vriture of some *unaccountable absolute import* attributed to the very tie itself" (p. 259; emphases added). Gordon (1964), discussing ethnic groups, wrote: "Common to all these objective bases [i.e., nationality, religion, and race] . . . is the social-psychological element of a special sense of both ancestral and future-oriented identification with the group. These are the 'people' of my ancestors, therefore they are my people, and they will be the people of my children and their children" (p. 29).

Although Gordon includes shared nationality as a possible basis for primordial attachments, others have contended that it is often the absence of national ties or the sense of alienation resulting from perceived injustice that enhances the primordial nature of ethnic group identity (e.g., Yinger 1981:258). This is the case with the Hmong refugees. Central to their sense of ethnicity is a tradition of political autonomy and social self-reliance that has been maintained and strengthened through four millenia of warfare, persecution, and forced migration, beginning in China, extending through Indochina, and culminating in their relocation here (Scott 1979). Moreover, their conflicts with the dominant population both in China and Indochina drove them far into the mountains where they lived alongside other "hill tribes" but in relative isolation from the assimilative forces of the lowland society. F. M. Savina (1930), the only European to have devoted an entire work to the history of the Hmong (then termed "Miao"), wrote:

> Beaten by the Chinese they had to give way. . . That is how the Miao became mountain men, in spite of themselves, some four thousand years ago, and that is how too they were always able to keep their independence in the middle of other peoples, keeping intact, along with their language and their customs, the ethnic character of the race (Savina 1930:175).[12]

Hugo Adolf Bernatzik, an early German ethnographer who worked in Indochina, attested to the Hmong's "indomitable desire for freedom" and their "aversion to being ruled by members of other peoples" (Bernatzik 1970:625), and added a warning to would-be "colonizers":

> Their urge for independence, their fearlessness bordering on defiance of death, their glowing love for freedom, which had been strengthened through thousands of years of fighting against powerful oppressors and has given them the reputation of feared warriors, will perhaps make difficulties for the colonizer (Bernatzik 1970:674).

This reputation made the Hmong attractive political allies for both the Royal Lao and the Communist sides at the outset ot the Indochina War. It was also known that their strong sense of ethnic pride and political autonomy would make them difficult to control and their loyality to the "larger" cause forever suspect (Dommen 1971:75; Toye 1968:195). Each side had to convince their Hmong allies that defeat would bring an end to their tribal freedom (Dommen 1971; Toye 1968), while victory could bring an autonomous Hmong state (Branfman 1970:252; Department of the Army 1970:654).

These primordial sentiments continue in San Diego and are especially evident whenever the Hmong identity is jeopardized, as when an outsider confuses the Hmong with other Southeast Asi.in refugees. For example, when this mistake is between teachers and students (both child and adult) or between welfare workers and clients, the response is usually a polite but firm reproof. If the mistake is in the public domain, the Hmong are outraged. For instance, when a large color photograph of a piece of traditional Hmong needlework was recently displayed on the front page of a local newspaper's "family section," with the caption, "Native Art of Vietnam," the president of Lao Family, who had not yet seen the picture himself, was besieged with telephone calls from irate community members demanding that he take action (not that he really needed their encouragement). They received a printed apology, but the unfortunate American refugee worker who was (wrongly) blamed for the error and who extracted the apology, was later berated by the president in front of several people for his "stupidity."[13]

Primordial sentiments are most readily formed around those kinds of intragroup interactions already possessing a high degree of solidarity ("congruities" in the words of Geertz [1973:259]), the archetype for which is kinship. It follows that any factors that impede interaction within the group and thus reduce solidarity would also weaken primordial sentiments. This is especially the case for ethnic populations that live in complex, industrialized societies where potentially disruptive factors abound, including, for example, residential dispersion, occupational diversification, and class stratification (Doornbos 1972; Hechter 1978; Yancey et al. 1976). The converse must also be true: factors increasing intragroup solidarity tend to reinforce primordial sentiments. It is quite possible for such factors to be present also in complex societies (Doornbos 1972; Epstein 1978; Johnston and Yoels 1977). I shall now demonstrate this for the Hmong.

The factors accounting for the unusual strength of Hmong ethnicity are of two kinds, those internal and those external to the Hmong community. Each of these can be further divided into the two categories of the Hmong's present cultural environment and those cultural aspects surviving from their past.

The Hmong community is strongly homogeneous[14] with respect to all the variables. There is little diversity of occupation, no effective class stratification, minimal spatial distribution, and no major differences in language, religion, or customs.[15] This homogeneity is both a continuation of the past and a product of the present. Swidden horticulture, practiced in the relative isolation of the mountains meant insufficient resources to require a diversification of labor or allow for economically differentiated and hierarchically arranged classes.

Recruitment into the higher commissioned ranks of the army and into higher government positions during the mid-1960's to the early 1970's, might ultimately have resulted in class differentiation. But the war did not continue and any tendency towards differentiation was erased by the refugee and relocation experience. Said one informant, "Since we have been here we say everybody is equal. . . . Everybody is on welfare, everybody have to go to work at the same place — even if you are a former general, former colonel, or former major, or whatever." In short, there are no occupational or class barriers that would effectively impede uniform interaction throughout the community.[16]

There were some regional differences within the Hmong population in Laos but they were not deeply felt or divisive, being mainly relatively minor clothing, ceremonial, and dialectic variations. Here, the fact that approximately 99% of the 4,500 or so refugees in San Diego now live in an area of not more than fifty square miles means that these differences survive as little more than memories in the minds of the older generation.

In addition, linguistic and religious homogeneity remain strong. What is new tends to be added rather than used as a substitute. English is increasingly being learned, mostly by the young, but as with French in Laos, not at the expense of Hmong; traditional animistic beliefs and, to a lesser extent, ritual, have been maintained, although with less certainty than before (Scott 1982), in spite of increasing Christian conversion.

Moreover, the community continues to be endogamous, which facilitates the maintenance of its sociocultural homogeneity (as well as demonstrating its strong degree of ethnic solidarity).

Let us now consider the factors external to the community that maintain the Hmong sense of identity. As Hechter (1978:298-299) has argued, whenever ethnic groups are distributed throughout the occupational structure of a society, ethnic solidarity will tend to be the strongest among those groups clustered at the bottom of the structure and will tend to diminish among those occupying the higher positions (all other factors of race, religion, and history being equal). "When one's life chances are seen to be independent of membership in a particular group, the psychic significance of membership in that group will tend to recede or to disappear all together" (Hechter 1978:299). The members of the more privileged ethnic groups will thus tend to act on an individualistic basis, while those less privileged will be more collectivistic, believing that their ethnic characteristics weigh more heavily in their life achievements. In a society with a strong egalitarian ideology, the latter groups may come to believe that it is precisely their distinctive ethnicity that causes their material disadvantage (Hechter 1978: 299). However, where different ethnicities are found within the same occupational groups, intergroup interaction begins to replace intragroup interaction, and class consciousness begins to replace ethnic consciousness as the basis for social action (Hechter 1978:308; see also Cohen 1974b: xxii).

Where would the Hmong fit into this range? Given their level of unemployment, it is obvious that they are clustered at the bottom of the American stratification system — probably more uniformly so than any other ethnic group. This can only enhance their traditional ethnic distinctiveness and the primordial sentiments attached to it. But they do not yet talk of discrimination. They may have felt this in Laos and China, but now, quite apart from resenting the other groups for their relatively privileged positions, the Hmong look on them with respect and admiration, and want to share in their fortunes as soon as possible. This, surely, is the point; when the local Hmong refugees look up, as it were, at the many American ethnic groups gathered around what must seem to them to be the highest reaches of the American economic mountain, it only serves to remind them that they too once held a similar (but literal) position in their own mountains, and that it was their strong sense of ethnic pride, their political autonomy, and their economic self-sufficiency that kept them there. It is around the desire to regain this pride that the primordial sentiments of Hmong ethnicity now revolve, and these sentiments are intensified accordingly.

Contrary to the expectations (and desires) of the local social service providers, the Hmong refugees are becoming more rather than less conscious of their ethnicity. It is helpful for us to see their experience as they see it.

When they first came to San Diego, the Hmong were apprehensive but also noticeably optimistic about their future. After all, they had recently enjoyed relative success in their experience with Americans and American culture as it was represented in Laos. They had quickly learned to use the weapons and tactics brought to them by the U.S. Military Forces and the CIA; they more than held their own in battle even against North Vietnamese regular army units, and they had grown accustomed to receiving respect and praise from their

American advisors and fellow combatants. That the war, and thus their homeland, had been lost was attributable to the devious and self-serving machinations of the Lao and American governments. Had U. S. support been continued, General Vang Pao [17] would have led them to victory by now, or at least would have wrested their mountains away from the Pathet Lao and North Vietnamese. What could be so difficult about adjusting to a peaceful life in America? If any problems did arise, an American government on whose side they had fought during the war and which had shown its gratitude by granting them asylum, would surely help to solve them.

As far as the Hmong were concerned, they had already been successful in acculturating, integrating, and even amalgamating (but not often marrying) into what seemed to be a representative sample of American society — and at little cost to their traditional ethnic identity. But they had no idea of just how small and unrepresentative this sample really was and, as a result, they were unaware of how ill-equipped they were for adjustment when they arrived. Nor could they have known that the American government's ability to help them with this adjustment would fall far short of its ability to destroy its enemies during war.

Soon after their arrival, the Hmong's initial optimism began to be replaced by a sober realization of their situation, of the wide gap between abilities and needs. There were two gradually unfolding responses. First, they returned shivering, as it were, from their brief foray into their new and alien world and avidly sought the warmth of their traditional culture and sense of ethnicity. What before had been accepted unhesitatingly as the "natural" ways of thinking and behaving became recognized as distinctive cultural elements that must be consciously and emphatically embraced so as to provide the security of a familiar identity in an alien environment.[18] The Hmong quickly learned what many immigrant

groups had known before them, i.e., it is always preferable to approach the unfamiliar from the security of the familiar (cf. Epstein 1978:100; Falk 1973:75; Kovacs and Cropley 1975:227-228; and Yinger 1981:258).

The second response was to create an interest-based ethnic movement in the form of a mutual-aid association — Lao Family. Yinger (1981) has expressed this process well, and his words have great relevance for the Hmong:

> Interest-based ethnic movements often occur when there are strong acculturative, integrative, and even amalgamative forces that have raised hopes for rapid status improvement. The hopes and expectations, however, soar above the more slowly changing reality. Thus group awareness is often increased, not lowered, by the. . .increase in the sense of shared relative deprivation caused by the gap between hopes and actual conditions (Yinger 1981:259).

The ethnic association pursues economic and political goals in order to reduce this gap, and it does so under the banner of its group's ethnicity, emphasizing the importance of maintaining strong ethnic attachments along the way (Cohen 1969, 1974a, 1974b; Hechter 1974; Young 1976).

This, then, is exactly the "interest" that the Lao Family leaders have in mind when they ask of their charges: "Do not forget who you are." They assume, probably correctly, that their group will receive greater attention on the part of the American public (in particular by those who hold the keys to economic and political advancement) if they are seen as a distinctive subculture, and as one that has a peculiarly disparate (and pitiable) background and thus with uniquely pressing needs for assistance when compared to the other Southeast Asian refugees. Indeed, it is the constant fear of being lumped together with the others into some general category, whether "Indochinese," "Boat People," "Vietnamese," or simply "refugees," that partly accounts for the vigilance that the leadership maintains against any attribution of mistaken or stereotyped identity by outsiders.

For the same reason the leadership carefully maintains a "VIP" guest list, which includes the directors and staff of all the local refugee social service agencies, public school administrators and teachers, police department representatives, county supervisors, and city council members, for use whenever a community-wide social gathering of some kind is planned.[19] Whether expressed during the New Year Celebration (Scott 1981), at the ceremony for the installation of new Lao Family officers and staff, or at the Awards Ceremony for Student Achievers, or whether the particular means is through the performance of traditional music, dance, and ritual, the showing of an ethnographic film,[20] or speeches and testimonials concerning war, resettlement, and adjustment — the message is always the external equivalent to the one given within the community: "Please remember we are the Hmong. We are a proud people, but we need your help."

Thus our explanation addresses the interaction of both primordial sentiments and social circumstances. In Daniel Bell's oft-quoted phrase: "Ethnicity has become more salient because it can combine an interest with an affective tie" (Bell 1975: 169).

Conclusion

Now that we have an explanation — a combined primordialist and circumstantialist one — for the assimilation-contra-assimilation paradox that exists in the San Diego Hmong community, we finally need to address the issue of how this understanding can be tailored to the interests of refugee policy makers and social service providers.

One understanding that may be reached from the above analysis is that the Hmong experience does not correspond to two deeply held American assumptions about the world. First, things do not always get better in time; they sometimes get worse. Second, adversity does not always bring out the best in people; it sometimes brings out the worst (relative to adjustment). The Hmong are accustomed to adversity, and in the past they always managed to survive. Given time, that will happen here. But our concern is the immediate future where they appear to be sinking farther into the impasse of unemployment and welfare support. There is also a message repeated with increasing regularity by public and private social service agencies which says, in effect, that "the government" will be spending less and less on the refugees, so they must start learning to take care of themselves.

This idea of "taking care of themselves" does not motivate the Hmong toward adjustment; rather, it makes them withdraw even farther. What is more humiliating than being turned down for a job time and again because one cannot speak, let alone read and write English; because one cannot understand American numbers and colors; because one does not know how to dress for and behave at job interviews? What is more frustrating than when one wants to be self-supporting, as one's ancestors had always been, but lacks the skills to become so? This kind of adversity they have never known before, and they respond by becoming *more* Hmong, rather than less so.

It is not only a matter of identity but also the enormous gap between their abilities and the needs of the larger society that causes their difficulties in adjustment. We noted above that this gap intensifies primordial sentiments. So they interact more and more with each other and less and less with outsiders, even with those whose task it is to help them.

Yet is also follows from our analysis and from Hechter's (1978) argument that different conditions might change the Hmong's response. If more money were to be spent on language and vocational training, if there were more and better trained teachers and better facilities, if there were more and better jobs available, the Hmong could move more effectively and extensively into the occupational system of this society. Then their "shared sense of relative - deprivation," their cultural homogeneity and entrenchment, their interest-based ethnic movement, and the intensity of their primordial sentiments (thus also the strength of their ethnic solidarity) would be reduced accordingly. Their identity would not be extinguished altogether — its primordial quality and their own determination to keep it alive are both too great for that — but at least it might be reduced to the extent that it allows them to take better advantage of the economic opportunities around them. This is, after all, what they themselves want — integration without complete identification, or a "stabilized pluralism" vis-a-vis the larger society (Barnett et al. 1954:990).

One thing is certain. The Hmong's present situation is unstable. Without any means of support of their own, their only hope lies first in the willingness of the government to continue funding the language and vocational training programs, and second in the willingness of those among them who are already capable of adjusting successfully to continue to lead them and to call attention to their predicament. If either source of support ends, the other is likely to follow. In that event, the majority of the present adult population, together with the generation to follow, is likely to fall backwards into a permanent lower class, or even "under class," watching with envy, and perhaps with rancor, as the more successful among them (even some of their own children and grandchildren) move away into the higher levels of American society. Told to "sink or swim," they will surely sink, carried under, but given some solace, by the weight of their own ethnicity.

NOTES

[1] The fieldwork on which this paper is based was conducted intermittently between August, 1979 and August, 1981. I wish to thank Robert Levy, Sandra Murray, Amina Namika Raby, and especially F. G. Bailey, for reading earlier drafts and offering helpful editorial and substantive advice.

[2] For ethnographic accounts of the Hmong in Laos, see Barney (1967); Lebar (1964); and Lemoine (1972); for the Hmong in Thailand, see Bernatzik (1970); Cooper (1978a, 1978b, 1979); and Geddes (1976). Owing to the slow but steady flow of Hmong migration between the two countries, primarily from the former to the latter, the cultural and linguistic differences between the two populations, with respect to traditional patterns, are minimal. The main difference is that these patterns persist to some extent in Thailand, while in Laos they have been largely disrupted by war, Communist opposition, and refugee relocation. It should also be noted that the name "Hmong," which the people use for themselves, has appeared in the literature only within the last decade or so. Before that time, the names used were those applied by dominant, neighboring peoples: "Miao," by the Chinese and "Meo," by the Lao and Thai, both of which are resented by the Hmong because of their perceived derogatory connotations.

[3] This policy of resettling refugees only with fellow members of their ethnic group, and in most cases, with close kinsmen, has been consistently followed by the major voluntary refugee resettlement agencies (VOLAGs), at least in San Diego. This has not been the case with the smaller sponsoring institutions, such as churches. See Trillin (1980) for the tragic consequences of a church-sponsored resettlement of a Hmong family into a small community whose refugee population was exclusively Lao.

[4] These figures refer only to persons within the employable age bracket of 18-65. The 1976 percentage is based on an estimate calculated for that period in 1979 by refugee vocational training personnel and corroborated by Hmong community leaders. The percentages for 1979 and 1981 are derived, respectively, from a non-random survey conducted by the Family Service Association of San Diego County (N=164, representing about 50% of the adult population; previously cited in Scott [1979]) and from a survey conducted randomly by the author (N=106, representing about 5% of the adult population).

[5] The term "formal leadership" refers to the officers of the association: a president, two vice-presidents, a secretary and vice-secretary, and a treasurer and vice-treasurer. The president is elected annually by the dues-paying members of the association, and he in turn nominates the other officers. All nominees are open to community-wide approval, but this process is largely pro forma, with serious opposition to any of the nominees seldom occurring. In fact, turn-over within the leadership as

a whole has been minimal since the association's inception three years ago; most of the movement instead has been internal, from office to office.

For the current (1981-82) term, the average age of the officers is approximately twenty-eight, the youngest being twenty-four (the second vice-president) and the eldest, thirty-five (the vice- secretary). The president is twenty-seven.

The average number of years of education among the seven officers is about thirteen; the most educated is the secretary (three years of college), and the least, the vice-secretary (ten years elementary). The president has two years of college. In addition, the president, both vice-presidents, and the secretary are currently attending local junior colleges in the evenings. All officers are literate in French, Lao, and Hmong, as well as in English. Finally, all are employed in skilled, refugee-related social service occupations (interpreting, counseling, case work, and elementary teaching). These attributes serve to demonstrate the distinction — indeed, the eminence — of the association's leadership when compared to the adult population as a whole, 93% of which, judging from the above 1981 survey, has had no more than six years of formal education (61% none at all) and, as pointed out earlier, 77% of which is unemployed.

⁶ In addition to the seven officers, the Articles of Incorporation of Lao Family provides for three committees (Public Relations and Information, Social Services, and Sports), six local area representatives, called "gatekeepers," and two senior advisors. As with the officers, tenure for all is one year. The officers, committee "chairpersons," and senior advisors meet every other week; the entire body, once every month. The level of education and employment among the chairpersons and advisors is equal to that of the officers, while the committee members' and gatekeepers' is slightly lower but still significantly higher than the adult population as a whole.

The several formally mandated duties of the association can be subsumed under four general categories: (1) The allocation of community resources, including food, clothing, money, and transportation, toward the assistance of needy families. This duty is primarily the responsibility of the Social Services Committee and is performed as a supplement to, not replacement for, already existing kinship networks from the extended family to the clan. (2) The transfer of information and management of relations between the community and outside institutions and individuals, which is under the specific supervision of the Public Affairs and Information Committee. (3) The mediation of any protracted or otherwise serious dispute within the community that has eluded the grasp of the appropriate kinship-based authorities (i.e., male elders). The officers, primarily the president, and the two

senior advisors together act as a centralized, impartial body of authority in such cases. (4) The implementation of strategies for sociocultural adjustment originating from among the national leadership of Lao Family, headquartered in Santa Ana, California (see Scott 1979). The Public Affairs and Information Committee, backed by the president and advisors, holds primary responsibility in this area. The immediate representation of the association's interests and responsibilities in all four areas is the duty of the gatekeepers, one serving in each of the six main population clusters.

The use of "Lao" instead of "Hmong" in the association's title is a reflection more of a political aspiration on the part of the central leadership toward Lao national recognition than of either an assumption of Lao ethnic identity or a representation of Lao refugees (Scott 1979).

⁷Actually, the social science "jury" is still out on this question. Nagata (1974), for example, argues that ethnic groups are quite capable of assimilating into the political and economic main-stream of their society while retaining their identities — indeed, while even oscillating freely between their own and others' identities according to which one is the most useful in the situation at hand. Baskaukas (1977) and Putnins (1976) agree that it is possible for assimilation to occur with the retention of ethnic identities but only at the expense of some degree of identity conflict and resulting anxiety. Finally, Broom and Kitsuse (1955) would have it that assimilation with ethnic identities intact is simply not possible.

⁸Cf. Gordon (1964:70-71) for a similar framework. For earlier, and in some respects, even more thorough treatments of the subject, see Barnett et al. (1954) and Spiro (1955).

⁹It should be noted that anthropologists usually view assimilation and acculturation as separate processes (see Teske and Nelson 1974) — a moot point as far as our analysis is concerned.

¹⁰ Thus far, only the leadership and staff of Lao Family, in addition to about an equal number of other adults, have achieved this goal — not more than 3% of the entire adult population. The remaining 20% or so who are employed have not really progressed beyond the initial stage of integration (i.e., employment), as evidenced by the fact that their occupations (e.g., electronics assembly, landscaping) require little, if any, interaction with non-Hmong fellow workers. For them, and to even a greater extent for those unemployed, assimilation has meant only a small amount of acculturation, and that primarily in the material dimension. It can be said, therefore, that acculturation and integration within the San Diego Hmong community has occured significantly only at the level of the *individual*, and with those individuals al-

ready possessing most of the requisite skills when they arrived; at the *group* level, the San Diego Hmong are largely unassimilated, in any sense of the term (see Teske and Nelson 1974 for a discussion of this distinction).

[11] Yinger (1981) uses the term "dissimilation" to refer to this paradox. But since it can hardly be said that the Hmong desire to become less assimilated than they already are, it seemed advisable to coin a term that more accurately reflected the Hmong's attitude, which is more properly expressed as being *against* assimilation.

[12] Cited in and translated by Geddes (1976:31).

[13] Although normally unafraid to speak his mind to Americans — which is one reason he had been elected to a second term in office — the president was uncharacteristically harsh in this instance. However, it was the eve of the Hmong New Year and according to traditional custom, he was quite drunk. He later apologized to the worker for his actions, expressing obvious embarrassment.

[14] This is not to say that the community is entirely harmonious. There does exist some interclan conflict, concerning mainly disputes over bride price payments, but this type of conflict cannot create the kinds of cleavages that would disrupt the sociocultural homogeneity of the community because it does not result in the formation of stable groups of people. The type of conflict that would prove more disruptive, e.g., occuring between differentially assimilated factions, may be in the offing but is presently too isolated and infrequent to have any serious effect.

[15] It is, in other words, the absence within the community of the same factors that are claimed to cross-cut other American ethnic groups, reducing their solidarity and weakening their identity. In all fairness to the circumstantialists, it should be pointed out that they also argue that the absence of these factors in an ethnic group would result in a heightening of its sense of ethnicity but they see no reason to include primordial sentiments in this process.

[16] It should also be pointed out, following Barth (1969), that it is the very existence of the cultural distinctiveness of this homogeneous community that helps account for the maintenance of the ethnic boundary drawn around it. This explanation, however, addresses the question of *how* ethnic boundaries are maintained, not *why*.

[17] Vang Pao was the Hmong commander of the U. S.-supported *Armee Clandestine*, which consisted primarily of Hmong guerrilla soldiers and mounted the only effective resistance to the Pathet Lao and North Vietnamese forces during the war. Subsequently, Vang Pao helped to establish Lao Family and today remains as its national president.

[18] It is perhaps ironic that the same alienating traits of this society that has led to the cultural entrenchment of the Hmong community — impersonality, universality, rationality, and instrumentiality — are also the very ones that allow the Hmong to move in and out of it with relative ease. Shopping at the supermarket requires little, if any, English and even less in the way of permanent, meaningful interaction with outsiders.

[19] Usually enough of these "VIPs" attend to require two large tables, which are always placed at the front of the hall where such activities are held. The anthropologist is given a seat farther back among the general audience — as much a sign that the leaders know who butters their bread as it is of his acceptance into the community.

[20] This film — *Miao Year* — is rented on each occasion from the University of California Extension Media Center in Berkeley.

REFERENCES CITED

BARNETT, H. G., LEONARD BROOM, BERNARD J. SIEGEL, EVON Z. VOGT, and JAMES B. WATSON
    1954 — Acculturation: an exploratory formulation. American Anthropologist 56:973-1002.
BARNEY, G. LINWOOD
    1967 — The Meo of Xieng Khouang province, Laos. *In* Southeast Asian Tribes, Minorities, and Nations. P. Kunstadter, ed. Princeton: Princeton University Press, pp. 271-294.
BARTH, FREDRIK
    1969 — Introduction. *In* Ethnic Groups and Boundaries. F. Barth, ed. Boston: Little, Brown and Company, pp. 9-38.
BASKUSKAS, LIUCIJA
    1977 — Multiple identities: adjusted Lithuanian refugees in Los Angeles. Urban Anthropology 6:141-154.
BELL, DANIEL
    1975 — Ethnicity and social change. *In* Ethnicity: Theory and Experience. N. Glazer and D. Moynihan, eds. Cambridge: Harvard University Press, pp. 141-174.

BERNATZIK, HUGO ADOLF
1970 — Akha and Miao: problems of applied ethnography in farther India. New Haven: Human Relations Area Files.
BRANFMAN, FRED
1970 — Presidential war in Laos, 1964-1970. *In* Laos: War and Revolution. N. S. Adams and A. W. McCoy, eds. New York: Harper and Row, pp. 213-218.
BROOM, LEONARD, and JOHN I. KITSUSE
1955 — The validation of acculturation: a condition to ethnic assimilation. American Anthropologist 57:44-48.
COHEN, ABNER
1969 — Custom and politics in urban Africa: a study of Hausa migrants in Yoruba towns. London: Routledge and Kegan Paul.
1974a— Two-Dimensional Man: an essay on the anthropology of power and symbolism in complex society. Berkeley: University of California Press.
1974b— Introduction: the lesson of ethnicity. *In* Urban Ethnicity. A. Cohen, ed. London: Tavistock, pp. ix-xxiv.
COOPER, ROBERT G.
1978a— Dynamic tension: symbiosis and contradiction in Hmong social relations. *In* The New Economic Anthropology. J. Clammer, ed. London: Macmillan Press, pp. 138-175.
1978b— Unity and division in Hmong social categories in Thailand. *In* Studies in ASEAN Sociology. P. S. J. Chen and H. D. Evers, eds. Singapore: Chopmen Enterprises, pp. 279-320.
1979 — The Yao Jua relationship: patterns of affinal alliance and residence among the Hmong of northern Thailand. Ethnology 18:173-181.
DEPARTMENT OF THE ARMY
1970 — Ethnographic study series: minority groups in Thailand. Pamphlet No. 550-107. Washington, D. C.: U. S. Government Printing Office: 1970 0-351-606.
DESPRES, LEO, ed.
1975 — Ethnicity and resource competition in plural societies. The Hague: Mouton Publishers.
DOMMEN, ARTHUR J.
1971 — Conflict in Laos: the politics of neutralization. New York: Praeger Publishers.
DOORNBOS, MARTIN R.
1972 — Some conceptual problems concerning ethnicity in integration analysis. Civilisations 22:263-283.
EPSTEIN, A. L.
1978 — Ethos and identity: three studies in ethnicity. London: Tavistock.
FALK, GERHARD
1973 — The assimilation process in America. International Behavioral Scientist 5:70-80.
FISHER, MAXINE P.
1978 — Creating ethnic identity: Asian Indians in the New York City area. Urban Anthropology 7:271-285.
GAMBINO, RICHARD
1974 — Blood of my blood: the dilemma of the Italian Americans. Garden City, New York: Doubleday.
GEDDES, WILLIAM R.
1976 — Migrants of the mountains: the ecology of the Blue Miao (Hmong Njua) of Thailand. Oxford: Clarendon Press.
GEERTZ, CLIFFORD
1973 — The integrative revolution: primordial sentiments and civil politics in the new states. *In* The Interpretation of Cultures. Clifford Geertz. New York: Basic Books, pp. 255-310.
GLAZER, NATHAN and DANIEL P. MOYNIHAN
1975 — Introduction. *In* Ethnicity: Theory and Experience. N. Glazer and D. P. Moynihan, eds. Cambridge: Harvard University Press, pp. 1-26.
GORDON, MILTON M.
1964 — Assimilation in American life. New York: Oxford University Press.
GREELEY, ANDREW M.
1974 — Ethnicity in the United States: a preliminary reconnaissance. New York: Wiley.
HALSEY, A. H.
1978 — Ethnicity: a primordial bond? Ethnic and Racial Studies 1:124-128.

HECHTER, MICHAEL
  1974 — The political economy of ethnic change. American Journal of Sociology 79:1151-78.
  1975 — Internal colonialism: the Celtic fringe in British national development, 1536-1966. Berkeley: University of California Press.
  1978 — Group formation and cultural division of labor. American Journal of Sociology 84:293-318.
HOROWITZ, DONALD L.
  1975 — Ethnic identity. In Ethnicity: Theory and Experience. N. Glazer and D. P. Moynihan, eds. Cambridge: Harvard University Press, pp. 111-140.
ISSACS, HAROLD R.
  1975 — Basic group identity: the idols of the tribe. In Ethnicity: Theory and Experience. N. Glazer and D. P. Moynihan, eds. Cambridge: Harvard University Press, pp. 29-52.
JOHNSTON, BARRY V. and WILLIAM C. YOELS
  1977 — On linking cultural and structural models of ethnicity: a synthesis of Schooler and Yancy, Ericksen, and Juliani. American Journal of Sociology 83: 729-736.
KOVACS, M. L. and A. J. CROPLEY
  1975 — Alienation and the assimilation of immigrants. Australian Journal of Social Issues 10:221-230.
LEBAR, FRANK, GERALD C. HICKEY, and JOHN K. MUSGRAVE
  1964 — Ethnic groups of mainland Southeast Asia. New Haven: Human Relations Area Files Press.
LEMOINE, JACQUES
  1972 — Un village Hmong vert du Haut Laos. Paris: Centre National de la Recherche Scientifique.
NAGATA, JUDITH A.
  1974 — What is a Malay? a situational selection of ethnic identity in a plural society. American Ethnologist 1:331-350.
NOVAK, MICHAEL
  1972 — The rise of the unmeltable ethnics: politics and culture in the seventies. New York: Macmillan.
PARKIN, DAVID
  1974 — Congregational and interpersonal ideologies in political ethnicity. In Urban Ethnicity. A. Cohen, ed. London: Tavistock, pp. 119-157.
PATTERSON, ORLANDO
  1975 — Context and choice in ethnic allegiance: a theoretical framework and Caribbean case study. In Ethnicity: Theory and Experience. N. Glazer and D. P. Moynihan, eds. Cambridge: Harvard University Press, pp. 305-359.
PUTNINS, ALDIS L.
  1976 — Immigrant adjustment: a note on Kovacs and Cropley's model. Australian Journal of Social Issues 11:209-213.
SAVINA, F. M.
  1930 — Histoire des Miao. 2nd ed. Hong Kong: Imprimerie de la Société des Missions. - Éstrangères de Paris.
SCOTT, GEORGE M., JR.
  1979 — The Hmong refugees of San Diego: initial strategies of adjustment. In Proceedings of the First Annual Conference on Indochinese Refugees. G. Harry Stopp and Nguyen M. Hung, eds. Fairfax, VA: Citizens Applied Research Institute of George Mason University, pp. 78-85.
  1982 — A new year in a new land: religious change among the Lao Hmong refugees in San Diego. In The Hmong in the West: Observations and Reports. Bruce T. Downong and Douglas P. Olney, eds. Minneapolis: The Center for Urban and regional Affairs, University of Minnesota, pp. 63-85.
SHILS, EDWARD
  1975 — Primordial, personal, sacred and civil ties. In Center and Periphery: Essays in Macrosociology. Vol. 2. Edward Shils. Chicago: The University of Chicago Press, pp. 111-126.
SIMPSON, GEORGE EATON
  1968 — Assimilation. In International Encyclopedia of the Social Sciences. D. Shills, ed. New York: Macmillan and the Free Press, pp. 438-444.
SPIRO, MELFORD E.
  1955 — The acculturation of American ethnic groups. American Anthropologist 57:1240-1252.
TESKE, RAYMOND H. C., JR. and BARDIN H. NELSON
  1974 — Acculturation and assimilation: a clarification. American Ethnologist 1:351-367.

TOYE, HUGH
  1968 — Laos: buffer state or battle ground? London: Oxford University Press.
TRILLIN, CALVIN
  1980 — U. S. Journal: Fairfield Iowa. Resettling the Yangs. The New Yorker, March, 24:83-100.
YANCEY, WILLIAM L., EUGENE P. ERICKSEN, and RICHARD N. JULIANI
  1976 — Emergent ethnicity: a review and reformulation. American Sociological Review 41:391-402.
YINGER, J. MILTON
  1981 — Toward a theory of assimilation and dissimilation. Ethnic and Racial Studies 4:249-264.
YOUNG, CRAWFORD
  1976 — The politics of cultural pluralism. Madison: University of Wisconsin Press.

SOUTHEAST ASIAN REFUGEES IN THE UNITED STATES: THE INTERACTION OF KINSHIP AND PUBLIC POLICY

DAVID W. HAINES

Office of Refugee Resettlement[1]

The formulation and implementation of federal refugee policy is conditioned by, and has pronounced effects upon, the structures and relations of kinship among Southeast Asian refugees. This is particularly true of three core policy issues. First, the federal government is explicitly committed to facilitating the rapid economic self-sufficiency of refugees, and must therefore be cognizant of the ways in which this process is the function of joint strategies on the part of sets of kin, particularly those within a household. Second, the federal government has, or is considered to have, responsibility for the geographic and residential distribution of refugees within the United States. Any attempts to control or guide this distribution must inevitably confront the social, often kin-based, dynamics of initial resettlement, and subsequent, so-called secondary migration of refugees. Third, the government has shown an increasing interest in the importance of ethnic communities and self-help organizations in the resettlement process, and must therefore possess an understanding of the kinds of kinship links that are core to such collectivities.

Over a half-million Southeast Asian refugees have come to the United States since 1975. Their adjustment, both short- and long-term, has engendered considerable interest among both researchers and the general public. In many ways, the experiences of these refugees after arrival in the United States mirror more general patterns typical of recent immigrants. In other ways, however, their experiences are relatively unique. Some of these differences involve the forced nature of their emigration and the links between their exodus and the previous involvement of the United States in Southeast Asia. Others reflect the effects of transit or prolonged stays in countries of temporary asylum.

One major difference involves the explicit involvement of the federal government in the adjustment of Southeast Asian refugees to their situation in the United States. Thus, while the effects of kinship are pervasive for almost all recent immigrants to the United States, it is only with refugees that the federal government remains directly involved with those aspects of adjustment which are so pervasively affected by the structure and behavior of kin groups, the rights and obligations that hold between particular categories of kin, and the resources that kinship presents in the development of adaptive strategies towards a new environment. The following paper addresses this interaction between Southeast Asian refugee kinship and public policy regarding these refugees.

"Family" and Public Policy

In recent years there has been a growing interest in, and debate about, the relationships between families and public policy in the United States. There has been work on the status of American families (e.g., Lasch 1977; Bane 1976; Masnick and Bane 1980), the effects on families of particular public policies (e.g., Greene and Blake 1980; Marans and Colten 1980; McDonald 1979; Girdner 1981), and the feasibility of developing comprehensive family policy that would both avoid unnecessary intrusion into family life, and tap the problem-solving capabilities of families as they exist (e.g., Gilbert 1979; Kamerman and Kahn 1976; Kinch 1979; Blehar 1979; White House Conference on Families 1980).

Such attempts to more effectively understand the interaction of family (kinship) and public policy have been instructive, but have faced three continuing problems. First, there has been limited effort outside anthropology to define what families are. Second, the understanding of family structure and behavior, however defined, is rendered difficult by the analytic problems in elucidating and documenting the structure and functioning of social groups, as opposed to the inventory of the attributes of individuals. This is a particular problem in mainstream social science relying so heavily as it does on survey methodology which is, almost by definition, a polling of individuals. Social interaction is usually measured as an artifact of individual characteristics, behaviors, or attitudes. Consequently, the reconstruction of the dynamics of the social unit becomes a tortuous process, both analytically and practically.

The third major problem in analyzing the interaction between families and public policy in the United States stems from the particular historical connection between the American state and the individual. Explicitly, the commitment of the state is to the individual (see Rice 1977). Any relationship of the state to the family is therefore likely to be implicit, derivative from a commitment to particular individuals, or very weak when brought into conflict with more explicit commitments to particular individuals. A rather telling description of this problem is presented by Girdner (1981) in her analysis of contested child-custody cases in an American court, where a presumed state commitment to the family as a whole must be subdivided into a prioritized inventory of *individual* rights, such as the overarching commitment to the best interests of the child.

Underlying all of these problems is the fact that most of the dialogue on family and public policy has been bounded by the current situation in the United States in which, by a long process of mutual accommodation, existing public plicy on families and the actual situation of families have been brought into some-

thing of a balance. That is, implicit though the process may be, public policies are likely to be somewhat attuned to the needs of those families from which those who make the policy come. Only when there is significant change in the structure of families, as with the increasing number of single-parent households, is the tension between families and public policy brought into relief. Without such change or juxtaposition of differences, the mutual effects between family structure and public policy defy cogent analysis.

The central difficulty, then, in refining the understanding of the interaction of family and public policy is the lack of a clear comparative context through which to assess the fit of family structure with public policy. One solution to the problem is to look for situations in which there has not been a long process of mutual accommodation and in which the structure of kin units, and the goals and process of public policy, remain in contrast. This paper addresses one such situation, that of the half-million refugees who have come to the United States from Southeast Asia during the last seven years. An analysis of their adjustment to the United States serves as a particularly cogent example of the way in which kinship structures can both facilitate and hinder the achievement of policy goals, and how specific policies can both hinder and facilitate the social (and psychological) aspects of refugee adjustment.

The following paper thus has its relevance on two levels. First, it presents an introduction to the importance of kinship in refugee resettlement. Second, it serves as an example of the potential lack of fit between family structure and public policy when a long process of mutual interpenetration of the two has not partially obscured the relationships. The following presents first, a review of the resettlement of Southeast Asian refugees in the United States; second, an overview of the structuring of kinship among the four major components of the refugee population; and third, an analysis of the interaction between kinship and three general policy directions that have characterized federal refugee policy. The subsequent conclusions address both the specific refugee resettlement implications as well as the more general implications for the generic understanding of family and public policy.

Southeast Asian Refugees in the United States

Immediately following the collapse of the American-supported Republic of Vietnam in April, 1975, approximately 130,000 people fled to the United States. The vast majority were Vietnamese, and most spent varying periods of time both overseas and then inside the continental United States, before being resettled into American society.[2]   This initial group of Southeast Asian refugees rapidly attained rates of employment similar to that of the United States population as a whole (Stein 1979; Marsh 1980; Opportunity Systems, Inc. 1977). However, their adjustment was not without problems. Most of the refugees remained significantly underemployed, felt profoundly the lack of family members either lost during the exodus or still remaining in Southeast Asia, and had a variety of cultural adjustment problems that received considerable notice, largely under the mental health rubric.

The succeeding two years brought what, with hindsight, were modest additional flows (14,000 people in 1976; 3,000 in 1977; 20,000 in 1978).[3]   1978, however, saw an increase in refugee flow out of Vietnam, and increasingly from Cambodia and Laos as well. By early 1979, the plight of the so-called boat refugees was drawing increasing public attention, and in June President Carter doubled the authorized monthly entry level into the United States to 14,000. In 1979, 81,000 Southeast Asian refugees entered the United States, and in 1980 the number doubled to 167,000. An additional 130,000 arrived in 1981, giving a total of well over one-half million. The resulting population is far from ethnically homogeneous. While the majority remain Vietnamese, many of these are, in fact, of Chinese origin. There are also increasingly

large numbers of Cambodians (Khmer), lowland Laotians (ethnic Lao), and highland Laotians (largely Hmong).[4]

Southeast Asian refugees, like other immigrants, have a variety of resources and problems that affect the course of their continuing adjustment to the United States. In the aggregate, their occupational qualifications in terms of basic census categories are similar to those of the general United States population, and to those of arriving immigrants in general (Taft, North, and Ford 1979; Opportunity Systems, Inc. 1977, 1981). However, there is often a lack of readily available and relevant employment, and lack of English language competence severely restricts the opportunities for employment that is commensurate with their existing skills.[5]   In recent years, refugees have arrived with a considerable backlog of medical problems that have further hampered the adjustment process (e.g., Center for Disease Control 1980a, 1980b, 1979; Erickson and Hoang 1980; Catanzaro and Moser 1982).

Many of such factors affecting adjustment can be understood as the function of individuals' characteristics. However, Southeast Asian refugees, again like other immigrants, maintain a set of beliefs about social relationships, and a set of actual continuing relationships with particular people. Such beliefs and relationships have direct effects on their subsequent adjustment to the United States. Since the federal government has a mandated role in that adjustment, kinship and public policy become explicitly intertwined.

The Structuring of Kinship in Southeast Asia

The three countries that were brought together during the colonial period as French Indochina all have long and independent histories. Cambodia, Laos, and Vietnam have interacted, as States, for centuries, but their common history has, as often as not, involved adversarial roles. The dominant population in each country is unique.[6]   Each has a distinctively different language, largely different religious patterns, very different colonial experiences under the French,[7]   and a variety of other cultural beliefs and patterns which are not shared. Further, within each of the national groups there are significant minority populations. Various of these, notably the Hmong from highland Laos and ethnic Chinese from Vietnam, are represented among the Southeast Asian refugee population in the United States.

The variation among the Khmer, Lao, Hmong, ethnic Chinese, and Vietnamese is seen not only in history, culture, language, and frequently ecology, but also in the basic structuring of kin relations. The Vietnamese, for example, are patrilineal.[8] While arguments are possible about the origin of patrilineality among the Vietnamese, particularly as to the effects of Chinese influence, there can be no argument about the importance of the patriline in Vietnam, and the way it functions as the basis for the possession and transmission of corporate land administered on behalf of the lineage by senior males within the line. While the lineages lacked the extent of those, for example, in South China they nevertheless had many of the same functions as holders of corporate property.

The Hmong are also patrilineal, but have a far greater extent and structure to the lineages, and also, compared to the Vietnamese, fully operational family alliances and clans (e.g., Geddes 1976; Dunnigan 1980). The Khmer and Lao, on the other hand, have decidedly more bilateral systems, with the lack of any strong lineality, any clear preference for the male side (rather the reverse), or the extensiveness of kin groups that characterize either the Vietnamese or the Hmong. These differences are reflected in the respective kinship terminologies of the four groups, with the Vietnamese and Hmong having classic descriptive (Sudanese) terminologies with their emphasis on distinguishing different kinds of collateral relatives, particularly between relatives on the male and female side.[9] The Khmer, on the other hand, have a bilateral (Eskimo) terminology, as does American society.

The extent of these differences is worth noting, particularly as it relates to the later argument of this paper about ethnic communities. And these differences can be conveyed most simply by comparing the structures of the Vietnamese and Khmer villages described respectively by Hickey (1964) and Ebihara (1964, 1977). In Khanh Hau, the Vietnamese village, the constituent neighborhoods were to a large extent segments of patrilineages comprised of sets of brothers residing as neighbors and cooperating on a regular basis. As children remained with their parents after marriage, a significant proportion of the households were extended. The village as a whole also had a strong kinship basis with its political organization running parallel to the structure of predominant lineages. This joint kinship/political structure was also reflected in religious affiliation. A new sect, for example, typically found adherents among a set of kin.

The Khmer village, on the other hand, had smaller kin groups. Kinship was also limited more exclusively to the household. In both cases, the Khmer are more similar to Americans than to Vietnamese. While a significant number of households were extended, most of these involved residence with the wife's parents (i.e., matrilocal) and there was strong indication of ultimate preference for nuclear households (i.e., neolocal residence). Neighborhoods thus tended to be based on relations of locality, rather than kinship. The cohesion of the village as a whole focussed on the religio-cultural axis of the pagoda. In contradistinction to the Vietnamese village, kinship, religion, and politics were thus not woven together into the fabric of the village.

A brief overview of kinship among the Lao, Khmer, Hmong, and Vietnamese fails to do justice to the complexity or nuances of social relations, but it can serve to indicate both the importance of kinship among these people and the significant variation among them in the structuring of kinship. In the following, Southeast Asian kinship will sometimes be treated as unitary. This is done for the sake of simplicity. However, at other times the variation among the populations will be of particular interest.

Policy Concerns

In adjusting to the United States, all immigrants are likely to make use of the resources of kinship in finding jobs and housing, leveraging salary and wage income into household self-sufficiency, deciding on areas in which to live, and generally implementing effective adaptive strategies toward their new environment. However, the situation of refugees differs in that the federal government continues to be directly involved in these processes, and explicitly committed to their outcomes. Because of this, the interface between kinship and public policy is far more extensive than is the case for other immigrants. The following is a discussion of three general areas of policy concern regarding the adjustment of Southeast Asian refugees and the way they affect, or are contingent on, the kinship structures of these populations. The three areas are, first, the economic adjustment of refugees and their rapid achievement of economic self-sufficiency; second, the geographic and residential distribution of refugees; and third, the general and specific support furnished to refugees by their ethnic communities and organizations.

1. Economic Adjustment. The attainment of economic self-sufficiency is the cornerstone of federal policy vis-a-vis refugees, and is indicated as such in the Refugee Act of 1980. Much of the concern about self-sufficiency has manifested itself in attention to the employment status of refugees. The existing research has consistently noted rapid progress toward employment on the part of Southeast Asian refugees (e.g., Bach and Bach 1980; Opportunity Systems, Inc. 1981; Kim 1980). However, self-sufficiency is not *per se* a function of employment. Rather, employment is an individual matter with considerable influence on a characteristic (self-sufficiency) of a particular social and kin-based group — the household.[10]

A particular kin group, the household, thus appears at the very core of self-sufficiency. And there is reason to believe that the ability of many Southeast Asian households to function as units of production goes beyond the dual wage-earner pattern that increasingly characterizes many mainstream American households. Specifically, for the Vietnamese there is illustrative data about the family as a particularly effective basis for entrepreneurship, and for the Vietnamese and Hmong some indication that the pattern of extended households (including adults other than husband and wife) raises the possibility of triple-wage-earner households (Opportunity Systems, Inc. 1981; Haines, Rutherford, and Thomas 1981).

On the other hand, the size of refugee families and the number of dependent children they include, mean that the household has greater needs than do the smaller households that are characteristic of the general United States population. The use of public assistance is, as the negative face of self-sufficiency, only partially related to the employment or income status of individuals; rather it is the artifact of the social unit that is the household. In either case — as a unit of production for self-sufficiency or a unit of consumption for public assistance — it is the social unit that is the core agent for the policy goal of refugee resettlement. The particular structuring of these kin units is thus at the basis of the entire resettlement effort.

In assessing the interface between kinship and policy concerns about refugee economic adjustment, the implications are both clear and simple. The policy concern, of necessity, entails a clear understanding of the social kin unit through which income will be matched with necessary expenditures.

2. Geographic and Residential Distribution. The second area of continuing policy concern regarding Southeast Asian refugees is their geographic distribution, as well as their residential distribution within particular communities. In 1975 there was an explicit decision on the part of federal officials to disperse refugees throughout the U.S. (Taft, North, and Ford 1979; Tran Tuong Nhu 1976). The decision had much to do with the government's previous experience with Cuban refugees who had been allowed to remain at will in Miami during the early 1960s, and with whom somewhat later efforts at resettlement away from Miami had been, at best, marginally successful.

Despite the policy, however, and despite initial placements that (from a current perspective) do appear dispersed, Southeast Asian refugees almost immediately began a series of continuing internal migrations, typically labelled 'secondary' migration, that show a pronounced shift toward the West and South and toward areas of higher refugee population. About two-fifths of the refugees, for example, now reside in California. And in California, the settlement patterns are far from random, with high concentration, in particular, around the Los Angeles area.

This process of concentration has a number of causes. The search for employment is, with little doubt, a major factor in secondary migration. Climate is undoubtedly also a factor. But underlying and related to both are likely to be the same kind of chain migration processes typical both of other immigrants, and of other internal migrants. While the initial placement of refugees in 1975 was not conditioned by existing ethnic communities — such communities were small and far between — since 1975 there have been both such communities and an increasing number of close relatives for new refugees to join. At present, at least two-thirds of incoming refugees are resettled near anchor relatives. Further, there is no doubt that reunion with relatives is a major factor in further moves once within the United States. Even where moves are ostensibly in search of employment, there are likely to be relatives of some kind at the place of destination. Little data exist to date on the extensiveness of kin reunion as a motivating factor in secondary migration, but it is instructive that surveys of refugees that inventory areas of personal concern find very high concern about missing relatives. One study (Kim 1980) found it to be the most widely shared "very serious" problem, and another (Human Resources Corporation 1979) found it to be the second most serious problem.[11]

In its social dynamics, the initial and subsequent geographical distribution of refugees probably differs little from that of other immigrant groups. Where the difference does lie is in the proactive role of the federal government in forstalling such concentration. Here the interface of kinship and public policy is more problematic than in the issue of economic adjustment. Public policy here goes to some extent against what might be called the natural process of immigrant geographic mobility.

A related policy concern involves the government's desire to avoid real or perceived impact of refugees on the localities in which they settle, or to which they move. This is not precisely the same as a desire to keep refugees more or less dispersed. Specifically, this is because significant impact is not a direct function of numbers. A relatively low number of refugees in a general area may well coalesce into a single housing complex, thus causing virtually no general impact on a community but a very specific and noticeable impact on the neighborhood.

While there are a number of areas in which refugees could conceivably cause significant impact on a locality, it is largely in terms of housing that the impact is noteworthy. This is for three reasons. First, there are simply not that many refugees in the United States to seriously threaten most resources. Refugees, for example, have been over the past years a significant but relatively small segment of total immigration to the United States. Second, refugees, even on the local level, are unlikely to be in direct competition over most kinds of economic resources. Most, at least initially, are moving into the labor market at entry-level jobs which are not in strong demand.[12] Third, refugees do need housing, and the kind of housing they need is in limited supply. This is partially the result of general trends in the housing market but also the result, again, of the effects of kinship.

Whether in New Orleans (e.g., Ward and Gussow 1979; City of New Orleans 1979), Denver (e.g., Afton 1980), or Minneapolis (e.g., Calderon 1981), the pattern appears similar. General demographic trends (the decrease in average household size) or

housing market characteristics (drop in
new starts and conversions to condomin-
iums) have resulted in extremely low
vacancy rates in most large cities. In
many, vacancy rates are now reputedly
below 1 percent. That is, there is very
little rental housing at all, for anybody.
This situation is further exacerbated by
two additional factors. First, the availability of moderately-priced rental housing,
which refugees are likely to need, is likely
to be even more limited. Second, refugee households are large, and the availability of multi-bedroom apartments is
demonstrably an even more limited
resource (see Ragas 1980). Kinship, in the
simple sense of large household size,
militates against the ready availability of
appropriate housing. Refugees must find
either virtually non-existent moderately
priced multi-bedroom apartments, or somewhat smaller apartments where rules about
the number of people in the residence are
either loose or not rigidly enforced. A
further possibility is a housing complex
where relatives can live together and
maintain something of a joint household
even if sectioned off in different apartments (see Thomas 1981 for a parallel
situation in France).

One logical outcome of this process is
that when refugees do find an area which
meets these requirements, they are likely
to move there in considerable numbers.
At such a local level, even a hundred
refugee families would have significant
impact, and possibly come into conflict
with Americans who, for their own reasons,
are also seeking the increasingly rare
resource of affordable housing. In New
Orleans, Vietnamese moved into a traditionally black housing complex, in Denver a Chicano one, and in Minnesota
Hmong moved into public housing previously occupied by Native Americans.

A lack of appropriate and available
housing thus lays the groundwork for
the perception of negative refugee impact
on a community, and consequently contributes to the potential for community
tensions and/or negative public opinion.
A general goal of avoiding real or perceived negative impacts is undermined

by long-standing trends in the housing
market, and exacerbated by the graphic
misfit between residential kin groups
and the buildings that are supposed to
house them.

3. *Ethnic Communities and Organizations.* The final issue of general policy
concern involves the ethnic community.
This comprises two distinct issues. First
is the need of refugees for a network of
social support that has both practical
(emergency aid, access to jobs) and social-psychological (reference group, emotional support) aspects. Second is the
more specific issue of ethnic organizations per se. Numerous of these have been
founded since 1975 (e.g., Bui 1980; Khoa
1980), and their ability to furnish services
to their co-ethnics has been raised as an
important alternative in facilitating the
resettlement process. These two ethnic
community issues are relatively distinct
from each other, but the importance of
kinship is pervasive for both.

The importance of the ethnic community as a general support network is the
easier side of the issue. If the function of
the community is to furnish help in times
of need, then the core of that community
is likely to involve kin, for whom obligations to aid will be more axiomatic. If
the purpose of such a community is to furnish emotional support, or to provide a
supportive environment in which a
reconciliation of the old and the new can
take place, again the core kin network —
what in the United States would automatically be called the family — is also likely
to be of paramount importance. However, the way in which the group provides
this support, and its internal functioning,
is likely to vary significantly among the
Khmer, Lao, Hmong, and Vietnamese. As
indicated earlier, the extent of relevant kin
is likely to be greater for the Hmong and
Vietnamese, and the people deemed appropriate to give advice and aid will also
vary. Siblings, for example, will have particular importance among Vietnamese (e.g.,
Haines, Rutherford, and Thomas 1981),
while brothers-in-law may be of crucial
importance for the Lao or Khmer.

The second side of the ethnic community issue involves more formal com-

munity organizations. Here, the central question involves the extent of kin relations, and the degree to which kinship is coterminous with the community. Ethnic organizations are likely to have particular characteristics that depend on the ethnicity of those involved. For the Hmong, as noted, kinship extends from the household to the lineage, family alliance, and clan. For the Khmer, kinship is more limited to the nuclear family itself, and community has its own separate existence based more on a general cultural consensus, and more on ties of locality. Thus both Khmer and Hmong may belong, with high frequency, to ethnic organizations (e.g., Kim 1980). However, the organizations have a totally different structural basis. Ultimately, ethnic organizations are an aspect of kinship for the Hmong, while for the Khmer they are not (though particular kin links may be important within the organization).

Neither the issue of ethnic communities as support networks nor ethnic communities as actual organizations is a simple one. Yet even a rudimentary look at the issue, and the background of the particular refugee groups involved, indicates the pervasive importance of kinship. While the self-sufficiency example indicates the importance of household structure, the dispersion example indicates the general importance of kin, the impact/housing example indicates more fully the importance of household structure, the ethnic-community issue raises more complex, and fine-grained, questions about the interactions of a far wider group of kin than typically receive attention in the United States. It is this final issue, more than the others, which raises questions about the particularities of specific kinship systems, rather than the general importance of kinship which might be assumed to only vary slightly between different societies.

Conclusions

The discussion in this paper is meant to demonstrate the general ways in which kinship among Southeast Asian refugees to the United States is inevitably wound into central policy concerns of the federal government. The precise implications of the examples vary. In one case (achieving self-sufficiency), there is a potential match between the policy goal and the relevant kin unit. In another case (dispersing refugees), kinship and public policy tend to be at odds. The issue of local impact raises both general questions about families and housing that have relevance to other sectors of American society (cf. U.S. Department of Housing and Urban Development 1980), and more specific questions about the structure and functioning of refugee families, and their consequent need for particular kinds of physical structures in which to live. Finally, as indicated, the ethnic community example stresses the need for more fine-grained analysis of the specifics of Vietnamese, Khmer, Lao, and Hmong kinship.

While this discussion of the pervasive importance of kinship for the entire process of refugee resettlement has relevance for the specific policy concerns of those dealing with refugees, it also has wider relevance. For those dealing with the more generic issue of family and public policy, this paper has presented additional examples of the implicit (and sometimes unexamined) nature of public policy toward some families, has indicated the internally contradictory nature of some of these implicit goals — as in the goals of dispersing and fostering ethnic communities — and, most importantly, is a reminder of what the American situation looks like when confronted with a different kinship system.

NOTES

[1] The views expressed are solely those of the author and do not necessarily reflect those of the federal government.

[2] There are a number of books and articles relating to the initial 1975 influx of Southeast Asian refugees. Kelly (1978) presents a compelling account of the exodus, and some interesting observations on one of the resettlement camps in the United States. Liu, Lamanna, and Murata (1979) present more aggregate type of information covering the same period. Justus (1976) indicates some of the problems with the aggregate-data approach, based on anthropological research in a refugee camp.

[3] The actual number of entries per year is as follows:

1975	—	130,394
1976	—	14,466
1977	—	2,563
1978	—	20,397
1979	—	80,678
1980	—	166,727
1981	—	132,447

All these numbers refer to fiscal years, and the figure for 1976 includes the transition quarter.

[4] Exact figures on breakdown by ethnicity are not available. Compilation of the 1980 Alien Address Report indicates that of the total population at that time about 79 percent were Vietnamese, 6 percent Khmer, and 16 percent Laotian (including both ethnic Lao and Hmong). The proportions of Laotian and Cambodian have risen since that time. The number of ethnic Chinese is far more difficult to estimate, since they are not indicated in any way on the major data files compiled by the federal government.

[5] There have been suggestions about the decline in the occupational levels of refugees over time. This would not be surprising. However, it should be cautioned that general surveys (e.g., Opportunity Systems, Inc. 1981) continue to show high occupational levels in country of origin despite the increasing number of recent arrivals who are included in such surveys. It should also be cautioned that the high percentage of recent arrivals who are joining relatives does not support assertions that more recent refugees are profoundly different in terms of general background than earlier arrivals.

[6] Despite the long, and expensive, American involvement in Southeast Asia, there has been very little basic social research. Had Hickey not done his work on Khanh Hau (1964) there would be virtually no baseline study for Vietnam. For Cambodia, there is a similar heavy reliance on Ebihara's (1964, 1977) work. It is quite possible that the Hmong are, from a social/cultrual point of view, the best studied of the refugee groups in country of origin.

[7] Cambodia, Laos, and Vietnam were not even united administratively under the French. French Indochina was, in fact, five more-or-less separate units comprised of Laos, Cambodia, Tonkin (north Vietnam), Annam (central Vietnam), and Cochinchina (south Vietnam). Not all five of the units were administered in the same way. Cochinchina, in particular, bore the brunt of direct administration by the French.

[8] It is important to stress, since there has been some confusion about this in regard to Vietnam in particular, that patriliny does not mean patriarchy. Both Hickey (1964) and Hoskins (1975) are quite clear on the autonomy and economic participation of Vietnamese women.

[9] For the present purposes, it is not necessary to specify precisely the relationship between the terminology and the relations of kinship. It is sufficient to suggest that they are likely to be consistent. For a more detailed discussion of Vietnamese kinship terminology see Haines (1980).

[10] The importance of the household as the vehicle for the achievement of self-sufficiency is underscored by research on the Cubans, who remain the largest group of refugees absorbed into the United States. The potential parallels are instructive. Analysis of 1970 Census data (Urban Associates, Inc. 1974) indicates three unique aspects to the Cuban-American population at that time. First, Cuban males had the highest labor-force participation rates of any identified ethnic group in the 1970 Census. Second, Cuban females had a rate of labor-force participation a full ten points above the average for the entire United States population. Third, Cuban-Americans had a high rate of intact marriages. The net result is that Cubans in the U.S., despite low income levels as individuals were demonstrably the most successful of Hispanic groups in economic terms as households (c.f. Prohias and Casal 1973). There are some interesting parallels in the analysis of women's roles among Cuban and Vietnamese refugees. For example, in both cases women appear to be very active economically but also maintain a ritually somewhat subordinant position within the household (e.g., Hoskins 1975; cf. Boone 1980, 1981; Ferree 1979).

[11] It is particularly interesting that in the two surveys cited, service providers were also interviewed about refugee needs and in both cases did not consider that the absence of family members was a serious problem. This was virtually the only area in which the prioritizing of problems by refugees and by service providers was divergent in more than a minimal way.

[12] The major case in which tensions have risen on directly economic grounds involves the fishery industry along the Texas Gulf Coast and eastward to Florida. It is a unique situation and, ironically, a tribute to the success and ingenuity of the fishermen (see Starr 1981; Chakroff and Mitchell 1979).

REFERENCES CITED

AFTON, JEAN
    1980 — Vietnamese immigrants in Denver: two seasons of fieldwork in Sun Valley. *In* Processes of Transition: Vietnamese in Colorado. P. Van Arsdale and J. Pisarowicz, eds. Austin, Texas: High Street Press, pp. 53-62.
BACH, ROBERT L., and JENNIFER B. BACH
    1980— Employment patterns of Southeast Asian refugees. Monthly Labor Review 103 (10): 31-38.
BANE, MARY JO
    1976 — Here to stay: American families in the twentieth century. New York: Basic Books.
BLEHAR, MARY C.
    1979 — Families and public policy. *In* Families Today: A Research Sampler on Families and Children. Eunice Corfman, ed. Washington, D.C.: U.S. Government Printing Office, pp. 971-989.
BOONE, MARGARET S.
    1980 — The uses of traditional concepts in the development of new urban roles: Cuban women in the United States. *In* A World of Women. Erika Bourguignon, ed. New York: Praeger, pp. 235-269.
    1981 — The social structure of a low-density cultural group: Cubans in Washington, D.C. Anthropological Quarterly 54(2): 103-109.
BUI, DIANA
    1980 — The Indochinese mutual assistance associations. Washington, D.C.: Indochina Refugee Action Center.
CALDERON, EDDIE
    1981 — The impact of Hmong refugees in Phillips and Elliot Park, Minneapolis. Paper presented at the Hmong Research Conference, University of Minnesota, October 1981.
CATAZARO, ANTONIO, and ROBERT JOHN MOSER
    1982 — Health status of refugees from Vietnam, Laos, and Cambodia. Journal of the American Medical Association 29 (32): 1303-1308.
CENTER FOR DISEASE CONTROL
    1979 — Health status of Indochinese refugees: malaria and hepatitis B. Morbidity and Mortality Weekly Report 28 (39): 463-464, 469-470.
    1980a — Health screening of resettled Indochinese refugees — Washington, D.C., Utah. Morbidity and Mortality Weekly Report 29 (1): 4,9-11.
    1980b — Tuberculosis among Indochinese refugees — United States, 1979. Morbidity and Mortality Weekly Report 29 (32): 383-384, 389-390.
CHAKROFF, PAUL, and LOUIS L. MITCHELL
    1979 — New economic and social opportunities for Americans and Indochinese on the Texas gulf coast. Washington, D.C.: TransCentury Foundation.
CITY OF NEW ORLEANS
    1979 — Impact analysis of Indo-Chinese resettlement in the New Orleans metropolitan area: a task force report. New Orleans: Mayor's Office of Policy Planning.
DUNNIGAN, TIMOTHY
    1980 — The importance of kinship in Hmong community development. Paper presented at the annual meetings of the American Anthropological Association, Washington, D.C.
EBIHARA, MAY
    1964 — The Khmer. *In* Ethnic Groups of Mainland Southeast Asia. Frank LeBar, Gerald Hickey, and John Musgrave, eds. New Haven: Human Relations Area Files Press, pp. 98-105.
    1977 — Residence patterns in a Khmer peasant village. Annals of the New York Academy of Sciences 293:51-68.
ERICKSON, ROY V., and GIAO HOANG
    1980 — Health problems among Indochinese refugees: results of 194 comprehensive evaluations. Paper presented at the First National Conference on Indochinese Education and Social Services, Arlington, Virginia.
FERREE, MYRA MARX
    1979 — Employment without liberation: Cuban women in the United States. Social Science Quarterly 60:35-50.
GEDDES, WILLIAM R.
    1976 — Migrants of the mountains. Oxford: Clarendon Press.
GILBERT, NEIL
    1979 — An initial agenda for family policy. Social Work 24:447-450.

GIRDNER, LINDA
    1981 — Contested child custody cases. Doctoral dissertation. The American University, Washington,
          D.C.
GREENE, JANE G., and GLENDA P. BLAKE
    1980 — How restrictive rental practices affect families with children. Washington, D.C.: U.S. Govern-
          ment Printing Office.
HAINES, DAVID
    1980 — The structuring of kinship in Vietnam: implications for refugee adaptation. Paper presented at
          the annual meetings of the Society for Applied Anthropology, Denver, Colorado.
HAINES, DAVID, DOROTHY RUTHERFORD, and PATRICK THOMAS
    1981 — Family and community among Vietnamese refugees. International Migration Review
          15:310-319.
HICKEY, GERALD C.
    1964 — Village in Vietnam. New Haven: Yale University Press.
HOSKINS, MARILYN
    1975 — Vietnamese women: their roles and their options. In Being female. Dana Raphael, ed. The Hague:
          Mouton, pp. 127-146.
HUMAN RESOURCES CORPORATION
    1979 — Evaluation of the Indochinese refugee assistance program in private agencies in California. San
          Francisco, California.
JUSTUS, JOYCE BENNETT
    1976 — Processing Indochinese refugees. In Exploratory fieldwork on Latino migrants and Indochinese
          refugees. Roy S. Bryce-Laporte and Stephen R. Couch, eds. Washington, D.C.: Smithsonian,
          pp. 76-100.
KAMERMAN, SHELIA B., and ALFRED J. KAHN
    1976 — Explorations in family policy. Social Work 21:181-186.
KELLY, GAIL PARADISE
    1977 — From Vietnam to America: A chronicle of the Vietnamese immigration to the United States.
          Boulder, Colorado: Westview Press.
KIM, YOUNG YUN
    1980 — Population characteristics and service needs of Indochinese refugees. Volume 3 of the Research
          Project on Indochinese Refugees in the State of Illinois. Chicago: Travelers Aid Society of Metro-
          politan Chicago.
KINCH, ROBERT, ed.
    1979 — Strengthening families through informal support systems: a Wingspread report. Racine, Wis-
          consin: Johnson Foundation.
LASCH, CHRISTOPHER
    1977 — Haven in a heartless world: the family besieged. New York: Basic Books.
LE XUAN KHOA
    1980 — Indochinese mutual assistance organizations as mechanisms in community mental health. Paper
          presented at the National Conference on Social Welfare, Cleveland, Ohio.
LIU, WILLIAM, MARYANNE LAMANNA, and ALICE MURATA
    1979 — Transition to nowhere: Vietnamese refugees in America. Nashville: Charter House.
MARANS, ROBERT W., and MARY ELLEN COLTEN
    1980 — Measuring restrictive rental practices affecting families with children: a national survey. Wash-
          ington, D.C.: U.S. Government Printing Office.
MARSH, ROBERT E.
    1980 — Socioeconomic status of Indochinese refugees in the United States: progress and problems.
          Social Security Bulletin 43 (10): 11-20.
MASNICK, GEORGE, and MARY JO BANE
    1980 — The nation's families: 1960-1990. Cambridge, Massachusetts: Joint Center for Urban Studies.
McDONALD, GERALD W.
    1979 — Family well-being and quality of life: humanistic concerns of the family impact analyst. Family
          Coordinator 28:313-320.
OPPORTUNITY SYSTEMS, INC.
    1977 — Fifth wave report: Vietnamese resettlement operational feedback. Washington, D.C.
    1981 — Ninth wave report: Indochinese resettlement operational feedback. Washington, D.C.

PROHIAS, RAFAEL, and LOURDES CASAL
1973 — The Cuban minority in the U.S.: preliminary report on need identification and program evaluation. Boca Raton, Florida: Florida Atlantic University.
RAGAS, WADE R.
1980 — Housing the refugees: impact and partial solutions to the housing shortages. Journal of Refugee Resettlement 1:40-48.
RICE, ROBERT M.
1977 — American family policy: content and context. New York: Family Service Association of America.
SARAN, PARMATMA, and EDWIN EAMES
1980 — The new ethnics: Asian Indians in the United States. New York: Praeger.
STARR, PAUL D.
1981 — Troubled waters. International Migration Review 15:226-238.
STEIN, BARRY N.
1979 — Occupational adjustment of refugees: the Vietnamese in the United States. International Migration Review 13(1):25-45.
TAFT, JULIA, DAVID NORTH, and DAVID FORD
1979 — Refugee resettlement in the U.S.: time for a new focus. Washington, D.C.: New TransCentury Foundation.
THOMAS, PATRICK
1981 — Indochinese refugees in France and the U.S. Journal of Refugee Resettlement 1 (4): 15-21.
TRAN TUONG NHU
1976 — Vietnam refugees: the trauma of exile. Civil Rights Digest 9 (1): 59-62.
URBAN ASSOCIATES, INC.
1974 — A study of selected socio-economic characteristics of ethnic minorities based on the 1970 Census, volume 1: Americans of Spanish origin. U.S. Department of Health, Education, and Welfare, Office of the Assistant Secretary for Planning and Evaluation, Washington, D.C.
U.S. DEPARTMENT OF HOUSING AND URBAN DEVELOPMENT
1980 — How well are we housed: large households. Washington,D.C.
WARD, MARTHA, and ZACHARY GUSSOW
1979 — Coping and adaptation: community response and the New Orleans Vietnamese. Paper presented at the conference on Indochinese Refugees, George Mason University, Fairfax, Virginia
WHITE HOUSE CONFERENCE ON FAMILIES
1980 — Listening to America's families: action for the 80's. Washington, D.C.

KENNETH A. SKINNER is an Assistant Professor of Anthropology at Widener College in Chester, Pennsylvania. Besides having conducted research among Indochinese in the United States, he has studied career paths and interpersonal conflict in a government bureaucracy in Japan.

VIETNAMESE IN AMERICA: DIVERSITY IN ADAPTATION

KENNETH A. SKINNER

INTRODUCTION

The thrust of Vietnamese presence in the United States dates from 1975. During the ensuing years Vietnamese have come to share membership in certain social categories spawned by their new socio-economic situation and residence. While they have language and former citizenship in South Vietnam in common, their diverse backgrounds mean that among themselves they share very little else. Suddenly Vietnamese found themselves classed together as "refugees," having shared the experience of exiling themselves from their homeland. For most, viewing themselves as "refugees" was disquieting, and the attributes of refugee status, notably being indigent and powerless, were incompatible with self-images largely derived from middle- and upper-class social positions in Vietnam.

As years pass and the Vietnamese become more incorporated into U.S. society, a new social category is supplanting that of "refugees." On the assumption that the Vietnamese will become U. S. citizens, they are increasingly being referred to as "Vietnamese-Americans." As in the case of the category "refugees," this classification, like most social categories, does not reflect the social and economic diversity among the people included.

Much of the diversity among Vietnamese in the United States stems from their backgrounds in Vietnam, such as differences in social status, occupation, wealth, religion, political orientation, education, and region of origin. During their residence in the United States, other differences have emerged. New status distinctions are being forged, involving differences in economic well-being, educational attainments, adaptations to U. S. society, and notions about self-identity. The diversity argues against associating behavioral and socioeconomic attributes with a social category based wholly on country of origin. That the Vietnamese are all "refugees" does not render these differences insignificant.

Moreover, "Vietnamese-American" is not a category which the Vietnamese as yet have adopted for themselves, but is being applied by institutions of U.S. society. The category carries with it another classification, that of ethnic minority status. Designation as an ethnic group can simply mark social and cultural boundaries of a segment of a population. Ethnic minority status, however, can also evoke stereotypical notions about a people's social position and behavior. Unfortunately, in many people's minds ethnic minority status connotes lower socioeconomic position, difficulties in functioning in society, and below average learning and achievement potentials. Abundant evidence to the contrary is only slowly moderating such views. While the classification is useful to institutions providing services to targeted clientele, we should recognize that it is likely to have an effect on how Vietnamese progress in their adaptation, as well as on the development of their own and others' notions about who they are and how they can relate to the society of which they are now part.

This article presents selected data on the history of the Vietnamese presence in the United States and on significant social factors affecting their adaptation. The diversity in Vietnamese demographic characteristics and patterns of adaptation is emphasized, and this provides a context for understanding the implications of an emerging social classification in ethnic terms. Data are drawn from two sources: first, extensive interviews conducted by the author among Vietnamese and Americans assisting the refugees in Minneapolis/St. Paul in 1977 and in Iowa in 1979; and second, published results of other recent research.

Arrival of the Vietnamese

Prior to 1975 only about 15,000 Vietnamese were residing in the United States. Most of these individuals were wives of U.S. servicemen or students/trainees on visas allowing temporary stays. With the collapse of the government of South Vietnam in April 1975, thousands of people fled their homeland. Concurrently, many Laotians and Cambodians left as their governments changed hands. The Vietnamese generally fled out to sea, not having frontiers allowing passage into Thailand. Vietnamese also had greater access to U.S. military and civilian transports than did their Laotian and Cambodian neighbors (cf. Kelly, 1977; Liu, 1979; Snepp, 1977). As a consequence a larger proportion of the Vietnamese exiles, estimated at 135,000, ended up in the United States during that year.

William Liu (1979) has provided extensive documentation of the reasons Vietnamese give for having left their homeland. The fear among military personnel, civil servants, employees of U.S. installations, and

Catholics that the new government would exact reprisals was a major reason. This was often combined with recognition that middle- and upper-class lifestyles could not be maintained under a new regime. With the rapid advance of enemy troops, many other people simply felt that the situation had deteriorated to such an extent that concern for physical safety made escape necessary. Most of these people expected to be able to return after a brief period during which the communists would be routed by American and South Vietnamese forces. A number of young military men found themselves unwillingly headed out to sea aboard boats commanded by officers who had decided to flee. In other cases, individuals having close relationships with Americans decided to take advantage of the chance to gain entry to the United States. Motivations for people's departures, as well as awareness that their act could result in permanent exile, were certainly not uniform among those who eventually arrived in the United States. As is true for most previous cases of largescale exodus connected with political change, application of the term "refugee" masks the diverse motives and events which contributed to people finding themselves exiled from their homelands (cf. Ex, 1966; Fagen et al., 1968).

Descriptive information about the 1975 arrivals reveals further diversity. Although the majority of household heads were in white-collar jobs in Vietnam (Liu, 1979:50), pre-evacuation occupations represent a broad spectrum, including military personnel, civil servants, businessmen, transportation workers, teachers, farmers, and fishermen. Educational backgrounds reflect a similar range, with highest educational levels among household heads being university or post-graduate for over one-quarter, secondary school for about half, and elementary school or none for slightly less than one-quarter (Task Force for Indochina Refugees, 1977:28). Because city dwellers had greater access to means of escape than did rural residents, people from Vietnam's urban areas, primarily Saigon, constitute a majority of the 1975 evacuees. Nearly half of the household heads were born in the northern part of Vietnam and had fled south after the 1954 defeat of the French (Liu, 1979:58). Catholicism is the preferred religion of about half of the evacuees, while adherents in South Vietnam did not exceed ten percent of the population (Rahe et al., 1978:188). Other religious orientations include Buddhist, Confucian, Protestant, and animist. While the number of extended family groups who were able to leave Vietnam is quite high, with sixty-two percent arriving in family units of five persons or more (Montero, 1979:24), a sizable number of individuals, especially young men, arrived unaccompanied by family members. Extremes of wealth are represented among the emigres, with some people being able to bring out suitcases of gold and U.S. dollars while others left with little more than the clothes they were wearing. As might be expected from the differing occupational and religious backgrounds, political orientations vary. For example, there are fervent anti-communists, religious conservatives, liberal intellectuals, and apolitical farmers.

Following the first wave of evacuees in 1975, many more Vietnamese, as well as smaller numbers of Laotians and Cambodians, arrived in the United States, bringing the total Indochinese refugee population above 240,000. While some of the post-1975 exiles left Vietnam for reasons similar to those of their predecessors, events in Vietnam and actions by recipient countries have served to add new motivations to the already diverse collection. Since 1975, Vietnam has experienced a succession of poor harvests, inability to replace lost capital equipment, denials of foreign markets and suppliers, and economic drain from continued military activity in Laos, Cambodia, and against the Chinese incursion (cr. Chanda 1979, Luce 1979). Loss of sources of livelihood, inability to continue in desired occupations, and poor economic conditions in Vietnam have contributed to decisions to flee. Most sought entrance to the United States, which has always been first choice for country of resettlement among Vietnamese in camps in Malaysia, Thailand, and Hong Kong (Weintraub, 1978; Kamm, 1977). Many decisions to leave were influenced by an awareness, gained from Voice of America broadcasts and letters from relatives who had left earlier, that the United States gives priority to reuniting family members and admitting former employees of U.S. government installations. The number of people leaving increased dramatically after 1977 as the result of internal events in Vietnam. Within the context of worsening relations between Vietnam and China, many of the assets of Vietnam's ethnic Chinese population, whose loyalties were suspect, were expropriated by the government. Another factor was the fear, or experience of being sent to re-education centers or rural work camps designed to re-establish agricultural production and drain off the excess urban population caused by the war. The tragic odysseys by boat in search of asylum captured the attention of the world.

The characteristics of recent arrivals add to the diversity among the Vietnamese population. Not only is a larger proportion ethnic Chinese, but indications are that people from lower socioeconomic levels and rural areas are represented in larger numbers (Rule, 1978; Weintraub, 1978). While many of the 1975 evacuees are highly educated and speak English or French, this is much less true of recent departees (Kamm, 1978; Roberts, 1978). Resettlement workers have expressed concern that these different characteristics may make adjustment more difficult for recent arrivals than it was for their predecessors. Some observers, however, suggest that the experiences in post-1975 Vietnam and during flight may have conditioned a greater willingness to make major changes in lifestyle and to accept a lower standard of living.

DIVERSITY IN ADAPTATION
Adapting to U.S. Society

The ability of the Vietnamese to adapt to United States society, of course, has been given much attention (e.g., Montero, 1979; Pisarowics, 1977; Starr et al., 1979; Stein, 1979; Vignes and Hall, 1979). In the activities of public and private institutions which have been assisting the Vietnamese, both explicit and implicit notions about what constitutes successful adaptation can be identified. Federal allocations for resettlement and monies contributed by Americans acting as sponsors have been aimed specifically at assisting people to become financially self-sufficient through the acquisition of language and work skills which will lead to employment (cf. Department of State, 1975). Federal funds have gone largely into occupational re-training programs, English language classes, and reimbursements to states for public assistance monies provided refugees.

Those who have aided the Indochinese have assumed that a certain amount of assimilation of American ways of doing things is necessary as a means for achieving financial self-sufficiency. Besides learning English, adoption of other behavioral and cognitive patterns were considered important in the development of an ability to manage in U.S. society. According to Gail Paradeise Kelly (1977), efforts to impose, whether conscious or unconscious, American norms began in the transit camps shortly after the Vietnamese arrived in this country. She cites language classes and camp newspapers in which American customs, including norms for relationships among family members, were presented as patterns to emulate. American behavioral patterns were presented not merely as things Americans did but as "things people who lived in America did" (Kelly, 1977:124). The assumption that Vietnamese should adopt American ways has even been incorporated in measures of successful adjustment, as evidenced by the conclusion of psychiatrists A. Joe Vignes and Richard C. W. Hall (1979:444) that Vietnamese have adjusted successfully partly because they "have accepted American social norms." Following stays in the transit camps, Vietnamese were placed with sponsors in communities throughout the United States. People who found themselves in communities where they were the only Vietnamese family were immediately confronted with the need to interact with their American hosts. Successful interaction often required not only an understanding of American patterns of behavior

211

but also adjustments in Vietnamese behavior. In well-meaning efforts to assist their charges, sponsors often encouraged behavior which conformed to American patterns and discouraged behavior which appeared strange in American eyes (cf. Conrad, 1979; Skinner and Hendricks, 1977). While the extent to which dispersal contributed to the adoption of American patterns of behavior and norms cannot be documented, the policy reflects an assumption that such behavioral and cognitive changes are unavoidable. Unlike the experiences of many other immigrants, there were few concentrations of Vietnamese already in the U.S. in which people could continue to perform occupational and social roles similar to those they were accustomed to in Vietnam.

While policies, programs, and actions by government agencies and sponsoring groups were not always overt attempts to encourage assimilation of American patterns, the "folk image" of the United States as a "melting pot" of many nationalities and races conditioned a belief that a certain amount of such assimilation was both acceptable and desirable in order to achieve financial self-sufficiency. This view was maintained despite a social climate different from that which existed when previous immigrants arrived. The civil rights movement and its offshoots during the 1960's have produced greater tolerance of ethnic diversity and less insistence on immigrants conforming to "Anglo culture" (cf. Schemerhorn, 1974). Both government agencies and the media have heralded people's rights to maintain cultural distinctiveness. The exigencies of providing economic, occupational, and educational opportunities for the refugees, however, seem to have made concern for allowing Vietnamese to maintain their own cultural patterns a secondary consideration for those devising assistance programs (cf. Liu and Muratta, 1978; Tran M.T., 1976; Tran T. N., 1976).

Most assessments of how the Vietnamese have adapted look at employment rates and average salaries, reflecting an assumption that occupational and economic adjustment tends to lead to socio-cultural adjustment. For example, surveys reported by Darrel Montero (1979:42-55) indicate that by October 1977 ninety-three percent of all refugees sixteen years and older were employed. Over eighty percent were working forty or more hours per week, and the average annual income of Indochinese households in 1977 was more than $9,600. Among former white-collar workers and military personnel there has been considerable downward occupational mobility, while blue-collar workers have been relatively successful in translating their skills to jobs in the United States. Less than ten percent of total household income came from public assistance, though nearly one-third of all households received some form of public assistance. Montero also reports that poor English language abilities have not prevented Vietnamese from securing employment, with almost nine out of ten who understand no English at all being employed.

Lower percentages of Indochinese labor force participation appear in reports based on smaller samples than the surveys presented by Montero (e.g., Social Security Administration, 1979; Starr et al., 1979). His data, therefore, seem to be slightly inflated. Perhaps this is the result of conducting the surveys by telephone, since people having telephones are more likely to be employed than those who do not. Also, Montero's data do not reveal whether employment was temporary, and significant numbers of Indochinese have only been able to secure employment for short periods.

It is not surprising that many people have been unable to transfer their social and occupational statuses in Vietnam to their situations in the United States. As a consequence the pre-evacuation status hierarchy has been severely disrupted. While many people have resigned themselves to loss of status, others have found the loss emotionally trying. Additional sources of emotional problems include homesickness, depression, and feelings of guilt for having left relatives in Vietnam (cf. Lie, 1978; Liu and Muratta, 1978; Nguyen, 1979; Slote, 1977; Social Security Administration, 1979). Psychiatrists Vignes and Hall (1979:443) conclude from their studies, however, that the refugees' "treated incidence and prevalence of major psychiatric disorders was no higher than for the population at large." Other mental health professionals, such as Nahan Nguyen (1979), suggest that the extent of emotional problems may be hidden because of the traditional practice of handling them in a family context rather than seeking professional help.

Employment data also reveal a wide range of economic situations among the Vietnamese, with relatively wealthy doctors and businessmen at one extreme and fishermen, janitors, and assembly line workers perhaps at the other. Evidence of the variety of economic situations, however, has not prevented the emergence of certain stereotypes of Vietnamese employment. Ironically, what may be the most alarming stereotype has been promoted by many of the people who are encouraging further admissions of Indochinese. In trying to counteract concerns that refugees will take Americans' jobs or become dependent on public assistance, advocates have argued that the Vietnamese have shown a willingness to accept the low-paying jobs most Americans do not want (cf. Committee on Human Resources, 1978:10; Cooney, 1979). The danger exists, of course, that the young generation of Vietnamese may have to fight being relegated to jobs at the lower end of the occupational spectrum and may even have their career aspirations thwarted. Research by Kenneth Skinner and Glenn

Hendricks (1977), for instance, suggested high career goals among the 200 Vietnamese students at the University of Minnesota in 1977. When asked to state desired career field, thirty-seven percent indicated engineering, eighteen percent health care, sixteen percent business, and eight percent computer science. Many Vietnamese parents, as Barry Stein (1979:35) points out, view their exodus as having been "for the children's futures" and have accepted the prospect that their own generation may be able to achieve only low-level jobs. Parents' efforts to provide educational and career opportunities for their children reveal that such resignation should not be interpreted as an acceptance that their low occupational standings will be transferred to the younger generation. The large number of young Vietnamese enrolled in post-secondary education is an indication of parents' expectations that their children will compete for high status jobs. For example, in Minnesota in 1977 over one-third of the Vietnamese between the ages of eighteen and twenty-four were enrolled in a college or university. Despite parents' low incomes and use of public assistance, significant amounts of family resources are being allocated for educational expenses.

While career aspirations provide some indication of what Vietnamese seek in their adaptation to U.S. society, we in fact do not have much information about what kinds of adaptations the Vietnamese want or would find acceptable. It is not known to what extent they wish to adopt American cultural and behavioral patterns. What aspects of Vietnamese culture do they wish to preserve and pass on to future generations? The diversity among the Vietnamese suggests that expected and/or desired adaptations vary to as great an extent as do occupational statuses, pre-evacuation social positions, and political orientations. Variations in willingness to assimilate, desire to achieve self-sufficiency, and need for association with fellow nationals are already in evidence. Changes seem to be occurring in sex roles and family roles, but little systematic research is available to indicate their extent. Vignes and Hall (1979:444) claim that Vietnamese wives are attracted to the greater "freedom" of American women, a prospect which distresses Vietnamese men. There have also been reports of Vietnamese parents expressing misgivings about children's adoption of the values and interests of American teenagers (Ha, 1979; Social Security Administration, 1979). In some families the father's inability to regain a previous occupational status has diminished his authority, while in other cases respect for familial norms has been maintained to the extent that children refuse offers of high-paying jobs until their fathers have secured respectable positions (Skinner and Hendricks, 1977). In the area of religious orientation, there is evidence both of

214

willingness to change, often taking the form of conversions to Christianity (Paine, 1977), and of desires to maintain traditional practices, as seen in efforts to establish Buddhist temples. How much cultural change occurs may be related to Vietnamese hopes and expectations of eventually returning to Vietnam, but we do not know what proportion of the population anticipates repatriation. An early survey indicated that forty-one percent of a sample of household heads said they planned to return to Vietnam to live (Norris and Dittemore, 1977), but no recent data are available to confirm an expected percentage decrease with time.

Internal Migration, Enclaves, and Conflicts

What positions in U.S. society individuals or the Vietnamese as a population will achieve remains to be seen. Their experiences during the past five years, however, reveal factors which have affected and will continue to affect their incorporation into U.S. society. These include 1) the geographic dispersal and subsequent internal migration, 2) conflict within the Vietnamese population, 3) federal programs to assist the refugees, 4) incidents of conflict between Vietnamese and U.S. nationals, and 5) the classification of the Vietnamese as an ethnic minority. By looking at these factors consideration of Vietnamese adaptation is moved beyond a focus on economic/occupational achievements and frequencies of emotional problems. Since these factors affect individual Vietnamese in different ways, giving attention to them contributes to a recognition that the present diversity in the Vietnamese situation is likely to extend into the future.

When the Indochinese began arriving, federal resettlement planners made the policy decision to disperse people thoughout the nation, rather than allowing them to concentrate in a few areas. Resettlement planners were responding to fears that a large influx of refugees in an area would exacerbate unemployment by taking jobs from Americans. A number of individuals and service groups recommended that the exiles be allowed the option of forming their own communities (Chau, 1975; Le, 1975). Federal officials ignored such recommendations, setting a pattern for later policy decisions in which political expedience and institutional convenience often took precedence over considerations of possible social and psychological consequences for the Indochinese (cf. Liu, 1979:153-172). Refugees were placed with individuals and organizations willing to act as sponsors. With the assistance of voluntary agencies having experience in resettlement activities, sponsors were expected to provide food, clothing, shelter, and assistance in finding employment during the initial months of adjustment. Geographically, these placements ranged from large cities

215

where Vietnamese could maintain contact with fellow nationals to small towns where a family was isolated.

Within a few months of being placed with sponsors, Vietnamese began moving away. By 1978 about half had moved from their original locations (Social Security Administration, 1978). This internal migration took two forms: movement from rural areas to cities and movement to states such as California, Texas, and Louisiana. In both cases people were seeking proximity to relatives and friends, though people also moved to states perceived as offering better job opportunities or higher levels of public assistance (cf. Hung, 1978; Montero, 1979; Stopp, 1978; Taft et al., 1979). California had about twenty percent of the Indochinese population in 1975, but by 1980 over forty percent (99,000) resided there (Pierce, 1980). While decisions to migrate and form ethnic enclaves were rational from the Vietnamese standpoint, one result has been that Americans in many communities have essentially lost interest in what happens to the Vietnamese. Since sponsors' help frequently did not result in their Vietnamese charges deciding to settle in a community, a certain amount of disillusionment has developed among Americans who had welcomed the refugees out of humanitarian sentiments (cf. Tielebein, 1979). In some instances abrupt departures were interpreted by sponsors as ingratitude. Disillusionment also set in as some sponsors became aware that they and their charges had dissimilar views about how refugees should act. Those sponsors who assumed that refugees should accept jobs at subsistence-level salaries and restrict purchases of "unnecessary" consumer items failed to appreciate the desire of many Vietnamese to regain lost status, a desire which frequently resulted in Vietnamese making demands for financial support which sponsors viewed as unreasonable (cf. Bache, 1978; Conrad, 1979). In contrast to these situations are many cases of Vietnamese remaining in areas of initial placement and becoming part of their adopted communities. While data allowing comparison of characteristics of those who migrated with those who did not are unavailable, it is interesting to speculate about general differences between the two. It may be that those who have not migrated are expressing a greater willingness to assimilate and to accept the primacy of rapid achievement of financial self-sufficiency, as encouraged by resettlement planners.

The concentration of Vietnamese in urban areas provides social networks through which people can obtain financial and psychological support. In many areas Vietnamese-organized associations have developed to provide social activities for members and to assist newly-arrived compatriots (cf. Afton, 1977; Ha, 1979; Pisarowics, 1977). While membership is generally based on locality of residence, some associations include only people of a particular religious faith, profession, or political orientation. Formation of associations and enclaves has not been without problems, however. Conflicts stemming from differing political convictions, competing ambitions of association leaders, and assertions of status distinctions have surfaced (Dickey, 1978). Ha Ton Vinh (1979) states that people from the lower classes have often refused to join organizations which included people from upper classes, fearing that such association would serve to perpetuate their traditional status even in the United States. The conflicts add to the emotional strains already being experienced and impede the emergence of individuals or organizations who can speak to the larger society on behalf of broad constituencies of Vietnamese.

While migration to urban areas and other states meant a loss of sponsorship, people have not been denied access to federally-supported occupational re-training programs and English language programs. Moreover, people relocating in a different state have generally maintained eligibility for government financial assistance in the form of Aid for Dependent Children monies, Medicaid, and food stamps.[1] The need for such assistance has decreased substantially, but Vietnamese in some states, especially states with fairly generous assistance levels, have had to face accusations by some Americans that refugees have become dependent on "welfare" or have benefited from government programs to a greater degree than have other groups at low income levels (cf. Pierce, 1980; Social Security Administration, 1979). Critics fault social service agencies for being excessively willing to allow the use of cash assistance rather than make efforts to find good jobs for people (Shearer, 1980). While some Vietnamese were quite willing to accept public assistance during initial years in this country, recent employment and public assistance data demonstrate movement away from reliance on public funds (Montero, 1979; Social Security Administration, 1978; Taft et al., 1979). The image of dependence and indigence, if it persists, provides additional barriers to Vietnamese adaptation in that it discredits actual accomplishments and implies a weakness in Vietnamese "character." Although this image has been promoted by Americans who wish to restrict further admission of Indochinese, its real effects are likely to be on those already here.

Vietnamese have generally been well received by Americans in their communities and workplaces, but incidents of conflict have occurred. This is not surprising, given the mutual lack of understanding of cultural differences. Media coverage of these incidents is often extensive, making them appear more common than is actually the case. Among reported conflicts is fighting between Americans and Vietnamese on shop floors of industries as a result of perceived insults.

While conflicts stemming from cultural misunderstandings are note-worthy, conflicts over access to economic and other resources are more significant because they reveal social junctures at which Vietnamese are experiencing problems with potentially long-term effects. In Texas and Florida, for example, American fishermen have been upset by Viet-namese fishing techniques which they believe violate accepted practices and threaten depletion of fishing areas (Associated Press, 1979; Raines, 1978).

It is significant that many of the conflicts involve Vietnamese and members of ethnic minority groups. For example, when the governor of Iowa announced that the state would welcome more "boat people" from Indochina, some Blacks who had earlier assisted refugees expressed frustration that refugees' needs appeared to have priority over those of Blacks (Brown, 1979). In a number of universities Blacks and Chicanos have confronted school administrators with complaints that financial aid monies provided to Vietnamese were disproportion-ately large and therefore decreased resources available to "indigenous" minority students (Skinner and Hendricks, 1977). Leaders in the Black community of New Orleans have expressed concern that the number of Indochinese applicants for public housing has made it more difficult for Blacks to gain access to these units (Brown, 1978). Threats and physical violence directed at Vietnamese living in a public housing complex in Denver seem to have been connected to feelings among Chicano residents that the material possessions of Vietnamese in the community indicated that they did not need access to public facilities and therefore had been given preferential treatment by city housing officials (Lopez, 1979; Martisius, 1979). In an analysis of the conflict in Denver, Marge Yamada Taniwaki et al. (1979) note that while the issue of access to public housing was not of either population's making, actions were aimed at each other rather than at the institutions and power structure to which both have been subject.

Vietnamese-American: Becoming an Ethnic Minority

Competition between Vietnamese and members of minority groups is to a certain extent a reflection of the fact that the Vietnamese, as well as other Indochinese, have been classified as ethnic minorities by some of the American institutions providing assistance. Specifically, many universities and colleges include Indochinese in minority student support programs designed for students who are members of the four categroies of ethnic minority status, i.e., Black, Chicano, Native American, and Asian-American, and who are educationally and/or economically disadvantaged. For the Vietnamese, "educational dis-advantage" has been interpreted as their English language deficiencies, rather than weaknesses in scholastic preparation, which in most instances is quite high. The major benefit of participation in these programs is that students are eligible for larger amounts of financial aid than is available to non-participants.[2] Also, employers are including Indochinese in headcounts of minority applicants for employment and of minority hired. Public housing and health officials include the Indochinese among their ethnic minority clientele.

Given the criteria used to define ethnic minority status, which for the Vietnamese is only their Asian ancestry, the Vietnamese cannot legitimately be excluded from the category and its benefits. Schools, employers, and public agencies have simply followed federal guidelines on what constitutes ethnic minority status and have sought to assist displaced persons by utilizing affirmative action and other programs originally intended to redress specific social and historical circumstances experienced by groups of longer standing in the United States. These institutional efforts to provide access to needed financial, occupational, and educational resources, however, often place the Vietnamese in unwanted competition with other segments of U.S. society. The fact that relatively few people of Asian ancestry, such as Japanese- or Chinese-Americans, have sought resources earmarked for ethnic minorities makes acquisition of benefits by Vietnamese appear to some people to be an intrusion of a competing group.

Following the dissolution of sponsorships and subsequent migrations, Vietnamese have come into more direct contact with institutions of U.S. society. Considering Vietnamese as an ethnic minority may seem to signify respect for their cultural distinctiveness. The designation, however, can be viewed as primarily a convenience for institutions because it permits provision of services according to established procedures for assisting others classified in this manner. "Refugee" is not an institutionally meaningful category, or at best it has short-lived utility as a way of marking boundaries of a sub-set of the population. Because refugee status denotes economic and social privation, it could easily be replaced by a category with similar attributes, but with greater utility and permanence, i.e., "ethnic minority." That the Vietnamese themselves, in terms of their diverse backgrounds and post-evacuation achievements, do not uniformly exhibit the presumed characteristics of either of these categories does not seem to have been taken into consideration as this transformation took place. Of course, previous classification as refugees alone did not bring about this reclassification. Other recent immigrants, such as Russian Jews and Hungarians, have been considered refugees but were not subsequently classified as ethnic minorities, despite obvious ethnic distinctiveness. In the final analysis it appears that it is racial distinctiveness, as expressed by the categories of ethnic minority status, which permits the shift in classification. That Vietnamese, Cambodians, and Laotians were also refugees simply contributed to allowing the shift to occur relatively unexamined.

In the process of adaptation by any immigrant group, people come into contact with institutions of their new society. Strategies are often devised for facilitating these contacts and for obtaining desired services and resources. The Vietnamese are becoming aware, as have other people,[3] that their status as an ethnic minority has strategic value in that it affords access to benefits in the areas of employment, housing, health, education, and eligibility for loans. Acquiescence to being classified as an ethnic minority has short-term advantages, just as being viewed as refugees was the basis on which assistance had been provided during the initial period of adjustment. In talking to Vietnamese, however, it is apparent that they are unaware of the social and historical bases for ethnic minority status in the United States.

Among Americans involved in assisting the Indochinese, a few have given thought to possible implications of ethnic minority status. For example, in a June 1979 speech before the National Coalition for Refugee Resettlement in Washington, D.C., Colleen Shearer, director of the Iowa Refugee Service Center, questioned the classification of Indochinese as minorities. Within an argument that public and private programs must respond to the demonstrated value placed on work among the Indochinese, Shearer warns that minority designation may encourage "second-class citizen attitudes and ethics" (Whitaker, 1979).

Shearer's inference is that it is important to examine whether encapsulating the Vietnamese in the category Asian-American ethnic minority represents the larger society's prescription for how Vietnamese should adapt to the United States. Specifically, are the Vietnamese expected to assimilate as a minority group? Vietnamese are already viewed by many Americans as willing to accept low-level jobs, and the connotations of minority status may reinforce the impression that there is what John U. Ogbu (1978) calls a "job ceiling" above which Vietnamese are not expected to be able to compete. As Colin Greer (1974) notes, when people make reference to ethnic groups they are often communicating quite specific implications about incomes and social class. Americans may be encouraged to view Vietnamese individuals' occupational and educational successes in the context of their being an ethnic minority, whom many Americans assume have difficulty achieving success, rather than viewing attainments solely on the basis of individual competence and effort. Moreover, the feeling among Vietnamese that they are "outsiders" in U.S. society may be reinforced by their formal designation not only as a culturally distinct group but also as people whose potentials are assumed to be inherently of a lower order. Minority status, as Joan Vincent (1974) points out, is a categorization of the political structure and serves to maintain the status quo rather than bringing about fundamental social change. Without minority designation, ethnic groups are more free to compete with each other and to confront extablished economic and political institutions, and such competition may contribute to reshaping society.

While the cultural distinctiveness of the Vietnamese is quite apparent, Vietnamese as individuals have not as yet defined their identities in U.S. society, identities which may or may not emphasize shared cultural or ethnic qualities. In the interim, the imposition of an ethnic minority classification carries connotations which achievement-oriented and formerly upper- and middle-class Vietnamese are unlikely to want to be included in their emerging redefinitions of social identities. People who were once in the lower strata of Vietnamese society but who are now striving to re-order status distinctions in Vietnamese communities may not find identification as a minority congruent with their aspirations. While acquiring skills necessary to manage in U.S. society, many Vietnamese are also trying to maintain their own cultural patterns. During this process Vietnamese may mistakenly interpret ethnic minority designation as an expression by U.S. institutions that such efforts are supported and that cultural assimilation is no longer expected of immigrants. For the short-term, at least, cultural maintenance may be facilitated by the economic resources which wearing an ethnic minority "badge" secures. There is the danger, however, that in the process of obtaining these resources Vietnamese may present themselves in a manner which confirms the larger society's assumptions about the attributes of minority status. Over time, young Vietnamese may be socialized into adopting patterns of behavior and notions about achievement potentials which are associated with minority status.

The diversity among the Vietnamese, both in social backgrounds and forms of adaptation, make a uniform definition of social identity unlikely, and so it is indeterminable how large a segment of the Vietnamese population will embrace the categorization as an ethnic minority. It is predictable, however, that individual Vietnamese will eventually react to the imposition of this category. It would not be surprising for some to express the feeling that the classification not only fails to reflect their abilities and aspirations, but also debases the integrity of Vietnamese culture. The emergence of self-defined Vietnamese identities, if they develop at all, will take time, and in the course of their development many Vietnamese are likely to express resentment at institutional assumptions that minority status and its attributes should be part of Vietnamese-American identity.

221

CONCLUSION

The American predilection of assuming that ethnically-defined sub-sets of the population basically share certain social and economic characteristics, not only within a sub-set but across sub-sets, is in evidence in the case of the Vietnamese. As is true for other ethnic groups, diversity characterizes the Vietnamese better than does homogeneity. Social and occupational backgrounds, political and religious orientations, and motivations for leaving Vietnam reflect this diversity. Vietnamese experiences and actions since arriving in the United States similarly defy population-wide generalizations. American institutions' failure to appreciate this diversity has contributed to the facile assumption that application of a social category, whether Vietnamese-American or ethnic minority, is appropriate and meaningful to the Vietnamese themselves. Besides having to deal with the very real problems of achieving social, economic, and psychological adjustment in the United States, the Vietnamese will increasingly find themselves combating consequences of imposed social categories.

NOTES

1. The major legislative base for assisting Indochinese refugees is the Indochina Migration and Refugee Assistance Act of 1975, which authorized 100 percent federal reimbursement to states for cash assistance provided to refugees through September 1977. The usual eligibility requirements for receiving public assistance (i.e., disability, over 65 years of age, or dependent child of single parent or unemployed father) have generally been waived for the refugees and funds have been provided on a case-by-case basis. In October 1977, Congress granted a one-year extension of authority for federal reimbursement at the 100 percent level. Starting in October 1978, reimbursement was to be phased down over a three-year period. In 1978, however, Congress extended the 100 percent reimbursement for one year, largely as a result of the large number of new arrivals from Indochina. Public officials of states and counties in which Indochinese had congregated also argued that it was unfair for local taxpayers to bear the burden of picking up assistance costs of a national program (cf. American Public Welfare Association, 1979; Committee on Human Resources, 1978). In 1979 full federal funding was extended for four years.

2. In 1975 Congress made refugees eligible for most federal financial assistance available to any U.S. citizen, including Basic Educational Opportunity Grants for post-secondary education (cf. Martin, 1976; Skinner and Hendricks, 1977).

3. Other recent immigrants have become aware of the value of being classified as ethnic minorities and have actively sought the recognition of occupying this status. Research by Maxine Fisher (1978) on Asian Indians in New York reveals interesting parallels with the Vietnamese situation. Like the Vietnamese, Asian Indians are a diverse population, including a number of language groups and religious orientations. An association embracing all Asian

222

Indians sought to develop a common ethnic identity and to change the federal government's classification of them from "white/caucasian" to "Indo-American ethnic minority." Despite the fact that Asian Indians in the United States have not been victims of gross discrimination and are highly successful professionals, they petitioned for ethnic minority status in order to extend and protect their economic attainments.

REFERENCES

AFTON, J.
　　1977　　"Vietnamese in Denver: the development of the Sun Valley enclave." Paper presented at meetings of the *Rocky Mountain Psychological Association,* Albuquerque, New Mexico, May.

AMERICAN PUBLIC WELFARE ASSOCIATION
　　1979　　"Indochinese refugees: an increasing population, a growing need for help." *Washington Report* 34(1):1-2.

ASSOCIATED PRESS
　　1979　　"Viet refugee fishermen flee town after slaying." *Denver Post* (August 9):10.

BACHE, E.
　　1978　　"No gold in streets, the Vietnamese found." *New York Times* (June 10):19.

BROWN, W.
　　1978　　"A different war: Vietnamese refugees caught in black-white friction in New Orleans." *Washington Post* (July 18):13.

　　1979　　"Blacks angered by Iowa refugee aid." *Washington Post* (February 13):A2.

CHANDA, N.
　　1979　　"Vietnam's battle of the home front." *Far Eastern Economic Review* (November 2):44-48.

CHAU, K. N.
　　1975　　"Refugee problems in the days ahead." pp. 118-123. in *Report of the San Francisco Research Planning Conference on Asian Migration.* National Science Foundation.

COMMITTEE ON HUMAN RESOURCES
　　1978　　*Hearing on Indochina Migration and Refugee Assistance Amendments of 1978.* U.S. Senate, August 9.

CONRAD, P.
　　1979　　"Living with refugees." *Newsweek* (August 13):15.

COONEY, P.
　　1979　　"Iowa opens its heart to 'Boat People.'" *Des Moines Register* (April 29):1E ff.

DEPARTMENT OF STATE
1975   *Special Report: Indochina Refugee Resettlement.* (August).

DICKEY, C.
1978   "Vietnamese politics still plagues refugees." *Washington Post*
(February 5):A10.

EX, J.
1966   *Adjustment After Migration.* The Hague: Martinus Nijhoff.

FAGEN, R. R., R. A. BRODY, and T. J. O'LEARY
1968   *Cubans in Exile.* Stanford, Calif.: Stanford University Press.

FISHER, M.
1978   "Creating ethnic identity: Asian Indians in the New York City
area." *Urban Anthropology* 7:271-285.

GREER, C.
1974   "Remembering class." Pp. 3-35 in C. Greer (ed.), *Divided
Society: The Ethnic Experience in America.* New York: Basic
Books.

HA, T. V.
1979   "The Indochinese mutual assistance associations as sociocultural settlement patterns." Pp. 32-39 in G. H. Stopp, Jr. and
Nguyen M.H. (eds.), *Proceedings of the First Annual Conference on Indochina Refugees,* Fairfax, Virginia.

HUNG, N. M.
1978   "Some observations on Vietnamese refugees in the United
States with special reference to Vietnamese refugees in northern
Virginia." Paper presented at the *Consortium for Asian Studies,*
Norfolk, Virginia, November.

KAMM, H.
1977   "Vietnamese boat refugees hope they will find home in U.S."
Minneapolis Tribune (September 11):18B.

1978   ". . . And Vietnamese refugees are still fleeing." *New York
Times* (January 22):IV4.

KELLY, G. P.
1977   *From Vietnam to America: A Chronicle of the Vietnamese
Immigration to the United States.* Boulder, Colo.: Westview.

LE, T. A.
1975   "The Vietnamese refugees: perspectives and recommendations."
Pp. 142-154 in *Report of the San Francisco Research Planning
Conference on Asian Migration.* National Science Foundation.

LIE, R.
    1978   "Mental health concerns of the Indochinese refugees." Paper
            presented at meetings of the *Society for Applied Anthropology,*
            Merida, Mexico, April.

LIU, W.
    1979   *Transition to Nowhere: Vietnamese Refugees in America.*
            Nashville, Tenn.: Charter House.

LIU, W., and A. MURATTA
    1978   "The Vietnamese in America, Part IV: mental health of
            Vietnamese refugees." *Bridge* 6(2):44-49.

LOPEZ, E.
    1979   "Lifeline tossed to refugees strains Denver resources." *Denver
            Post* (August 5):27.

LUCE, D.
    1979   "The boat people: America can best help them by recognizing
            its complicity." *The Progressive* (September):27-29.

MARTIN, J.
    1976   "Vietnamese students and their American advisors." *Change*
            (November):11-14.

MARTISIUS, B.
    1979   "Many Viets abandon Denver housing project homes." *Denver
            Post* (August 22):1 ff.

MONTERO, D.
    1979   *Vietnamese-Americans: Patterns of Resettlement and Socio-
            economic Adaptation in the United States.* Boulder, Colo.:
            Westview.

NGUYEN, N.
    1979   "An emotionally disturbed Vietnamese child refugee in a
            residential treatment center: a case presentation." Pp. 73-77 in
            G. H. Stopp, Jr. and Nguyen M. M. (eds.), *Proceedings of the
            First Annual Conference on Indochina Refugees*, Fairfax,
            Virginia.

NORRIS, V. T., and D. DITTEMORE
    1977   "Vietnam in retrospect: a history of Indochinese migration and
            the 1975 exodus." Paper presented at meetings of the *Rocky
            Mountain Psychological Association,* Albuquerque, New
            Mexico, May.

OGBU, J. U.
    1978   *Minority Education and Caste: The American System in
            Cross-Cultural Perspective.* New York: Academic Press.

PAINE, J.
    1977   "The still-displaced Vietnamese." *Los Angeles Times* (June 2):IV1 ff.

PIERCE, N. R.
    1980   "Carter's refugee settlement time bomb." *Des Moines Register* (March 1):7A.

PISAROWICS, J. A.
    1977   "Vietnamese in Denver: influence of the refugee community on individual psycho-sociological adjustment." Paper presented at meetings of the *Rocky Mountain Psychological Association,* Albuquerque, New Mexico, May.

RAHE, R. H., J. G. LOONEY, H. W. WARD, TRAN M. T., and W. T. LIU
    1978   "Psychiatric consultation in a Vietnamese refugee camp." *American Journal of Psychiatry* 135:185-190.

RAINES, H.
    1978   "Vietnam fishermen in Florida in net-length-dispute." *New York Times* (June 11):26.

ROBERTS, S. V.
    1978   "Boat people brave adversity to seek new lives in U.S." *New York Times* (January 2):10.

RULE, S.
    1978   "Boat refugees find adjusting to U.S. another hard journey." *New York Times* (December 18):B8.

SCHEMERHORN, R. A.
    1974   "Ethnicity in the perspective of the sociology of knowledge." *Ethnicity* 1:1-14.

SHEARER, C.
    1980   "Doing better at doing the right thing." *Des Moines Register* (March 1):7A.

SKINNER, K. A., and G. L. HENDRICKS
    1977   "A new minority: Indochinese refugees in higher education." *Office for Student Affairs Research Bulletin* 18(4), University of Minnesota. ERIC Reproduction Services No. ED 148274.

    1979   "The shaping of ethnic self-identity among Indochinese refugees." *Journal of Ethnic Studies* 7(3):25-41.

SLOTE, W. H.
    1977   "Adaptation of recent Vietnamese immigrants to the American experience: a psychocultural approach." Paper presented at the meetings of the *Association for Asian Studies,* New York, March.

SNEPP, F.
1977   *Decent Interval.* New York: Random House.

SOCIAL SECURITY ADMINISTRATION
1978   *Report to the Congress: Indochinese Refugee Assistance Program.* Washington, D. C.

1979   *Secretarial Report: Indochinese Refugee Assessment.* Washington D. C.

STARR, P. D., A. E. ROBERTS, R. G. LENOIR, and THAI N. N.
1979   "Adaptation and stress among Vietnamese refugees: preliminary results from two regions." Pp. 110-119 in G. H. Stopp, Jr. and Nguyen M. H. (eds.), *Proceedings of the First Annual Conference on Indochina Refugees,* Fairfax, Virginia.

STEIN, B. N.
1979   "Occupational adjustment of refugees: the Vietnamese in the United States." *International Migration Review* 13:25-45.

STOPP, Jr. G. H.
1978   *Indochinese Refugee Resettlement Patterns in the Washington, D. C. Area.* Fairfax, Virginia: Chesapeake Regional Research Papers.

TAFT, J. V., D. S. NORTH, and D. A. FORD
1979   *Refugee Resettlement in the U.S.: Time for a New Focus.* Washington, D.C.: New TransCentury Foundation.

TANIWAKI, M. Y., C. VALENCIA, and R. WARNER
1979   "Denver's westside community: the impact of Indochinese resettlement on a predominantly Chicano neighborhood." Pp. 57-72 in G. H. Stopp, Jr. and Nguyen M. H. (eds.), *Proceedings of the First Annual Conference on Indochina Refugees,* Fairfax, Virginia.

TASK FORCE FOR INDOCHINA REFUGEES
1977   *Report to Congress* (June 20). Washington, D.C.

TIELEBEIN, A.
1979   "Refugees: moving again." *Cedar Falls Record* (Iowa) (June 28-30).

TRAN M. T.
1976   "The cry for help: problems of mental health among the Indochinese refugees." Unpublished.

TRAN T. N.
1976   "Vietnamese refugees: the trauma of exile." *Civil Rights Digest* 9:59-62.

VIGNES, A.J., and R. C. W. HALL
    1979   "Adjustment of a group of Vietnamese people to the United
            States." *Americal Journal of Psychiatry* 136:442-444.

VINCENT, J.
    1974   "The structuring of ethnicity." *Human Organization* 33:375-
            379.

WEINTRAUB, P.
    1978   "The exodus and the agony." *Far Eastern Economic Review*
            (December 22): 8-10.

WHITAKER, R.
    1979   "Refugee coalition meeting in Washington, D.C." *Iowa Orient-
            ing Express* 2(2):3.

Elites and Ethnic Boundary Maintenance:
A Study of the Roles of Elites in
Chinatown, New York City

Bernard Wong

Department of Anthropology
University of Wisconsin, Rock County Campus

ABSTRACT: Most of the studies about elites, as demonstrated in the literature of the social sciences, have been on their various roles as leaders, rulers, patrons, and culture brokers in developing countries. Very few studies have been undertaken on the roles of elites in urban ethnic communities in developed societies. This study examines the nature and functions of two groups of elites — their conflicts, their differential use of ethnicity, and their influence on the ethnic boundary of an urban Chinese community. The present study finds that ethnic boundary maintenance and transformation are principally the consequence of the activities of the elites. The transformation of the Chinese ethnic group in New York from a culture-carrying unit to that of an interest group in present-day Chinatown is, among other factors, also the by-product of the activities of the new elite.

Introduction

The study of elites in urban ethnic communities, especially in the various urban Chinese communities in America, presents a challenging opportunity to a social scientist. Generally, the elite have been studied in relationship to their various roles as leaders and rulers (Weber 1947; Pareto 1935; Mills 1969), patrons and culture brokers (Wolf 1956, 1966; Foster 1963a, 1963b; Boissevain 1966; Mayer 1967; Kenny 1960; Campbell 1964; Paine 1971; Strickon and Greenfield 1972; Geertz 1963; Misra 1961; Bottomore 1964). Few studies, however, have been conducted on the roles of elites in urban ethnic communities in developed societies. There are virtually no ethnographic accounts of the activities of the elite, or their management of ethnic identities in the various urban Chinatowns in America.

The purpose of this paper is to describe and analyze the nature and functions of the elite in Chinatown, New York.[1] Within this general framework, the following questions will be asked:

1. Who are perceived to be the elite of the community? What are the sociocultural attributes of the elite?
2. What are the self-perceived identity or identities of the elite of Chinatown?
3. How do the elite use various symbols, identities, and resources for pursuing individual and collective goal-seeking activities?
4. What are the rules adopted by the elite in their interaction with each other, with the community, and with outsiders?

The elite of New York's Chinatown are of particular interest because of their heterogeneous composition as well as their diversified adaptive strategies within the elite categories, and because the elite have been the pillars of the social activities of Chinatown. Unlike the Chinese communities of Sarawak (Tien 1953), Bangkok (Skinner 1958), Manila (Amyot 1960), and Lima (Wong 1971), where elites are much more assimilated, those in the Chinese community of New York until recently were eager to use the Chinese ethnicity, values, and traditional social organizations to maintain the community's internal "law and order" and to preserve the integrity of their ethnic boundaries. Historically, New York's Chinatown has long been a relatively closed or "segregated" community. From its inception in the 1880s, Chinatown has relied on the elite for its general well-being. They have been instrumental in assisting members of the community to obtain employment and financing, and in settling disputes within the community. Even the average New Yorker recognizes the important role played by the president of the Chinese Consolidated Benevolent Association and attributes to him the title of "unofficial major" of Chinatown. Rose Lee (1960), Virginia Heyer (1953), Leon Gor Yun (1936), and Stuart Cattell (1962) allude to the "wheelings and dealings" of the power elite of New York's Chinatown. None of these authors, however, focused their attention on the nature, functions, and activity systems of the elite. The elite of Chinatown are of interest to anthropologists because of their differential use of ethnicity and self-identification. A study of the elite of Chinatown will contribute to an understanding of their role in the urban ethnic community, the community-city integration process, and the multifaceted aspects of ethnicity in an urban environment.

Sociocultural Characteristics of the Elite of Chinatown, New York City

New York City's Chinese population in 1970 was 69,324, according to the U.S. Bureau of Census. There has been a steady increase of 10,000 per year in the Chinese population since 1970, bringing the number of Chinese in New York City in 1976 to approximately 120,000. Of this number, 60,000 are said to reside in the Chinatown area on the Lower East Side of Manhattan. Other areas of Chinese concentration are in the vicinity of Columbia University in Manhattan, Flatbush in Brooklyn, Jackson Heights and Amherst in Queens. However, our concern here is the Chinatown area.

The term *elite* has usually been defined from an objective, *etic* point of view (Bottomore 1964:1; Cole 1955:102-103; Pareto 1935:1422-1423; Nadel 1956:415). The present study on the other hand is interested in the subjective perceptions and categorizations of the elite in the community.

Members of New York's Chinese community distinguish two kinds of elites or "big persons." One group is called the *Kiu Ling*[2] (literally, the leaders of the overseas Chinese). The other group are supervisors of, or social workers in, the social service agencies and are called *Chuen Ka*[3] (literally, experts on social problems).

The elite were identified by the reputational approach. Names of elites were solicited from key informants and the list of names was subsequently verified by checking randomly with the general public in the community.

Generally, members of the community and all my informants considered the "big persons" as the "upper crust" in the community, but "middle-class or upper-middle-class" people in the larger U.S. society (Wong 1976). The income range of most of the elite (in 1974) is approximately $16,000 to $22,000 per year. Some elite persons, especially the *Kiu Ling,* are said to earn more than this because they are owners of firms.

Members of the community perceive differences within the elite in terms of age, birthplace, life-style, occupation, dialect, and language ability (see Table 1). *Kiu Ling* are China-born immigrants who came to this country many years

TABLE 1. Sociocultural Backgrounds and the Elites in Chinatown, New York City

	Traditional elite (or Kiu Ling)	New elite (or Chuen Ka)
Birthplace	China	U.S.A.
Age	Above 50	25 to 50
Occupation	Owners of Chinese-type business units: grocery stores, restaurants, novelty stores, department stores	Professionals: social workers, lawyers, accountants
Power base	Family name, territorial dialect associations, and Chinese Consolidated Benevolent Association	Social agencies, nonprofit community service organizations
Language	Sze Yup, Sam Yup, and Toysanese (mainly), with some knowledge of English	English; with some Cantonese-speaking assistants
Life-style	With exception of clothing, traditional rural Chinese	American middle class

ago. The number of *Kiu Ling* who are active in community affairs is said to be about 70. These individuals hold important positions in the 60-odd major family name, dialect, and regional associations, and in the Chinese Consolidated Benevolent Association. Serving as officers in the various traditional associations can bring both prestige and a solid following which may be helpful for future goal-seeking activities. Thus, the associations serve as a power base for the *Kiu Ling*.

A majority of the *Kiu Ling* are from the rural areas of Kwangtung province and generally speak the Sze Yup and Sam Yup dialects. They are entrepreneurs in typically Chinese businesses in Chinatown: laundries, chop suey restaurants, groceries, and gift stores. They are generally older, averaging 55 years of age, and have little formal education. Their many years of residence in the United States has brought some practical knowledge about this country and thus the *Kiu Ling* are familiar with two cultural systems — Chinese and American.

Frugality is proverbial among the older Chinese immigrants. Many of them have accumulated some wealth through years of hard work and saving. If there had not been a Communist takeover, they could have returned to China to be rich landlords or entrepreneurs, or simply to live a life of elegant retirement.

The second group of elites, known locally as *Chuen Ka,* are mostly Chinese-Americans who are social workers, or volunteers (whose actual occupations range from accountants, lawyers, and students to politicians) affiliated with a dozen social agencies. They can be second-, third-, or fourth-generation male or female Chinese-Americans. Very few of them speak any Chinese dialect. Because of this inability and their lack of knowledge of Chinese culture, they are frequently labeled by *Kiu Ling* as the *Juk Sing* — bamboo sticks (meaning rootless in either the Chinese or the American culture). *Chuen Ka* are generally college-educated in the U.S. and are professionals employed in American establishments. They are much younger than the *Kiu Ling*. While the *Kiu Ling* are more familiar with the Chinese culture, these new elites are more familiar with the English language and American society. As a group, the new elite are determined to upgrade the living standards of the Chinese community. They may also have certain self-interests, such as establishing an electoral power base or attracting customers to their accounting, law, and employment firms. Some of these Chinese-American elites are social workers who went to Chinatown to establish community services with funds available from the city, state, or federal government, and draw competitive salaries for their services. Other *Chuen Ka* volunteer their services for ideological or altruistic reasons. Almost all of the new elite use the social agencies to contribute their services to the community and to enlist followings.

The life-style of the new elite also differs from that of the *Kiu Ling*. The former tend to live according to the standard of the American middle class.

Although they may work in Chinatown, they prefer to live in other suburban neighborhoods. A great deal of their money is spent for housing and for the purchase of automobiles, recreational equipment, and household furnishings. This explains why the new elite do not accumulate handsome savings like the *Kiu Ling,* who live frugally and humbly, putting their money in the bank or investing it in profit-generating enterprises. The traditional *Kiu Ling* often criticize the new elite for drawing salaries for their community service or for having ulterior motives such as obtaining votes. The *Kiu Ling* consider themselves to be altruistic since they give money and time to the community. The new elite respond by calling the *Kiu Ling* "obsessed name-seekers," or "prestige-seekers" who spend money to buy prestige.

The older elites are the merchants and businessmen who strive to secure the leadership positions from the traditional associations and hope to rule the community through the offices of the associations. Hence, they resemble the "governing elites" mentioned by Pareto (1935). The new elite, on the other hand, are U.S.-educated professionals who use the social agencies as their power base to recruit followers and to contribute their service to the community. Thus, these new elites are similar to those middle-class elites in the developing countries who are eager to initiate sociocultural change (Bottomore 1964; Geertz 1963; Misra 1961; Niel 1960).

Management of Ethnic Identity

Jean Briggs's (1971:55-73) ethnographic data from the East Arctic has shown that an elite's (or patron's) goals, the strategies available to him, and the likelihood of his achieving his goals are influenced by the identity or identities he has chosen and that others have attributed to him. The identities selected by the two groups of elites in New York's Chinatown differ in many respects. Further, the ways in which they manipulate these identities for goal-seeking activities also vary.

First, the traditional elite tend to assume three identities: "Overseas Chinese," the "real Chinese," and "Chinese-Americans." When transacting with the Taiwan government, they assume the identity of Overseas Chinese because in so doing they are likely to be given special preference by the Taiwan government in all official interactions. Historically, the term *Kiu Ling* was used by the Nationalist (Kuomintang) government to refer to the exemplary Overseas Chinese who were leaders in championing the causes of the Kuomintang. The Nationalist government expects the *Kiu Ling* to play a bridging role between the community and Taiwan. Because of this expectation, a majority of the *Kiu Ling* take up an anti-Communist ideology and are hostile to groups that are sympathetic to the People's Republic of China. As leaders of the Over-

233

seas Chinese, *Kiu Ling* can obtain visas, export permits, and privileges under favorable export quotas of certain merchandise from Taiwan.

In dealing with the members of the community, the traditional elite tend to claim that they are the "real Chinese," as opposed to the second- and third-generation Chinese-Americans. A "real" Chinese means one who speaks and writes the Chinese language, interacts with other Chinese in a "humane," "Chinese" way, practices all the Chinese customs, celebrates the important Chinese festivals, etc. The occasion for proclaiming oneself as a real Chinese is generally during the course of elections in the various traditional associations. That is to say, in the recruitment of followers in the community and in the accumulation of political power in the community, it is believed that assuming the identity of a "real Chinese" is advantageous. The real Chinese identity is most often used in the context of opposition to the new elite.

Taking the identity of a Chinese-American is a necessity in transacting with the United States government, for only a citizen can benefit from the privileges and rights extended to the American public. Hence, when the *Kiu Ling* work with the United States government on behalf of the Chinese to protect their economic or political interests, they take up their Chinese-American identity.

Every American who has full or part Chinese blood, irrespective of language and birthplace, is a Chinese-American according to the new elite. The traditional elite, on the other hand, stress that only the "real Chinese" can understand the Chinese community and its problems and that outsiders should not interfere with the internal problems of the community. The new elite feel that every Chinese who is concerned with the community has the right to engage in community service. They feel that they are the middlemen who help the Chinese-American to participate in the resource distribution of the larger society in general and of New York City in particular. The *Chuen Ka* have been assisting members of the community in various ways: to adjust their visa status in the U.S., to obtain Social Security benefits, to secure funds from the city government to operate day care centers, to find jobs, and to provide free legal counsel. Through such endeavors, the new elite are winning the respect of the community and gradually attracting a clientele that usually has had to depend on the *Kiu Ling*.

The *Chuen Ka* also use a larger ethnic identity — Asian-American. The manipulation of regional ethnicity for goal-seeking activities is recognized by Lyman and Douglas (1973), as they point out that there are situations which dictate the use of a larger ethnic identity. Many of the *Chuen Ka* realize that to fight racism they need more participants in their movement. However, it is not only the need for more members that has caused Chinese-Americans to cooperate with other Asians and to assume the Asian-American identity.

Common interests and destiny are also important bases for such behavior. Japanese, Chinese, Koreans, and other Asians are frequently referred to in official legislation and documents as Asians or Orientals. Thus, if one Asian group — for example, the Japanese — breaks a racist barrier, it is likely that the Chinese and other Asians can also benefit. Using the Asian-American identity, many Asian groups have cooperated in their struggle for equal opportunity and human rights.

Values and Symbols Used by the Elites

In Chinatown, the two groups of elites circulate and use different symbols and values for their goal-seeking activities.

Since they have assumed the identity of the real Chinese, the *Kiu Ling* envision themselves as "models to copy" by members of the community. To show their "Chineseness," they are eager (1) to participate in the twice-a-year ancestor worship and to direct the celebration of the traditional Chinese festivals, (2) to secure membership in many traditional associations, and (3) to involve themselves in the affairs of the associations. It is not uncommon to find a *Kiu Ling* simultaneously holding membership and offices in four or five associations. Membership and official titles in many associations are not only signs of popularity, but also symbols of wealth, power, and "Chineseness."

As a "real Chinese" a *Kiu Ling* feels that he is obligated to preserve Chinese culture in New York City. To them, an ethnic group is a unit of cultural transmission (Greeley 1971, 1972). In this respect, the *Kiu Ling* are similar to the elites of Tabanon who see themselves as the preservers of their cultural tradition (Geertz 1963). Participation in associations and organizing the sweeping-the-grave ceremonies and other ancestor-worship rituals are considered to be important in validating their roles as culture preservers and in expressing their devotion to the traditional customs of China. Usually a Sunday during spring and during autumn are selected by the *Kiu Ling* as the days on which to bring members of the associations in chartered buses to Brooklyn's Evergreen Cemetery to visit the graves of former members of the community. The *Kiu Ling* usually make generous contributions to these ceremonies and are patrons for many other traditional celebrations such as the Chinese New Year. The colorful banners, the Lion Dance Troupe, and the Chinese firecrackers used for the Chinese New Year are financed chiefly by the voluntary contributions of the traditional elite.

As mentioned earlier, the *Kiu Ling* are usually older Chinese who are pro-Nationalist China (Taiwan). They do not hesitate to publicly demonstrate their pro-Kuomintang ideology. For example, pictures of Chiang Kai Shek and Sun Yat Sen are displayed in the offices of the various family, regional, and dialect associations, and in the Chinese Consolidated Benevolent Association. Both the Chinese (Kuomintang) and American flags are prominently displayed in the various parades sponsored by the *Kiu Ling*.

Not only do the traditional elites validate their "Chineseness" and their prestige through their active participation in Chinese festivals and their extravagant donations to cultural activities, but they also promote traditional Chinese values: *Lai* (or *Li* in Mandarin) — politeness and propriety; *Yee Hey* (*I Chi* in Mandarin) — trusting righteousness; *Kam Ching* (*Kan Ching* in Mandarin) — sentimental friendship; *Yan Ching* (*Jen Ching* in Mandarin) — human feelings; *Mien* (*Lien* in Mandarin) — face; and *Chang Ching* (*Chin Ching* in Mandarin) — warmth of kinship. These values are the basis for the operation of many transactional relationships such as the patron-client relationship, friendship, and kinship. Many of the traditional elite lamented that these basic values have become only a facade for many second- and third-generation Chinese and that consequently they do not feel confident in any dealings with them.

The new elite also use symbols and circulate social values, but for a different reason. The *Chuen Ka* fully realize that the continual expression and validation of Chinese culture are necessary for ethnic solidarity. Symbols are used and the memories of the tragic history of the early Chinese immigrants in America are recalled. Chinese are encouraged to wear Chinese clothes, especially during the parades and demonstrations. Buttons like "Asian power" and "Chinese power" are worn during demonstrations. In this case, the ethnic group is used not principally as a carrier of cultural traditions, but as an interest or pressure group for political and economic activities (Glazer and Moynihan 1970). Leaflets are distributed by some social agencies to inform the Chinese public on how to protect their human rights, perform their civic duties, and file discrimination complaints. As a community worker or social worker, a *Chuen Ka* feels that he is an "educator" and an "agent of social change."

The *Chuen Ka* recognize that if they have a solid following it will be possible for them to secure more funds and other resources for the community. In order to build a sizable following among the Chinese, these elites proceed in a manner similar to that of many ethnic politicians, i.e., by way of "consciousness raising" (Novak 1972). Such an effort is reflected in the newly installed mural near Chatham Square depicting the plight of the Chinese in America, in which an attempt is made to tell the history of the Chinese in America. On the left side of the mural is the infamous massacre of the Wyoming Rock Stream. On the right side of the mural there is a train symbolizing the contributions of the early Chinese immigrants who helped construct the Central Pacific Railroad. It is said that this mural was painted for the residents of Chinatown, not for its tourists. Thus, the message of this art work is clear: "Chinese should learn from their past experience."

While raising the ethnic consciousness of the Chinese, the *Chuen Ka* are at the same time purveying the values of the larger society such as "government exists for the individual," and "equality for all." Thus, the efforts of the new elite aim at preparing the members of the Chinese ethnic group to participate in the larger society.

Interaction Patterns

The two groups of elites follow different rules in dealing with the members of the community — outsiders and themselves as well. To the traditional elite, the Chinese community is for the "real Chinese." Thus, the second- and third-generation Chinese are to be excluded since they are "Americanized Chinese." According to the traditional elite, Chinese-Americans, including the new elite, should not interfere with the affairs of the Chinese community. In fact, Chinese-Americans who cannot speak the language are prohibited from competing for offices in the traditional Chinese family, regional, and dialect associations since they use Chinese as a medium of communication and as an official language for the settlement of disputes. Chinese-Americans are thus excluded from participating in the associations which, according to the traditional elite, constitute the structure of the community.

The Chinese Consolidated Benevolent Association is the highest level overall organization of Chinatown. It coordinates the 59 trade, recreational, tong, regional, dialect, political, and family name associations, and the fongs. The lowest level of organization is the village association known locally as *fong.* The hierarchical structure of the community's associations is shown in Figure 1.

Membership in these associations varies. The number of active members at the mid-level (trade, recreational, tong regional, dialect, political, and family

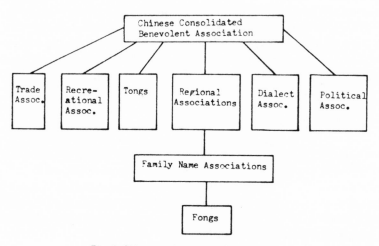

Fig. 1. Chinatown's community structure.

237

name) associations averages 300. Membership in the low-level associations (fongs) ranges from a handful to a few dozen. All the associations send their representatives to the CCBA, and these representatives constitute the Assembly of the CCBA.[4].

Due to the differences in language, life-styles, and mentality, there is little interaction between the new elite and the traditional elite. However, verbal attacks on each other's leadership qualifications are frequent. One traditional leader of the Chinese Consolidated Benevolent Association who is also president of a powerful merchant association said that only the *Kiu Ling* of Chinatown can solve the problems of the community: "How could those social agencies such as the Community Service Society, the Chinatown Planning Council, the Chinese Development Council, help us? They are all outsiders. We know our problems, and we have the means to solve them."

In other words, the *Kiu Ling* believe that they alone are the legitimate resource personnel of the community. The *Chuen Ka* (the new elite), on the other hand, contend that the *Kiu Ling* and the Chinese Consolidated Benevolent Association cannot speak for the community for a variety of reasons. First, the CCBA includes only 59 community organizations; many others are not invited to participate in the decision-making processes of the CCBA because of ideological differences. Second, the leaders of the CCBA are unfamiliar with U.S. politics and the methods for tapping resources of the larger society. Third, the *Chuen Ka* say the CCBA is not concerned with the needs of the ordinary Chinese, but rather with the needs of business and employers in Chinatown. So far, attempts to reconcile the differences and bring about cooperation between the two groups of elites have not been successful. Thus, a power struggle between the two groups continues. Each tries to gather in the followers of the other. The new immigrants — the majority of the population — tend to use the social agencies and are more comfortable dealing with the new elite, who seem to be more "modern," more "urban," and more "knowledgeable" about New York City. Even some of the old immigrants found the new elite to be more efficient in alleviating their problems, for example, in obtaining medical care or social security benefits from the government.

Elites vis-à-vis the Chinese Community

According to the traditional elite, the hierarchical social order of Chinatown, which is patterned after the traditional peasant organization in China, should be maintained. All members of the community should affiliate with their respective regional, family, trade, dialect, and village associations. Members of the community should approach the *Kiu Ling* of the lower organizations before they approach the leaders of the higher level associations.

The traditional *Kiu Ling* still believe that Chinatown is a self-sufficient community that can take care of its welfare problems, solve its own disputes, and police its own people. Efforts are made to prevent intervention from the larger society. One of the most serious community concerns recognized by these elites is Chinese education. They are interested in having a Chinese school in the community for their children as well as for the children of their followers. The *Kiu Ling* perceive themselves as preservers of Chinese culture and see the Chinese school as a powerful vehicle for this preservation. Also, education is valued highly by the Chinese, and being a donor or patron for the community's educational concerns will bring great respect and prestige.

The Chinese school is supported financially by the *Kiu Ling* of the community. The richest and most powerful *Kiu Ling* will sit on the Executive Committee of the Board of Trustees. The leaders of the various family, regional, dialect, and trade associations are trustees of the Chinese school. At present, the president of the Board of Trustees is also the president of the Chinese Consolidated Benevolent Association, who has said that for reasons of autonomy the school has no intention of seeking help from the state or federal governments. It is generally feared that if the Chinese school received financial support from the city or state governments, the *Kiu Ling* would lose control of the school. Thus, there is an isolationist policy enacted by the community's *Kiu Ling* to deliberately prevent the possible intervention by the larger society. This phenomenon is not unique to Chinese ethnic groups. In *The American Minority Community*, Judith Kramer points out that most Jews and Catholics in America have not demanded equality and the complete abolition of social distance because they want to maintain their autonomy in their own communities (Kramer 1970:65).

The Chinese school teaches not only the Chinese language but also Chinese culture. For example, it teaches Chinese folk music and folk dances, and sponsors special programs to educate Chinese youngsters on "filial piety." The schedule of the school is specially designed so that the children who study in American public schools can attend the Chinese school. The Chinese grade school runs daily from 4:00 to 7:00 p.m.; it begins shortly after the children are dismissed from regular public schools. There are Chinese language programs on Saturday and Sunday for high school age and adult Chinese. Due to generous donations and close supervision of the *Kiu Ling,* the school budget is always balanced.

Not only do the traditional elite refuse to seek financial aid from the larger society for the Chinese school, but they also hesitate to ask for assistance in other areas, such as welfare, housing, medicare, etc. Nevertheless, they still insist that they are the legitimate channels through which the community's transactions with the larger society must be conducted.

The new elite conduct their community service through the various social agencies in Chinatown. They believe that the traditional associations are vestigial structures that probably served the recreational and welfare needs of the immigrants of the past, but can no longer adequately meet the needs of a Chinatown whose population differs substantially from that of the earlier period. In the past (1880s-1960), the Chinese community was composed mainly of adult males who were sojourners in this country. Since the 1960s, young and old, male and female, single and married Chinese have come to this country with the intention of making it their permanent home. Prior to 1965, the immigrants were from the rural areas of China and were enculturated in a traditional social environment — peasant organization and traditional Chinese values. The new immigrants are principally from urban areas such as Canton, Hong Kong, Macao, and Taipei.

The new elite are particularly hostile to the Chinese Consolidated Benevolent Association, the stronghold of the traditional elite, because of its lack of flexibility in serving the pressing needs of the more recent immigrants: employment, housing, medical care, English education, social control, etc. Most of the new elite neither discourage nor encourage the Chinese to join the traditional associations. However, they do encourage all the Chinese to use the facilities and services of the social agencies. In fact, they have made inventories of the various types of services performed by all social agencies and have published several pamphlets to inform the Chinese public on how to make the most effective use of these agencies. The pamphlets give particular emphasis to these attractions: no fee, no favor, and no obligation.

The new elite plan to replace the welfare functions once performed by the *Kiu Ling* and the family and regional associations with the services of the social agencies. Members of the community are constantly reminded that they do not have to depend on the *Kiu Ling* to gain employment or credit, or to settle disputes.

The new elite are interested in assisting the Chinese in assimilating into U.S. society. For example, they favor the establishment of a school or center to teach English to adults and new immigrants, thus enabling them to find employment in non-Chinese businesses.

Elite vs. the Larger Society: New York City and the U.S.

The traditional elite have adopted the following strategies in dealing with the United States: (1) Participate in some sectors of the larger society while retaining significant aspects of their cultural identity; (2) retain some ties with the larger society while securing community control for themselves (cf. Barth 1969; Lyman and Douglas 1973).

Looking through the personal histories of the *Kiu Ling*, it is not difficult to discover why they follow these strategies. As mentioned earlier, they are older Chinese, mostly over 50, who have spent many years in the U.S. When they first came to this country, they were laborers, small merchants, or employees. They witnessed the discrimination practiced by the larger society against the blacks and other minority groups, including the Chinese. Hence, they are generally skeptical about the possibility for racially distinctive minority groups being integrated into the larger society.

The *Kiu Ling* intend to participate in some sectors of activity in the U.S., but hope to retain their cultural identity and secure community control. The sectors in which they participate in New York are restaurants, laundries, garment factories, Chinese groceries, and gift shops. They are concerned with the steady increase of customers in the Chinese restaurants, the image of Chinatown, New York, as a safe place, the number of tourists visiting Chinatown, and parking and traffic problems that can affect the Chinese businesses. Any regulations and policies enacted by the city government affecting these typically Chinese businesses (the lifelines of Chinatown) cause concern among the traditional elite. This is partly because they themselves are entrepreneurs in these fields and partly because they represent the interests of the Chinese business community as a whole. Hence, the Kiu Ling are concerned with the continued property of the Chinese ethnic niche.

The traditional elite generally feel that a good "appearance" for Chinatown is good for Chinese business. They play host to many visiting dignitaries from the city, state, and federal governments. These *Kiu Ling* stress harmony and friendship. Peaceful coexistence with other ethnic groups such as the Puerto Ricans and Jews on the Lower East Side and the Italians in Little Italy is emphasized.

The new elite's basic strategies in dealing with the larger society are: (1) to emphasize ethnic identity to develop new positions and patterns to organize activities in those sectors formerly not found in the U.S. society (Barth 1969; Lyman and Douglas 1973; Wirth 1945); and (2) to form coalitions with other ethnic groups for the attainment of similar institutional goals. Knowing that Chinese restaurants, garment factories, and laundries are still the most important businesses of the Chinese, the new elite attempt to render services to people in these businesses. Thus, for instance, the Chinatown Planning Council has been trying to get federal and city subsidies to run day care centers for the Chinese mothers who work out of economic necessity in garment factories or as waitresses in restaurants, thus leaving young children unattended. Several marches to City Hall to petition for day car subsidies have been conducted in the past several years.

The new elite, however, want to widen the job horizon and opportunities for the Chinese. They encourage Chinese-Americans to seek employment in all fields, from hospital administration, civil service, construction, and commercial positions to the professional sectors. Notices on the possibilities of employment with the police and FBI are posted in many social agencies. The new elite of the social agencies are interested in placing qualified Chinese in positions in the larger society where they were not found formerly, such as New York Telephone, Consolidated Edison, the U.S. Postal Service, city government, and the broadcasting industries. They also take complaints concerning violations of human rights, Equal Opportunity, and Affirmative Action programs and forward these complaints to the proper authorities.

The new elite are alert to the available resources which the Chinese ethnic group can utilize. In order to compete for these resources, American politicians are enlisted to assist the cause of the Chinese. The new elite are interested in enlisting community support for Chinese candidates who are running for government offices in New York. However, due to the limited number of registered voters, it is unlikely that any Chinese candidates will have mass support from the Chinese community. Nevertheless, the need to have Chinese politicians is gradually being felt in the community. Due to the efforts of the new elite, many Chinese have registered to vote.

The new elite also differ from the traditional elite in the procedures and techniques of dealing with the dominant society. While the *Kiu Ling* insist on harmony, patience, and inaction unless other measures are absolutely necessary, the *Chuen Ka* believe in the conflict approach — not conflict in the sense of physical force, but in the sense of social pressure and of militant attitudes. The new elite feel that it is American to fight for equality and freedom. They are fond of using methods commonly resorted to by many interest groups in America, such as protests and strikes, to obtain their goals.

Many of the traditional *Kiu Ling* think that publicity and high visibility will provoke envy from members of the larger society, which will lead to unhappy consequences for the Chinese. The new elite, on the other hand, believe that the mass media may publicize the plight of the Chinese and thus arouse the sympathy of the public toward the community. Not only are the new elite determined to fight with protests, demonstrations, and strikes, they also want to form coalitions with other ethnic groups to fight for equal rights and create new social positions for the ethnic groups.

The ethnic groups with which the Chinese tend to ally themselves are the Japanese, Koreans, Filipinos, and other Asians. So far, the new elite have published a journal to arouse the consciousness of the Asians and thus attempt to form a united front to fight racism. Thus, the new elite follow a strategy directly opposed to that of the traditional elite in dealing with the larger society. The former use ethnicity to participate in the social, economic, and political life of the larger society. The latter wish to limit contact with the larger society and hence preserve the autonomy of the community.

Elites vis-à-vis China

Concerning transactions with China and Overseas Chinese communities, there are also differences between the traditional and the new elite. The *Kiu*

Ling perceive themselves to be the indispensable link between the Chinese community of New York and China (Taiwan) and with other Overseas Chinese communities in the world. For the *Kiu Ling,* the legitimate government of China is the Republic of China. The Nationalist government in Taiwan is glad to have the *Kiu Ling* as its middleman and openly supports the *Kiu Ling* as the official spokesmen for the community. The Chinese Nationalist Consulate in New York still requires the leaders of the family, dialect, and regional associations as character references for the Chinese in the community.

Rules of propriety must be followed when a member of the community wants to transact business with the Nationalist Chinese Consulate in New York. One has to approach the lower level association first before he approaches the higher level association and ultimately the Chinese Consulate. Likewise, in dealing with the other Overseas Chinese communities, the activities of the *Kiu Ling* of the lower level associations have to be coordinated by the *Kiu Ling* of the intermediate levels who, in turn, are coordinated by the *Kiu Ling* of the highest level. Thus, for instance, in the relief aid to the Chinese earthquake victims in Managua in 1973, the New York Chinese were asked to deliver relief materials to the appropriate family associations first; from threre they would be forwarded to the CCBA, which collected all the materials and sent them to the equivalent organizations in the Chinese community of Managua.

The various Chinese associations in the United States are coordinated by two major centers: the Chinatowns of New York and San Francisco. Thus, if a leader is accused of usurpation and is subsequently ejected from his association in New York City, his name will be circulated immediately to the different branches of the same association (in Boston, Washington, D.C., Philadelphia, Detroit, Miami, Chicago, San Francisco, and other cities) in the United States (see Figure 2).

This associational network was established during the Tong War days (Lee 1960). News of Tong wars traveled quickly. If the On Leong Tong declared war on the Hip Sing Tong in New York, the On Leong Tong and Hip Sing Tong in Chicago and San Francisco would immediately go to war with one another (Leong 1936).

The leaders of the local associations have to confer with the leaders of the same association in other cities on major decisions. For example, if the Lee Association in Detroit wants to sell its old building to rebuild a new office, the leaders of the association are required to confer with the Lee Association in New York.

While the *Kiu Ling* are pro-Kuomintang, the *Chuen Ka,* or the new elite, are sympathetic to the People's Republic of China. They are proud of the achievements of China. Because of the emergence of the People's Republic of China, many of the new elite interviewed showed considerable pride in being of Chinese descent and expressed their interest in visiting China. However, the new elite have not shown interest in being bridges between the community and the People's Republic of China or with other Overseas Chinese communities.

243

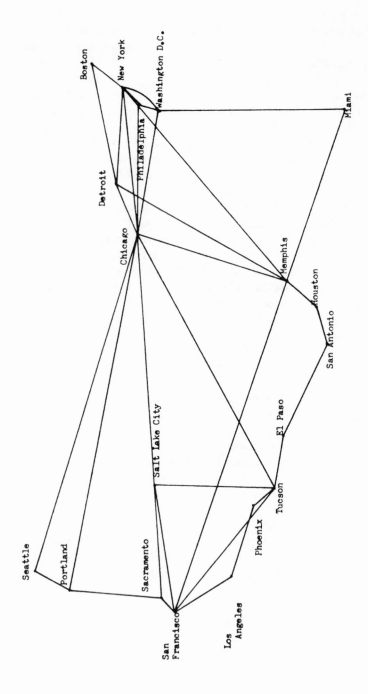

Fig. 2. Chinese associational network in the United States.

In fact, they identify themselves more with the U.S. than with Chinese culture. Their goal is to link the Chinese community with New York City and the larger U.S. society.

Discussion

The present study found that there are two kinds of elite in New York's Chinatown. When evaluated according to the community's standards, they are both the top-level people; when viewed against the larger U.S. society, they are considered by members of the community to occupy a middle-class status.

The traditional elite (*Kiu Ling*) of the community are the cultural preservers. They are not the "literati," as expected by Max Weber (1947), but rather are entrepreneurs in the ethnic businesses who have no high formal education, but control the means of production. They use their wealth, influence, and connections to recruit followers, to obtain the leadership positions in the traditional associations, and to oppose the presence and activities of the new elite. Thus, there is intense conflict between the traditional and the new elite in the community. The latter (*Chuen Ka*) are the "white-collar" professionals, educated in U.S. colleges, who seek an unreserved acceptance by the larger society and organize efforts to fight racism. The new elite from the social agencies and nonprofit service organizations follow a strategy directly opposed to the old elite. The former use ethnicity to assist members of the community to participate in the social, economic, and political life in New York City. Specifically, the new elite use ethnic status to obtain funding from city, state, and federal governments for their agencies and the minority status to gain employment and financial aid for the Chinese. In such endeavors, they attract many followers and users of the social agencies. Thus, their power base is expanding and their prestige is increasing. For those new elite who are social workers, job security is enhanced by a large clientele.

The traditional elite use ethnicity — traditional Chinese values, symbols, social organizations — to maintain a segregated community in which they are the prestigious rulers. They wish to limit contact with the city, state, and federal governments and preserve the status quo. The traditional elite have been diligent and successful in protecting the Chinese ethnic niche and in preserving the Chinese culture in New York City, but at the cost of isolation. This introversion is counterbalanced by the outreaching efforts of the new elite who, in assisting the Chinese to participate in the resource distribution of the larger society, bring the community into direct contact with other ethnic groups in New York and the larger society.

The traditional elite assume the roles of leaders and cultural stabilizers. The new elite's roles are as change agents and culture brokers between the

245

Chinese subculture and the U.S. culture, mediators between the community and the city. Thus, the old and new elite of an encapsulated ethnic community are not homogeneous. They can be agents of either cultural stability or cultural change, depending on a host of interwoven factors: cultural identity or identities chosen, birthplace, language ability and education, past experience of discrimination, occupation, type of self-interest, desire to maintain an ethnic group's cultural purity, desire to integrate into the dominant society, familiarity with the larger society, etc. As a consequence of the new elite's activities, the Chinese community of New York has become more outwardly oriented, and the ethnic boundary of the community has assumed a different character. Formerly, the Chinese ethnic boundary in New York was almost impenetrable; today, it does not isolate the members of the community from the larger society, particularly from city welfare assistance. The new elite enable members of the ethnic group to participate in the social, economic, and political life of America.

Some questions remain: Why is the new elite gaining more power at the expense of the old elite? What is the nature of the new ethnic boundary of Chinatown? The data obtained from my field research indicate that there are several variables for the gradual replacement of the old elite by the new elite. One is the change in the goals of the clientele. The new elite's followers are the new immigrants — the majority of Chinatown's population. The second variable is the changed population composition of Chinatown after the 1960s. Prior to the 1960s Chinatown was composed of old immigrants, principally China-oriented adults, males, sojourners. Chinatown's population since 1960 is far more heterogeneous. There are males and females of different ages, professionals, merchants, students, and laborers from the urban areas of China. The traditional associations, geared to the emotional needs of the rural, adult, male sojourners, cannot meet the wide range of social problems of the new immigrants: juvenile delinquency, housing, day care, medical care. These new immigrants are better educated and aspire to the affluent American life-style. They intend to make America their permanent home and their problems include not only finding a job in the community, but finding a *better* job and participating in the "good life" of America.

The third variable is the changing social relationships in Chinatown. In the past, social action was based on kinship, clanship, hometown-network, association-network. The operation of the traditional elite is based on these personal relationships. Today, Chinatown's social relationships are complex and relatively impersonal. In addition to the traditional social relationships, the new immigrants are involved in relationships of employer-employee, teacher-student, customer-owner, friendship, and patron-client. The traditional elite that ruled the community on the bases of kinship and clanship are thus losing their social sanctions. The fourth variable is the population size. In the pre-1960s era, Chinatown was relatively small. The Chinese population in New

York City increased from 18,329 in 1950 to 69,324 in 1970 (U.S. Census of Population: 1970). The resources of the traditional elite and their associations are simply inadequate to meet the needs of such a large population.

Accompanying the replacement of the old elite by the new elite, there is a change in the nature of the Chinese ethnic boundary in New York City. The Chinese ethnic group, which was formerly a carrier of Chinese culture and an autonomous, self-contained social unit for the perpetuation of Chinese ethnic businesses, is today perceived to be diversified by the members themselves. Common destiny and ethnic background are viewed as a basis for the formation of an interest group by means of which members of the community can participate in the resource distribution of New York City and the larger society. The new ethnicity is used as a resource by which ethnic group members can branch out of their ethnic niche/enclave. This new ethnicity is principally initiated and energized by the new elite of the community. Thus, the new elite is at least partially responsible for the transformation of the Chinese ethnicity in New York City. Whether this change in the Chinese community of New York is representative of other urban ethnic groups remains to be determined. However, the present study suggests that the research on ethnic boundaries and ethnic groups should focus on their power elite since the nature of the ethnic boundary and the transformation of ethnicity are frequently the by-products of the activities of their elite.

NOTES

[1] The data on which the present paper is based were obtained from fieldwork conducted in New York City in 1972-1973. The author is indebted to the National Science Foundation and the Ford Foundation for supporting the fieldwork and to Dr. Arnold Strickon of the University of Wisconsin-Madison for his helpful comments on the paper.

[2] This is a Cantonese transliteration, since the informants were Cantonese.

[3] *Chuen Ka* is the abbreviation of *She Hui Man Tai Chen Ka*, "social problem experts." Again, this is a Cantonese transliteration.

[4] A complete exposition of the structure of the CCBA would require many pages. For more detail, consult James Lee (1972).

REFERENCES CITED

Amyot, Jacques
    1960   The Chinese Community of Manila: A Study of Adaptation of Chinese Familism to the Philippine Environment. Philippine Study Program, University of Chicago, Research Monographs, No. 2.

Bailey, F. G.
    1969   Stratagems and Spoils. New York: Schocken Books.

Barth, Fredrik (ed.)
1969   Ethnic Groups and Boundaries. Oslo: Universitetesforlaget.

Boissevain, Jeremy
1966   Patrons in Sicily. Man 1(1):18-23.

Bottomore, T. B.
1964   Elites and Society. Baltimore: Penguin Books.

Briggs, Jean
1971   Strategies of Perception: The Management of Ethnic Identity. *In*
                    Patrons and Brokers in the East Arctic, Robert Paine (ed.). New-
                    foundland: Institute of Social and Economic Research, Memorial
                    University of Newfoundland, pp. 56-73.

Campbell, J. K.
1964   Honour, Family and Patronage. Oxford: Clarendon Press.

Cattell, Stuart H.
1962   Health, Welfare and Social Organization in Chinatown, New York City.
                    New York: Community Service Society.

Cole, G. D. H.
1955   Studies in Class Structure. London: Routledge and Kegan Paul.

Foster, George
1961   Interpersonal Relations in Peasant Society. Human Organization
                    19:174-175.

1963a   The Dyadic Contract: A Model for the Social Structure of a Mexican
                    Peasant Village. American Anthropologist 63:1173-1192.

1963b   The Dyadic Contract in Tzintzuntzan, II: Patron-Client Relationship.
                    American Anthropologist 65:1280-1294.

Geertz, Clifford
1963   Peddlers and Princes. Chicago: University of Chicago Press.

Glazer, Nathan and Daniel P. Moynihan
1970   Beyond the Melting Pot. Cambridge, Massachusetts: M.I.T. Press.

Greeley, Andrew
1971   Why Can't They Be Like Us? New York: E. P. Dutton & Co.

1972   That Most Distressful Nation. Chicago: Quadrangle Books.

Heyer, Virginia
1963   Patterns of Social Organization in New York's Chinatown. Ph.D.
                    dissertation. Ann Arbor: University Microfilms.

Kenny, Michael
1960   Patterns of Patronage in Spain. Anthropological Quarterly 33(1):14-23.

Kramer, Judith
1970   The American Minority Community. New York: Thomas Y. Crowell Co.

Lee, James
    1972   The Story of the New York Chinese Consolidated Benevolent Associa-
           tion. Bridge Magazine 1(5):15-18.

Lee, Rose Hum
    1960   The Chinese in the United States of America. Hong Kong: Hong Kong
           University Press.

Leong, Gor Yun
    1936   Chinatown Inside Out. New York: Barrows Mussey.

Lyman, Stanford and William Douglas
    1973   Ethnicity: Strategies of Collective and Individual Impression Manage-
           ment. Social Research 40(20):345-365.

Mayer, Adrian
    1967   Patrons and Brokers: Rural Leadership in Four Overseas Indian Com-
           munities. In Social Organization, Maurice Freedman (ed.). Chicago:
           Aldine Publishing Co., pp. 167-188.

Mills, C. Wright
    1969   The Power Elite. New York: Oxford University Press.

Misra, B. B.
    1961   The Indian Middle Classes. London: Oxford University Press.

Nadel, S. F.
    1956   The Concept of Social Elites. International Social Science Bulletin
           8(3): 415.

Niel, R. Van
    1960   The Emergence of the Modern Indonesian Elite. The Hague: W. Van
           Hoeve.

Novak, William
    1972   The Rise of the Unmeltable Ethnics. New York: MacMillan Co.

Paine, Robert (ed.)
    1971   Patrons and Brokers in the East Arctic. Newfoundland: Institute of
           Social and Economic Research, Memorial University of Newfoundland.

Pareto, Vilfredo
    1935   The Mind and Society. London: Jonathan Cape.

Passwell, Harold, Daniel Lerner, and Easton Rothwell.
    1952   The Comparative Study of Elites. Stanford: Hoover Institute Studies.

Skinner, William
    1958   Leadership and Power in the Chinese Community of Thailand. Ithaca:
           Cornell University Press.

Strickon, Arnold and Sidney Greenfield (eds.)
    1972   Structure and Process in Latin America. Albuquerque: University of
           New Mexico Press.

Stuart, William T.
1972   The Explanation of Patron-Client Systems. *In* Structure and Process in Latin America, Arnold Strickon and Sidney Greenfield (eds.). Albuquerque: University of New Mexico Press, pp. 19-42.

Tien, Ju-kang
1953   The Chinese of Sarawak. London: London School of Economics and Political Science.

Weber, Max
1947   The Chinese Literati. *In* From Max Weber, H. H. Gerth and C. Wright Mills (eds.). New York: Oxford University Press, pp. 416-444.

Wirth, Louis
1945   The Problems of Minority Groups. *In* The Science of Man in the World Crisis, Ralph Linton (ed.). New York: Columbia University Press, pp. 347-372.

Wolf, Eric
1956   Aspects of Group Relationships in a Complex Society: Mexico. American Anthropologist 58:1065-1078.

1966   Kinship, Friendship and Patron-Client Relations in Complex Societies. *In* The Social Anthropology of Complex Societies, Michael Banton (ed.). London: Tavistock, pp. 1-22.

Wong, Bernard
1971   Chinese in Lima. Manuscript. Fieldwork report submitted to the Ibero-American Studies Program, University of Wisconsin-Madison.

1974   Patronage, Brokerage, Entrepreneurship and the Chinese Community of New York. Unpublished Ph.D. dissertation, University of Wisconsin-Madison.

1976   Social Stratification, Adaptive Strategies, and the Chinese Community of New York. Urban Life 5(1):33-52.

Why There Are No Asian Americans in Hawai'i: The Continuing Significance of Local Identity

Jonathan Y. Okamura

The term "Asian American" is not commonly used in Hawai'i except by academics and the media. In everyday discourse, the much more frequently used related term is "Oriental," although it tends to be applied primarily to Chinese, Japanese, and Koreans and less so to Filipinos, Southeast Asians, and South Asians. In other contexts, individual Asian American groups will be specified, since there are only four major groups (the first four noted above), rather than a collective term being employed. At the individual level, people in Hawai'i claim to be Chinese, Filipino, Japanese or Korean, as the case may be, rather than Asian American.

Beyond the use of the term, the concept, Asian American is even less recognized and advanced in Hawai'i. There is essentially an unfamiliarity with the political significance of the concept rather than a conscious disavowal of it. There are very few specifically Asian American organizations or social movements in Hawai'i. Communities, cultural activities, and other social processes also tend not to be referred to or identified as Asian American. The newer terms, "Asian and Pacific American" or "Asian and Pacific Islander American," are even less commonly used in Hawai'i despite the presence of several Pacific Islander groups including Native Hawaiians, Samoans, Tongans, and Guamanians.

One of the factors that contributes to the marginality of Asian American identity in Hawai'i is the significance of another panethnic identity that Asian American groups and individuals can affirm, i.e., local identity. This paper reviews various economic and political developments and changes in and beyond Hawai'i during the past decade and assesses their impact on the significance and meaning of local identity. These developments include: substantially increased investment from Japan during the latter half of the 1980s, the tremendous expansion of the tourist industry in the economy of Hawai'i, the continued development of the movement for Hawaiian sovereignty and for recognition of their rights and claims as the indigenous people of Hawai'i, and the widening social cleavage between Japanese Americans and other ethnic groups, particularly Filipino Americans, Native Hawaiians, and haole or white Americans. In very different ways, all of these economic and political developments have contributed to the continuing significance of local identity in Hawai'i. However, it is argued that tourism development and Japanese investment have had the greatest impact on the maintenance of local identity through their increasing marginalization of Hawai'i's people to external sources of power and control. Continued affirmation of local identity over the past decade represents an expression of opposition to outside control and change of Hawai'i and its land, peoples, and cultures.

Local Versus Asian American Identity

Over ten years ago, an article on local identity and culture in Hawai'i discussed their historical and contemporary sources and accounted for the increasing salience of local identity since the 1960s (Okamura, 1980). In particular, various external social and economic forces of change perceived as detrimental to the quality of life that local people had come to value with living in Hawai'i were specified. These factors included substantial inmigration of Whites from the U.S. mainland, increased immigration from Asia and the Pacific, and the tremendous growth in the tourist industry. As a result, it was argued that the notion of "local" had come to represent the common identity of people of Hawai'i and their shared appreciation of the land, peoples and cultures of the islands. Given this commitment to Hawai'i, *local* also had evolved to represent the collective efforts of local people to maintain control of the economic and political future of Hawai'i from the external forces noted above.

On the U.S. mainland during the 1960s, Asian Americans were engaged in a similar movement to develop a panethnic identity and consciousness for themselves (Wei, 1993). However, the concept of Asian American identity has never taken hold in Hawai'i even though there are several Asian American groups that represent significant proportions of the population including Japanese (22.3%), Filipino (15.2%), Chinese (6.2%), Korean (2.2%), Vietnamese (0.5%) and other Southeast Asian (e.g., Laotian and Kampuchean) (Hawaii, 1993:44). Asian Americans collectively comprise a little less than one-half of the state population of 1.1 million. Because of the considerable populations of Japanese, Filipino, and Chinese Americans and the overall structure of ethnic relations in Hawai'i, these groups have not found it necessary to establish and affirm collectively a specifically pan-Asian American identity or movement. Instead, there are separate organizations to represent the interests and regulate the affairs of those groups such as chambers of commerce and statewide ethnic community associations.

The political and economic necessity to develop such a panethnic organization and consciousness prevailed during the pre-World War II period of plantation labor recruitment to Hawai'i. Local identity has its historic origins in this period based on the common working class background of Native Hawaiians and the immigrant plantation groups including Chinese, Filipinos, Japanese, Koreans, Okinawans, Portuguese and Puerto Ricans. Together these groups shared a collective subordinate social status in opposition to the dominant *haole* (white) planter and merchant oligarchy. Over the years, local identity gained greater importance through the social movements to unionize plantation workers by the International Longshoremen's and Warehousemen's Union (ILWU) in 1946 and to gain legislative control by the Democratic Party in 1954.

The emergence and significance of local identity can be viewed as ultimately contributing to the nonsalience of Asian American identity in Hawai'i, especially since both movements developed in roughly the same time period, i.e., the mid-1960s to early 1970s. Japanese, Chinese, Filipinos, etc. may lack an appreciation of Asian American identity since they already share another panethnic identity with one another that also includes several non-Asian groups such as Native Hawaiians, Portuguese, and Puerto Ricans. Furthermore, the notion of local is essentially specific to Hawai'i, emerging as a result of its particular social history, whereas Asian American is a much broader category with relevance in communities throughout the United States.

The larger political and economic structure of ethnic relations in Hawai'i is the primary factor in the nonemergence of Asian American identity. While the socioeconomic status of Asian Americans in Hawai'i and on the continental United States is generally similar, the former, particularly Japanese and Chinese Americans, wield much greater political power at the state level than do their mainland counterparts. The lesser political power of mainland Asian Americans is indicated by their relative representation in the population. In California, the 2.7 million Asian Americans—including Filipinos (732,000), Chinese (705,000), Japanese (313,000), Vietnamese (280,000), Koreans (260,000), and Asian Indians (160,000)—far outnumber their counterparts in Hawai'i but represent only 9.1 % of the California population of 29.9 million (Los Angeles Times, 1990). In the context of much larger White (17 million) and Hispanic (7.7 million) groups and a substantial African American (2.1 million) population, Asian Americans face a much greater need for coalescing their numbers in pursuit of their common political and economic interests than they do in Hawai'i.

Similarly, at the national level the 6.9 million Asian Americans, who together represent a minimal 2.8 % of the U.S. population, need to view themselves as a collectivity with shared problems and concerns in relation to the larger dominant society. But in Hawai'i, certain Asian American groups, such as Chinese, Japanese and locally born Koreans, can be considered part of the dominant society, thus lessening the political and economic relevance of Asian American identity for them.

Local Culture and the Ethnic Rainbow in Hawai'i

It is widely believed by both academic researchers and laypersons that ethnic relations in Hawai'i are qualitatively "better" than oᵢ. the U.S. mainland and in other parts of the world. The multiethnic riot in Los Angeles and violent outbreaks in other cities in April 1992, following the verdict in the Rodney King case, will certainly not go unnoticed by the proponents of this argument. The latter also maintain that "Hawai'i's ethnic rainbow of shining colors, side by side" has valuable lessons to offer to the rest of the nation: "If America's mushrooming minority populations are to live together in harmony, perhaps they should take a close look at our multicultural test tube" (Yim 1992:B1). One reason advanced for the more tolerant ethnic relations in Hawai'i is the "unique" local culture of the islands, which is a "prime example of the ability of diverse peoples to live harmoniously together" (Ogawa 1981:7). Even Hawai'i's governor, John Waihee, has argued that, "we've tried to call that culture which allows everybody to kind of exchange, go in and out of, enjoy various things . . . in its best sense, local culture. What glues it all together is the native Hawaiian culture" (quoted in Yim 1992: B1).

This view of local culture as the result of "blending, sharing and mixing" processes is not especially insightful (Okamura 1980:122-123). These are highly imprecise and misleading terms that ignore the far more complex political and economic processes that were involved in the development of local culture and identity, in particular the historical oppression of Native Hawaiians and the immigrant plantation groups prior to World War II. Nonetheless, Ogawa (1981:7) has stated that "Hawaii's peoples have created a culture in which everyone feels they can make a contribution, be a part of. It is a culture which provides a sense of shared experiences or 'points of commonality' where people come together and create a mutually beneficial and enriching experience." These points of commonality would include eating certain foods (e.g., plate lunches), the practice of particular customs and habits (e.g., "low keyed" and considerate interactions), modes of entertainment (e.g., ethnic jokes) and shared folklore (e.g., supernatural beliefs). With the exception of social interactions, all of the above common areas are trivial and can hardly serve as the collective basis for a shared culture that is supposed to underlie social relations in Hawai'i.

With regard to ethnic interactions in Hawai'i, an argument could be made that they do involve a certain degree of tolerance and acceptance, at least compared to the mainland (Kirkpatrick 1987:310). This cultural emphasis, popularized as the "aloha spirit," is very much part of the public code of ethnic relationships in Hawai'i, which maintains that ideally such interpersonal relationships should proceed without reference to ethnic stereotypes or prejudice. However, as noted by Odo, the danger of idealizing ethnic interactions is that it tends to deny the reality of ethnic conflicts. Odo states, "It's kind of a mythology that allows us to cover up bad interethnic, interracial relations" (quoted in Yim 1992:B1). The tradition of tolerance allows for Hawai'i's people to avoid acknowledging and confronting the institutionalized inequality among ethnic groups and the resultant tensions and hostilities that are generated. This, perhaps, is the primary reason for the continued emphasis on the tradition of harmonious ethnic relationships despite evidence and knowledge to the contrary. In fact, it has been argued that the cultural emphasis on tolerance and the presence of ethnic antagonisms are "complementary" rather than contradictory insofar as interethnic ties become even more valued in the context of harsh ethnic stereotypes (Kirkpatrick 1987:310).

Without recourse to the notion of a shared or mixed culture, local identity can be seen to derive its significance primarily from structural rather than cultural factors. This structural dimension of local identity is based on the categorical opposition between groups considered local and those considered nonlocal, including haole, immigrants, the military, tourists, and foreign investors. Local is essentially a relative category; groups and individuals are viewed or view themselves as local in relation to others who are not so perceived. From this perspective, local identity is very exclusive rather than all inclusive and serves to create and maintain social boundaries between groups. The political and economic changes described below have heightened the boundaries between local and nonlocal groups and thereby enhanced the salience of local identity.

Japanese Investment in Hawai'i

Clearly, the most dominant economic force in Hawai'i during the 1980s, especially the latter half, was dramatically increased Japanese investment in tourism, resort development, and real estate. Local economists have maintained that virtually all of the economic growth in Hawai'i in the late 1980s was due to Japanese investment and, as a result, the state had experienced its "greatest period of prosperity since the boom years of the 1970s" (Honolulu Star-Bulletin (HSB) 1990a:A8). Between 1986 and 1990, Japanese investment in Hawai'i, including purchases of real estate and businesses, totaled more than $11 billion with well over one-half of this amount in 1989 ($2.8 billion) and 1990 ($3.8

billion) alone (*Sunday Star-Bulletin & Advertiser (SSBA)* 1991a:A1). In 1990, Japanese expenditures were divided among hotels and resorts ($1.52 billion), land ($919 million), office buildings and other commercial property ($885 million), residential property ($413 million), and businesses ($44 million) (*SSBA* 1991b:A8). Japanese corporations presently own 65 % of the hotel rooms in Hawai'i, more than 50 % of the office space in downtown Honolulu, and over one-half of the private golf courses. In addition, Japanese investors purchased about 5,900 higher-priced homes and condominiums valued at $3.2 billion between 1986 and 1990 and thus own 11 % of the total value of real estate in Hawai'i (*SSBA* 1991a:A9).

The cumulative economic impact of Japanese investment in Hawai'i is evident from estimates of the multiplier effect their expenditures have on the state economy. In 1989 direct and indirect economic activity resulting from Japanese investment and tourist expenditures generated $9.5 billion, which, by one way of calculation, was equivalent to 45 % of the $21.3 billion gross state product for that year, although not all of the former amount represented original expenditures from Japan (*HSB* 1990a:A1). (Private sector economists laud Japanese investment in overly positive terms. They maintain, for example, that such investment has reduced unemployment and underemployment in the state. It is evident however that the economy of Hawai'i and thousands of jobs are now dependent on a single foreign country). Japanese corporations accounted for the great bulk (86%) of foreign investment in Hawai'i between 1986 and 1989 (*HSB,* 1990d:A1). Of necessity then, economic developments in Japan, especially their economic, business, and financial problems, have to be of major concern to the local economy and population.

The substantially increased Japanese investment in Hawai'i and throughout the world in the late 1980s was due to the specific convergence of several factors in the Japanese financial sector. These factors included the doubling in value of the yen in relation to the U.S. dollar, the tripling of stock-market values, very low interest rates along with an aggressive lending drive by banks, and runaway urban land prices. However, for various reasons including a crash of the Japanese stock market, these factors are no longer present. As a result, Japanese investment in Hawai'i has declined tremendously from the boom period of the late 1980s; for example, Japanese real estate purchases dropped from $2.9 billion in 1990 to $328 million in 1992 (*HSB* 1993a:A1). Since 1991, Japan-financed construction projects, particularly resort compexes and hotels, have been stalled or canceled resulting in a downturn in the Hawai'i economy, especially in the construction and tourist industries. These are clear indications of the fundamental vulnerability of the economy and the local people to unpredictable and uncontrollable forces from outside the Islands.

During the past decade, Hawai'i's people have become increasingly aware of their expanding economic subordination to Japan and Japanese investors. In a statewide survey of Hawai'i's registered voters (n=408) conducted in 1990, 46 % of the respondents agreed with the statement that "Hawai'i is on the verge of becoming a colony of Japan," although 52 % expressed disagreement (HSB 1990b:A8). Two-thirds (67%) of the respondents believe that Japanese nationals "don't care about Hawai'i except as a place to play or make money," and 60 % do not "trust the political motives" of Japanese investors. These responses are consistent with the view that Hawai'i already is an economic colony of Japan, especially as a result of tourism investment (Kim 1993:239).

Tourism Overdevelopment

Tourism continues to be the mainstay of the Hawai'i economy representing a whopping 38.3 % of the gross state product (GSP) of $28.6 billion in 1991, far exceeding military expenditures (10.9%) as the second largest contributor to the GSP (Hawaii 1993:343). The annual number of visitors currently totals 6.5 million or almost six times the state population of 1.1 million (Hawaii 1993:185). On any given day, there are more than 150,000 tourists in the islands who would represent about 14 % of the resident population. On the neighbor islands with their much smaller population, the average daily number of tourists comprises substantial percentages of the resident population, e.g., Maui (41%) and Kaua'i (37%) (Hawaii 1993:187). However, after years of consistent growth the annual number of tourists to Hawai'i began to decline from its high of seven million in 1990 as a result of the mainland recession and the Persian Gulf War. Visitors from the mainland and Canada have decreased from 4.7 million in 1990 to less than 4 million just two years later, with a consequent decline of $1.1 billion in visitor expenditures in 1992 (*HSB* 1993b:A1). These are clear indications that the Hawai'i tourist industry has entered the maturation, if not saturation, phase of its development in which such decreases are inevitable (Mak and Sakai, 1992:188).

The overall social and economic impact of tourism in Hawai'i extends far beyond the physical presence of tourists. Direct visitor-related expenditures totaled $11 billion in 1991, which represented nearly a doubling since 1985 (Hawaii 1993:203). Tourism generated $6.5 billion in household income and another $1.2 billion in state and county tax revenues in 1991 which was about

257

40 % of total tax revenues collected (Hawaii 1993:203). Most significantly for working people, 140,000 jobs are generated directly and 250,000 jobs are created directly and indirectly by tourism, which represents about 40 % of the employment positions in Hawai'i (Hawaii 1993:204). These generally low pay, low mobility, and low security jobs in the tourist industry are primarily in service and sales work: hotel services (28%), "eating and drinking places" (24%), other retail trade (19%) and other services (13%) (Hawaii 1992:200).

Overdependence on tourism has essentially resulted in a "locked-in economy" in Hawai'i in which economic diversification becomes increasingly more difficult to develop (Aoudé, 1993). The state economy was recently rated the worst in the nation by U.S. News and World Report, particularly in terms of decline in unemployment, business bankruptcies, and income growth rate (*HSB* 1992b). A tourism-dependent economy, with its generally low wage and insecure jobs, provides limited opportunities for socioeconomic mobility or even for maintaining a certain standard of living (Okamura, 1992). It is not surprising then that a recent statewide survey (n=419) reported that 81 % of the respondents believe that Hawai'i is "too dependent" on tourism (HSB 1993d:E5).

The restricted economic opportunities that result from tourism dependence are compounded by the extremely high cost of living in Hawai'i, with Honolulu having the dubious distinction as the second most expensive metropolitan area in the nation (*HSB* 1992a:A1). Housing costs in Hawai'i also are among the highest in the country and prevent an estimated 80 to 90 % of renters from becoming homeowners. It is estimated that it costs 38 % more to live in Hawai'i, the so-called paradise tax, than on the mainland (*Honolulu Advertiser (HA)* 1992), a price that local residents have been forced into paying.

Because of the overdependence on tourism, the overall quality of life for Hawai'i's people is especially vulnerable to worldwide fluctuations in economic activity and to uncontrollable international political events. Recent state budget reductions for government services and programs have been necessitated by a substantial decline in government tax revenues, which have resulted from a slowing down of the economy beginning in 1991, especially in tourism. As a consequence of the economic downturn, unemployment has reached its highest level (5%) in over five years, particularly in the neighbor island tourist industry.

With regard to Japanese investment in tourism, particularly in hotel and resort development, the economy of Hawai'i has never been as dependent on foreign investment and control. Because Japanese corporations have so heavily invested in hotels, resort complexes, golf courses, and other sectors of the tourist industry, there is concern for their trend toward "enclave investment." Enclave investment establishes a closed system for the ultimate benefit of investors in which profits flow out from an investment site back to the investors' base. Japanese purchases and development of hotels, resorts, golf courses, restaurants, and shopping centers in Hawai'i—in collaboration with travel agencies, airlines and tour companies in Japan—comprise all the necessary elements for enclave investment. The result is that profits from Japanese tourism activity return to Japan rather than benefit the local community, aside from the creation of low paying sales and service jobs.

Japanese represent about 25 % of the annual number of tourists to Hawai'i (*HSB* 1993c:A1). However, in contrast to the substantial decline in visitors from the U.S. mainland, and Canada in recent years, Japanese tourists have more than doubled in number since 1986 to over 1.6 million in 1992. Like Japanese investment in Hawai'i in the latter half of the 1980s, this considerable increase also can be attributed to the enhanced value of the yen. While there are considerably fewer visitors from Japan than from the United States, and their average stay of six days is shorter than that of mainland visitors, Japanese tourists spend $344 a day as opposed to $141 for their mainland counterparts (Hawaii 1993:197). Japanese tourists contributed $2.8 billion directly into the Hawai'i economy in 1991 (compared to $5.8 billion by American tourists), which represented almost a tripling since 1985 (Hawaii 1993:201). Thus, Japanese tourists have a disproportionate impact on the state economy in relation to their absolute numbers due to their greater purchasing power and also their supposedly greater potential for market growth compared to mainland visitors. Hawai'i has recently dropped to third place behind Australia and Europe as the destination choice among the ten million Japanese who annually travel abroad. This is another indication of the fickleness of the tourist market that can have disastrous consequences for local working people and their quality of life.

Hawaiian Sovereignty and Identity

One of the most significant changes in ethnic relations in Hawai'i during the past decade has been the further development of the Hawaiian sovereignty movement. Its more recent origins can be traced to the 1970s with the emergence of various politically-oriented Native Hawaiian organizations concerned with protesting land abuses and advocating their rights and claims to a land base (Trask 1984:122). Since then, the movement has developed to include occupations of restricted areas and finally to declarations of sovereignty based on indigenous rights to the land (Trask 1984-85:119).

Trask (1984-85:121) distinguishes the "Hawaiian Movement" from other protest struggles in Hawai'i by its demand for a land base, which follows from the native rights of Hawaiians as the original inhabitants of the islands. Other community struggles, such as those against the eviction of residents of Waiahole and Waikane valleys and Ota Camp, advocated the rights of local people to maintain their cultural lifestyle in their established communities (Okamura 1980:134). However, Trask (1984-85:121) notes that as the 1970s proceeded, the indigenous rights of Native Hawaiians as "historically unique" from the rights of local groups began to be asserted in other community struggles.

During the 1980s several organizations were established to advocate either sovereignty or independence for Native Hawaiians. Perhaps the largest and best organized of these groups is *Ka Lahui Hawai'i* (The Hawaiian Nation), which was formed at an islands-wide constitutional convention in 1987. Ka Lahui Hawai'i has over 16,000 members, a formal constitution, elected officials and representatives from each island, and executive and legislative government branches. Its approach to establishing a sovereign nation is to have Native Hawaiians recognized under the U.S. government policy that gives all Native American peoples the right to self-governance (*Ka Lahui Hawai'i* 1991:4). The land base for the Hawaiian nation would include half of the 1.4 million acres of ceded lands presently under state control, the 190,000 acres of land administered by the State Department of Hawaiian Home Lands, and additional lands provided in compensation for the overthrow of the Hawaiian monarchy in 1893 (Trask 1992:255).

In addition to the sovereignty movement, the past decade also has been distinguished by continued expression and affirmation of Native Hawaiian identity, particularly through its cultural revitalization of values, beliefs, and customs. Hawaiian traditional dance, arts and crafts, and music have continued to flourish. Interest has been renewed in traditional health and healing practices and in religious rituals and beliefs. Most importantly, the Hawaiian language, at one time prohibited to be used in the public schools, continues its revival with the establishment of the Punana Leo language immersion schools in which Native Hawaiian children are taught in their own language. These and other similar manifestations represent continued revitalization and articulation of Hawaiian culture and identity, a process that began in the early 1970s as the Hawaiian *renaissance* (Kanahele 1982:25).

The development of the sovereignty movement and the general affirmation of Native Hawaiian identity have implications for local identity insofar as they have undoubtedly influenced many Native Hawaiians to view themselves as Na

Kanaka Maoli, the indigenous people of Hawai'i. As the indigenous people, Hawaiians have native rights to own and control land, to worship, to fish, hunt, and gather natural resources, and other ancestral rights that distinguish them from other local groups. It is not clear what proportion of the Native Hawaiian population considers themselves more as indigenous than as local, but they can claim both identities without contradiction.

Asserting their collective identity as the native people of Hawai'i may create divisions between Native Hawaiians and other local groups, but these divisions are not necessarily absolute cleavages. Many non-Hawaiians have kinship ties with Native Hawaiians through marital relationships. The attitudes toward and the extent of support for Hawaiian sovereignty among non-Hawaiians are presently unknown, but some local groups have expressed support. The Hawai'i chapter of the Japanese American Citizens League (JACL) introduced and adopted a resolution at their 1992 national convention that called for JACL support for Hawaiian sovereignty.

Cleavage Among Ethnic Groups

Since the 1970s there has been a widening social cleavage between Japanese Americans and other ethnic groups in Hawai'i including Filipinos, haole, and Native Hawaiians. Native Hawaiians have expressed resentment against Japanese American "racial exclusiveness in social relations and their patronage system" (McGregor 1985:2 cited in Kent 1989:114). Filipino Americans along with haole have been quite vocal in accusing Japanese Americans of discriminating against them in employment, particularly for state government positions. Filipino Americans (12.9%) and haole (22.8%) were underrepresented among permanent state employees (excluding Department of Education teachers and University of Hawai'i faculty) hired in fiscal year 1989. Japanese Americans (31.9%) were hired at a much higher rate, proportional, however, to their representation in the Hawai'i labor force (HSB 1991: A4). These hiring imbalances contribute to the widespread perception that Japanese Americans "control" state government employment through favoring their own applicants, thereby discriminating against non-Japanese.

Hostility against Japanese is not a new phenomenon; it has been present in various forms throughout much of their historical presence in Hawai'i. As a result of their participation in the sugar plantation strikes of 1909 and 1920 and their growing American-born population, Japanese encountered tremendous racism and discrimination from the larger society during the 1920s. However, the more recent antagonism against them differs from previous such expressions insofar as it has been described as an "anti-Japanese backlash" (Kotani 1985: 174; Boylan 1986: 1). The use of this term indicates that the more recent hostility against Japanese Americans is a response to their perceived higher political and economic status and thus to a perceived division between them and other ethnic groups in Hawai'i.

The anti-Japanese backlash resulted from a prevalent negative stereotype of Japanese Americans that they "dominate" Hawai'i both politically and economically. As noted by Odo (1984), this stereotype is based more on a "mythology of AJA power and arrogance" that is partially attributable to various types of mid-level administrative, professional, and clerical occupations they hold, particularly in the public sector. Japanese Americans are especially well-represented in the state Department of Education as school administrators (52%), elementary (63%), and secondary (50%) schoolteachers, and clerical staff (50%) (*HSB* 1990c:A3). In those positions, they come into direct contact with a considerable segment of Hawai'i residents and their children, and oftentimes are made to bear the burden of blame for the failures of the long underfunded public educational system.

In the larger economic sphere, contrary to popular misconception, Japanese Americans do not have the highest occupational status in Hawai'i. Chinese Americans and haole have such status, based on their substantial overrepresentation in professional, management and executive positions (Okamura 1990:5). Japanese American men continue to be well-represented in blue-collar work in Hawai'i where they comprise 36 % of construction workers, 40 % of mechanics, and 41 % of precision production workers. (Kotani 1985:154). Japanese American women constitute 41 % of secretaries and 26 % of sales cashiers. Given their older median age, Japanese Americans are the largest group in the Hawai'i labor force (although a rapidly declining one with the ongoing retirement of the Nisei second generation), which also contributes to a perception of economic power and employment discrimination against non-Japanese.

The supposed economic dominance of Japanese Americans in Hawai'i is especially absent in terms of corporate power. Of the 50 largest corporations in Hawai'i (based on sales in 1992), only four, i.e., Servco Pacific (no. 12), Tony Management Group (no. 44), Kuakini Health System (no. 45), and Star Markets (no. 46) are owned and controlled by local Japanese Americans (Hawaii Business, 1993). The largest corporations in Hawai'i still include a few of the former "Big Five" companies, i.e., Castle & Cooke (now known as Dole Food, no. 1) and Alexander & Baldwin (no. 6), along with other multinational corporations. Japanese Americans also tend to be considerably underrepresented among the leading business executives who wield corporate power in Hawai'i through holding multiple directorships in locally-based corporations (Kotani 1985: 172). In essence, as argued by Kent (1989:114),

> the AJA elite has never *constituted a legitimate ruling class in Hawai'i.* Instead, they have skilfully performed a multitude of roles—front men, middle men, mediators, agents, and power brokers—in the service of the authentic ruling class, much of which does not reside in the islands and which prefers invisibility as one element of its power. (emphasis in original)

The real sources of power over the Hawai'i economy are multinational corporations based on the U.S. mainland or abroad, including United Airlines, Torray Clark, Prudential Life Insurance Co., Jardine Pacific in Hong Kong, and Kyo-Ya Co., Azabu Group, Seibu Group and Kumagai Gumi Co. in Japan.

Despite the fallacious nature of the "dominating" stereotype, the backlash and cleavage against Japanese Americans are very real in their consequences. In many ways, Japanese Americans have replaced haoles as the scapegoat group in Hawai'i toward which the hostilities of other ethnic groups, including haoles, are directed.   As scapegoats, they may perceive their collective identity and acceptance as local being threatened, especially since the negative stereotypes applied to them, such as "dominating," "arrogant," and "clannish," are clearly nonlocal characteristics.

Japanese Americans, particularly those of the third and fourth generations, have responded to the backlash against them not by reorganizing themselves to maintain their social status or to advance their collective concerns but by downplaying their Japanese American identity. They can be seen as emphasizing the local dimension of their ethnic identity in their appreciation of Hawai'i and its peoples and cultures. In doing so, they reaffirm their social ties with other local groups and to Hawai'i as a special place for them to live, work, and maintain family and friendship bonds. Twenty years ago, Yamamoto (1974:101) argued that the increasing identification of third-generation Sansei Japanese with being local served as a compromise resolution of a developing cultural identity crisis between being Japanese and being committed to Hawai'i and its people. This identity dilemma is still with local Japanese but has been made more problematic by the widening cleavage with other ethnic groups.

In the 1970s, in response to the influx of Philippine immigrants who appeared to pose a threat to their collective identity, local Hawai'i-born Filipinos engaged in a similar process of asserting the local component of their ethnic identity . Filipino immigrants were perceived by their local-born counterparts as reinforcing derogatory stereotypes that had originated with the predominantly uneducated and lowly employed plantation labor recruits. To emphasize their local identity and to dissociate themselves from immigrant Filipino stereotypes, Hawai'i-born Filipinos engaged in violent conflict with the immigrants and avoided them (Okamura, 1983).

Conclusion

The continuing salience of local identity can be attributed to various external and internal forces of development and change, discussed above, that gained considerably in their scope and intensity during the past decade. In particular, substantially increased Japanese investment, especially in tourism, and the continued overdevelopment of tourism, have had the greatest impact on the meaning and significance of local identity. In the 1970s, Yamamoto (1979:114) argued that "Being local assumes that while social, cultural, and economic changes are going to move the overall social structure of Hawai'i further away from traditional community, the changes need not entail the total Americanization of Hawaii's people." However, the decade of the 1980s has resulted not so much in the Americanization of people in Hawai'i but in the ongoing internationalization of the islands through their further incorporation into the global capitalist economy.

Globalization of Hawai'i's economy and other political and economic processes are contributing to the increasing marginalization of Hawai'i's people to external sources of power and control. As a result, local identity has been maintained as an expression of resistance and opposition, albeit unorganized, to such outside domination and intrusion. The designation *Local* continues to represent the shared identity of people in Hawai'i who have an appreciation of and a commitment to the islands and their peoples, cultures, and ways of life, which are perceived as being threatened by external forces of development and change, e.g., tourism and foreign investment. However, while there has been increasing recognition among local people of their peripheral status in Hawai'i, there has not been a resulting collective effort to regain control of political and economic forces in the islands from external sources.

In the late 1970s, such an effort was described as *Palaka* Power, named for the durable cloth used to make the work clothes of plantation laborers, stevedores, and other working-class people in Hawai'i. Palaka Power, or what might be termed local advocacy, sought especially to promote and protect the interests and values of local people during the 1978 State Constitutional Convention;

however, it never developed into an organized social movement. State Representative David Hagino, the principal theorist of the Palaka Power initiative, attributed its failure to the yuppie generation of political leaders currently in power who are more concerned with "grandiose projects, ostentatious spending and conspicuous consumption" than with social justice and equality (*HA* 1993: B1).

In his 1989 address at the 18th annual meeting of the Japan-Hawai'i Economic Council in Nagoya, even Hawai'i's governor acknowledged the ongoing process of marginalization of Hawai'i's people.

> while there is no doubt that Hawaii's residents have benefited from an economy that is fueled by dollars from Tokyo, Vancouver, Sydney and Chicago, there is also no doubt that Hawaii's residents are experiencing a sense of loss—loss of their land to others and, more important, loss of control. (*Hawaii Business* 1990:29)

While the governor may speak about loss of land and control to outside investors, his and previous state government administrations have not done very much to limit those losses and, in fact, have facilitated them through their subsidizing of the tourist industry with taxpayer monies. In typical response to the ongoing slump in the tourist industry, the Hawai'i Visitors Bureau received an additional $8.5 million from the State Legislature in 1993 so that it could lure tourists from Germany, Taiwan, Hong Kong, and other far flung places to Hawai'i even though its supplementary promotional funding the previous year had not resulted in an increased number of tourists. The lack of political leadership and long-term vision on the part of elected government officials towards the development of an alternative economic future for Hawai'i, at least one not so heavily constrained by tourism and foreign investment, only contributes to the growing feeling of loss of control to outside forces among local people.

The perception of powerlessness among local people to change the economic and political future of Hawai'i is evident in the increasing migration of tens of thousands of island residents to the U.S. mainland each year. This movement of "voting with one's feet" indicates the growing level of dissatisfaction with life in Hawai'i, particularly in terms of the high cost of living, the relative lack of financially rewarding jobs, and the high cost of housing. The mainland migration (excluding military personnel and their dependents) to only four western states (California, Washington, Oregon, and Nevada) has been estimated at almost 11,000 annually (*SSBA* 1992: B1), while the total civilian movement to the mainland is estimated at 21,740, nearly 2 % of the state population (Miklius 1992:242) which is a considerable percentage considering the cost of moving to the mainland.

Local identity, while not organized into a viable social movement, will continue in its significance for Hawai'i's people if only because of their further marginalization through the ongoing internationalization of the economy and overdependence on tourism. Because of this overdependence, it may well be too late for the necessary changes to be initiated that can give power and control to the people of Hawai'i.

References

Aoudé, I.G. 1993. "Tourist Attraction: Hawaii's Locked-in Economy." In P. Manicas (ed.), *Social Process in Hawai'i: A Reader*. Pp. 218-235. New York: McGraw Hill, Inc.

Boylan, D. 1986. Interview in *Hawaii Herald*. "Japanese Americans and Elections '86." September, pp. 1, 5, 12.

Hawaii Business 1990. "The Japaning of Hawaii." January.

_____. 1993. "The *Hawaii Business* Top 250." August.

Hawaii. Department of Business, Economic Development and Tourism (DBEDT). 1992. *The State of Hawaii Data Book 1991*. Honolulu: DBEDT.

_____. 1993. *The State of Hawaii Data Book 1992*. Honolulu: DBEDT.

Honolulu Advertiser 1992. "Paradise Tax Highest Ever, But May Start Falling." September 25.

_____. 1993. "Another View: Much Endures." April 4, pp. B1, B4.

Honolulu Star-Bulletin 1990a. "Japanese Money Fired Isle Growth." April 11, pp. A1, A8.

_____. 1990b. "Half Believe State Nearly a Japan Colony." April 25, pp. A1, A8.

_____. 1990c. "Most Education Jobs Held by 1 Racial Group." August 16, pp. A3.

_____. 1990d. "Investors Fear Backlash in Islands." November 20, pp. A1, A8.

_____. 1991. "Judiciary Tallies its Ethnic Hires." August 2, pp. A4.

_____. 1992a. "Mastering Isles High Living Cost Takes Scrimping." August 11, pp. A1.

_____. 1992b. "Isle Economy is Rated Worst." September 16, pp. D1.

_____. 1993a. "Japanese Investing Falls 80%." March 18, pp. A1.

_____. 1993b. "Spending by Tourists Shows Sharp Decline." May 8, pp. A1, A8.

_____. 1993c. "HVB Report Full of Facts on Tourists." May 15, pp. A1.

_____. 1993d. "Isle Residents Don't Want to Foot the Bill on Tourist Promotion." June 16, pp. E1, E5.

Ka Lahui Hawai'i 1991. "Ka Lahui Hawai'i, The Sovereign Nation of Hawai'i." A Compilation of Legal Materials for Workshops on the Hawaiian Nation.

Kanahele, G.S. 1982. "The New Hawaiians." *Social Process in Hawaii*, 29:21-31.

Kent, N.J. 1989. "Myth of the Golden Men: Ethnic Elites and Dependent Development in the 50th State." In *Ethnicity and Nation-building in the Pacific*. Pp. 98-117. Tokyo: The United Nations University.

Kim, K. 1993. The Political Economy of Foreign Investment in Hawai'i. In P. Manicas (ed.), *Social Process in Hawai'i: A Reader*, Pp. 236-245. New York: McGraw Hill, Inc.

Kirkpatrick, J. 1987. "Ethnic Antagonism and Innovation in Hawaii." In J. Boucher and D. Landis (eds.), *Ethnic Conflict: International Perspectives*, Pp. 298-316. Beverly Hills: Sage Publications.

Kotani, R.M. 1985. *The Japanese in Hawaii: A Century of Struggle*. Honolulu: The Hawaii Hochi, Ltd.

Los Angeles Times 1990. May 11, pp. 5.

Mak, J. and M. Sakai 1992. "Tourism in Hawai'i: Economic Issues for the 1990s and Beyond." In Z.A. Smith and R.C. Pratt (eds.), *Politics and Public Policy in Hawai'i*. Albany: State University of New York Press.

McGregor, D. 1985. The Hawaiian Perspective on Japanese in Politics and Business. Unpublished paper.

Miklius, W. 1992. "Outmigration." In R.W. Roth (ed.), *The Price of Paradise: Lucky We Live Hawai'i?* Honolulu: Mutual Publishing.

Odo, F. 1984. "The Rise and Fall of the Nisei." *Hawaii Herald*, August-November (six part series).

Ogawa, D.M. 1981. "Dialogue: What is Local?" *Humanities News* 2(1):1, 7.

Okamura, J.Y. 1980. "Local Culture and Society in Hawai'i." *Amerasia* 7(2):119-137.

_____. 1983. "Immigrant and Local Filipino Perceptions of Ethnic Conflict." In W.C. McCready (ed.), *Culture, Ethnicity and Identity*, Pp. 241-263. New York: Academic Press.

_____. 1990. "Ethnicity and Stratification in Hawaii." *Operation Manong Resource Papers*, No. 1. Operation Manong Program, University of Hawai'i.

_____. 1992. "People of Color in Hawaii's Ethnic Rainbow." Paper presented at Annual Conference of the Hawai'i Sociological Association, Honolulu, Hawai'i, March 21.

Sunday Star-Bulletin & Advertiser 1991a. "Japan Investors Pull Back After Record Haul in 1990." November 24, pp. A1, A9.

_____. 1991b. "Japanese Investment in Hawaii During 1990." November 24, pp. A8.

_____. 1992. "Moving to Mainland: Trail of Plastic Hints at Growing Migration." April 19, pp. B1.

Trask, H.K. 1984-85. "Hawaiians, American Colonization and the Quest for Independence." *Social Process in Hawaii*, 31:101-136.

_____. 1992. "Kupa'a 'Aina: Native Hawaiian Nationalism in Hawai'i." In Z. A. Smith and R. C. Pratt (eds.), *Politics and Public Policy in Hawai'i*. Albany: State University of New York Press.

Wei, W. 1993. *The Asian American Movement: A Social History*. Philadelphia: Temple University Press.

Yamamoto, E. 1974. "From 'Japanee' to Local: Community Change and the Redefinition of Sansei Identity in Hawaii." Senior thesis, Department of Sociology, University of Hawaii.

_____. 1979. "The Significance of Local." *Social Process in Hawaii*, 27:101-115.

Yim, S. 1992. "Hawaii's Ethnic Rainbow: Shining Colors, Side by Side." *Sunday Star-Bulletin & Advertiser*, January 5, pp. B1, B3.

Cultural and economic boundaries of Korean ethnicity: a comparative analysis

Pyong Gap Min

Abstract

This article explains Korean immigrants' ethnicity in the United States, focusing on their cultural homogeneity and economic concentration. Korean immigrants are a culturally homogeneous group in terms of a common language, a set of common customs and values, and a commonality in historical experiences. This cultural homogeneity and lack of subgroup differences provide a cultural basis of Korean ethnicity. Moreover, the vast majority of Korean immigrant families are affiliated with Korean immigrant churches, which facilitates Koreans' fellowship and retention of the Korean cultural tradition. In addition, Korean immigrants concentrate in a limited range of small businesses, and this occupational segregation provides an economic basis of Korean ethnicity.

The extent to which members of an ethnic/immigrant group maintain their native cultural tradition and social interactions with co-ethnic members is referred to as 'ethnic attachment' or 'ethnicity' (Hurh and Kim 1984; Reitz 1980; Yinger 1980). Korean immigrants in the United States maintain a high level of ethnicity. That is, the vast majority of Korean immigrants speak the Korean language, eat mainly Korean food, and practise Korean customs most of the time. Most Korean immigrants are affiliated with at least one ethnic organization and involved in active informal ethnic networks. For example, Hurh and Kim (1988) report that 90 per cent of Korean immigrants in Chicago mainly speak the Korean language at home and that 82 per cent are affiliated with one or more ethnic organizations. A comparative study of three Asian ethnic groups – Korean, Chinese, and Filipino – indicates that a much larger proportion of Korean Americans (75 per

Ethnic and Racial Studies Volume 14 Number 2 April 1991
© Routledge 1991 0141–9870/91/1402–225 $3-/1

cent) than Filipino (50 per cent) or Chinese Americans (19 per cent) have joined one or more ethnic associations (Mangiafico 1988: p. 174).

Theorists of ethnicity have emphasized two major factors as bases of ethnicity. First, commonalities in culture and historical experiences that members of a group share provide an important basis of ethnicity (Glazer and Moynihan 1963; Gordon 1964; Greeley 1971; Greeley 1974). A minority group that has a common language, a common religion, and/or other cultural and historical commonalities is likely to maintain higher levels of ethnic identity and ethnic subculture than other minority groups. Second, productive activities, particularly associated with job-market concentration, also contribute to ethnic solidarity and ethnic identity (Bonacich 1973; Bonacich and Modell 1980; Olzak 1986; Reitz 1980; Yancy *et al.* 1976). Minority/immigrant groups usually concentrate in certain occupations, and the occupational concentration puts them in conflict and competition with the majority population or other minority groups over economic interests. Inter-group conflicts for economic survival enhance also in-group solidarity.

When cultural boundaries coincide with boundaries defined by pro-ductive activities, 'ethnic solidarity is doubly reinforced' (Olzak 1986; see also Bodnar *et al.* 1982). Korean immigrants in the United States maintain a high level of ethnicity exactly because of this coincidence of cultural and economic boundaries. That is, Korean immigrants are a culturally homogeneous group, and at the same time they occupa-tionally concentrate in a limited range of small businesses. This article intends to explain Korean immigrants' strong ethnic attachment, focus-ing on their cultural homogeneity and occupational concentration. The extent to which Korean immigrants are culturally homogeneous or economically segregated can be effectively assessed in comparison with other immigrant/ethnic groups. Thus, this article will very often compare Korean immigrants with other minority/immigrant groups in the United States, particularly with other Asian ethnic groups, in order to explain Korean ethnicity.

Cultural homogeneity

The 1970 US census estimated that the Korean-American population was less than 70,000. It increased to more than 350,000 in 1980 (US Bureau of the Census 1983, p. 125) and has probably reached one million in 1990 (*The Central Daily*, 29 May 1989). This suggests that the predominant majority of Korean Americans are the post-1965 immigrants from South Korea. South Korea is a small and culturally homogeneous country, and Korean immigrants sustain a high level of ethnicity partly because of their strong cultural and historical ties.

The cultural homogeneity of Korean immigrants becomes clearer when they are compared with other immigrant groups in the United

States. It is a well-known fact that Filipino immigrants consist of a number of subgroups based on language and place of origin. The absence of a common native language and regional differences partly contribute to factionalism and disunity characterizing Filipino-Americans' community organization (Pido 1986, p. 95). Asian-Indian immigrants, like Filipino immigrants, consist of many linguistic-regional subethnic groups. Thus, close friends and visiting patterns among Indian immigrants usually involve people from the same region or the same language group (Saran 1985, p. 114). Moreover, Indian immigrants consist of religiously heterogeneous subgroups, which is one major source of internal conflicts (Williams 1988).

Researchers have described earlier Chinese immigrants as having maintained strong in-group ties (Light 1972; Lyman 1968, 1974). This generalization is, however, no longer applicable to recent Chinese immigrants, who are composed of several nationality groups: Chinese immigrants from Taiwan, Hong Kong, Singapore, Vietnam, and mainland China. Immigrants from Taiwan and mainland China differ significantly in political ideology, socio-economic background, and other characteristics (Kwong 1987; Mangiafico 1988). Even immigrants from mainland China consist of several linguistic-regional subgroups and thus are not a culturally homogeneous group. Another national-origin immigrant group that has significant subgroup differences is the Iranian. The Iranian immigrant-group contains four ethnic-religious subgroups: Armenians, Baha'is, Jews, and Muslims. Each Iranian ethnic-religious subgroup has its own economy, which is only weakly tied to an encompassing Iranian ethnic economy (Light *et al.* 1990).

By contrast, Korean immigrants have only one native language and regional differences are insignificant in their ethnic identity. South Korea is a small country, smaller than the state of Georgia. More than half of recent Korean immigrants have come from Seoul, the capital of South Korea, and more than three-quarters of them have come from the five largest cities (Park *et al.* 1990, p. 31). The vast majority of them have received high-school and/or college education in Seoul and other large metropolitan cities. Thus, alumni associations, which play an important role in maintaining Koreans' friendship networks, can include most Korean immigrants. Schools in the homeland may well be an important basis for ethnic organizations for Chinese, Indian, and Filipino immigrants as well. Yet, since the source country of each of these other Asian immigrant-groups is so large, alumni associations can tie only a small proportion of immigrants.

Koreans in the US, with the exception of Koreatown in Los Angeles, do not maintain a territorial community. Widely scattered in the whole metropolitan area, they maintain a non-territorial community. Ethnic media play the central role in integrating geographically dispersed Korean immigrants. Ethnic media seem to be more effective in enhancing ethnicity for Korean immigrants, especially since Koreans have only one native language. Almost all Korean immigrants can read Korean-language newspapers and understand Korean-language television programmes. Native-language media, however, can serve only a small proportion of Indian or Filipino immigrants, who consist of several language groups.

Affiliation with ethnic churches

The vast majority of Korean immigrants are affiliated with Korean immigrant churches, which also facilitates Koreans' ethnic attachment. Christianity is a minority religion in Korea, with approximately 16 per cent of Koreans affiliated with Protestant churches and another 5 per cent with Catholic churches (Korean National Bureau of Statistics 1987). However, Christians are overrepresented among Korean immigrants. In a pre-departure survey conducted in Seoul, 54 per cent of the 1986 Korean immigrants to the US reported that they were affiliated with a Christian church in Korea (Park *et al.* 1990, p. 60). Korean immigrants have largely come from the urban, middle-class segment of the Korean population in which the Christian religion is very strong. This is one of the major reasons why Christians are overrepresented among Korean immigrants. Many Christians fled from North to South Korea before and during the Korean War, and North Korean refugees, who have no strong family ties in South Korea, have immigrated to the US in a greater proportion than the general population in South Korea. This is another reason for the overrepresentation of Christians among Korean immigrants. Finally, Korean Christians are more likely to choose immigration to the US than are Buddhists or Confucianists, which has also contributed to the disproportionate Christian background of Korean immigrants.

Many Korean immigrants, who were not Christians in Korea, probably attend the Korean ethnic church for practical purposes. Thus, an overwhelming majority of Korean immigrants are involved in ethnic churches. In a survey conducted in Los Angeles in 1986, 66.8 per cent of the Korean respondents were found to attend the Korean ethnic church at least every two weeks. The 1988–89 Korean Churches Directory of New York shows that there were 165 Korean churches in five boroughs of New York City. Assuming that the Korean population of New York City in 1988 was 72,000, there was one Korean church for every 436 Koreans in New York City.

Korean immigrant churches serve several practical functions for Korean immigrants, which are indispensable to Koreans' adjustment in the United States (Min 1992). Two of these practical functions contribute to Korean ethnicity. Many Korean immigrants attend ethnic church for the purpose of fellowship. In this connection, it is useful to note the findings from the 1986 Chicago study of Korean immigrants (Hurh and Kim 1988, p. 63). In the study 23.6 per cent of the church-going respondents indicated fellowship or meeting friends as the primary motive for attending church. After Sunday service all Korean immigrant churches have a fellowship hour, which usually lasts half an hour to one hour. During the fellowship hour, church members exchange greetings and enjoy informal talks with fellow church-members. All Korean churches serve refreshments during the fellowship hour, and a significant proportion of them serve a Korean-style full lunch (Min 1992).

Korean immigrant churches are usually small. A survey of Korean churches in New York City indicates that the median number of members is eighty-two. The small congregations of Korean immigrant churches can be explained by the need of Korean immigrants for small-group, primary social interactions. As I. Kim (1981, p. 199) rightly points out, the ethnic church plays the role of 'a pseudo-extended family' for many Korean immigrants. Korean immigrants attending a small church enjoy intimate friendship networks with church members not only inside the church but also outside it. A significant proportion of Korean immigrants seem largely to establish informal friendship networks with other members of their church by inviting them to dinner or to go picnicking, by playing sports with them or by taking trips together. In this connection, it is important to note that 45 per cent of those Korean immigrants in Chicago with one or more intimate Korean friends in the same city first made friends with them in the ethnic church (Hurh and Kim 1987).

Whereas a large Korean church provides more formal programmes for church members, it is less effective than a small church when it comes to providing Korean immigrants with an intimate social environment. However, even large Korean immigrant churches have made adjustments in such a way that they meet the needs of Korean immigrants for fellowship and belongingness. Korean immigrant churches usually divide church members into several groups by area of residence, and help each group to hold regular district meetings called *Kuyok Yebae*. It has been found that nearly 80 per cent of Korean churches in New York City have district groups, and that they hold district meetings once or more a month (Min 1992). A district meeting combines a religious service and a dinner party at a member's private home, thus providing members with ample opportunity for informal social interactions. Church members who belong to the same district rotate hosting the meeting, usually offering a prepared dinner.

The other practical function of Korean immigrant churches that contributes to Korean ethnicity is maintenance of the Korean cultural tradition. Korean churches help to preserve Korean culture in several different ways. First, they contribute to the maintenance of Korean culture partly because the Korean language and customs are more strictly observed inside the Korean ethnic church than outside it. Korean pastors give sermons in Korean for almost all adult services of worship. Even for children's services, they use the Korean language more often than English. A survey reveals that only 20 per cent of the New York City Korean churches provide services for children in English alone, and the others use either Korean (24 per cent) or a bilingual mix (55 per cent) (Min 1992). Moreover, a large proportion of Korean immigrant churches provide a Korean-language programme for children, which is central to language retention for the Korean American community.

Exposure to Korean culture in the Korean immigrant church is not limited to the Korean language. All Korean immigrant churches celebrate religious and Korean traditional holidays such as Easter, Thanksgiving, and New Year's Day by serving a variety of traditional Korean food. Many Korean church participants wear traditional Korean dress on important Korean holidays. Korean churches also teach children traditional Korean values, such as filial piety, in a number of ways. For example, the youth programme in some Korean immigrant churches teaches children to prepare breakfast for parents on Mothers' Day. Almost all Korean churches organize an end-of-year party at a member's private home on New Year's Eve, when church members usually play a traditional Korean game called *yoot*.

Of course, ethnic churches contribute to maintaining ethnicity for other immigrant groups. However, they seem to be far more effective for sustaining ethnicity for Korean immigrants than for other current immigrant groups, since Koreans have a much higher level of affiliation with ethnic churches than do other groups. Although more than 80 per cent of Filipino immigrants are Catholics (Pido 1986), most of them seem to attend American Catholic churches. A survey (Mangiafico 1988, p. 174) shows that only 17 per cent of Filipino immigrants are affiliated with their ethnic churches. A much smaller proportion of Chinese immigrants than Korean immigrants have a Christian background (B. Kim 1978). As previously noted, Asian-Indian immigrants consist of religiously heterogeneous groups such as Hindus, Sikhs, Muslims, and Jains. Although Judaism is considered to have played a significant role in uniting Jewish Americans, less than 50 per cent of Jewish Americans are affiliated with synagogues. A survey conducted in Boston, for example, shows that only 38 per cent of Jewish Americans are affiliated with synagogues (Cohen 1985, p. 56).

The Christian religion is not an indigenous Korean religion, whereas Judaism is a Jewish religion. Some readers may wonder how Korean immigrants can revive Korean ethnicity through a religion adopted from the West. Participation in an ethnic church in itself enhances Korean ethnicity regardless of religious dogmas and rituals, because it helps Korean immigrants to get together for fellowship. Moreover, Korean immigrants have modified the Christian religion in such a way that it is supportive of Korean ethnicity. Of course, part of the reason why the Christian religion has gained such popularity in Korea is because it has embraced some of Korea's indigenous principles, particularly Confucian ethics and shamanism (Y. Kim 1982). In their efforts to preserve Korean culture and Korean identity through ethnic churches, Korean immigrants have further Koreanized the Christian religion. In spite of the great influence of Korean indigenous thought on the Korean Christian religion, Christians in Korea are on average less Korean than other Koreans. By contrast, Korean immigrants affiliated with ethnic churches are more Korean than those not so affiliated. This nationalization of the Christian religion is not unique to Korean immigrants. Different Catholic groups in the United States – French, Irish, Italian, and Polish – have modified the Catholic religion in such a way that its religious way of life fits into their ethnic subculture. This is why Greeley argued that 'the various nationality groups were, at least to some extent, quasi-denominations within American Catholicism' (Greeley 1972, p. 119).

Concentration in small businesses

Korean immigrants concentrate heavily in a limited range of small businesses and their economic segregation also enhances ethnic attachment and ethnic solidarity. The 1980 Census shows that Korean immigrants had the highest self-employment rate, with 12 per cent among seventeen recent immigrant groups (US Bureau of the Census 1984, p. 8). The Census reports greatly undercounted the self-employment rate of Korean immigrants as well as those of other groups. Moreover, the self-employment rate of Korean immigrants has substantially increased since 1980. Thus, more recent case-studies show Koreans' exceptionally high levels of small-business concentration and economic segregation. For example, a survey conducted in 1986 shows that 45 per cent of Korean workers in Los Angeles are self-employed and that another 30 per cent are employed in Korean firms (Min 1989). The New York Korean community is even more entrepreneurial than the Los Angeles Korean community. A 1988 study (Min 1990) revealed that 61 per cent of married male and 49 per cent of married female Korean workers in New York City were engaged in their own businesses and that only 14 per cent of the Korean labour force was in the general labour market.

Whereas Korean immigrants' family and group ties facilitate their entrepreneurial activities, their involvement in small businesses further strengthens ethnic ties. Korean immigrants' occupational concentration in small businesses enhances ethnic attachment in three different ways.

First, it contributes to Korean ethnicity by bonding Koreans together. Korean proprietors depend mainly upon family members and other co-ethnic employees for their operation of businesses. Korean workers employed in Korean firms in Los Angeles are found to have an average of 93 per cent of Korean workers, in comparison to 22 per cent for those Koreans employed in non-Korean firms (Min 1989). Thus, only a small proportion of adult Korean immigrants maintain social interactions with Americans at the workplace, since most Koreans are segregated in the ethnic subeconomy. Korean immigrants, both proprietors and ethnic employees working for Korean stores, speak the Korean language, eat Korean lunch, and practise Korean customs during most of the working hours. Of course, Korean businesses largely serve non-Korean customers and thus need to speak English for business transactions. However, their English is limited to basic conversation and to the names of merchandise items.

Moreover, Koreans segregated in the ethnic market extend frequent social interactions with fellow Koreans to off-duty hours. In the 1986 Los Angeles survey, 47 per cent of Koreans in the ethnic market reported that they met other Koreans for dinner or picnics at least once a week, whereas only 23 per cent of Koreans employed in the general labour market said that they did (Min 1989). The same survey indicated that Koreans in the ethnic market exhibited a higher level of ethnicity than those in the general labour market in terms of the frequency of speaking Korean at home, the frequency of watching Korean television programmes, and the number of subscriptions to Korean newspapers and magazines.

No comparative study has examined the differentials in the proportion of workers in the ethnic market among different Asian immigrant-groups. Nevertheless, the vast majority of Filipino and Indian immigrants are believed to work for American firms, since their self-employment rates are much lower than those of Korean immigrants (Kim *et al.* 1989; Min 1986–87). This suggests that most Filipino and Indian immigrants speak English and observe American customs at least at the workplace, whereas a marked majority of Korean immigrants remain faithful to the Korean cultural tradition both at home and at the workplace.

Second, Korean ethnic business strengthens ethnic solidarity partly because Korean immigrants in each Korean community concentrate in a few types of business. When a minority/immigrant group specializes in small business, it is usually in a few or several business lines, for instance, Chinese restaurants and garment-manufacturing for Chinese Americans (Kwong 1987). Koreans in Los Angeles concentrate in the grocery/liquor trade, dry-cleaning service, and Korean-imported items such as wigs, handbags, clothing, and jewellery (Min 1989). Koreans in New York City concentrate heavily in the greengrocery business

(I. Kim 1981; Min 1990). Korean grocers in Los Angeles feel a strong sense of group solidarity because their class and ethnic interests overlap. That is, Korean grocers in Los Angeles as a *petit-bourgeoisie* maintain a higher level of class unity than white grocers in Los Angeles because they share brotherhood associated with the same nationality. Few Korean immigrants in Los Angeles would be interested in white-dominant trade-associations or labour-unions. Yet, most Korean grocers in Southern California are affiliated with the Korean Grocers' Association and active in protecting their group interests.

Third, Korean immigrant entrepreneurship enhances ethnic solidarity because the operation of small businesses involves conflicts with out-group members. The fact that minority/immigrant groups are segregated in certain business specialities may not be a sufficient condition for stimulating ethnic solidarity. The clustering of ethnic businesses can increase internal solidarity because minority/immigrant proprietors engaged in the same line or similar lines of business face conflicts with outside interest groups for economic survival. Middleman-minority theory posits that middleman groups specializing in small businesses receive a high level of hostility from the host society, which in turn strengthens ethnic solidarity (Bonacich 1973; Turner and Bonacich 1980). Korean immigrant proprietors have come into conflict with several interest groups: (1) minority customers, (2) white suppliers, (3) white landlords, (4) local residents, (5) white labour unions, and (6) government agencies such as the State Labor Department.

The most serious intergroup conflicts have arisen between Korean ghetto merchants and black customers. A large proportion of Korean immigrant businesses are located in low-income black areas (Kim and Hurh 1985; Light and Bonacich 1988; Min 1988). Korean immigrant merchants in black ghettos take the role of middleman minorities in that they distribute merchandise produced by big corporations to low-income black customers (Bonacich and Jung 1982; Light and Bonacich 1988). Korean store-owners operating businesses in black areas, like middleman minorities in other societies, have faced a high level of hostility and violent reaction from black customers. Blacks have indicted Korean merchants for treating black customers disrespectfully, for failing to contribute money to the black community, and for not hiring black employees (I. Kim 1981; Light and Bonacich 1988, pp. 318–19). For these and other reasons, blacks in New York, Baltimore, Philadelphia, Los Angeles, and other Korean centres have reacted against Korean ghetto-merchants by resort to murder, arson, boycott, demonstration, and mass-media attack.

Korean/black intergroup conflicts have probably been more serious in New York than in any other city. Several large-scale black boycott movements against Korean merchants have occurred in New York City. The boycotting of two Korean-owned greengrocery stores in

Flatbush Avenue, Brooklyn, New York is probably the most serious one. The boycott started in January 1990 after a scuffle between a black female customer, who allegedly tried to steal merchandise from a Korean greengrocery store, and Korean employees, who allegedly beat up the customer. The boycott, led by Mr. Sonny Carson, the president of the December Twelfth Movement, has received wide coverage by the national media. The New York City government, the Federal Bureau of Investigation, and the Department of Justice have all intervened to stop the five-month-old boycott, but have so far not produced any fruitful results.

A series of conflicts with blacks has made Korean store-owners aware of the potential collective threat in this country from black ethnics and has thus contributed to the fostering of Korean ethnic solidarity. In many Korean communities various business associations have been established mainly to deal with intergroup conflicts associated with Koreans' involvement in black-ghetto businesses. Korean community leaders and ethnic newspapers identify attacks on Korean merchants with attacks on the Korean community as a whole. Thus, problems related to Korean ghetto-businesses have led not only business proprietors but also other Koreans to be concerned about their common fate and marginal status in the USA.

The positive effects of business-related conflicts with blacks on Korean ethnic solidarity are clearly exemplified in the current boycott of the two Korean greengrocery stores in Brooklyn, New York. The sales volume for each store has been reduced to almost nothing since the boycott started in January 1990. However, both stores have been able to stay open for approximately five months largely because of the contributions made by various Korean organizations and individuals. The Korean Green Grocers' Association of New York has raised a fund of more than $50,000, mostly from its members, to help the two Korean greengrocery stores in trouble (*Sae Gae Times*, 28 May 1990). Many Korean ethnic churches and ethnic newspapers in the New York metropolitan area have also participated in fund-raising campaigns to help them. Korean business associations in Los Angeles, Philadelphia, Atlanta, and other cities have also contributed money to these Korean small-business owners. Moreover, many Koreans from New York and other parts of the country have individually donated money to help the Korean business-owners, whom they consider to be 'victims of black racism against Koreans'. One Korean lawyer has provided free legal services for the two business-owners (*Sae Gae Times*, 24 May 1990). In addition, the boycott has led to the establishment of the Civil Rights Committee under the Korean Association of Greater New York to deal with intergroup relations effectively. The committee consists of fifty well-known Korean community leaders in the New York metropolitan area – lawyers, university teachers, journalists, educational leaders, pastors, social workers, and business tycoons. No other Korean ethnic organization in New York includes so many experts in different fields as this organization.

Korean immigrants' concentration in small businesses has also led to intergroup conflicts with white wholesalers, and this, too, has strengthened ethnic solidarity. Korean retailers in all lines of business, with the exception of those who sell Korean-imported items, find themselves in conflict with white wholesalers. They have encountered discrimination by white wholesalers in the quality, prices, and speed of delivery, of merchandise, in parking allocations, and in other aspects of service to customers. As a large number of Korean retailers in each major Korean centre concentrate in a few business lines, they have resources to make collective responses to discriminatory practices by white wholesalers.

One can document a number of cases in which Korean retailers have taken collective action against white wholesalers to protect their common interests. For example, in 1977 approximately a hundred Korean greengrocers in New York staged a demonstration against a Jewish wholesale store at the Hunts Point Market to protest about an ethnic slur made by an employee of the store (I. Kim 1981). In 1988 Korean fish-retailers in New York boycotted a large fish-wholesaler, Slain and Sons, Inc., to protest against 'selling rotten fish', 'cheating in scaling', and 'unkind treatments' (*Sae Gae Times*, 29 July 1988; 16 November 1988). The boycott lasted five months, until the wholesaler, who had experienced a significant reduction in sales, sent a written apology to the Korean Fish Retailers' Association. Also, the Korean Grocers' Association in Atlanta was established in 1983 to take concerted action against 'monopolistic prices' by white wholesalers (Min 1988, p. 112). Korean grocers through their organization have negotiated with white wholesalers over prices of some grocery items and they have been moderately successful in protecting their common interests.

Korean entrepreneurs also clash with white landlords over economic interests, and this conflict, too, has contributed to fostering in-group ties. Many Korean immigrants buy a failing business or open a new one and then within a few years make it thrive (Min 1988, p. 114). As Korean-owned businesses become more successful, so white landlords raise rents by significant margins over a short period. This escalating-rent problem is most serious in the New York Korean community. A large number of Korean immigrants operate general-merchandise shops and greengrocery stores in Manhattan. Most of these Korean merchants have experienced rent increases by white landlords, especially by Jewish landlords, two or even three times over a period of between three and five years. Many Korean store-owners in Manhattan have to stay open twenty-four hours to cover the high rents

279

(*Korea Times of New York*, 15 December 1988). Korean business-owners in New York have held demonstrations several times, asking the city government to legislate on the regulation of rents. In 1988 a group of Korean leaders representing the Korean American Association and other Korean business associations in New York joined the New York Small Business Coalition for Regulating Commercial Rents and was active in lobbying the city council to pass a law regulating commercial rents (*Sae Gae Times*, 16 November 1988). In the 1989 mayoral election, Korean business owners endorsed Mr David Dinkins, the current black mayor, mainly because he promised to take some measures, if elected, to regulate commercial rents.

The effects of Koreans' small-business operations on their ethnic solidarity become evident when the Korean group is compared with other Asian immigrant-groups. Other non-entrepreneurial Asian immigrant-groups also specialize in certain occupational categories. For example, 15.1 per cent of Asian Indian immigrants work as medical professionals (US Bureau of the Census 1988, p. 465). Indian medical professionals in the New York metropolitan area maintain a higher level of class unity than white medical professionals in the city because they belong to the same 'ethclass' in which ethnic and class interests overlap. However, group solidarity is far less strong for New York Indian medical professionals than for New York Korean greengrocers because the former have not experienced the kinds of intergroup conflict for economic survival that the latter have.

By emphasizing the effects of Koreans' concentration in small businesses on ethnic solidarity, I do not fail to recognize that it also encourages intragroup conflict and competition. It has been well documented that Korean store-owners face strong competition from co-ethnics (I. Kim, 1981; Kim and Hurh, 1985; Min, 1988). However, competition among Korean store-owners, largely limited to the individual level, has never destroyed unity on the community level. Moreover, many Korean business associations in different Korean communities have been established partly to regulate excessive competition among Korean merchants in the same business specialty.

Finally, some readers might quickly point out that the conflict between Korean immigrant proprietors and co-ethnic employees will destroy ethnic solidarity. Several researchers have stressed class conflicts between Chinese business-owners and co-ethnic employees in Chinatown (Light and Wong 1975; Sanders and Nee 1987; Thompson 1980; B. Wong 1987). They have indicated that Chinese workers employed in co-ethnic firms are subject to a high level of exploitation and that Chinese ethnic employees are very conscious of their class interests against co-ethnic employers. However, the Korean community basically differs from the Chinese community in terms of business structure and the socio-economic background of new immigrants and thus it does not have the class cleavages existent in the Chinese community. On the one hand, the Korean community is more entrepreneurial than the Chinese community, as indicated by the differentials in the self-employment rate and the number of firms per 1,000 persons (Min 1989). On the other hand, the Chinese community annually receives a large number of new immigrants from mainland China, who are severely handicapped in employment in the general labour-market and who thus look for employment in the ethnic market. These differences suggest that there is a great demand for ethnic employees in the Korean community, whereas there is an oversupply of ethnic employees in the Chinese community, especially in Chinatown, where most immigrants from mainland China are settled.

Chinatown immigrants are vulnerable to exploitation by co-ethnic firms not only due to their oversupply of labour for Chinese firms, but also due to their lack of resources to avoid starvation wages. Nearly all immigrants from mainland China come here with almost no resources and thus have no alternative to low-wage employment (Kwong 1987). In contrast, most Korean immigrants bring a certain amount of money to this country at the time of immigration (Park *et al.* 1990), and a significant proportion of Korean immigrants have started their own businesses with the money brought from Korea (Kim and Hurh 1985; Min 1988, p. 80). Thus, many Korean immigrants have personal resources that enable them to avoid exploitation by co-ethnic employers. They work in Korean-owned stores mainly to acquire business experience and then move into their own business rather quickly. Most Korean ethnic employees seem to consider their employment as a temporary state to acquire business training and thus approach labour issues from the viewpoints of the owner. A very small proportion of Korean ethnic employees feel themselves exploited by co-ethnic employers, and labour movements are almost non-existent in the Korean community (Min 1989). By contrast, Chinatown workers employed in co-ethnic firms seem to be trapped in the working-class position more or less permanently and thus they are more class-conscious than Korean ethnic employees.

Summary and conclusion

Recent Korean immigrants are interesting to scholars of minority groups partly because they maintain a high level of ethnicity. The vast majority of Korean immigrants speak the Korean language, adhere to Korean customs and values, and maintain social interactions mainly with fellow Koreans. Moreover, they have developed within a short period of time strong ethnic solidarity in protecting their interests against outsiders.

Theorists of ethnicity have emphasized two major factors as bases of ethnicity. First, commonalities in culture and historical experiences that members of a group share provide an important basis of ethnicity. Second, productive activities associated with occupational concentration contribute to ethnic solidarity and group identity. This article has analysed Korean ethnicity, focusing on Korean immigrants' cultural homogeneity, affiliation with ethnic churches, and economic concentration.

To summarize the foregoing analyses. South Korea is a small, culturally homogeneous country, and Korean immigrants maintain a high level of ethnicity partly because of their strong cultural and historical ties. Other current US immigrant groups such as Asian-Indian, Filipino, Chinese, and Iranian groups are characterized by subgroup differences in language, customs, values, religion, and political ideology, which hinder the development of national ethnic consciousness. Korean immigrants share one language, the same customs and values, and the same historical experiences. These commonalities in culture and historical experiences provide a cultural basis of Korean ethnicity.

The vast majority of Korean immigrants are affiliated to Korean immigrant churches, and their high affiliation to ethnic churches further reinforces Korean ethnicity. Korean immigrant churches first of all contribute to Korean ethnicity by providing places for fellowship and social interactions. They also contribute to Korean ethnicity by helping to maintain the Korean cultural tradition. The Christian religion is not a Korean indigenous religion. However, Korean immigrants have modified the Christian religion in such a way that it fits into their need for Korean ethnic subculture and Korean ethnic identity. Historically, this nationalization of Christianity has occurred to black and white-Catholic ethnic groups as well.

Korean immigrants concentrate in a limited range of small businesses, and their economic segregation also enhances ethnic attachment and ethnic solidarity. First of all, Korean immigrant businesses contribute to Korean ethnicity by binding ethnic members together, as they depend upon family members and co-ethnic employees for business operation. Furthermore, Korean immigrants' concentration in small businesses has strengthened ethnic solidarity because Korean merchants have been involved in conflicts with outside interest groups for economic survival. Korean ghetto-merchants have received rejection and hostility from black customers. Moreover, Korean entrepreneurs have clashed with white wholesalers, white landlords, and white labour unions over economic interests. These business-related conflicts with outside interest groups have motivated not only Korean business proprietors but also other Korean immigrants to be concerned about their common fate and marginal status in the USA.

Acknowledgement

This article is based on works supported by the National Science Foundation under Grant Number SES–8608735 and PSC-CUNY Award (No. 661303). Any opinions, findings, conclusions, or recommendations expressed in this article are those of the author and do not necessarily reflect the views of the National Science Foundation or PSC-CUNY.

References

BODNAR, J. R., *et al.* 1982 *Lives on Their Own: Blacks, Italians, and Poles in Pittsburgh, 1900–1960*, Urbana, IL: University of Illinois Press

BONACICH, EDNA 1973 'A theory of middleman minorities', *American Sociological Review*, vol. 37, no. 5, pp. 583–94

BONACICH, EDNA and JUNG, TAE HWAN 1982 'A portrait of Korean small business in Los Angeles', in Eui-Young Yu *et al.* (eds), *Koreans in Los Angeles: Prospects and Promises*, Los Angeles, CA: Center for Korean-American and Korean Studies, California State University, pp. 75–98.

BONACICH, EDNA and MODELL, JOHN 1980 *The Economic Basis of Ethnic Solidarity: Small Business in the Japanese American Community*, Berkeley and Los Angeles, CA: University of California Press

COHEN, STEVEN 1985 *American Modernity and Jewish Identity*, New York: Tavistock Publications

GLAZER, NATHAN and MOYNIHAN, DANIEL 1963 *Beyond the Melting Pot: Negroes, Puerto Ricans, Jews, Italians, and Irish of New York City*, Cambridge, MA: M.I.T Press

GORDON, MILTON 1964 *Assimilation in American Life: The Role of Race, Religion, and National Origin*, New York: Oxford University Press

GREELEY, ANDREW M. 1971 *Why Can't They Be Like Us?*, New York: Dutton

—— 1972 *The Denominational Society: A Sociological Approach to Religion*, Glenview, IL: Scott, Foresman, and Company

—— 1974 *Ethnicity in the United States: A Preliminary Reconnaissance*, New York: John Wiley & Sons

HURH, WON MOO and KIM, KWANG CHUNG 1984 *Korean Immigrants in America: A Structural Analysis of Ethnic Confinement and Adhesive Adaptation*, Madison, NJ: Fairleigh Dickinson University Press

—— 1987 *Korean Immigrants in the Chicago Area: A Sociological Study of Migration and Mental Health*, Interim Report submitted to the National Institute of Mental Health, US Department of Health and Human Services

—— 1988 *Uprooting and Adjustment: A Sociological Study of Korean Immigrants' Mental Health*, Final Report submitted to the National Institute of Mental Health, US Department of Health and Human Services

KIM, BOK-LIM 1978 *The Asian Americans: Changing Patterns, Changing Needs*, Monteclair, NJ: The Association of Korean Christian Scholars in North America

KIM, ILLSOO 1981 *New Urban Immigrants: The Korean Community in New York*, Princeton, NJ: Princeton University Press

KIM, KWANG CHUNG and HURH, WON MOO 1985 'Ethnic resources utilization of Korean small businessmen in the United States', *International Migration Review*, vol. 19, no. 1, pp. 82–111

KIM, KWANG CHUNG, *et al.* 1989 'Intra-group differences in business participation: a comparative analysis of three Asian groups', *International Migration Review*, vol. 23, no. 1, pp. 73–95

KIM, YOUNG CHUN 1982 'The nature and density of Korean churches in the United

States', in Seong Hyung Lee and Tae-Hawn Kwak (eds) *Koreans in North America: New Perspectives*, Seoul: Kyung Nam University Press, pp. 215–30

KOREA TIMES OF NEW YORK 1988 'Korean merchants forced to open 24 hours', 15 December

KOREAN NATIONAL BUREAU OF STATISTICS 1987 *1985 Population and Housing Census*, Seoul: Korean Economic Planning Board

KWONG, PETER 1987 *The New Chinatown*, New York: The Noonday Press

LIGHT, IVAN 1972 *Ethnic Enterprise in America: Business and Welfare among Chinese, Japanese, and Blacks*, Berkeley and Los Angeles, CA: University of California Press

LIGHT, IVAN and BONACICH, EDNA 1988 *Immigrant Entrepreneurs: Koreans in Los Angeles, 1965–1982*, Berkeley and Los Angeles, CA: University of California Press

LIGHT, IVAN, *et al.*, 1990 'The four Iranian ethnic economies in Los Angeles', Unpublished Manuscript, University of California at Los Angeles

LIGHT, IVAN and WONG, CHARLES C. 1975 'Protest or work: dilemmas of the tourist industry in American Chinatowns', *American Journal of Sociology*, vol. 80, no. 6, pp. 1342–65

LYMAN, STANFORD 1968 'Contrasts in community organization of Chinese and Japanese in North America', *Canadian Journal of Sociology and Anthropology*, vol. 5, no. 1, pp. 51–67

—— 1974 *Chinese Americans*, New York: Random House

MANGIAFICO, LUCIANO 1988 *Contemporary Asian Immigrants: Patterns of Filipino, Korean, and Chinese Settlement in the United States*, New York: Praeger

MIN, PYONG GAP 1986–87 'A comparison of Filipino and Korean immigrants in small business', *Amerasia Journal*, vol. 13, no. 1, pp. 53–71

—— 1988 *Ethnic Business Enterprise: Korean Small Business in Atlanta*, Staten Island, NY: Centre for Migration Studies

—— 1989 *Some Positive Functions of Ethnic Business for an Immigrant Community: Koreans in Los Angeles*, Final Report submitted to the National Science Foundation

—— 1990 'Immigrant entrepreneurship and wife's overwork: Koreans in New York City', paper presented at the Annual Meeting of the American Sociological Association

—— 1992 'The structure and social functions of Korean immigrant churches in the United States', *International Migration Review*, vol. 26

OLZAK, SUSAN 1986 'A competition model of ethnic collective action in American cities, 1877–1889', in Susan Olzak and Joane Nagel (eds), *Competitive Ethnic Relations*, New York: Academic Press, pp. 17–46

PARK, IN-SOOK HAN, *et al.* 1990 'Korean immigrants and U.S. immigration policy: a predeparture perspective', Paper of the East-West Population Institute, No. 114, Honolulu: East-West Center

PIDO, ANTONIO J. A. 1986 *The Philipinos in America: Macro/micro Dimensions of Immigration and Integration*, Staten Island, NY: Center for Migration Studies

REITZ, JEFFREY 1980 *The Survival of Ethnic Groups*, Toronto: McGraw-Hill

SAE GAE TIMES 1988 'Koreans' anger roared Fulton fish market', 29 July

—— 1988 'The Slavin sent a letter of apology to the Korean Fish Retailers' Association', 16 November

—— 1990 'Preparation of six-million dollar litigation', 24 May

—— 1990 'Let's Help Two Korean Green Grocers', 28 May

SANDERS, JIMMY and NEE, VICTOR 1987 'Limits of ethnic solidarity', *American Sociological Review*, vol. 52, no. 6, pp. 745–67

SARAN, PARMATMA 1985 *Asian Indian Experience in the United States*, Cambridge, MA.: Schenkman Books

THE CENTRAL DAILY 1989 'The Korean-American population has reached one million', 29 May

—— 1990 'Korean-American civil rights coalition established', 25 May

THOMPSON, RICHARD H. 1980 'From kinship to class: a new model of urban overseas Chinese social organization', *Urban Anthropology*, vol. 9, no. 3, pp. 265–93

TURNER, JONATHAN and BONACICH, EDNA 1980 'Toward a composite theory of middleman minorities', *Ethnicity*, vol. 7, no. 2, pp. 144–58

US BUREAU OF THE CENSUS 1983 *1980 Census of Population*, PC80–1-B1, Washington, DC: United States Government Printing Office

—— 1984 *1980 Census of Population*, PC80–1-D1-A. Washington, DC: United States Government Printing Office

—— 1988 *Subject Reports, Asian and Pacific Islander Population in the United States: 1980*, Section 1

WILLIAMS, RAYMOND B. 1988 *Religions of Immigrants from India and Pakistan: New Threads of American Tapestry*, New York: Cambridge University Press

WONG, BERNARD 1987 'The Chinese: new immigrants in New York's Chinatown', in Nancy Foner (ed.), *New Immigrants in New York*, New York: Columbia University Press, pp. 243–72

YANCY, WILLIAM E., *et al.* 1976 'Emergent ethnicity: a review and reformulation', *American Sociological Review*, vol. 41, no. 3, pp. 391–403

YINGER, MILTON 1980 'Toward a theory of assimilation and dissimilation', *Ethnic and Racial Studies*, vol. 4, no. 2, pp. 249–64

PYONG GAP MIN is Assistant Professor in the Department of Sociology at Queens College, City University of New York.

ADDRESS: Department of Sociology, Queens College of City University of New York, 65–30 Kissena Boulevard, Flushing, NY 11367–0904, USA.

Acknowledgments

Nee, Victor and Herbert Y. Wong. "Asian American Socioeconomic Achievement: The Strength of the Family Bond." *Sociological Perspectives* 28 (1985): 281–306. Reprinted with the permission of JAI Press Inc.

Kibria, Nazli. "Household Structure and Family Ideologies: The Dynamics of Immigrant Economic Adaptation Among Vietnamese Refugees." *Social Problems* 41 (1994): 81–96. Reprinted with the permission of the University of California Press. Copyright 1994 by the Society for the Study of Social Problems.

Johnson, Colleen Leahy. "The Principle of Generation Among the Japanese in Honolulu." *Ethnic Groups* 1 (1976): 13–35. Reprinted with the permission of Gordon and Breach Science Publishers.

———. "Interdependence, Reciprocity and Indebtedness: An Analysis of Japanese American Kinship Relations." *Journal of Marriage and the Family* 39 (1977): 351–62. Copyright 1977 by the National Council of Family Relations, 3989 Central Avenue, NE, Suite 550, Minneapolis, MN 55421. Reprinted by permission.

Fleuret, Anne K. "Incorporation into Networks Among Sikhs in Los Angeles." *Urban Anthropology* 3 (1974): 27–33. Reprinted with the permission of Institute Inc.

Okamura, Jonathan Y. "Filipino Hometown Associations in Hawaii." *Ethnology* 22 (1983): 341–53. Reprinted with the permission of *Ethnology*.

Yu, Elena S.H. "Filipino Migration and Community Organizations in the United States." *California Sociologist* 3 (1980): 76–102. Reprinted with the permission of California State University, Los Angeles.

Light, Ivan, Im Jung Kwuon, and Deng Zhong. "Korean Rotating Credit Associations in Los Angeles." *Amerasia Journal* 16, no.2 (1990): 35–54. Reprinted with the permission of the *Amerasia Journal*.

Chung, Sue Fawn. "The Chinese American Citizens Alliance: An Effort in Assimilation, 1895–1965." In *Chinese America: History and Perspectives* (San Francisco: Chinese Historical Society of America, 1988): 30–57. Reprinted with the permission of the Chinese Historical Society of America.

Scott, George M., Jr. "The Hmong Refugee Community in San Diego: Theoretical and Practical Implications of Its Continuing Ethnic Solidarity." *Anthropological*

Quarterly 55 (1982): 146–60. Reprinted with the permission of *Anthropological Quarterly*.

Haines, David W. "Southeast Asian Refugees in the United States: The Interaction of Kinship and Public Policy." *Anthropological Quarterly* 55 (1982): 170–81. Reprinted with the permission of *Anthropological Quarterly*.

Skinner, Kenneth A. "Vietnamese in America: Diversity in Adaptation." *California Sociologist* 3 (1980): 103–24. Reprinted with the permission of California State University, Los Angeles.

Wong, Bernard. "Elites and Ethnic Boundary Maintenance: A Study of the Roles of Elites in Chinatown, New York City." *Urban Anthropology* 6 (1977): 1–22. Reprinted with the permission of Institute Inc.

Okamura, Jonathan Y. "Why There Are No Asian Americans in Hawai'i: The Continuing Significance of Local Identity." *Social Process in Hawaii* 35 (1994): 161–78. Reprinted with the permission of the University of Hawaii, Sociology Club.

Min, Pyong Gap. "Cultural and Economic Boundaries of Korean Ethnicity: A Comparative Analysis." *Ethnic and Racial Studies* 14 (1991): 225–41. Reprinted with the permission of Routledge.